# In from the Cold

Published in Cooperation with
the Peace Research Institute Frankfurt, Germany

# In from the Cold

## Germany, Russia, and the Future of Europe

EDITED BY

## Vladimir Baranovsky
## and Hans-Joachim Spanger

FOREWORD BY

### Eduard Shevardnadze

Westview Press
BOULDER·SAN FRANCISCO·OXFORD

Published in 1992 in the United States of America by Westview Press, Inc., 5500 Central Avenue, Boulder, Colorado 80301-2877, and in the United Kingdom by Westview Press, 36 Lonsdale Road, Summertown, Oxford OX2 7EW

A CIP catalog record for this book is available from the Library of Congress.
ISBN 0-8133-8624-1

Printed and bound in the United States of America

The paper used in this publication meets the requirements of the American National Standard for Permanence of Paper for Printed Library Materials Z39.48-1984.

10    9    8    7    6    5    4    3    2    1

# Contents

# Foreword

Europe, a continent literally brimming with history, has gone through periods of rise and decline, exhilarating eras of remarkable flourishing, and dark times of deep decay. A mere decade ago, "Europessimism" was the predominant mood on the continent: while rapidly losing its influence on the world stage, Europe was turning into a field of sharp confrontation between East and West. Who would have thought then that the waning years of the twentieth century would usher in a brand-new age in European history?

By the end of the 1980s a wave of sudden and fundamental changes had washed over Europe, clearing the way for a qualitatively new stage in the evolution of the Old World. Europe was entering the last decade of the century looking younger, casting off the load of the past, coming to life after the confrontations of "cold war," finding a kind of second breath. This centuries-old civilization, which is deeply rooted in classical antiquity and has assimilated the greatest spiritual and material achievements of humankind, seemed acquiring a chance to develop its full potential.

The revolutionary reconstruction of the USSR initiated in 1985 became the most important event of international significance. As a result, the perennial image of the Soviet Union changed radically. The Western countries ceased to regard the USSR as totally alien, abnormal, hostile, and threatening. A number of substantial adjustments in Soviet foreign policy contributed greatly to this new perception. They found their expression in a thorough reevaluation of the fundamental aims and means of the country's foreign policy as well as in a new and much more constructive and flexible approach to various major international problems.

To be sure, effecting such revolutionary changes was by no means an easy undertaking. It proved necessary not only to overcome traditional ideological dogmas and stereotypes but also to translate the "new political thinking" into a new foreign policy. The latter was increasingly opposed by reactionary forces in the Soviet Union. They were criticizing as "concessions to imperialism" virtually everything that had made possible the normalization of the situation in the world, reduced the threat of war, eroded the enemy image of the USSR, and encouraged confidence and sympathy for the Soviet Union in other countries.

The steps taken under *perestroika* have stirred much sympathy abroad for the USSR and created favorable conditions unprecedented and unique in the history of the Soviet state. Moreover, the changes in the Soviet Union gave a powerful stimulus for the positive developments on the European continent. In fact, *perestroika* also stimulated the revolutionary reforms in the countries of Central and Eastern Europe. New political forces appeared on the scene there, and within a few months a fundamental transformation of the whole economic and political system was initiated. Accordingly, relations between the countries in the eastern part of the continent have been radically altered. They are no longer based on "mutual solidarity" (i.e., categorically rejecting the West while largely staying under Soviet control) but on a balance of interests and on principles such as equality and mutual respect of political choices.

Only on this basis did German reunification become possible -- though not so long ago almost nobody could have thought of this as a goal of practical policy. The division of the country, absent a post-World War II peace treaty, festered into a sore at the very heart of Europe that could not but be excised. All the talk about the right of nations to self-determination would have remained mere palaver had the Germans been refused such a right. All the arguments about the necessity to overcome the division of Europe would have been vacuous had they failed to address its most visible symbol -- the division of Germany. The settlement of this problem has become one of the major contributions to the cause of strengthening peace and stability on the European continent.

New perspectives for progress in pan-European cooperation are coming to light. The "Charter of Paris for a New Europe," signed on 21 November 1990 by the 34 participants in the CSCE meeting in Paris, proclaims that the era of division and confrontation in Europe has come to an end. Human rights, democracy and the rule of law, economic freedom and responsibility, friendly relations between nations, strengthening international security, and cooperation with other parts of the world are actually laid down in this document as common European values. It is no less important to note significant policy shifts being effected by the North Atlantic Treaty Organization. Its recent decisions actually mark a dramatic turning point; once fully implemented, they will have a tremendous impact on international politics.

It is no exaggeration to say that the old idea of a united Europe is being given a chance. The European countries now proceed from the assumption that they have a common destiny, common problems, and common interests. These include better living conditions, a secure and lasting peace, guarantees for basic rights and freedoms, material wealth, an adequate intellectual development, a healthy environment, etc. It is Europe that faces the noble task of showing the rest of the world that the further progress of our civilization is possible only on the basis of the universal human values.

However, most recent developments in Europe have equally demonstrated that the continent is confronted with a number of serious risks for peace and stability. In the eastern part of the continent the aggravation of problems that have remained unsettled for many years could become a source of tension and encourage extremist tendencies in both domestic and foreign policy. Issues of interethnic relations are on the agenda again and have significant international implications. Phantoms of nationalism creep out of their deep holes. The dramatic events in Yugoslavia have turned a whole European country into a battlefield and at the same time highlighted the lack of adequate instruments available to the international community to tackle these reemerging problems.

The Soviet Union, due to its extremely aggravated socioeconomic difficulties, the failure of its traditional economic model, its rapidly proceeding disintegration, and the lack of confidence in the political administration at different levels, became a special problem for Europe. After the failed coup in August 1991 new opportunities appeared to have been opened up for reconstructing the country on the principles of parliamentary democracy and on the basis of equal rights between the republics. In addition, it also cleared the way for straightforward measures to facilitate transition from the centrally planned to a market economy. However, centrifugal forces, on the one hand, and the inherent risks of economic transformation in conditions of political and economic disarray, on the other, have put the country on the brink of catastrophe.

Economic collapse, social unrest, civil wars, violent interethnic clashes, and -- not least -- disorganization and desperate moods among the military not only threaten the future of what used to be the Soviet Union but will also have a serious impact on the rest of Europe and even the world as a whole. Only if utmost responsibility, readiness for compromise, and democratic determination govern political behaviour, both in Moscow and in the capitals of the other successor states, can the deep crisis be overcome. And the West cannot and should not remain aloof when faced by this dramatic situation.

I would like everybody to understand clearly: the political future of Europe cannot be separated from the fate of our young countries, and our future is not isolated from the fate of Europe. And while *perestroika* has substantially determined the movement toward a new united

Europe, Europe itself, if it intends to become really new, can and must provide maximum support for overcoming the destructive processes in the former Soviet Union.

Not least because this book, which I have the pleasure to introduce, was jointly researched and written by distinguished scholars from Frankfurt and Moscow would I like to point to the special importance of the relations between Germany and the successors to the Soviet Union for the future of Europe. Actually, the entire modern history of Europe has been greatly influenced by the interaction between Germany and Russia (and later the Soviet Union), which were, so to speak, doomed to form the axis of any international system embracing the whole of the continent. In terms of their internal development, however, they are now at rather different stages: Germany has just reunified and become stronger, whereas the former Soviet republics are in the painful process of determining the future shape of their relations while facing the most serious economic, social, and political problems. But if we look ahead, say, five, ten, or fifteen years hence, it becomes clear that, whatever changes the political map of Europe might undergo, Germany in the center and the new states in the east will be among the most important actors on the continent.

In my view, relations between Germany and these new states seem to have great potential. True, they are not entirely without problems -- inherited from the past and connected with the present. Although the wounds of the past can be psychologically painful, they are not incurable if treated cautiously and with care. And present challenges should be perceived not only as a matter of concern but as an incentive for getting to know each other and also for learning to live together -- as, for instance, in the case of the stationing of Soviet troops on German territory until 1994.

Among many other areas of bilateral cooperation, I would like to emphasize here the joint intellectual work on all the problems related to international politics. This volume is a good example of constructive efforts of academics from both sides of the former divide in a field that until recently was a source of sharp ideological controversies. Now the very nature of the debate has changed radically. We no longer try merely to express respective "credos." Instead our objective now is to find *together* the answers to uneasy questions raised on the continent, to determine *together* better prospects for the Old World. And Europe is definitely worth such efforts.

*Eduard Shevardnadze*
Moscow

# Preface

Europe has entered a new phase in its historical development. The division of the continent into two blocs, at loggerheads with each other for more than forty years, is over. So too is the order instituted at Yalta, which made Europe into a mere appendage of the only two powers able, after the Second World War, to shape the world as they saw fit: the United States of America and the Union of Soviet Socialist Republics. It is now up to Europe itself to reshape its fate. However, the first two years of the new era have shown that, contrary to the promising signs at the time of the 1989 turning point, this process will require much effort and a considerable time span. Despite the fact that history is now open once again after decades of Manichean bipolarism, this requirement of time and effort applies no less to the precipitately declared triumph of liberal values in politics, the economy, and society throughout Europe and indeed on a global scale.

The iron curtain may have fallen in 1989, but a deep rift continues to divide the continent into a western and an eastern part. The dual legacy of the two mass movements of the nineteenth century -- socialism and nationalism -- weighs heavy in the eastern part of Europe. Socialism, particularly in its Marxist-Leninist variant, was unable to triumph over capitalist methods of production, as it claimed ideologically to be able to do. It managed only to lay the foundations of an industrial society and to do so only at a slower rate and by resorting to the methods of the authoritarian centralized state. Yet the more economic development progressed, the more socialism itself became a barrier to the growth of productive forces, and, in the age of information, it ultimately foundered on its inability to process information adequately in a centralized manner. Socialist internationalism was to suffer a similar fate. Its attempt to solve the national question via the class struggle, and to overcome national fragmentation through social integration, remained tied to the authoritarianism of the communist party. The latter's demise revealed that, against the background of only partial socialist modernization in Eastern Europe, the various forms of national atavism had been largely preserved and had lost nothing of their virulence. Indeed, serving as it did as a synonym for political liberation and economic and social emancipation, nationalism acquired an extra boost which, notoriously, resulted in its translation into physical violence.

The legacy of erstwhile real socialism and the revival of European nationalism constitute challenges which, though having their origins in the eastern part of the continent, nevertheless affect the whole of Europe. Although the future of the East today lies in the West, that future can only be secured if the western side too demonstrates a willingness to accommodate, to open up, and to engage in joint conflict resolution. This is all the more important in that virtually all political actors have been utterly surprised by the pace of change in Europe and have not really, to date, acquired adequate tools to bring under control the risks of multipolar disorder which have replaced the former unbending bipolar order. The changes in the political map of Europe provide a graphic example of this. German unification, spurred on by the impatience of the people in the GDR, took place relatively quickly and with the agreement of all the powers involved. In the case of Yugoslavia, on the other hand, people's impatience ended in a bloodbath which even the international community has made little headway in stemming.

Nevertheless, the war in Yugoslavia has not yet managed, as it did once before during this century, to disrupt European equilibrium and stability and bring rival alliances onto the scene. The situation could be otherwise in the case of the erstwhile Soviet empire, where a geopolitical realignment of unprecedented proportions and totally unforeseeable outcome has begun. Actual and potential interethnic conflicts and border claims, the possible use of military force, and the prospect of external interference -- these are the most disturbing factors that could undermine stability both in the region east of the Bug river and beyond.

A serious reassessment is therefore needed, both of the very notion of international security in Europe and of the methods and means of preserving it. This concerns the major actors of international politics -- the nation-states -- as well as residual alliances (NATO) and integrating bodies (EC) and, not least, what continues to be the sole pan-European forum, namely the CSCE. Only joint efforts can ensure that old risks do not become new threats and that the current problems of transformation do not end in new division and confrontation but are overcome through integration and cooperation.

It is against this background that the authors of the present volume analyse the changes that have taken place on the European continent, tracing their appearance from the beginnings of *glasnost* and *perestroika* in 1985 and their acceleration in the wake of the European revolutions of 1989. The analysis is made to a large extent from the perspective of the two states which in the past have played a prominent role in shaping European antagonism and which have been most affected by the sea change, albeit in opposing ways: Germany and the former Soviet Union/Russia. "Perspective" here relates not only to the actual subject matter under discussion, namely the significance and role of the two states within the concert of European powers, but also to the fact that the present volume is the product of a two-year period of co-operation between researchers from these two countries and that, as a result, national perceptions, priorities, and emphases are reflected, both implicitly and explicitly, in the analysis.

In the first part of the book, under the title "Continuity and Change," stock is taken of the situation, and an assessment is made of the background to, and nature of, the changes that have occurred since 1985 and of the chances and risks they present in regard to the prospect of a new, and henceforward pan-European, order. *Gert Krell* highlights the fact that, in contrast to the previous modern-day attempts to found such an order -- in 1815 (Vienna), 1919 (Versailles, Trianon), and 1945 (Yalta and Potsdam) -- there is now an opportunity of establishing a European peace order that is more than just a post-war order; that is to say, it would not be hamstrung by the fact of having emerged from the ruins of a war. In addition, following the demise of Marxist-Lenin-ist socialism, there is now no longer any ideological antagonism; instead, all the states of Europe feel bound to the common principles and norms laid down in 1990 in the Paris Charter for a New Europe. Finally, the rivalry between the (great) powers of Europe that was a characteristic feature of the nineteenth and first half of the twentieth century is now largely a thing of the past -- not least because of the historically unprecedented mutual transparency and interdependence that now exists.

This means that the preconditions for the establishment of a new order, integrating both halves of Europe, are much more favourable today than they ever were in the past. This applies particularly to prospects for far-reaching arms reductions. However, the disintegration of the bipolar order has, as Krell argues, another side to it, which is expressed in the fact that the established mechanisms of war prevention and conflict management between the blocs, and also the avoidance of conflict within the blocs, are scarcely applicable in today's changed conditions. But an increasing need for conflict prevention and management arises from the revival of nationalism and the growing potential for ethno-national conflict. The latter has led to the emergence of new, multifarious types of East-East conflicts in the place of the unidimen-sional clash between East and West. They are what largely shapes the new security agenda in Europe. The successful implementation of that agenda will determine whether the peaceful integration of the two still very disparate parts goes ahead successfully, and therefore also whether one of the major preconditions for the solution of the two greatest challenges facing the world -- the development crisis and the ecological crisis -- can be fulfilled.

Like Gert Krell, *Yuri Borko* claims that one of the outstanding results of the revolutionary changes of 1989 is the fact that it is now possible for the first time to conduct the European dialogue in the universal language of modern civilization. This was not possible under real socialism. Although socialism had its roots in some of the greatest achievements of European thinking, in the wake of the modifications introduced by Lenin and, above all, by Stalin, with his creation of Marxism-Leninism, it turned increasingly into a totalitarian ideology, which, with its myths and dogmas, cut itself off on principle from Western enlightenment. However, by the beginning of the 1980s at the latest, this ideology had lost its power of persuasion, and with the coming of *glasnost*, as Borko explains, the bell finally tolled for it. Socialism proved unable to overcome capitalism -- even in the sense of a synthesis as mooted in the convergence theory; nor was Mikhail Gorbachev's attempt to lead socialism back to civilization and secure it an equal place in the "common European home" granted success. And the situation is accentuated by the fact that Russia, as a result of all this, is now faced with an alternative as familiar as it is novel: to turn towards the West or once again set off on a separate Russian path.

The transition from the bipolar, confrontational order to a pan-European structure of cooperation and security calls for a rethinking of existing institutions and procedures. In this connection, says *Peter Schlotter* in his contribution, the Conference on Security and Cooperation in Europe (CSCE) must be regarded as being of particular significance. With its fifty-plus members, it is the only body to embrace all the states of Europe as well as those which have a direct influence on European security. It has a mandate to deal with all problems which, in the broadest sense, relate to security on the European continent. Finally, since its foundation in the mid-1970s, the CSCE has acquired a wide-ranging fund of experience in conflict management. However, this is also the area in which its obvious weaknesses are rooted. The CSCE too is a product of the East-West conflict, and its achievements in the past were a direct function of the readiness of the two blocs to cooperate. It therefore needed to adapt to the radically different conditions of multipolarity, but developments in this direction have so far only been rudimentary. Peter Schlotter discusses a range of new procedures and institutions which might considerably increase what has up to now been the extremely limited effectiveness of the CSCE as an organ for conflict prevention.

In this connection, the relationship of the CSCE to other institutions and organizations in Europe -- notably NATO -- is significant. This is the theme tackled by *Harald Müller*. It is evident that NATO has lost the real justification for its existence, namely to provide a counter-weight to the obvious, massive Soviet threat. It therefore needs a new legitimation, and the much-quoted residual risks are not sufficient here. From this, Müller concludes that NATO must become an integral component in a pan-European security system based on the CSCE. In view of the originally Dutch initiative to entrust NATO with peace-keeping missions within the framework of the CSCE, such an idea shows how quickly the previously inconceivable can today become a political reality.

However, this kind of model depends not only on NATO's flexibility and readiness to reform but also on the interests prevailing in the eastern part of Europe, where expectations are currently directed more at the proven guarantees of collective defense available within NATO than at the uncertain prospects of a collective security based on the CSCE. Of particular importance in this regard is the former Soviet Union and its two most important successor states, Russia and Ukraine. Two themes related to this are dealt with in detail here: the evolution of Moscow's policy on Europe, in the chapter by *Vladimir Baranovsky*, and the change in Moscow's military policy, discussed by *Yuri Streltsov*. Both analyses begin with the start of *perestroika* and close with a look into the uncertain future both of the Commonwealth of Independent States and of Russian policy following the demise of the Soviet Union.

They paint a detailed picture of the convoluted and, quite often, inconsistent paths taken by Moscow's foreign and military policies, of the increasingly complex internal political environment, and of the rapidly changing demands being imposed from outside. Thus, although Moscow's policy over the last seven years has shown an unprecedented degree of readiness and ability to adapt, one cannot talk of a coherent strategy. This is also true to some extent of Russian policy in the post-Soviet era, which, although it has rid itself of many of the half-truths of the past, is now confronted with the problem of defining the country's new role in a radically altered environment. Thus, although Russia in many ways, particularly from the military point of view, has the potential of a great power, it no longer has the ability unilaterally to shape the international system. Given that the country will be dependent on European cooperation for the foreseeable future, and in view of virulent fears of Russian dominance, greater ambitions will be subject to relatively strict limits.

The legacy of the Soviet Union is also the main topic on the present arms control agenda in Europe, and it is this subject which *Matthias Dembinski* and *Hans-Joachim Schmidt* tackle in their contribution. The Soviet Union did not ratify the two most important arms control treaties of recent years, START and CFE, nor have its successor states as yet been able, in a concerted and lasting manner, to deal with the legacy of the Soviet armed forces in a way consonant with these two treaties. Although some important advances have been made in the reduction of strategic and tactical nuclear weaponry, we are left, for the foreseeable future, with the problem that there is now not *one* nuclear power, with a reliable system of centralized control, but *four* -- and four whose intentions are fairly unclear. The situation is similar in regard to the reduction of conventional arms in Europe, which, because of the dictates of economic requirements, is currently being conducted mainly on a unilateral basis. The basis on which arms control in Europe has taken place to date, the alliance approach, had already become obsolete when the CFE treaty was signed in December 1990, but no new approaches are yet in sight. It is therefore likely that, after the various desiderata have been dealt with within the framework of the CFE IA negotiations, negotiated arms control will once again fade into the background, to be replaced by joint efforts to achieve military confidence-building.

From the time of its foundation in 1871, Germany -- or rather the German nation-state -- had always presented a problem as far as the balance of power on the European continent was concerned. It was from Germany that the two devastating world wars were launched, and the attempt, in the wake of those wars, to found a European order, was always guided by the notion that Germany's potential must be contained. The reemergence of the unified German nation-state is, after the disintegration of the Soviet Union, the clearest sign of the end of the Cold War and the beginning of a new age. Against this background, *Bruno Schoch* examines the question of whether there is any likelihood that history -- in whatever form -- will repeat itself. His conclusion remains ambivalent. On the one hand, he points to far-reaching changes, to the integration of Germany into the international community, to the radical turning point of 1945, and to the modernization of German society, all of which make a resurgence of German great-power politics unlikely. On the other hand, however, the conditions underlying the basic German consensus of the post-war period -- manifested internally in postnational constitutionalism and externally in unconditional acceptance of European integration -- have undergone radical alteration. As a result, it seems questionable that the Federal Republic's past will also be the future of united Germany. At any rate, the first foreign-policy test to occur after unification, the Gulf War, was, according to Schoch, not passed.

That the unification of the two German states provoked both fears and, above all, far-reaching expectations from the Eastern point of view, is explained by *Aleksandr Kokeev*. He describes the complex relationship between Bonn and Moscow in the forty years since the end of the Second World War. He also emphasises the central role played by the Federal Republic during the period of detente and the latter's efforts to achieve East-West understanding during the often tense 1980s. This prepared the way for the ultimate consent of the Soviet Union to German unification, after a series of half-hearted and inconsistent attempts to slow down the process, and to its consent on conditions that largely coincided with Bonn's wishes. It also gave rise to the notion that Germany was predestined for the task of bridge-laying between East and West, though this is an expectation that can be fulfilled only when the necessary political and economic preconditions have been satisfied on the Russian side.

The bridge picture, with its insinuation of a special mission for Germany in Europe, and against the background of the *Sonderwege* (special ways) Germany has followed during history, has met with many reservations, particularly in the West. Nevertheless, there is probably no question that, in the long term, a pan-European order will only be conceivable if the two halves of Europe move closer together, if there is political and economic assimilation, and if the two halves are finally united under a common roof. As an important central European country, Germany undoubtedly plays a very prominent role in this process, but an even more prominent role is played by the European Community, as explained by *Vladimir Zouev* in his contribution. The EC is not only an object of desire for the eastern half of the continent, in line with Vaclav Havel's formula about a "return to Europe"; it is also the nucleus on which the new Europe is to be built. Moreover, the community represents an example of a new pattern of international relations as well as a model of a new economic, social, and political organization -- a model that could probably open the way for overcoming the problems being generated by the current preponderance of nation-states.

However, at the present time neither the EC nor the states of Eastern Europe are sufficiently well prepared to do justice to this kind of once-in-a-century mission. By according priority to a deepening of integration rather than to a possible extension, the community has signalled that its efforts continue to be directed primarily inward. Nor is it clear when the desired membership will be granted to the reforming states of the East: the EC's priorities in this regard lie primarily with the EFTA countries. However, the further integration advances, the greater become the barriers for new members: even now there are considerable reservations in Eastern Europe about renouncing recently secured sovereignty in favour of inclusion in a powerful supranational organization.

For the foreseeable future, therefore, the former socialist countries will remain "at the gates," and will continue to be dependent on outside help in their efforts to bring about the transformation of their economic and social systems. This situation has given a new boost to ideas about these countries' creating their own system of regional integration. Why COMECON, dissolved in mid-1991 after a series of vain attempts at reform, was not a suitable basis for such a system, is explained by *Aleksandr Nekipelov*. As an alternative model of international socialist economic relations, it not only laboured under the systemic defects of the planned economies, it actually increased them. Because of the systematic problems with price-fixing, multilateral payment, and mutual coordination of planning, it was never possible, within the framework of COMECON, to fully exploit the advantages of the international division of labour. Despite the obvious defects, a relatively well-developed network of reciprocal supply-links did establish itself within COMECON. Just how important these links were, however, became painfully obvious when, in 1991, in the wake of unilateral measures by its members, the organization went under, along with trade in Eastern Europe.

The collapse of commerce between the former socialist countries placed another considerable burden on their efforts to bring about transformation. The tasks that must be tackled in this area are discussed in the last two contributions -- by *Pavel Kandel*, who deals with the political and social aspects, and by *Hans-Joachim Spanger*, who looks at the economic reforms that are being introduced. Although the goal of the 1989 revolutions -- namely the overcoming of the totalitarian order and the creation of pluralist societies based on individual competition -- is not really in doubt at the moment, obstacles which cannot be ignored are piling up on the path that leads to it. The first two years of the new age have shown that institutional reforms in politics and the economy are scarcely adequate, and that what is really needed is a radical change that reaches right down into individual behavioural attitudes. Given the burden of the socialist legacy, given various historical factors that reach back further than this, and given the profound economic depression, the conditions for such a change are extremely poor. Internal fragmentation, bringing a growth in populism and nationalism; the adoption of hostile stances in external relations, with the risk this brings of a bal-kanization of the region; and the paralyzing coexistence of Manchester-style capitalism on the one hand, and bureaucratic immobility on the other -- these are all clear warning signals. Without comprehensive Western support -- this much should at least have become clear -- the transformation will not succeed. And this support is all the more urgent in that the future of the whole continent will be decided in Eastern Europe.

*Vladimir Baranovsky*
*Hans-Joachim Spanger*

# Acknowledgments

This book is the outcome of a joint project under the auspices of the Peace Research Institute Frankfurt and the Institute of World Economy and International Relations in Moscow. Its aim was not just to assemble a number of articles in a volume but to enter into a truly cooperative research effort on the future of Europe. For this reason, the project included fellowships as well as two major conferences held in Frankfurt in June 1990 and in Moscow in March 1991.

Conceptualized and agreed upon in summer 1989, the manuscript was prepared at a time when revolutionary changes were sweeping over the European continent. Though intellectually highly stimulating, this made writing on current developments a sometimes hazardous endeavour. Therefore, the editors wish to thank the authors for their patience, their readiness to keep track with the evolving situation, and for updates and revisions they were forced to introduce into their chapters more than once. Among the many people who were involved in organizing the conferences, in proof reading, and in preparing the camera-ready manuscript, we are particularly grateful to Claudia Buckenmaier, Beate Jahn, and Andreas Scholz for their invaluable support. Similarly, we wish to thank Margaret Curran as well as Gerard Holden, Michael Schatzschneider, and Bernard R. Unden, who successfully tackled the demanding task of translating and language editing.

Finally, the editors along with the authors wish to thank the John D. and Catherine T. MacArthur Foundation, Chicago, whose generous support made possible a project which in many aspects proved a journey into unknown territory.

*V.B.*
*H.-J.S.*

# About the Contributors

**Vladimir Baranovsky**, professor of political science, is currently senior researcher at Stockholm International Peace Research Institute and main researcher at the Institute of World Economy and International Relations (Russian Academy of Sciences, Moscow), where he was also head of the department of European studies during 1988-1992. Since 1991 he has served as member of the Scientific Council of the Russian Ministry of Foreign Affairs. He has authored and edited numerous books on West European integration (in Russian) and has written extensively on Soviet and Russian foreign policy.

**Yuri Borko** is professor of economics and head of department at the Institute of Europe (Russian Academy of Sciences, Moscow). From 1970 to 1989 he was head of department at the Institute of Information on Social Sciences (Academy of Sciences of the USSR). He is also president of the Russian Association of European Studies. His books include (in Russian) *Social Progress and Economic Integration* (1984) and *The Common European House: What We Think About It* (1991).

**Matthias Dembinski** is currently visiting fellow at the Center for Science and International Affairs, Harvard University. From 1989 to 1991 he was a research fellow at the Peace Research Institute Frankfurt. He is the author of many articles and reports on nuclear arms control in Europe.

**Pavel Kandel** is a historian who worked at the then Institute of Economics of the World Socialist System (Academy of Sciences of the USSR, Moscow) during 1979-1990. In 1990 he moved to the Institute of Europe. He has published numerous articles on the efforts at reform, the revolutionary changes, and the process of transformation in Central and Eastern Europe.

**Aleksandr Kokeev** is a senior fellow at the Institute of World Economy and International Relations, Moscow. He has specialised on Germany and has contributed to many Russian publications on the Federal Republic of Germany and on relations between Moscow and Bonn.

**Gert Krell** is head of the research group on European security at the Peace Research Institute Frankfurt. From 1983 to 1984 he was Assistant Director for Regional Security of the International Institute for Strategic Studies, London. He is the author and editor of several books on international security, arms control, and German foreign policy, including most recently *Internationale Politik: Eine Einführung* (1991) and *Friedensgutachten* (1987-1992).

**Harald Müller** is senior fellow and Director of International Programs at the Peace Research Institute Frankfurt. During 1984-1986 he was senior fellow at the Center for European Policy Studies, Brussels, and, since 1984 he has been visiting professor at the Center for International Relations, Johns Hopkins University, Bologna. His recent books include *Vom Ölembargo zum National Energy Act* (1989) and *How Western European Nuclear Policy Is Made* (1991).

**Aleksandr Nekipelov**, professor of economics, is deputy director of the Institute of International Economic and Political Studies of the Russian Academy of Sciences in Moscow (the former Institute of Economics of the World Socialist System). He is the author of some forty books and articles on COMECON-related problems.

**Peter Schlotter** is senior fellow at the Peace Research Institute Frankfurt. In 1990 he served as policy adviser to the then GDR foreign minister Markus Meckel, and in 1992 he was visiting professor at the Technical University, Darmstadt. He has written extensively on arms control, East-West detente, West European security cooperation, and the CSCE.

**Hans-Joachim Schmidt** is a research fellow at the Peace Research Institute Frankfurt. He has specialised on conventional arms control in Europe and has published numerous articles on MBFR, CDE, and CFE.

**Bruno Schoch** is senior fellow at the Peace Research Institute Frankfurt. He is the author of some thirty articles on international marxism, eurocommunism, and German unification. His books include *Marxismus in Frankreich seit 1945* (1980), and *Die internationale Politik der italienischen Kommunisten* (1988). Most recently he edited *Deutschlands Einheit und Europas Zukunft* (1992).

**Hans-Joachim Spanger** is senior fellow at the Peace Research Institute Frankfurt. In 1987-1988 he was research associate at the International Institute for Strategic Studies in London. He has written several books and many articles on the two Germanys, including *Die SED und der Sozialdemokratismus* (1982), *Die beiden deutschen Staaten in der Dritten Welt* (1987), and *The GDR in East-West Relations* (1989).

**Yuri Streltsov**, colonel (ret.), served from 1964 to 1974 on the General Staff of the Soviet Army. Afterwards he headed the section on disarmament at the Institute of the United States and Canada (Academy of Sciences of the USSR, Moscow). In 1978 he became head of department at the Diplomatic Academy of the Foreign Ministry of the USSR and in 1985 senior fellow at the Institute of World Economy and International Relations in Moscow. He has published numerous books and articles on the arms race, arms control, NATO, and US foreign policy.

**Vladimir Zouev** is head of the section on the European Community at the Institute of World Economy and International Relations in Moscow. Since May 1992 he has been economic advisor to the Russian Ministry of External Economic Relations. He is the author of *Great Britain and the European Community* (1988, in Russian).

# In from the Cold

# PART ONE

# Continuity and Change

# 1

## The Transformation of East-West Relations and the New Security Agenda in Europe

*Gert Krell*

### Introduction

Historical years reckon up differently from calendar years. The cumulation of political events between 1989 and 1991 in Eastern Europe, in the Soviet Union, and in East-West relations has led to a radical transformation of the international system -- and this is even before the full consequences of those events have become apparent. The reform process has brought a dismantling of structures integral to the East-West conflict. In November 1990, the members of the CSCE solemnly declared the end of that conflict with the proclamation of the Paris Charter. The socialist world system is also being dissolved. This process reaches beyond the East-West conflict as it had developed after the Second World War, and embraces the origins of the antagonism between capitalism and socialism, the first international expression of which came with the Russian Revolution. Finally, the transformation of the current international system is reaching into the old Russian/Soviet Union, affecting structures dating back to the 19th century and earlier.

Although the current historical situation remains open, it is important to stress the radical nature of the changes that have taken place. They rank alongside other major events that fundamentally transformed the international system -- the two world wars, for example, or the Russian Revolution itself. The present hiatus will lead to new constellations in world politics; it will offer new options for world history, but it will also raise a number of new problems, or revive old questions under changed circumstances.

The radical change which the "European Revolution of 1989-91" has brought about in the international system is embedded in two longer-term global trends that raise fundamental questions about the possibility of progress in the world system as a whole. Those trends are: the structural crisis being experienced by developing countries, and the fundamental ecological crisis now threatening the world. The European revolution, the structural crisis in the developing countries, and the fundamental ecological crisis, constitute the starting-points for world politics at the beginning of the final decade of the twentieth century -- or, if we count in historical rather than calendar years, the starting-points for a new century.[1]

In this chapter, I concentrate (1) on political developments and (2) on developments in Europe itself, particularly those which affect the security agenda. I first look back on the East-West conflict -- its contents, its importance for the structure of European (and world) politics, and its dissolution. I then discuss the transformation of East-West relations in both its positive and its negative dimensions. I begin with the more promising aspects of the new international order, including the process of, and further prospects for, demilitarization. On the negative side, I mention some of the problems which the old order has left behind and which are as yet unresolved, and I go on to introduce the new category of conflict which seems to have replaced the former East-West antagonism, namely the clash of nationalist and ethnic aspirations, mainly in what used to be "the East." In the conclusions, I summarize the major security challenges facing western Europe, eastern Europe, and Europe as a whole.

## The East-West Conflict

To give an adequate scientific definition of the East-West conflict is difficult. Most interpretations remain within the framework of influential theoretical models explaining what holds the world -- i.e. international relations -- together.[2] As a result, stress is laid on various conflictual aspects: conflicts between political orders, between differing systems, conflicts of power, conflicts over security. The turn taken by events would seem to vindicate those who always maintained that the true cause of the East-West conflict lay in the communist party's claim to power, lacking as it did any kind of democratic legitimation, whether internal or external. This does not, however, necessarily provide a retrospective justification for the policy of strength. On the contrary, militarized anti-communism -- this at least is Ernst-Otto Czempiel's thesis, and one that he was already advancing before the turning-point came -- actually helped to conceal the true causes of the conflict, to extend the conflictual configuration, and thus to prolong it beyond its normal life-span.[3] Miscalculations of the socialist "alternative" are easy to condemn now, and they must indeed act as a spur to self-critical examination, not only by social movements and political parties but by *realpolitik* itself.[4] Nonetheless, in undertaking such critical and self-critical reflection, one should not lose sight of the circumstances in which the conflict originated, namely the serious asymmetries in the international system, and the problem of unequal development -- a problem that has still not been resolved in what is now once again an alternativeless international capitalist system.[5]

One fact that cannot be disputed is that the East-West conflict was the dominant conflictual configuration in the international system after the Second World War. Even during detente, it remained antagonistic in nature, because the decisive precondition for that detente was, precisely, the recognition that the world was divided: into opposing military blocs, into differing social orders and economic systems, and into rival political ideologies each claiming universal validity. It is important to bear this in mind: that frequently cited formula "the end of the Cold War" is not applicable to the process we are currently witnessing, since the Cold War embraced only one part of the East-West conflict and had already given way to detente during the 1960s and 1970s.[6]

The conflictual configuration engendered by the East-West conflict did not just influence relations in the northern hemisphere, it was global in its tendency. The "Third World" was made into a tool of the two sides -- through the installation of military bases, through arms sales, client relationships, and even proxy wars. The actions of the "Third World," for its part, were governed by the East-West conflict. At times, it tried to team up with the "Second World" against the "First," or else it attempted to extract advantages from the clash between East and West. Even where, as a "third" world, it consciously rejected bloc-formation, the East-West conflict constituted one of its preconditions. Wherever its specific roots may lie, this conflict between East and West was conducted as a hegemonic clash between two superpowers, using military, economic, and political means; and the resultant costs moulded and distorted structures and decision-making processes in all the countries involved, particularly the USA and the USSR. But the hegemonic conflict was not resolved militarily, a fact which may -- but need not necessarily -- be an effect of nuclear deterrence.[7]

The East-West conflict was related to -- not identical with -- the clash between capitalism and socialism on the world scale. Originally, socialism was conceived, both theoretically and in political practice, as a further stage of development, as a level superior to bourgeois-capitalist society; only later did it become a strategy for alternative, "catching-up" development in an international economic system dominated by the developed capitalist countries. The importance of the socialist economic system of course remained slight, particularly in comparison with the military status of the Soviet superpower.

Finally, the East-West conflict was also related to -- but even less identical with -- the communist world-movement, the origins of which lie in the Western system itself and which, despite many schisms and ruptures (social democratic revisionism, Maoism, Titoism, Eurocommunism) and despite a steady decline in legitimation, continues, even after the demise of the Soviet Union, to have its place within that system.

The East-West conflictual configuration resulted in the formation of certain structures and the establishment of a certain order. Not a peace order, since the configuration continued to be marked by antagonism and a serious lack of legitimation -- without antagonism and a lack of legitimation, it would not have become a conflictual configuration. It was an order in the sense that norms, agreements, and procedures for regulating the conflict and the division of influence were developed.[8] The "prevention of war" became a central, if not evenly reflected, element in this order. War-prevention in the East-West conflict was inconsistent and inadequate, because it was a method of war-prevention secured by military means; but it was by no means futile. The civilizing of the conflict through arms control, for instance, always remained prey to certain dangers, but it managed ultimately, as early as the old days of detente, to establish itself on a permanent basis.[9] The CSCE process, which was also born out of the need for some form of conflict-regulation, evidently contributed to the transformation of the system. It was originally inaugurated by the Eastern side as part of a strategy for safeguarding the territorial status quo -- but one that was by no means seen as purely politically defensive; however, it then began to have a critical effect, in that it organized co-operation, reduced external pressure (although this was desired as a stabilizing mechanism), and exposed the nub of the confrontation -- real socialism's lack of legitimation -- turning it into a subject of open debate.

Over and above this, the East-West conflict offered a solution to the German question, even though the majority of Germans did not see it this way. As far the community of states was concerned, this was the third successful solution to the problem, despite the manifest and onerous internal deficiencies of this variant of division. But Germany had twice failed as a united union-state, and the chief precondition for the East-West conflict, and thus also for the separation and repression of one half of the German people, was, after all, the Second World War, which Germany itself had unleashed.

In addition, the clash between East and West resulted in the containment of the potential for conflict within the two alliances. However, the achievements of the prevailing order in this regard were at best indirect -- that is to say they resulted from the fact that particular conflicts were neutralized by being absorbed into a higher -- and more dangerous -- conflictual configuration. Economic relations within the OECD area come under this category: the East-West conflict had a disciplining effect on them. The process of West European unification was probably also boosted by the East-West conflict -- which is not by any means to imply that it was the major cause of it. In the Soviet sphere of power, the whole nationality issue in eastern central and south-eastern Europe, in the Caucasus, Central Asia, and the core countries of the Union, was put on ice during the period of the East-West conflict; it was not constructively worked through, however, but was repressed or poorly disguised under the mantle of socialist internationalism. Hence, one can only speak in cynical fashion here of achievements of the prevailing order.

The East-West conflict began heading for its own dissolution the moment the Soviet leadership started to call its own claim to power -- devoid of democratic legitimation -- into question. The irony -- or indeed tragedy -- of the story lies in the fact that Gorbachev at first believed he could provide a new justification for that claim to power. From the very start of *glasnost* and *perestroika* -- with which the CPSU Secretary General intended merely to effect a reform, albeit a comprehensive one, of Soviet communism -- vistas were opened up which would sooner or later destroy the framework of the old East-West order. At some point, the new detente inaugurated in 1985 would, even under Gorbachev's early premises, have so transformed the relationship that it was no longer possible to speak of the East-West conflict in its original sense. Even the reforming version of socialism, which ranked universal human rights over the class struggle, which sought to strengthen the United Nations, and which undertook credible steps towards demilitarizing foreign policy (this was how the Soviet Union initially looked under Gorbachev) marked a decisive departure from the realms of "coexistence" -- which had ultimately been conceived as tactical in nature -- and thus also from the realms of a conflictual configuration, which, despite detente, remained antagonistic in character.[10]

The fact that the reform of the socialist system of states was not (or no longer) possible proved that Gorbachev's premisses were false, though only in a dialectical sense. This time, the reforms were not intended merely to be cosmetic; and they turned out not to be revocable any more. Whatever half-heartedness there was within Soviet society in specific terms, the socialist system of states, the socialist economic and military community began to break up. It was inevitable that they should break up, because they were not true communities; and it was possible for them to break up because this time the reform came from the Soviet Union itself and was determined to remain true to itself as a reform -- even though it ran counter to its socialist premisses.[11] The upshot was that both the ideological and institutional preconditions for the East-West conflict ceased to exist.

## The Transformation of East-West Relations

### *The New International Order*

Whatever the problems that will have to be tackled, and whatever the issues to be discussed in detail, we should begin by noting the peaceful resolution of the East-West conflict as a historic event. The termination of a hegemonic conflict in time of peace, without recourse to war, is an unusual occurrence, albeit not as extraordinary as is claimed by the realist school.[12] Peaceful resolution was possible because the Soviet Union declared that its own policy in the conflict had been a failure and withdrew from the conflictual configuration it had played a decisive role in creating with its ideological and foreign-policy claims to power. The American side contributed to the peaceful resolution to the extent that it did not exploit the withdrawal of its old rival in the classic way, in order to extend its power. This too runs counter to the assumptions of realism.

The old conflictual configuration also carried with it the threat of a third -- nuclear -- world war. This threat was probably never as great as was feared by the peace movement or by peace researchers, but it was definitely greater than zero. It had to be greater than zero, since the logic of nuclear deterrence both presupposes and produces the possibility of nuclear war. Statistically speaking, an accumulation of crises over time, all of them involving some risk of war, would ultimately have been bound to increase the risk. Of course, the various crises produced some learning-effects, but there were also instances of regression as far as conduct in conflict was concerned. With the dissipation of the East-West conflict, the risk of a nuclear world war tends towards zero, although the military infrastructure of nuclear deterrence -- and particularly of strategic nuclear deterrence -- will not be completely removed.[13]

Even during the era of the East-West conflict, the international system of states could only be described as bipolar with reservations. The term "bipolarity" was most applicable in the military field, where the prominent status of the two superpowers was particularly manifest. The Soviet Union has largely lost its superpower status -- at any rate, the preconditions for an active global role have all but disappeared for the foreseeable future. The new power configuration in the international system of states will oscillate between unipolarity and multipolarity -- if, that is, these categories are at all applicable. One cannot really talk of polarity any more, because there are no longer any significant security-problems between the remaining great powers -- and definitely no conflictual configuration. Others have proposed the term "imperfect oligopoly."[14] Dieter Senghaas speaks simply of an "OECD gravitational centre," with a few questionable candidates who are not yet -- or are no longer -- globally active (China, India, Russia, Brazil) and a "marginal remainder."[15]

If one uses other criteria than the mere technical capability to project power or to initiate nuclear war, then the USA is the only remaining superpower, in the classical sense that it has at its disposal, and is politically capable of using, military instruments of power across the world. But the USA is not a clear hegemon; in implementing policy on the international order, and even more so in regard to international economic affairs, it is dependent on co-operation. The USA's victory in the East-West conflict is a very relative one; it too has been weakened by the arms race, albeit not to the same extent as the former USSR. Even though the Gulf war may have seduced many people into thinking so, the international order that has emerged since the end of the East-West conflict is not an order governed by a *Pax Americana*.[16]

The USA continues to be -- or is now more than ever -- the most important of the great powers, but it finds itself politically and economically in a position of mutual dependence with the EC and Japan, with whom it forms a security partnership. Nor will there be any use of military force between these powers, or power-groups, in the future. This constitutes a favourable precondition for the establishment of an international peace order, in which there is no sign of any new global hegemonic conflict and which offers the United Nations the opportunity of greater achievements.[17]

The preconditions for a peaceful European order are also favourable, particularly in comparison with, and in contrast to, earlier attempts to achieve this (1815, 1919, 1945). The new European order will not be an order of the victors over the vanquished; it does not lie in the shadow of a large-scale war. It involves no fundamental ideological clash but can instead be built up from a fund of common notions of political order which, though not irreversible, are rooted in a mature consensus.[18] It is characterized by a high degree of transparency and -- particularly in western Europe (which includes the north, the south, and the centre) -- by complex interweavings. The western European process of unification precludes certain violent conflictual constellations -- such as Franco-German antagonism -- which have shaped European history for centuries.

Moreover, there is every prospect that the third attempt to reconcile the German nation-state and the European peace order will not this time fail.[19] Both at the systemic and at the actor level one may observe structural changes that are of greater moment than the remaining legacies of the first and second German dictatorships.[20] The degree to which Germany is politically embedded in, and contractually bound to, the West is greater than ever before, and this situation has come about voluntarily, so that it will not be affected by the return to full sovereignty. Furthermore, Germany has given a number of guarantees on security -- also voluntarily and on the basis of a broad consensus. It is not least for this reason that unification has been accepted by all of Germany's neighbours and all the major powers -- although there are still clear reservations about it. But unification was not pushed through against the will of third parties, let alone by force. The peaceful and democratic way in which unification was achieved "from below" must be regarded as a particularly significant advance compared with the foundation of the *Reich* in the nineteenth century. Finally, the democratization and demilitarization of German society and German foreign policy provide effective guarantees that Germany will not once again become a security risk for Europe. It will no longer develop any expansionist tendencies. And even if it did, it would not be able to put them into effect. Only a -- highly improbable -- extreme right-wing German government would seek an independent nuclear option, and this would be precisely the kind of government that would be unable to secure it.[21]

Another item to be recorded on the credit-side is the fact that the contemporary "great powers" of Europe are not so great any more and are satisfied with their positions -- with the possible exception of a radically nationalistic Russia. The new regional conflicts which are currently taking place or are beginning to emerge in Europe are no longer linked to hegemonic conflicts, in all probability they will not escalate into large-scale clashes; the kinds of rival alliances of great or medium-sized powers to whose level these conflicts could be raised do not exist. The civil war in Yugoslavia, however problematic and regrettable it is, will not now be the cause of another world war.

### Demilitarization

Alongside the political dismantling of the old conflictual configuration there is a dismantling of the military apparatus similar in proportion to a post-war demobilization. The historically unique backdrop of military threat in Europe -- whether in the form of a "Soviet or Western menace" or of the "danger of the arms race" -- is breaking up. The largest military machine in the world, the Soviet Army, is withdrawing, being drastically reduced, collapsing internally and externally. The "Treaty on Conventional Forces in Europe" (CFE) decrees the abolition of around 150.000 major army and air-force weapons-systems and establishes an extraordinarily detailed system of verification and control. But this is far from being the end of arms reductions. It is already obvious that manpower and weaponry will be reduced even further, regardless of whether any further arms control negotiations take place. In the case of the ex-Warsaw Pact countries, the planned figures already lie well below the ceilings agreed on in Vienna. On the NATO side too, it is clear that there will be further reductions.

In the case of nuclear weapons, it was the INF Treaty that marked the start of developments. It was the product of a highly contradictory amalgam of Soviet reformers, European peace-movements, and American "hardliners," yet it marked -- particularly in regard to the co-operation between Reagan and Gorbachev -- a major milestone on the road to a qualitative change in East-West relations.[22] The START treaty, which followed after a number of delays, is lagging well behind in substance, despite its incredibly detailed treatment and its radical provisions on verification. Although it brings some important advances in comparison with its predecessors, SALT I and SALT II -- above all, it comprises some arms reduction as well as arms regulation -- it no longer corresponds to the state of political relations. President Bush has acted on this and, on the basis of INF and START, has taken a clear step forward by initiating the abolition or withdrawal of all land- and sea-based tactical nuclear weapons and the reduction of air-based ones, and by suggesting further reductions in strategic weaponry. Gorbachev's response exceeded this, aiming amongst other things at a comprehensive test-ban. And there are good prospects for a complete ban on chemical weapons, which is still being negotiated in Geneva.

In their totality, the changes mentioned above signal the start of a radical demilitarization of relations between the industrial nations and also promise the release of urgently needed resources for tackling the real tasks facing humanity.

### Lasting Burdens

People cannot simply opt out of their history. The East-West conflict not only consumed a huge amount of productive potential; it also left behind some stubborn traces. This applies firstly in a literal sense to the military detritus -- the pollution of earth and water by nuclear tests and on conventional training-grounds. The cost of the clearing-up operation for Soviet bases in the German state of Brandenburg alone runs to tens of billions of DM, while that for military nuclear sites in the USA is around 100 billion dollars.[23] Disarmament too costs money: this applies to verification and to the scrapping of weapons -- the technical and political problems of which (e.g. the burning of chemical warfare agents) are far from all being solved. The conversion of the military-industrial complex to more productive activity involves financial costs and political and economic difficulties -- not least because of the privileges which this sector has long enjoyed, and because of its specific conditions of production.[24] The lack of housing for military personnel in the former Soviet Union, especially for the families of officers, has attracted particular attention because of its internal and external explosiveness.

But much of the legacy is contained in people's heads -- and I allude here not only to the end of totalitarianism or to the collapse of the Soviet Union: the East-West conflict shaped and distorted political thinking in the West as well. Polarization allowed for large-scale collective projections and thus absorbed creative socio-critical potential -- through each side's idealization of itself or of the other side. And it absorbed aggressive potential in enemy images, a potential that is now looking for other outlets. In the words of György Konrad: "If there is no longer one major enemy, there will be many small ones; the enemy image will split into parts. . . . Those who have learned to be afraid will reproduce the enemy: they need him."[25]

The dissolution of this structure -- the profound effects of which are not the usual subject-matter of reflection in political science -- and the willingness to give oneself up to the chances and risks of a completely new historical situation requires adjustments by more than just those groups in society who were very prominently and clearly linked with the East-West conflict.

## New States and New-Cum-Old Nationalism

Until the advent of the East-West conflict, European history of the nineteenth and twentieth century was decisively marked by nationalism and national movements. This nationalism appeared in two variants: emancipatory and aggressive-cum-expansionist. The two dimensions were not always clearly distinguishable, and even the defensive variant produced fuel for disputes between legitimate rival claims. The formation of nation-states left a trail of blood, even in the pioneering Western democracies, and even those countries continue to have their problems with it up to this day. Nationalism proved all the more explosive in the break-up of the old dynastic multi-nation states -- a process which we can now say was merely interrupted by the Russian Revolution and the East-West conflict. Europe has succeeded only at some points and times in delimiting the newly established nation-states from one another in an ethnically satisfactory manner, and in securing peaceful co-existence between various ethnic groups within these nation-states. In many areas, the fact of living side by side, being the natural product of history, was accepted as a matter of course, but many of the mixed communities were forcibly broken up by expulsions, ethnic displacement, or indeed genocide. Through its annihilation of the European Jews and its subjection and partial liquidation of other peoples and ethnic groups, National Socialism accomplished the unique feat of bringing this historical trend as it were to its perverse, apocalyptic expression.

Within the East-West conflict, the nationalist inheritance, in both its variants, was largely put on ice. In the West it was able to continue to express itself (viz. the civil wars in Ireland and Cyprus, Basque separatism, the French-Canadian movement), but its dynamic was defused to a great extent in a process of democratic integration backed by a historically unprecedented improvement in living conditions and welfare. In western Europe, supranational loyalties are replacing national references, social distances have decreased, and the various nationalities trust each other.[25]

In eastern central and south-east Europe, and in the Soviet Union itself, developments were much more complicated in this regard, and on the whole much less favourable. On the one hand, here too, as in the West, economic growth created new loyalties stretching beyond old ethnic boundaries; and after the end of the national-socialist conquest (or after the end of collaboration with Nazi Germany), the integrity of the nation-states and thus "national security" was guaranteed through Soviet dominance. On the other hand, constructive treatment of historical rivalries was seriously lacking in the whole socialist camp -- notwithstanding some substantial and partially successful attempts at correcting traditional economic asymmetries, such as between Bohemia/Moravia and Slovakia. In many cases the foundations for such rivalries were strengthened, or indeed newly laid, during the socialist period. The repressive Stalinist nationalities policy is a prime case, deliberately combining as it did the suppression of ethnic-national ambitions with the dissolution of traditional settlement-structures. The official denial -- supported by tenets of Marxist ideology -- of ethnic or national conflict in intra- or inter-state relations, together with the granting of favours to privileged ethnic groups or nationalities in a position of power, has given rise to special problems, in the Soviet Union and elsewhere.

In eastern Europe, traditional enemy images and national stereotypes have remained essentially intact, and this not only between eastern central Europe and the nationalities in the west of the former Soviet Union. Even between Poles, Czechs, and Hungarians there is more distrust than trust; and the majority of Poles, Czechs, and Slovaks see themselves as living in a hostile environment.[26]

With the dissipation of the East-West conflict, nationalism and the formation of nation-states has been reactivated. This also means calling into question not only the territorial boundaries established after the Second World War -- which had also been "frozen" by the East-West conflict -- but also the Paris treaties of 1919 and after. Indeed, there is more at stake now than old disputes about boundaries; what is at stake is the configuration of European nation-states in the twentieth century. Yugoslavia and the even older Russo-Soviet Union are already in the process of breaking up; the continued existence of Czecho-Slovakia is by no means certain.

The difficulties that will be encountered in the formation of successor states are already evident: the war in Yugoslavia, which is half civil, half national, is merely a clear expression of a whole series of latently violent, or already overtly violent, conflicts. In addition to the conflicts over boundaries between the successor nation-states, there is a need for regulations governing old and new ethnic minorities, since the majority of these potential new states or half-states will house more than one major ethnic group or nationality. Almost all the Yugoslavian and Soviet republics have significant minorities. The process of fragmentation reaches right into these republics, and the schismatic emancipation that is taking place -- the new republican nations unshackle themselves from the old, global states, but at the same time the indigenous or acquired minorities within them are suppressed or disadvantaged -- lays the foundations for further conflicts such as may be observed in various forms in Lithuania, Latvia, Croatia, Moldavia, Georgia, etc. In addition to this cynical division of the liberation process, there is a tendency for emancipation to be directed against the former "state-nations."[27] But if the Ingush, Chechen, and Tatars, for example, demand withdrawal from the Russian Federation, do the Russians in non-Russian republics not have the right of entry into it? Given that the Croats are withdrawing from the Yugoslav Federation, why should the Serbs not be allowed to withdraw from Croatia? The reference to historical borders is not much help here, since almost all borders are artifical, i.e. are political boundaries, a fact that is merely highlighted by the very desire for the dissolution of the old federations. Many ethnically mixed regions could not be disentangled even by correcting borders or shifting territory, however. The mythologization of nation or history serves little purpose here: only a strict ban on violence and the undivided right to self-determination can provide opportunities for compromise, the only other alternative being the questionable course of exchanging homelands via mutual resettlement.

Even on the optimistic assumption that there will be a gradual process of consolidation as the nation-states form or reform, with effective safeguards for minorities and new federative or confederative forms, the constellation of states in Europe and Asia will still be completely new. It cannot be clearly enough stressed that there is much more on the agenda than simply the dissolution of the East-West conflict. Assuming there will be no violent reshaping of the Russo-Soviet Union -- this cannot be entirely excluded, but seems unlikely -- what we have in prospect is the continuation of the process of break-up of the imperial multi-nation states (the Ottoman Empire, Austria or Austria-Hungary, Russia/the Soviet Union; in Africa, Ethiopia may be mentioned in this connection) which have for centuries made history.

This process will cause considerable changes to the political map of eastern Europe, the Caucasus, and Central Asia. New political regions will emerge, with new areas of political conflict and far-reaching political effects. In eastern Europe, new rivalries may develop betweeen Poland, Russia, and the Ukraine, perhaps involving the risk of new regional arms races. Hungarian revisionism and the Ukraine-Moldavia-Rumania triangle are also potential sources of trouble, whilst the Balkans are notoriously explosive.[28] The Chinese leadership, meanwhile, is keeping a nervous eye on the emancipation of ethnic politics on China's northern border, and on the repercussions this may have on Inner Mongolia and the Xin-Jiang province.[29] The civil war in Afghanistan is hardly an East-West problem any longer, it is now largely an internal islamic conflict. Fundamentalist groupings are endeavouring to establish solidarity from Teheran right into the north-west of India and, from this bridge, to extend their gaze to the Muslim republics of the former Union. In the erstwhile Soviet Union itself (and in China), pro-Islamic tendencies are stirring. This is another dimension in which the dissolution of the East-West conflict leads to the unbounding of former demarcations, in this case the political-cultural border between Islam and Christianity, which runs geographically (or politically) right through the middle of some countries or republics of the old configuration.

One special problem is that posed by Soviet nuclear weapons in the radically changed conditions of a fragmented USSR.[30] This concerns, firstly, the question of nuclear control from the centre. After the failed putsch, the new defence minister, Shaposhnikov, together with Gorbachev and Yeltsin, gave assurances that Soviet nuclear weapons had been in safe hands during the coup. In addition, the leadership of the Soviet strategic forces took measures signalling a reduction in battle-readiness to American reconnaissance. However, the confusion that surrounded the president's military command-centre and the three cases containing the electronic command-codes was clearly so great that it casts doubt on the current scheme of security, regardless of who is to take over the nuclear weapons belonging to the collapsing superpower.

The civil-war-like disputes in some republics have also raised the problem of "ethnic grab." The danger that one of the many parties to the civil war could forcibly acquire tactical nuclear weapons cannot be completely excluded. In addition there is the question of discipline amongst those guarding the weapons or amongst the relevant sections of troops. An army whose soldiers sell weapons and uniforms on the black market can, in principle, also lose fissile material by this route.

These risks may be small, and they may well be removed altogether if the planned elimination of most tactical nuclear weapons goes ahead. However, this does nothing to elucidate the problem of control of centrally regulated strategic nuclear weapons and the whole related infrastructure. Strategic weapons have become bargaining-counters in the negotiations between the republics over the new shape of the Union. Rumours about a preventive attack by Russia against the Ukraine (the rumours were immediately described as politically misguided and the attack as not even possible technically) revealed new sensitivities and anxieties.[31] What shape the new unitary strategic leadership will take is still an open question. Depending on how this debate and decision-making process develop, the Non-Proliferation Treaty may also be affected. Besides the "warheads," there are the "eggheads" -- i.e. the scientific-technical nuclear apparatus -- who are now also a matter of grave concern. Because of the desperate economic situation and the shrinking military-industrial complex, many experts will hawk their knowledge and contacts on the international nuclear market, in particular to aspiring third-world regimes. Rather than seeing these experts hired by Iran or Libya, for example, the West may try to buy them off first.

## The New Security Agenda in Europe

During the East-West conflict the main security issues were those involving East and West. They were so dramatic and overpowering that all other security issues paled in comparison. Even at that time, however, major asymmetries could be discerned in the behaviour of the two camps in regard to conflict. In the West, conflicts were mostly allowed to run their course in the open, even to the extent of producing inter- and intra-state wars -- albeit only in a very few cases. In the East, these kinds of conflicts were forcefully and sometimes violently repressed. In the West, the rare instances of organized inter- or intra-state violence were offset by a much stronger trend, a genuine transnationalization of values and institutions, of production, trade, and finance. No such developments took place in the East. In spite of some genuine achievements, particularly in the fields of education, training, and science and technology, the countries which experienced Soviet socialism are still (now openly again) confronted with a number of old problems of European history -- in addition to the grave and complex tasks of economic and political reconstruction.

Ironically, the capitalist parts of Europe were "communized" to a much greater extent after the Second World War than was Eastern Europe or the Soviet Union. This is the major reason why the new security agenda in Europe -- totally different from the Cold War order -- is highly asymmetrical. The West has greatly improved its security situation: the OECD zone of gravitation will continue to constitute a security community where inter-state conflict will not lead to large-scale violence; and domestic conflicts, inasmuch as they reach quasi-military dimensions at all (e.g. Northern Ireland, the Basque Provinces, Corsica), will only have local effects. This does not mean that the West will have no other security problems, but there is no clear, imminent danger any more. The possibility of direct military threat is an extremely remote one.

The East, on the other hand, has exchanged the old security problem of the East-West conflict for the new one of East-East conflicts -- a direct result of the bankruptcy of the old socialist system. Hence there has been no actual dissolution of security problems in the old East-West area, only a shift. By this I mean that, thanks chiefly to the break-up of alliances, states, and even republics, and to the rise of old and new nationalism, there has been a proliferation of conflictual constellations, and these now preponderate in the East. Since both the economic and internal political structures of the old and new countries in the region are very weak, and will remain so for quite some time, the tendency to intra-state or inter-state violence will not easily be held in check.

Fortunately -- and this makes the situation quite different from pre-1945 constellations -- these East-East conflicts are not linked to any superior conflictual formation. At their peripheries, however, they may overlap with other regions and their conflicts. This is all the more likely, as the political and geographical boundaries of former Yugoslavia and of the former Soviet Union become fluid. The resultant risks, which may be direct (trans-border violence or alliances) or indirect (general lawlessness, the collapse of economic and political structures, migration) transcend the East-East conflicts proper.

The major challenge for Europe as a whole is to find ways of preventing these violent conflicts, or at least of containing them. As for the possibility of controlling military conflict among third parties through external intervention, the prospects for such a course have never been very good at any time, either militarily or -- even less so -- politically. The use of military intervention to control violent conflict raises serious ethical questions and is often counterproductive. Political responsibility and legitimation for major operations can be shouldered only by collective organizations, and the consensus needed in such organizations constitutes a strong barrier to action, a barrier which will only be overcome in exceptional situations. Rapid reaction forces such as those planned by NATO could only control minor conflicts.

Thus preference must be given to non-military instruments -- this is already the principle underlying the UN covenant and the CSCE agreements. It is here that strategic planning and strategic imagination should concentrate their energies. Moreover, there should be a long-term policy aimed at preventing situations in which there is no alternative to the use of outside force or sanction. Any strategy that addresses major sources of conflict can be helpful in this regard: co-operative security policy; military strategies based on the notion of defensive defense; support for democratization; economic assistance; ecological cooperation.

Addressing the non-military dimensions of security has become a more urgent task *per se* as far as the survival of all societies is concerned, rich as well as poor, eastern as well as western. Such a course can also help avoid the explosion of the more classical security problems. The end of the East-West conflict offers a historic opportunity to demilitarize and to redirect scarce resources to more productive uses. Building an all-European community of peace, prosperity, and freedom as envisaged in the Paris Charter will be a difficult task. Without such a community, however, Europe will not be able to play the role it needs to play if the world is to move from the Cold War to a genuinely new world order.

## Notes

1. For an overview of the world system after the East-West conflict, see Gert Krell, *Aufbruch und Krise: Das Weltsystem nach dem Ost-West-Konflikt und die aktuelle Friedens- und Sicherheitsproblematik* (Frankfurt: HSFK-Report No. 6, 1991).

2. On the East-West conflict, see Werner Link, *Der Ost-West-Konflikt*, 2nd edn., (Stuttgart: Kohlhammer, 1988). Various approaches are discussed by Thomas Risse-Kappen, "The End of the Cold War and Theories of Change in International Relations," paper presented at the workshop "The End of the Cold War -- Evaluating International Relations Theories," European Consortium for Political Research, Essex, England, March 22-8, 1991.

3. Ernst-Otto Czempiel, "Friedenspolitik im europäischen Ost-West-Konflikt," in: Franz Böckle, Gert Krell (eds.), *Politik und Ethik der Abschreckung*, (Mainz, München: Kaiser, Grünewald, 1984), pp. 84-7.

4. The statist approach to detente is now the butt of criticism from those groups who opposed socialist regimes. Nevertheless, statist detente was one of the external preconditions for the changes that occurred.

5. See the sociological analysis of Soviet communism by Andrew C. Janos, "Social Science, Communism, and the Dynamics of Political Change," *World Politics*, Vol. 44, No. 1, 1991, pp. 81-112. His discussion of basic problems of development in an asymmetrical world system results in a very pessimistic prognosis of new possibilities of "revolutionary militancy" in the post-socialist period.

6. One could only argue that this period of détente was replaced by a new cold war at the beginning of the 1980s. The correction back to détente started

even before Gorbachev, however, and certainly before the "European revolution." Cf. Raymond Garthoff, *Détente and Confrontation. American-Soviet Relations from Nixon to Reagan* (Washington: The Brookings Institution, 1985), and Ernst-Otto Czempiel, *Machtprobe: Die USA und die Sowjetunion in den achtziger Jahren* (München: Beck, 1989).

7. On this, see, amongst others, John Lewis Gaddis, "The Long Peace: Elements of Stability in the Postwar International System," *International Security*, Vol. 12, No. 1, 1987, pp. 3-21; Robert Jervis, "The Political Effects of Nuclear Weapons: A Comment," *International Security*, Vol. 13, No. 2, Fall 1988, pp. 80-90; John Mueller, "The Essential Irrelevance of Nuclear Weapons: Stability in the Postwar World," *International Security*, Vol. 13, No. 2, Fall 1988, pp. 55-79.

8. See, for instance, Volker Rittberger (ed.), *International Regimes in East-West Politics* (London: Pinter, 1990).

9. On this, see, for instance, Alexander George, Philip J. Farley, Alexander Dallin (eds.), *US-Soviet Security Cooperation: Achievements, Failures, Lessons* (New York, Oxford: Oxford University Press, 1988). Also, Uwe Nerlich, Trutz Rendtorff (eds.), *Nukleare Abschreckung: Politische und ethische Interpretationen einer neuen Realität* (Baden-Baden: Nomos, 1989).

10. On the Soviet doctrine of coexistence, see Egbert Jahn, "Friedliche Koexistenz und Entspannungspolitik in sowjetischer Sicht," in: DGFK (ed.), *Zur Lage Europas im globalen Spannungsfeld, DGFK Yearbook 1982/3* (Baden-Baden: Nomos, 1983), pp. 67-90.

11. For a political justification of this process see Edvard Shevardnadze, *Die Zukunft gehört der Freiheit* (Reinbek: Rowohlt, 1991).

12. See Robert W. Tucker, "1989 and All That," *Foreign Affairs*, Vol. 69, No. 4, Fall 1990, pp. 93-114: "There does not appear to be an instructive modern historical parallel of a hegemonic conflict simply being terminated by the default in time of peace on one side" (p. 95). Perhaps not in the strict sense, but see Stephen R. Rock, *Why Peace Breaks Out: Great Power Rapprochement in Historical Perspective* (Chapel Hill and London: University of North Carolina Press, 1989).

13. I will mention new risks of proliferation, and indeed of regional nuclear war, later on.

14. Roberto Aliboni, Gianni Bonvicini, Cesare Merlini, Stefano Silvestri, "Three Scenarios for the Future of Europe," *The International Spectator*, Vol. 26, No. 1, 1991, pp. 4-29.

15. Dieter Senghaas, *Internationale Politik jenseits des Ost-West-Konflikts*, (Ebenhausen: Stiftung Wissenschaft und Politik AP 2722, 1991).

16. Much-needed correctives to the exaggerated expectations or fears regarding the USA's role after the East-West conflict are provided by Christoph Bertram, "Pax Americana Akt II," *Kursbuch* No. 105, September 1991,

pp. 37-44. On the controversy over the decline of the USA, see, e.g., Paul Kennedy, *The Rise and Fall of the Great Powers* (New York: Unwin Hyman, 1987); Joseph S. Nye, *Bound to Lead: The Changing Nature of American Power* (New York: Basic Books, 1990); Susan Strange, "The Persistent Myth of Lost Hegemony," *International Organization*, Vol. 41, No. 4, Fall 1987, pp. 551-74; Barry P. Bosworth, Robert Z. Lawrence, "America's Global Role: From Dominance to Interdependence," in: John D. Steinbruner (ed.), *Restructuring American Foreign Policy* (Washington: The Brookings Institution, 1989), pp. 12-47; Stephen Krasner, "Declining American Leadership in the World Economy," *The International Spectator*, Vol. 26, No. 3, 1991; Rudolf Witzel, "Der Niedergang Amerikas: Mythos oder Realität?," in: Bernd W. Kubbig (ed.), *Transatlantische Unsicherheit* (Frankfurt: Fischer, 1991), pp. 105-24.

17. There will continue to be disputes about regional supremacy, particularly in the Middle East, in southern Asia, and, in the longer term, in the four-way system made up of the USA, Japan, China, and Russia.

18. This was where the central problem of the otherwise very constructive nineteenth-century concert of powers was to be found. On the latter's achievements, see Paul W. Schroeder, "The 19th-Century International System: Changes in the Structure," *World Politics*, Vol. 39, No. 1, 1986, pp. 1-26.

19. On this, see, amongst others, Karl Kaiser, "Germany's Unification," *Foreign Affairs*, Vol. 70, No. 1, 1990/91, pp. 179-205; Gert Krell, "Gleichgewicht aus der Mitte? Deutschland und die europäische Friedensordnung im neuzeitlichen Staatensystem," in: Bruno Schoch (ed.), *Deutschlands Einheit und Europas Zukunft. Friedensanalysen 26* (Frankfurt: Suhrkamp, 1992), pp. 257-79.

20. On this legacy, see, for instance, Ralph Giordano, *Die zweite Schuld oder Von der Last Deutscher zu sein* (Hamburg: Rasch und Röhring, 1987), and Hans-Joachim Maaz, *Der Gefühlsstau: Ein Psychogramm der DDR* (Berlin: Argon, 1990). The socio-psychological issues associated with unification are discussed by Michael Lukas Moeller, Hans-Joachim Maaz, *Die Einheit beginnt zu zweit: Ein deutsch-deutsches Zwiegespräch* (Berlin: Rowohlt, 1991).

21. Inaccurate in their analysis and recommendations in this regard are both John Mearsheimer's "Back to the Future: Instability in Europe After the Cold War," *International Security*, Vol. 15, No. 1, Summer 1990, pp. 5-56, particularly pp. 37-40 and pp. 54-55; and Stephen van Evera's "Primed for Peace: Europe After the Cold War," *International Security*, Vol. 15, No. 3, Winter 1990/91, pp. 7-57. Both consider a German nuclear option as stabilizing.

22. See Thomas Risse-Kappen, *The Zero Option: INF, West Germany, and Arms Control* (Boulder, Colorado: Westview, 1988).

23. *Der SPIEGEL*, No. 20, 1991, p. 55 and *Handelsblatt*, October 30, 1991, p. 7.

24. *SIPRI Yearbook 1990. Armaments and Disarmament* (Oxford-New York-Toronto: Oxford University Press, 1990), pp. 344ff.

25. In a speech to the PEN-Congress in Vienna, as quoted in *Süddeutsche Zeitung*, November 6, 1991, p. 14 (author's translation). On the question of projections and enemy images see also Moeller, Maaz (*op.cit.* in note 20), pp. 131 and 143: "The offical enemy images have broken down, but not the internal ones -- the structures which we have described. These still need outlets via scapegoats. ... We both needed and used each other, in order to pacify our internal troubles: We imagined in you the greatness and freedom that we were not allowed to live -- and for you we represent the narrowness and poverty which you do not want to recognize on your own side. We use these projections to divert attention from our internal situations. If we really want to move closer, then we must take back these separations and release our counterparts from the projections. Then we would be confronted to a much greater extent with ourselves" (author's translation).

26. This does not exclude conflicts over immigration. Indeed, there is a risk of renationalization in western Europe, too.

27. See the polls in *Eurobarometer* of December 1990, pp. A-47.

28. That these formerly privileged groups will have to surrender something, is obvious and is implied in the very term "emancipation." The abolition of privilege does not mean merely changing places in an asymmetrical structure, however.

29. See, e.g., F. Stephen Larrabee, "Long Memories and Short Fuses: Change and Instability in the Balkans," *International Security*, Vol. 15, No. 3, Winter 1990/91, pp. 58-91.

30. See Lena H. Sun, "China Fears Spillover from Soviet Agitation," *International Herald Tribune*, September 21/22, 1991, p. 2.

31. See Christian Schmidt-Häuer, "Die Suche nach dem verlegten Schlüssel," *Die Zeit*, September 19, 1991, p. 9.

32. *Süddeutsche Zeitung*, October 25, 1991, p. 7.

# 2

---

# Beyond Antagonism:
# In Search of a New Identity
# After "Real Socialism"

*Yuri Borko*

The history of the 20th century has made clear that the character and structure of international relations depend to a great extent, if not completely, on the specifics of the social systems and on the level of development in the countries involved. Europe's experience in this respect is of particular significance, as two fundamentally different social systems developed and coexisted side by side there over many decades. Their interaction formed a pan-European social system, as it were, with basically antagonistic elements that had achieved a certain degree of mutual accommodation. During the course of the last two decades, however, this antagonism was challenged in at least two respects: first at the level of the intellectual debate, and later at the level of actual politics. This, one hopes, will eventually spawn a real pan-European system -- this time nonconfrontational, organic, and homogeneous.

## First Attempts to Overcome Antagonistic Coexistence

The anti-Hitler coalition of Stalinist totalitarianism and Western democracies, brought to life by extraordinary circumstances, fell apart immediately after the war. For Western Europe, not only did victory over the common enemy mean a reinforcement of democratic values but it also led to a critical reassessment of the tragic experience of the two world wars, the great economic depression of the 1930s, of fascism and of Stalinism. As for the Stalinist regime, it used this victory for a further strengthening of the totalitarian system and its expansion on the European continent to an area reluctantly recognized by the West as the zone of Soviet influence.

Each of the systems had its own logic of development. It stemmed from the basic features of these two systems and from the general course embarked upon by their respective political elites. Although both systems represented real alternatives in historical terms, in the end, history made an unmistakably clear decision. The total collapse of "real socialism" in Central and Eastern Europe and in the Soviet Union has unequivocally shown this path to lead nowhere. It was not until the end of the 1980s that the total failure of "real socialism" became evident, however. For more than 40 years, the two systems seemed similarly viable, forming the main axis of intersystemic security and, to a limited degree, even of cooperation. Security and cooperation were rather difficult to achieve, however, not least because of the mutual perceptions of the two antagonistic blocs. Both proceeded from the assumption that the two systems were virtually incompatible, being based on mutually exclusive principles of societal organization with fundamentally different relations between the individual and the state.

In the socialist countries, the perception of "the opponent" was largely determined by Lenin's theory that "imperialism was the final stage of capitalism," and by the related concept of "the general crisis of capitalism," which allegedly began after 1917, was steadily "deepening and worsening," and would finally end with the total collapse of world capitalism. This concept was reaffirmed even in the latest platform of the CPSU, adopted at its 27th congress in 1986.[1] In Western Europe, Soviet "real socialism" and its East European variants were regarded predominantly as the main models of a totalitarian society. Those advocating this view were no less categorical in judging the historical causes of "totalitarian communism" and its peculiarities than were their socialist counterparts in their analysis of capitalism. No doubt, their perception was reinforced by the cold war, especially in its initial stages. According to Stephen F. Cohen "the study of the Soviet Union by the 1950s had become an extremely politicized occupation, inseparable from time-serving political objectives and the spirit of crusades, and based on the principle "Study your enemy."[2] Although times then changed to the point of even gradually softening the mutual enemy images, on the whole, until the onset of *perestroika*, the concept of totalitarianism remained central to explaining the character of "real socialism."

Nevertheless, it was in the West that the idea of a fundamental similarity between the capitalist and the socialist systems -- beyond all their obvious differences -- emerged and even gained some popularity. This so-called theory of convergence, elaborated in the early 1960s, was initially much discussed in both the Western social sciences and Soviet Marxism-Leninism, before it faded away in the 1970s. The names of its founders and followers testify to the popularity this theory enjoyed until then. They include: Pitirim Sorokin, Walt Rostow, John Kenneth Galbraith, Raymond Aron, François Perroux, and Jan Tinbergen.

Gnosiologically connected with theories of modernization and industrial society, the theory of convergence proceeded from the fact that in the developed countries, on either side of the divide, the systems were characterized by an industrial, highly urbanized civilization that determined individual behavior and motivation as well as social needs. This similarity, it was argued, created and developed a trend toward a gradual rapprochement of values, politics, and organizational structures of capitalist and socialist societies. Raymond Aron wrote that the very idea of convergence was "brought to life by the desire to avoid at the very beginning any counterposing of socialism and capitalism, and was a way to analyze both of them as two variants of industrial society."[3] Some of the evolutionary processes under way in both the East and the West during those years were interpreted as proof of the theory of convergence. In Western Europe, state intervention in the economic and social spheres was on the rise. John Maynard Keynes's model of macroeconomic regulation and the policy of the "welfare state" were being put into effect. But even greater importance was attributed to the changes occurring in the USSR after Stalin's death. The proponents of convergence regarded these changes as tangible proof that the imperatives of industrial civilization were as valid in the socialist countries as they were in the capitalist ones.

In the USSR, as in the other socialist countries, the theory of convergence was subject to sharp criticism, being viewed and dismissed as "an attempt to falsify the facts and discredit socialism in the eyes of millions of people."[4] In the West, too, there was some criticism -- though for quite different reasons. The idea of convergence turned out to be discredited there because attempts at economic reform, along with cautious moves toward political liberalization in the countries of "real socialism," not only ended in failure but also spawned a stiffened conservatism, as in the USSR, the GDR, Poland, and Bulgaria, or were militarily suppressed with the "fraternal help" of the Soviet Union, as in Czechoslovakia.

But even though the hypothesis of a progressive rapprochement of the two social systems was not supported by reality, the theory of convergence, nevertheless, played a useful role. It was the first attempt to escape the rigid dichotomy "capitalism versus socialism." The advocates of this theory have pointed to the theoretical and political importance of the fact that, despite all the fundamental differences between them, both systems have common interests resulting from similar or at least closely related needs for social development. Actually, the theory of convergence precipitated the "discovery" of what later became universally recognized -- the global interdependence of all peoples, nations, and social systems. But before this happened, another, more practical, attempt to re-establish constructive intersystemic relations, albeit conceptually on a much narrower basis, was made: East-West détente. The basic goal of détente in the 1970s was not to change the two social systems but to complement by "normal" cooperation East-West relations that up to that point had been based almost exclusively on a military balance of confrontation between the two blocs. This required a formal recognition of the territorial and sociopolitical status quo, and of "rules of the game" agreed upon by the two systems.

The Helsinki Final Act, signed on August 1, 1975, was the first international document to manifest such an approach, and this makes it unique. But from the very beginning, this document contained time bombs, which started exploding only a year after its signature. The Final Act's principles were based on the Universal Declaration of Human Rights and thus modeled on Western patterns. Why did the then Soviet leader, Leonid Brezhnev, and his allies sign the Helsinki Final Act? Perhaps they underestimated the "danger" of using it to disregard cynically any of the declarations and norms of civilized behavior enunciated therein. Or perhaps they overrated the official Western recognition of what had been achieved during 60 years of "struggle for socialism." Anyway, the Soviet Communist Party and state bureaucracy showed very quickly that they were not prepared to respect human rights in the USSR, to stop the "ideological war" against the West and to terminate their support of extremist movements and regimes in developing countries. And they showed no inclination whatsoever to curb their frenzied and economically disastrous military programs. The Soviet invasion of Afghanistan gave the death blow to détente, which was already moribund anyway, and which, after all, proved incompatible with totalitarian socialism. As a result, in the early 1980s the two blocs in Europe turned back to what they had started with almost 40 years before. Again, the "enemy image" dominated the mutual perception, their respective values, norms, and socioeconomic principles appeared as irreconcilable as ever. All this ruled out the possibility of any substantive discussion about a common European architecture different from the one established during the cold war. After all, it had maintained the peace on the continent and promised to do so in the future as well.

The collapse of totalitarianism in Central and Eastern Europe has achieved what seemed rather utopian before: it opened the way for eventually overcoming an incompatibility that had persisted for decades. For the first time in postwar history, the European dialogue is being conducted in the universal language of modern civilization. This "rapprochement," however, is taking place in a manner quite different from the one the proponents of the theory of convergence visualized thirty years ago. Essentially, it is one side engaging in catching up with the other: the formerly "real socialist" countries have embarked on the long and difficult path of transition to a Western-type social system -- that of the market economy and multiparty democracy. This transition will no doubt be a painful process -- especially for the successors to the Soviet Union, where "real socialism" looked back on a much longer history and left deep imprints on the public consciousness.

## How to Overcome Totalitarianism?
## The Soviet Debate About the Future

In effect, *glasnost* and *perestroika* in the Soviet Union sounded the death knell for the moribund East European system. The democratic revolutions that swept Eastern Europe in late 1989 have irrevocably eliminated the totalitarian system there. Up to the failed putsch of August 1991 in Moscow, the USSR remained the only country in which that system, despite its complete lack of prospects, was still frantically resisting change. Seven decades of Marxist-Leninist ideology had solidly anchored the foundations of communist totalitarianism. Marxism-Leninism had been turned into a code of unquestionable dogmas and myths, subject to no other interpretation than the one suggested or approved "at the top."

One of the paradoxes of Soviet-type socialism was that this social system, alien to the fundamentals of European civilization, grew out of the greatest achievements of European thinking. Both the "utopian socialists," whose projects go as far back as early Christian morals, and the "scientific socialists" (such as Marx and Engels), who claimed to have developed socialism further (from "utopia to science"), had no doubts that they had discovered a universal remedy for all social ills: the substitution of public ownership for private ownership. As simple as this cure might have seemed to them, while moving on from "utopian science" to political practice, they failed to address the crucial question as to whether such a radical remedy would be compatible with basic values of European civilization such as humanism, freedom, justice, equality, and peace. But real life soon began dealing staggering blows to their optimism: it was not long before a monstrous gap between goals and means opened up in the first country of "victorious socialism." And while being put into practice, theory underwent two further, rather "anti-European," modifications, first at the hands of Vladimir Lenin and then at those of Joseph Stalin.

One cannot say that Lenin really falsified Marxism. But he changed its emphasis when he attributed an absolute character to revolution as a "locomotive of history" and declared "the dictatorship of the proletariat" the quintessence of Marxism. One might come to the conclusion that Lenin actually combined the socioeconomic theory of Karl Marx with the traditional Russian revolutionary maximalism. On the other hand, it is also true that, at a later stage, Lenin launched his "New Economic Policy," a novel approach to socialism running counter to Marx's anti-market orientation and Lenin's own adherence to the twofold dictatorship -- that of the state over society, and that of the communist party over the state. But this particular deviation of "Leninism" from "Marxism" was quickly and radically "smoothed away" by Stalin. Finally, Lenin appended to Marxism a theory of imperialism that justified the construction of socialism even in an economically backward country and foresaw the future confrontation between the rising socialist state (i.e. the Soviet Union) and the "dying capitalist states" (i.e. at that time, the European states ).

As far as Stalin is concerned, his contribution to the theory of communism is quite a specific one. From the work of his predecessors Marx, Engels, and Lenin, he borrowed only what could be used to bear out the theory of a totalitarian state, and the indispensable role of violence in history. The theories on class struggle and dictatorship of the proletariat were "enriched" by the concept of the inevitable escalation of the class struggle with the advance of socialism. A theory on the general crisis of capitalism and on the struggle of the two antagonistic social systems was added to the theory of imperialism. The list of Stalin's theoretical innovations of this kind can be expanded. But his major contribution to the theory of communism goes beyond it. It was he who created the simplified and schematic summary of Marx's, Engels's, and Lenin's ideas, known under the name of Marxism-Leninism. This "ultimate" version of Marxist thinking was canonized during Stalin's lifetime, its major concepts, arguments, and logical structure remaining valid until the introduction of *glasnost*. While Lenin's anti-European approach was sociopolitical, the one promoted by Stalin had a fundamentalist quality and rejected in every respect the basic values of European civilization. And finally, as an ideology, Stalin's brand of Marxism-Leninism held sway through physical and cultural terror. This was no accident but the quintessence of the totalitarian state, especially in its initial stage. And even more was required: a uniform system of propaganda and education to "reach" people throughout their entire lives; an "iron curtain" to cut them off from the outside world; a string of real and fictitious victories of the totalitarian regime over its capitalist enemy to back up the ideological myths.

All the aforementioned conditions prevailed in the USSR during Stalin's rule, especially from the early 1930s until his death in 1953. The three decades that followed saw a gradual decay of this social system and its underlying ideology. The unrelenting feeling of fear, most acute during the successive waves of mass repression and the recurring purges, began to subside. External trade ties had to be established for the sake of the country's economy, and this inevitably led to a vastly increased flow of information from abroad. Thus, in view of capitalism's scientific and technological achievements, it became harder and harder to simulate the "advantages" of socialism over capitalism. As a result, dogmatic and myth-permeated Marxism-Leninism (or "scientific communism") lost a great deal of its integrity and plausibility, and the huge propaganda apparatus lost some of its efficiency.

Intellectuals, who exposed Stalinism during the first "thaw" in the 1950s, were the first to play an important role in undermining the official Soviet ideology, before the so-called dissidents -- who formed the first ideological and political movement in the USSR, openly began opposing the totalitarian system. By the early 1980s, the deep crisis besetting the official ideology had become obvious. A petrified Marxism-Leninism had largely lost its capacity to extol the existing system. But tens of millions of people were still blinded by myths and prejudices. So, in order to break the spell a further element was needed -- akin to the boy in Andersen's fairy tale, who cried out in the middle of a crowded square "the emperor has no clothes." This role was performed by *glasnost*. Initially, it was primarily a flood of sensational information poured out on the public. Every day, the mass media came up with previously unknown facts and newly discovered aspects of society that had been kept secret for decades. Much of the information thus exposed literally had a shock effect.

Public consciousness in the Soviet Union, stifled by decades of totalitarianism, began to flower with the advent of *glasnost*. A kind of revolution swept through the mass media -- not in terms of technological innovations but in terms of the multisided information now offered to the public by the print and electronic media. At the time, public attention to new ideas breaking with the traditional official dogmas was enormous. Each new interpretation of history, politics, economic development, and political philosophy received a strong echo in public opinion. Articles written in a new and unorthodox spirit, and suggesting a re-evalutation of anything that had been considered "sacred cows" before, were widely discussed all over the country. Many of the authors challenging the "taboos" of the totalitarian ideology became almost national heroes -- a circumstance some of them later used as a springboard to a political career. It is against this background that we are able to make out a number of turning points in the evolution of Soviet society.

In 1987, the whole of society became involved in qualitatively new debates on the nature of the social system, the causes and consequences of current events and processes, and the correlation between the theory and practice of "scientific communism." And this time again, the debate focused on those "eternal questions" that Russian writers and philosophers had tried to solve as far back as the 19th century: Who is to blame? What is to be done? It is hard to say which publications actually played the role of the battering ram that first breached the solid wall of official ideology. At least two of them should be mentioned, however. In 1987, in an article he wrote for *Novy Mir* (New World), one of the most popular literary "heavies" in the Soviet Union, Professor Nikolai Shmelev -- who later became a member of parliament and an influential economic advisor to the Soviet leadership -- outlined the advantages of a market economy and a program of transition to the market.[5] And Professor Gavriil Popov -- the former editor in chief of the academic magazine *Voprosy Ekonomiki* (Problems of the Economy), later one of the leaders of the Russian democratic movement and mayor of Moscow -- in an article published in another broadly circulated magazine *Nauka i zhizn* (Science and Life), introduced the notion of command and administrative system into the Soviet vocabulary.[6] In fact, he was the first Soviet writer openly to highlight the link between the centralized planned economy and the repressive political regime.

In 1988, the debate over the key problems of Soviet society gained momentum. The monopoly of the official party and state ideology in the mass media and the scientific literature came to an end. For the first time in 70 years, "one-dimensional" thinking and ideological censorship were giving way to free thinking. It seems impossible to enumerate even the most significant books and articles published since then. But we certainly have to mention the *Perestroika, Glasnost, Democracy, Socialism* series, which has had such a large echo in a society redefining its own identity. The first book of this series, *No Other Choice*, contained about 30 articles written by well-known intellectuals and leaders of the democratic movement. It was followed by more volumes: *Realization* (1989), *To Comprehend the Cult of Stalin* (1989), *The Drama of Renewal* (1990), *Over Thorns* (1990), *Sinking into the Quagmire* (1991).[7] This series might well be called the anthology of Soviet public and political thought in the period of *glasnost* and *perestroika*.

The character of the social system created in the USSR was a pivotal issue in this debate. At least three interpretations of this system can be identified.

(1) The first wholly orthodox interpretation was based on the idea that the system created by Stalin was fully consistent with Marxism-Leninism and was truly socialist. A most pathetic illustration of this approach is a notorious article titled "I Cannot Compromise my Principles" by Nina Andreeva, a professor at the Leningrad Technological Institute (who became leader of the most orthodox faction of the communist movement in the USSR and later in Russia).[8] Though the author admitted that during the purges of the 1930s a great many innocent people had suffered, she believed such purges could be justified because of the class struggle raging at the time. According to Andreeva, any criticism of Stalin, "the pioneer of socialism," was a clear indication that this class struggle was being revived by the "successors of the expropriated classes." In a February 1990 interview with the Finnish newspaper *Viikkolehti*, she said that all the current problems were a result of the steady promotion of capitalism in the Soviet Union, starting as far back as the time of Khrushchev and having gained strength in recent years. She also insisted that currently "there is no real leader in the country, none like Stalin."[9]

At present, the proponents of a Stalin-type totalitarian socialism are politically marginalized. They are an obvious minority group, trying to turn back the clock of history and using ultraleftist phraseology. These neo-Stalinists, who favor Stalinism without the "gulag archipelago," can be found in all walks of life, but as a rule they belong to one of two groupings: those who have been part of the totalitarian system, worked for it and benefited from it; and those who have failed to achieve much in life but have adjusted to the system in which they have lived for all or most of their lives, and now are simply incapable of changing their way of thinking or living. This aggressive minority, however, represents a serious threat, for with growing unrest and instability in the country, it could attract millions of people yearning for security and order.

(2) The second point of view was expressed in the concept of a "deformed socialism," which had many supporters both among the CPSU leadership and among intellectuals.[10] This concept was adopted by Mikhail Gorbachev in many of his speeches and articles, beginning with his report "*October and Perestroika: The Revolution Continues,*" which he presented at the official meeting marking the 70th anniversary of the October Revolution. According to this approach, the introduction of public ownership of the means of production put an end to capitalist exploitation and established a truly socialist basis in the USSR. But the very essence of socialism was deeply affected by some of the serious deformations that occurred after 1917. Two of these are of fundamental importance and, as such, gave birth to many other distortions. In the political sphere, socialist democracy was supplanted by the openly repressive regime of Stalin's personal power, which developed into the dictatorship of the state bureaucracy, the *nomenklatura.* In the socio-economic sphere, a solely technocratic policy prevailed. Neither had the producer's alienation from his work been overcome, nor had the principles of socialist justice and socialist distribution of social product been sufficiently observed.

Most advocates of this concept referred to Stalinism as the major cause of the alleged deformations, i.e. specifically to the person who usurped power and to his policy. Fyodor Burlatsky, then editor in chief of *Literaturnaya Gazeta,* expressed this in a bold statement: "Let's answer a simple question: Had Lenin lived ten or twenty more years, would the country have gone through this ordeal, through 1937-38? Never!"[11] It is true that those who advocated such an explanation of "socialist deformations" in the Soviet Union also drew on the extremely unfavorable conditions the Soviet Union had to develop in, such as its economic and cultural backwardness, the hostility of the West, the bitter forms of social struggle, and the overall moral degradation. But still, the essential idea was that Lenin, with his "new economic policy," was regrettably succeeded by a man whose course of accelerated industrialization and collectivization, carried out by a militarized and centralized state and by the use of force and repression, proved disastrous.

The attempt to draw a dividing line between Lenin and Stalin is almost the focal point of criticism of the "deformed socialism." According to Mikhail Gorbachev, "it is obvious that the founders of Marxism and the theory itself cannot be held responsible for the deformations of socialism during the periods of personal cult and stagnation."[12] And others even referred to Lenin as "the last frontier" of communists in their ideological struggle with the opponents of socialism.[13] This approach came to the conclusion that both the renewal of socialism and an elimination of its deformations were directly linked to the resurrection of a "true" Marxism-Leninism, which should not be viewed as some ready-made design for a future social system but as a creative method of philosophical cognition and societal development. Even more, it was suggested that, from now on, the most valuable ideas from Marx's and Lenin's heritage should be chosen, i.e. the priority of the personality and the adherence to humanism and universal human values, but not the eternal class struggle, the dictatorship of the proletariat, or the large-scale nationalization of the means of production.

(3) The third concept maintained that no socialism at all was built in the Soviet Union. For example, the historian Yury Afanasyev, who also became a member of parliament and one of the most radical leaders of the democratic movement, argued that the Soviet society could not even be called "deformed socialism," since these deformations "hit its vital structures, the political system, the ways of production, and the rest."[14] So, if "everything" was deformed, what was left of socialism? According to this logic, the Soviet social system may be labeled "command and administrative," "state bureaucratic," "partocratic," or even "semifeudal," but it had nothing to do with socialism as conceived by Marx and Lenin. Ironically, this judgement is true both for the champions of a "new, humane and democratic socialism," as adopted by the new 1990 CPSU program,[15] and for their opponents. But whereas the former dismissed the criticism merely by trying to convert an insufficient "real socialism" into a true socialism, the latter argued that there was no country in the world where a socialist system was ever built along the lines of Marxism-Leninism. Thus, instead of tinkering anew in the spirit of "scientific socialism," one should turn to the values and achievements of world civilization.

There is one common element in all three approaches: a model of perfect (or ideal) socialism serves as a criterion for accepting or rejecting the socialist nature of Soviet society. And this is a truly unique approach, for no one has ever tried to assess feudalism or capitalism this way. However, for two reasons such a criterion is very subjective, too. First, it has become clear that different models of socialism exist; Marx and Engels, as well as the post-revolutionary Lenin and Stalin, were the originators of (at least) three different concepts of socialism.[16] Second, existing societies are never perfect, and it is actually impossible to measure precisely how close this or that society has come to an ideal. As a historical phenomenon, Soviet society was born and developed under circumstances that shaped its content and form as well as its general appearance. Therefore, if the question is raised as to what extent it corresponds to the idea of socialism, this very idea must be clearly defined.

All concepts and models of socialism included, on the one hand, basic values and ideas rooted in antiquity and early Christianity, and, on the other, systemic features that differentiated socialism from the previous stages of social development. The presence or lack of these features was a decisive criterion, which could prove or disprove the socialist character of any society. Starting with Thomas More and throughout the history of socialist thinking, the liquidation of private ownership was the undisputed core of any socialist society. And if socialism is understood as a society with collective forms of ownership and centralized control over production and distribution, then it is only logical that this was regarded as the system-creating quality of socialism. Exactly such a society was set up in the USSR. And albeit a far cry from an ideal of "social justice," it is nonetheless a historical reality looking more like the anti-utopias of Aldous Huxley, George Orwell, or the Russian émigré writer Yevgeny Zamyatin than the city of the sun or the society of emancipated labor. And nevertheless, this was socialism, implemented in the form and to the degree that a specific society in a specific country and under specific historical circumstances had proved capable of.

A broad variety of definitions of this "real socialism" could be found in Soviet publications: "initial stage," "primitive," "barracks," "state bureaucratic," "authoritarian," and so on. By way of summing up all these definitions, the Soviet political scientist Yevgeny Plimak came up with what we think is an interesting, comprehensive definition of his own: "In reality, the 1930s witnessed the creation of a specific social system with no historical parallels in the USSR. Insofar as it reflected a number of socialist features, it was indeed a socialist one. In some of its essential aspects, however, it was presocialist or even quite antisocialist."[17] All these definitions point to two dominant features of the system: its underdeveloped and its antidemocratic, repressive character. Both are dramatically reflected in Stalinism. Why Stalin and Stalinism became the center of the debate on the lessons of the postrevolutionary history of the country need hardly be explained.

This is certain to be a topic of discussion for many years to come. In the book *To Comprehend the Cult of Stalin*, it was justly pointed out that Soviet society "on a painfully long way with various halts and much turning back is approaching the vital process of de-Stalinization," but also that it was not until the advent of *glasnost* that it had become possible to study openly and freely "the brutal mechanism of total compulsion, moral and intellectual drainage, and physical extinction of the people, with Stalin being the creator and idol of this system."[18] This last quotation starkly shows the predominant perception of the tyrant and his tyranny in the last stages of the USSR. There remain a great many adherents of Stalinism, however. This is not reflected in direct apologies for Stalin but in the efforts to reestablish "the system," to revive the cult of an omnipotent state, and to dress the society in the straitjacket of the old ideology. "Stalin died yesterday," this frequently quoted phrase from a Russian historian, Mikhail Gefter, makes it abundantly clear that the tyrant's spirit still haunts the society.

Nevertheless, the public at large in Russia and the other independent states now definitely rejects Stalinism and is eager to comprehend its nature, its causes and consequences. It is virtually impossible to present the whole range of opinions and explanations. Literature on Stalin and Stalinism consists of hundreds of titles in which the multiplicity of thoughts has reached a peak, at least for now. Thus, it is more appropriate to delineate the main approaches in the analysis of the phenomenon. First there are the notorious neo-Stalinist approaches. Secondly, there is the uncompromising rejection of Stalinism as a major source of "deformed socialism," which is to be converted into a "humane democratic socialism" on the ideological basis of a "true" Marxism-Leninism. It should be noted, however, that the conceptual framework of this approach appears quite restrictive, thus preventing a profound analysis of the roots and nature of "the dictatorship of the proletariat," which ended up as a monstrous mechanism killing its own people and eventually starting its own self-destruction.

The alternative approaches no longer remain within the simplistic dichotomy of socialism versus nonsocialism. Thus, both Stalinism and "barracks communism" are explored as a cultural and social psychological phenomenon pointing, for instance, to the specific correlation between Stalinism and Russia's history, culture, and spiritual traditions. In this approach, history is referred to as a natural and ascending process of human civilization turned upside down by the official ideology. The way the country has developed since the "Great October Revolution" clearly shows that it was not able to reach a new stage of civilization, cut off as it was from the cream of world civilization. A new and more highly developed society cannot be built if almost everything that existed before is destroyed, if everything that contradicts Marxism-Leninism and the official political extremism is simply declared reactionary rubbish. This gives a clue about how to understand the essence and role of Stalinism.

The frontiers separating one part of public thinking from another are not so distinct as state boundaries. Nevertheless, there are good reasons for arguing that during 1990/91 social thinking in Russia and other Soviet republics underwent a thorough overhaul, which manifested itself in different ways. For one thing, public opinion tended to identify itself less and less with the Soviet Union and more and more with each particular nation, or nation-state, that had declared its independence and sovereignty. Again, the last taboos and self-restraints in discussing "blank spots" and "sacred cows," i.e. the most difficult issues of the past, present, and future, were lifted. Discussion of the nature of existing and conceivable models of socialism gradually gave way to sometimes heated debates about other questions: What is the true nature of our social system? What were the real reasons for its rise and fall? How was October 1917 connected with the earlier history of Russia, and what was Russia like on the eve of the revolution? What was the real role of Lenin and Leninism in all that happened? What is Marxism, and what historical blame and historical justification attaches to it? What are the options for reconstruction, and how might world experience, and especially the experience of the industrialized Western countries, be applied?

In fact, the first signs of this change in the public debate had emerged earlier, when people began discussing the concept of totalitarianism. Back in 1988 the philosopher Mikhail Kapustin said in an interview that totalitarianism and Stalinism were "almost synonymous," and that in some ways Stalinist totalitarianism was "close to fascism." It is important to note that this judgement came from an academic who also believed that Soviet society should be rebuilt on the basis of "neo-Marxism and neo-Leninism."[19] Among those who did not share Kapustin's political objective, the totalitarian label was applied not only to Stalinism but also to the period that followed it and is sometimes characterized as "post-Stalinism."[20] In their view, the dismantling of the totalitarian system in the USSR did not begin until the end of the 1980s. Thus in 1988/89 the philosopher Aleksander Tsipko published a series of articles under the general title "Sources of Stalinism,"[21] in which he addressed the question of the ideological relationship between Marxism and Stalinism. He concluded that "Stalin's idea of socialism and its primary tasks could not have differed much from what other Marxists at that time thought of it, since the basic social and philosophical ideas were the same." According to Tsipko, Marxism itself, by suggesting an extremely daring program for humankind's transition from pre-history to real history, made maximalist demands.[22]

But all this was only the beginning. The decisive change, or rather the break-through to a "revaluation of values," started in 1990. A great role in it was played by widespread publication of émigré and dissident literature, which had previously been kept in "specialized storehouses" or had been circulated illegally as *samizdat*. Names such as A. Denikin and L. Trotsky, N. Berdyaev and D. Merezhkovsky, P. Florensky and A. Chayanov, A. Avtorkhanov and M. Voslensky, A. Sakharov and A. Solzhenitsyn -- three generations of the post-October emigration, victims of the Gulag, and expelled dissidents -- gradually appeared in journals and bookshops. One cannot say that it was unknown to Soviet society. Its underground distribution began in the 1960s and played a significant role in the erosion of the official ideology. However, this literature was accessible mainly to the intellectual elite in Moscow and Leningrad and only rarely in the other cities. Nowadays, it is available to the general public and has become a vital reference in debates on the fundamental problems of social progress. Historians will have to analyze to what degree the émigré and dissident thinking has influenced (and will influence) the development of Russia and the other states on the territory of the erstwhile USSR. But even today it is evident that this literature has given a powerful stimulus to the debates and raised their intellectual and moral level.

But apart from the impact of émigré and dissident literature, it was the last agony and final collapse of the totalitarian communist system that played a decisive role in changing public thinking in 1990/91. Society badly needed new ideas, and it found them in a literature that had not only been prohibited and made virtually unaccessible, but had remained cut off from public opinion because of widespread prejudice and stereotypical thinking. This invisible barrier is now being dismantled -- not completely but to a considerable extent. One hopes that Russia has entered that period of spiritual renaissance without which it will be impossible to overcome the national catastrophe and bring about a substantial renewal of the country. Indeed, intellectual life in Russia has become very exciting, and the intellectual debate has undergone a profound change. That process of change has greatly accelerated since the last attempt by the old guard, in August 1991, to resurrect their dogmatic stereotypes. The present debate has become wide-ranging and fluid, but its main characteristics can be described as follows. Canonized Marxism-Leninism has not only been deprived of its monopolistic role in society, it has in fact almost ceased to exist in the traditional sense. Different versions of Marxism-Leninism are competing with one another, and the restoration of the previous ideological edifice is inconceivable. Instead, a climate of theoretical pluralism has developed, giving rise to a variety of strands of thinking that no longer accept Marxism-Leninism, or even Marxism, as a theory of political action or as a scientific method. On the other hand, the intellectual elite, and the public at large, are only just making their first steps toward fundamental renewal. The speed of this process depends on the development of society as a whole. If reactionary forces were to take over, even if only temporarily, free thinking and public opinion would be placed under enormous pressure, with witch-hunts and the old brainwashing. But even in such a situation, a mere restoration of ideological totalitarianism seems impossible. Its time has passed.

At one end of the spectrum of current political thinking we find neo-communism, with its extreme neo-Stalinism. It is supported not only by former CPSU bureaucrats, who formed the core of the *nomenklatura*, but also by a great part of the former "ideological staff" of the party, such as lecturers specializing in Marxism-Leninism, journalists, and editors. After a brief period of shock following the failure of the August 1991 coup, neo-communists and neo-Stalinists swiftly revived. The recovery was reflected in their attempts to adjust Marxism-Leninism to the new situation, to renovate it "on the cusp of the 21st century,"[23] and to develop new political programs. This spectre of orthodox Marxism-Leninism is opposed by non-communist and anti-communist views, and these have definitely gained the upper hand in intellectual debate and public opinion in Russia. The spectrum of these views is wide, ranging from social-democratic reformism, with its corresponding reinterpretation of Marx's concept of history, capitalism, and social progress, to a variety of Western liberalism and conservatism calling for a market economy and pluralistic democracy. One can hardly claim that any of these trends is brand new; most are based on established Western ideas and concepts. The main task is therefore to find out how Western theories and experience can be applied to the specific conditions prevailing in present-day Russia.

One of the hottest topics of the present debate, however, is the question of the "Russian national identity," i.e. Russian national self-consciousness, and Russia's place in world history and in the modern community of nations. The significance of this issue stems from the necessity not only to rethink the past, but also to determine a course for the future. The question is actually whether we are heading for a resurgence of the old dispute which had begun as early as the middle of 17th century, in the times of Nikon and Abakum, and reached its culmination in the well-known debates between Westerners and Slavophiles in the last century. Today's "neo-Slavophiles" and "neo-Westerners" share a clear negative assessment of the October revolution and the whole period after it. But this is the only view they have in common. Whereas "neo-Slavophiles" consider 1917 as a fatal seal on the protracted Westernization of Russia which had started with the reforms initiated by Peter the Great, the "neo-Westerners" regard the post-October alienation of Soviet Russia from Europe as the major disaster. And whereas the former talk of Russia's "special way," and the unique and mysterious "Russian soul," the latter link the country's future to its return to Western civilization, and more specifically to its return to Europe. Both parties have their extremist groups. But from a political point of view the real danger today comes from the aggressive "ultra-patriots," who intimidate society with the ghost of "Russophobia," a "hostile West," and a "Jewish-Masonic plot," calling for a restoration of law and order and of "millennial Great Russia."

For a while, it seemed as if the discussion about the nature and achievements of *perestroika* was to become one of the main issues in the public debate, and indeed, in 1989-91 the arguments became very heated. They continued even after Mikhail Gorbachev was forced to resign, but they soon faded, and this is not surprising. The failure of *perestroika* and the defeat of its initiator are clear. To prolong the discussion as to why *perestroika* had failed and what should have been done for it to succeed is absurd and inappropriate now. However, it must be said that the real significance of *perestroika* for Russia will not become clear until some time in the future. Only then will historians be in a position to analyze and evaluate this short period (from spring 1985 to the end of 1991), which not only profoundly changed the course of events in Russia and other ex-Soviet republics, but also had a marked impact on the world as a whole.

### Western Europe: A Model for the Future?

It will take a long time for a fundamentally reconstructed and truly post-totalitarian society really to take root in what was once called the "socialist community." Serious contradictions and difficulties have surfaced without exception in every one of the countries that have embarked on the new course. The initial euphoria about the unexpected and rapid success has given way to sober assessment. It has already become clear, however, that all the former socialist countries of Central and Eastern Europe have adopted Western society as a model for their own development. As President Vaclav Havel of Czecho-Slovakia has pointed out in a concise and highly significant phrase, their common aim is "their return to Europe."

As far as Russia and the other successors to the USSR are concerned, their own prospects of joining Europe are much less certain. In this case, however, it is not a question of geopolitical and economic choices, for, even in the Brezhnev era of "soft totalitarianism," the USSR showed interest in setting up an all-European system of security and cooperation. But again, and in a much more fundamental sense, Russia is confronted with a choice of historical dimensions: should it rebuild the system along "European lines" or start looking again for a "special, original way" of social progress? The answer to this question depends on what direction political consciousness will take, both at "the top" and at "the bottom." Before society can reconstruct itself, it must become aware of the need for change. And the only way to do this is to discard illusions and "unshakeable" dogmas. And exactly this process is currently under way in Russia. Its outcome depends on how honest and consistent society is in evaluating its historical experience. This does not concern only its self-perception, since a realistic self-image can be attained only through open and unbiased comparison with other countries and social systems and, in the case of Russia in particular, through comparison specifically with Western Europe.

It is no accident that, with the onset of *perestroika*, the experience of world civilization in resolving social problems has become a focal point in the efforts of the Soviet Union and its successors at social engineering. In this sense, the question of how to of overcome the official Marxist-Leninist dogma of "decaying capitalism" is by no means an academic one, but one of great practical importance. It should be mentioned here that the first attempts at overcoming this dogma in the Soviet academic world go back as far as the first "thaw" in the 1950s. For quite some time, however, these attempts failed to produce any practical results, and, by the 1980s a big gap had opened up between the level of concrete knowledge and the official theoretical paradigms applied to the world economy and international relations. Although *glasnost* did away with many ideological "taboos," it is still too early to speak of fundamental changes in economic and political theory. All one can do is identify some trends in the evolution of new theoretical concepts.

First of all, one should note the trend toward the "deideologization" of considerations of modern Western society. This trend is reflected in public criticism of yesterday's "sacred catchwords" -- "the total crisis of capitalism," "the bourgeois state" and of stereotypes such as that. which identified the market economy with "capitalist exploitation," or social relations with "the class struggle between capital and labor."[24] Russian scholars are seeking new methodological approaches to the analysis of Western society and of the various factors underlying its evolution. Among them, efforts at overcoming the traditional Marxist concept of "capitalist contradictions" are particularly important. It is well known that Marx and Lenin were convinced that these contradictions would inevitably result in the socialist revolution. But the experience of the 20th century has proven that this was far too simple an analysis. There is a more relevant methodological approach, namely, the analysis of the mechanisms of "self-regulation," whereby society "regularly resolves its accumulating contradictions and deals with the crises that arise."[25] The evolutionary potential of social systems depends largely on the flexibility of their self-regulating mechanisms. In fact, Western societies have shown themselves sufficiently flexible. Taking into account the profound changes that have occurred in Western countries (especially in Western Europe) since the end of World War II, we can conclude that "after the Second World War, a new regulation system for social processes has been formed, which helps neutralize worsening contradictions . . . These changes are so significant that we can speak of a qualitatively new stage in the development of capitalism in the second half of this century."[26]

Another approach goes even further in overcoming the Marxist theory of socioeconomic formations, and it expresses a direct interest in concepts of civilization. In 1989, two journals, *Voprosy Filosofii* (Questions of Philosophy) and *Mirovaya Ekonomika i Mezhdunarodnye Otnosheniya* (World Economy and International Relations) simultaneously initiated a debate on the concept of the integrated world, on the essence of civilizing progress, on the types and stages of the development of world civilization, and on the correlation between "civilization" and "formation."[27] One of the most controversial topics was whether the term "capitalism" could be applied to modern Western society. Summing up the polemic, a political scientist, the editor in chief of the journal *Mirovaya Ekonomika i Mezhdunarodnye Otnosheniya*, German Dilighensky wrote: "How can one define the society that we call capitalism? Undoubtedly it is a capitalist system from the economic point of view. But when one analyzes its policies and political systems, social goals and priorities, cultural life, i.e. everything referred to as the superstructure in Marxist terminology, it is practically impossible to reduce all these spheres of social reality to aggregating notions such as "capitalism" and "capitalist formation."[28] Moreover, within the framework of this new approach, the history of the European societies of the last centuries can hardly be described as the history of a capitalism driven solely by the development of the "production forces." On the contrary, it appears much more as a stage in the development of a

European civilization deeply rooted in ancient Greek and Roman traditions and in Christianity.

One might add one further touch to this picture by noting that the return to the idea of civilization has been accompanied by a return to the idea of a community of culture and of peoples in at least the European part of the former USSR and Europe. There is a distinct revival of the Western tradition in countries such as Russia, the Ukraine, and Belarus. It manifested itself in Russia as early as the 17th century, reaching its climax at the beginning of the 20th century before going into the near-seven-decade hiatus that followed the Bolshevik Revolution of 1917. Against this background, the rising interest in the West European social model carries conviction. And this interest is shared by all the former socialist countries now busy trying to overcome the heritage of totalitarianism. In their rush to emulate the Western model, however, they tend to overlook its various problems and serious inherent contradictions. All the same, when contemplating the social structures and the future political architecture of Europe, the former socialist countries should, and no doubt will, first of all analyze the West European achievements in creating an efficient, democratic, and modern society. The essence of this West European success story is that, since the end of World War II, Western Europe has been engaged in a continuous process of fundamental reform in which it gradually reorganized all the structures and mechanisms determining its economic, political, and social development. The Old World has undergone profound changes, and, as a result, it has constantly gained sufficient "breathing space."

To understand the significance of these changes, one should look back into the past. Since the Enlightenment and the French Revolution, Europe has achieved a real breakthrough in creating a unique civilization. It is unique because of the following three components: a developed industrial economy, a free civil society, and individuals with a specific personality -- active and determined, but at the same time self-critical; pragmatic and selfish, but at the same time imbued with, and reared in, the spirit of Christian ethics. But despite the magnificence of European civilization, its values, its spiritual and material culture, Europe's recent history is full of contrasts. The first half of this century was particularly tragic, marked as it was by the advent of chauvinism and militarism, two world wars, deep economic crisis, and violent social conflicts. And it was also in Europe that the two evil systems of our time raised their ugly heads: that of communist totalitarianism in the Soviet Union and that of national-socialist totalitarianism in Germany. One can hardly deny that these tragedies were at least by-products of European civilization. When contrasting the latter's remarkable achievements and tragic failings, one cannot but notice that many of the negative traits of individual behavior and social life are the reverse side of those traits we usually regard as positive. Just to mention a few of these opposing features: respect for the individual and individualism versus selfishness; economic freedom and private ownership versus lust for profit, cult of consumerism, and exploitation; the emergence of nations and nation-states versus nationalism, chauvinism, and colonialism; scientific and technological progress versus the arms race and ecological devastation; the promotion of democracy versus populism; and finally the ideas of social justice and social equality, which were eventually perverted into an egalitarian communism with total control over society and the individual.

A number of prominent thinkers have analyzed these paradoxes of European civilization and have each put forward ideas and concepts to try to overcome them: Thomas More and his *Utopia*, Jean-Jacques Rousseau and his "social contract," Karl Marx and his revolutionary socialism, Leo XIII and his *Rerum Novarum*, the encyclical proclaiming the Catholic church's social doctrine, to name but a few. Nevertheless, it would not be an exaggeration to assume that Europe needed the tragic experience of the first half of this century in order to mobilize and fundamentally change the social consciousness of its peoples. It served as a kind of shock therapy that helped them understand that the root causes of those cataclysms were to be found in European society itself. One could quote a number of authors who have dealt with this subject.[29] In his seminal book on European civilization, the well-known historian and sociologist, Samuel Eisenstadt, professor at the Hebrew University of Jerusalem, analyzes why Europe became the motherland of totalitarianism and in what way the latter was connected with either European modernism or European traditionalism.[30] The same theme was touched upon by Vittorio Strada, an Italian historian and journalist, in an article published in the Soviet weekly *Literaturnaya Gazeta*. When contemplating the phenomena of Hitlerism and Stalinism, he concluded, "A critical mind cannot agree with the reassuring and false thesis that totalitarianism was a kind of evil invasion of healthy and beautiful societies, something like the devilish revelry in the pious world. Both types of totalitarianism were borne by the European culture. But having delivered the "totalitarian syndrome," Europe invented the medicine as well -- liberal democracy as a prerequisite for its natural evolution to social democracy."[31]

The major result of this self-analysis was that West European societies began to overcome their habit of thinking in categories of confrontation in all its forms: social antagonism, ethnic intolerance, and political extremism. Gradually, the idea of social consensus was accepted, to be achieved, maintained, or restored only by means of constant dialogue and compromise. And a new intellectual, political, and psychological climate helped reconstruct regulatory mechanisms facilitating the solution of social problems and the resolution even of major contradictions. The Russian word *perestroika* entered the international political vocabulary only a few years ago, but the process it denotes has been under way in Western Europe since the late 1940s, i.e. nearly half a century earlier. It could be called the West European variant of *perestroika*, and it has led to the formation of a new type of society characterized by market and mixed economies, social security, pluralistic democracies, democratic participation, and constitutional states. In principle, all these components of the modern social system are present in all countries referred to as "the West." But West European society has some distinctive features, as compared, for instance, with American society. This is reflected in Western Europe's more pronounced adherence to the idea of social justice, common welfare, and "subsidiarity," all traditional values of both social democratic and christian democratic governments. An additional and very important feature of European culture (in the broadest sense of the word) is its unique combination of the common and the diverse, a natural result of the Babylonian mixture of peoples and languages in Europe from antiquity to the present.

The history of the Old World is full of pages written in the blood of innumerable wars. But this history has retained an idea of common fate as well, an idea of indivisible European civilization. It was the post-World War II period that resurrected this idea. As an integral part of this process, a radical restructuring of relations between the West European states took place. It is most convincingly reflected in the development of the European Community. The reasons for its success can be found both in its philosophy and in political practice. Most importantly, it has become a reality because of the renunciation of nationalism and chauvinism, of imperial and militaristic traditions -- which in the past exerted a decisive influence on the policies of the leading European states. This new course was proclaimed by leading West European statesmen immediately after the Second World War. The outstanding representative of British nationalism, Winston Churchill, delivered a sensational speech at Zurich in September 1946 in which he demanded an end to the "frightful nationalistic quarrels" that had turned into "the tragedy of Europe," and called for a return to the idea of the United States of Europe. Four years later, the French foreign minister, Robert Schuman, repeated the same *leitmotiv* in his famous *Déclaration du 9 Mai 1950*, calling for the establishment of a "Community of Coal and

Steel" as a first step toward a European federation that would unite peoples who "for ages have been divided by bloody discords."[32] Now, in retrospect, one can conclude that Western Europe has largely succeeded in overcoming traditional nationalism and prejudices, and the distrust and hostilities stemming from them.

Some other important elements of the European integrationist philosophy should be mentioned as well. They are:

(1) The recognition that economic interdependence is not only inevitable but also beneficial, and that open economies have definite advantages over protectionist ones.

(2) The firm conviction that integration can be developed only on the basis of free and equal participation of all the states involved, and that a necessary prerequisite of such participation is democracy.

(3) The recognition that contradictions and crises may not only slow down the process of integration or even stop it but also serve as signals for mobilizing intellectual and political pro-integration efforts in order to overcome the obstacles on the basis of mutually acceptable compromises.

Analysis of the changes that occurred in Western Europe after World War II, with respect both to the social system and to relations between states, reveals that at least this part of Europe has become qualitatively different from what it was before the war. One can even speak of a new stage in the development of West European civilization. "Mixed," "postindustrial," "new industrial," "technotronic," "informational," or even (in Alvin Toffler's words) "third wave" are some of the labels often applied to post-World War II West European society.

All this does not mean that this new social organism is flawless and faces no difficulties -- quite the contrary. On the cusp of both a new century and a new millennium, Western Europe sees itself confronted with a number of three-dimensional and extremely challenging problems: (1) internally, stemming from the evolution of the respective West European societies; (2) at the pan-European level, problems no longer connected with the cold war but with a new search for stability after the collapse of "real socialism" in Central and Eastern Europe; and (3) global problems without precedent in history and jeopardizing the very existence of mankind.

The internal problems of Western society seem less acute today than they were in the first half of the century or immediately after World War II. Nevertheless, they could threaten stability. It seems as if the main danger may lie in a new division of society into a two-tier entity -- a side effect of the new technological revolution that dictates structural and organizational adjustments of the economy, thereby leading to unemployment on an even large scale. This new cleavage pits a majority of the population (its competitive first tier) against its "left-behind" second tier, a substantial minority condemned to sporadic earnings, low living-standards, and moral degradation. The most disturbing aspect is that this marginalized category is being constantly swelled by young people responding to societal inertia and indifference with demonstratively antisocial behavior such as "hippyism" in various guises, drug addiction, or vandalism. Such destabilizing threats stem not only from the new technological revolution but also from the growing crisis of the "consumer society." The core of this crisis is to be found in our modern system of production and distribution, which tends to turn people into addicts of consumerism, at the same time undermining the primacy of moral and social values such as work, upon which modern Western civilization rests. So far, Western capitalism has done nothing to curb such unbridled consumerism and to alleviate this acute alienation of a sizeable segment of Western society. In his latest encyclical, *Centesimus Annus*, Pope John Paul II condemned both communism and unrestrained capitalism.[33]

In addition to these domestic challenges, there are global problems, among which the devastation of the environment and the gap between the rich "North" and the overpopulated, undernourished, and poor "South" are probably the most serious. These two interrelated problems necessitate a substantial reconsideration of the very idea of "social progress." This notion first appeared in Europe at the time of the industrial revolution, but today it seems to apply only to a rather small minority of mankind. Because of its integrity, however, the modern world requires a definition of "social progress" acceptable to the entire global community. The developed countries have not yet indicated that they might be ready for such a reorientation, which, barring a miracle, will probably have to identify "progress" with "survival." The latter envisages radical changes in life style, behavior, economic activities, and social policies, to enumerate but a few requirements. So, the situation is not overly encouraging, and the prospects are not at all clear. And yet, the modern European social system is very resilient. Its self-regulating mechanisms have developed over many years and have acquired sufficient flexibility. But the greatest treasure of modern European civilization is its spiritual potential, its unique moral and social experience, which has been radically reconsidered and renewed in the 20th century.

In his famous speech marking the 40th anniversary of Germany's liberation from Nazism, the German president, Richard von Weizsäcker, said: "Our own history shows us what can be done by man. This gives us no ground to view ourselves as a different and better type of people. Ultimate moral perfection does not exist -- nobody, nowhere, can achieve it. As human beings, we have learned something; as human beings, we are constantly exposed to dangers. But we are capable of overcoming them all over again."[34] This moral strength, this political will and ability to overcome all kinds of obstacles give us reason to believe that, in the near future, Western Europe will play a stabilizing role on behalf of the whole European continent. It will be a nucleus of integration and a guarantor of a future democratic, peaceful, and united Europe.

## Notes

1. *Materialy XXVII sjesda Kommunisticheskoi Partii Sovietskogo Sojusa* (Documents of the XXVII Congress of the Communist Party of the Soviet Union), (Moscow, 1986), p. 124.

2. S.F. Cohen, *Rethinking the Soviet Experience. Politics and History since 1917* (New York, Oxford, 1985), pp. 9-10.

3. R. Aron, *Dix-huit leçons sur la société industrielle* (Paris, 1962), p. 50.

4. *Sovremennye burzhuaznye teorii o slyanii kapitalizma i sotsialisma* (Modern Bourgeois Theories on the Convergence of Capitalism and Socialism), (Moscow, 1970), pp. 6-9.

5. N. Shmelev, "Avansy i dolgi (Promises and Debts)", *Novy Mir*, No. 6, 1987, pp. 142-58.

6. G. Popov, "S tochki zreniya ekonomista (From the Point of View of an Economist)," *Nauka i zhizn*, No. 4, 1987, pp. 54-5.

7. *Inogo ne dano* (No Other Choices), (Moscow, 1988); *Postizhenie* (Realization), (Moscow, 1989); *Osmyslit kult Stalina* (To Comprehend the Cult of Stalin), (Moscow, 1989); *Drama Obnovleniya* (The Drama of Renewal), (Moscow, 1990); *Cherez ternii* (Over Thorns), (Moscow, 1989); *Pogruzhenie v tryazinu* (Sinking into the Quagmire), (Moscow, 1991).

8. *Sovetskaya Rossiya*, March 13, 1988.

9. *Izvestia*, February 23, 1990.

10. A. Butenko, "Realny Sotsializm. O soderzhanii ponyatiya (Real Socialism. On the Content of the Notion)," *Obshchestvennye nauki*, No. 4, 1988, pp. 5-16; A. Butenko, *Sovremenny sotsializm. Voprosy teorii* (Modern Socialism. Problems of Theory), (Moscow, 1989); E.V. Zolotukhina-Abolina, V.E. Zolotukhin, *Sotsializm: problemy deformatsii* (Socialism: Problems of Deformation), (Rostov na Donu, 1989).

11. F. Burlatsky, "Kakoi Sotsializm narodu nuzhen? (What Socialism is Necessary for People?)," *Literaturnaya Gazeta*, April 20, 1988, p. 2.

12. M. Gorbachev, "Sotsialisticheskaya ideya i revolutsionnaya perestroika (The Socialist Idea and the Revolutionary Perestroika)," *Pravda*, November 26, 1989.

13. "Leninizm i perestroika (Leninism and Perestroika)," *Pravda*, February 1, 1990.

14. Yu. Afanasyev, "Otvety istorika (Answers of an Historian)," *Pravda*, June 26, 1988.

15. "K gumannomu, demokraticheskomu sotsializmu. Programnoye zayavleniye XXVIII sjesda KPSS (To a Human, Democratic Socialism. Programmatic Statement of the XXVIII Congress of the CPSU)," *Pravda*, June 15, 1990.

16. V. Kisselev, "Skolko modely sotsializma bylo v SSSR (How Many Models of Socialism were there in the USSR?)," in: *Inogo ne dano*, (Moscow, 1988), pp. 354-69.

17. E. Plimak, *Politicheskoye zaveshchaniye Lenina. Istoki, sushchnost, vypolneniye* (Lenin's Political Testament. Sources, Content, Fulfillment), (Moscow, 1989), p. 199.

18. *Osmyslit kult Stalina* (Moscow, 1989), pp. 5-6.

19. *Knizhnoye obozreniye*, No. 38, 1988, pp. 4-5.

20. L. Gordon, E. Klopov, "Stalinizm i post-stalinizm: neobkhodimost preodoleniya (Stalinism and Post-Stalinism: The Need of Overcoming)," in: *Osmyslit kult Stalina*, (Moscow, 1989), pp. 460-96.

21. A. Tsipko, "Istoki stalinizma (Sources of Stalinism)," *Nauka i zhizn*, No. 11, 1988, pp. 45-55; No. 12, 1988, pp. 40-8; No. 1, 1989, pp. 46-56; No. 2, 1989, pp. 53-61.

22. A. Tsipko, *Nauka i zhizn*, No. 11, 1988, p. 51; No. 1, 1989, p. 47.

23. "Marksizm na poroge 21-go veka (Marxism on the Threshold of the 21st Century)," *Knizhnoye obozreniya*, No. 9, 1991.

24. V. Sheinis, "Kapitalizm, sotsializm i ekonomicheski mekhanizm sovremennogo proisvodstva (Capitalism, Socialism and the Economic Mechanism of Modern Production)," *Mirovaya ekonomika i mezhdunarodnye otnosheniya* (MEMO), No. 9, 1988, pp. 5-23; "Zapadnaya demokratiya i problemu sovremenogo obshchestvennogo razvitiya (Western Democracy and Problems of Contemporary Development of Society)," *MEMO*, No. 11, 1988, pp. 5-18; No. 1, 1989, pp. 71-84; Yu. Shishkov, "Teoriya imperializma: retrospektivy vzglyad v kontse stoletiya (Theory of Imperialism: A Retrospective View at the End of the Century)," *Nauka i zhizn*, No. 9, 1990, pp. 34-42; No. 10, 1990, pp. 16-24.

25. Yu. Borko, "O mekhanismakh samorazvitya sovremennogo kapitalizma (On Mechanisms of Self-development of Modern Capitalism)," *Kommunist*, No. 11, 1988, p. 106.

26. *Ibid.*, p. 113.

27. "Problemy tselostnogo mira (Problems of the Indivisible World)," *MEMO*, No. 9, 1989; "Formatsii ili tsivilisatsii? (Formations or Civilizations?)," *Voprosy filosofii*, No. 10, 1989, pp. 34-59.

28. G. Diligensky, V. Lektorsky, "Povodya itoghi diskussii (Summing up the Discussions)," *MEMO*, No. 12, 1990, pp. 55-6.

29. E. Posdnyakov, "Formationnye i tsivilisationnye podkhody (Approaches to Formation and Civilization)," *MEMO*, No. 5, 1990, pp. 49-60; Yu. Kochevrin, "Kapitalizm s positsii istorii i sovremennosti (Capitalism in View of History and Capitalism Today)," *MEMO*, No. 8, 1990, pp. 5-16; A. Fursov, "Vosnikoveniye kapitalizma i evropeiskaya tsivilisatsiya, sotsiogeneticheskiye interpretatsii (European Civilization and the Birth of Capitalism: Socio-Genetic Interpretations)," *Sotsiologicheskie isledovaniya*, No. 40, 1990, pp. 26-42; Yu. Borko, "O sotsialnom progresse v menyayushehemsya mire (On Social Progress in the Changing World)," *Kommunist*, No. 11, 1990, pp. 121-7.

30. S.N. Eisenstadt, *European Civilization in a Comparative Perspective*, (Oslo, 1987).

31. Vittorio Strada, "Novy stary spor (New Old Dispute)," *Literaturnaya Gazeta*, July 25, 1990, p. 15.

32. H. Brugmans, *L'idée européene 1920-1970*, (Bruges, 1970), pp. 373-6, pp. 382-4.

33. *Encyclical letter Centesimus Annus addressed by the Supreme Pontiff, John Paul II, to the Venerable Brothers in the Episcopate, the Priests and Deacons, Families of Men and Women Religious, All the Christian Faithful, and All Men and Women of Good Will on the 100th Anniversary of Rerum Novarum*, (Vatican City, 1991), p. 71, 77-82.

34. *Novoe Vremya*, No. 40, 1990, p. 43.

# PART TWO

# Security and the Future Architecture of Europe

# 3

---

# Beyond the East-West Conflict:
# Institutionalizing Security
# and Cooperation in Europe

*Peter Schlotter*

The upheavals in Central and Eastern Europe and the dramatic events in the Soviet Union since autumn 1991 have led to the end of the East-West conflict. This will substantially affect the significance and function of the CSCE process. Up to now, that process has been geared primarily to managing the East-West conflict -- through linkages and compromises, through rules of conduct and debates about policy implementation, and through regular conferences and meetings of experts. But in the future, the CSCE will have to act without reliance on the structural pattern set by the old East-West conflict.

It is an open question which role the CSCE will play in the future, especially in comparison to other multilateral European institutions. Presently, the specificity of CSCE is threefold: first, all European states, the United States, Canada and the Asian republics of the former Soviet Union are participants in the process, thus the CSCE encompasses all states involved in European security; second, it functions as a platform for discussing and deciding upon a broad variety of issues affecting European security and cooperation; last, it has been successful in managing many problems during the East-West conflict and has helped to overcome it. In this chapter, I will present an argument for enhancing the CSCE toward becoming the central platform for a new European peace architecture. However, conditional for such a role is a substantial revision of CSCE mechanisms in line with the new challenges to peace and security in Europe.

This chapter consists of four main parts. First, the major conflicts and challenges confronting Europe will be briefly enumerated. Then, some considerations in the context of integration theory and the concept of regime-building will be presented, which, in my view, help manage these problems. Thirdly, I will explain why CSCE -- in order to facilitate future conflict resolution in Europe -- should become the main organization for developing regimes. Finally, the question of how the CSCE should be delimitated from other European institutions, namely NATO, the European Community, and the Council of Europe will be dealt with.

The following considerations about a new European architecture are neither purely normative nor purely descriptive. They try to steer between the Scylla of speculation and the Charybdis of just describing current political trends. Though relying on present political tendencies as much as possible these ideas must also contain a certain degree of speculative, value-oriented utopia.

## The Challenges of the 1990s

The dissolution of the prevailing conflict structure has led to fundamental new problems. Western liberal democracies have won the "Cold War" (as a cypher for the East-West conflict in general). But -- as after every war -- making peace is often more difficult than waging war. In this case, however, establishing a peace order seems to be easier: the Cold War has not caused such terrible wounds, economically and mentally, as a hot war would have done, and the East-West conflict came to an end peacefully and cooperatively. So, much of the old confrontation is history, but it needs manifold endeavors to clear away the "scrap heaps" and to tackle the new problems. In Western Europe, a relatively dense economic integration is growing as well as more cooperation in political and military affairs, whereas in Eastern Europe -- after the dominance of the Soviet Union and the single party power of the Communists have vanished and the economic relations between the former socialist states have been largely interrupted -- at best nation-based policies, at worst nationalism and chauvinism are surfacing again. Multinational states like the Soviet Union and Yugoslavia are desintegrating, mostly into smaller states which will also be multinational.

Europe has lost its dominant or hegemonic "pacifiers." In the case of the Warsaw Treaty Organization, the alliance itself was dissolved. In the case of NATO, its cohesion will be greatly reduced, because the Soviet threat has disappeared: no one in the "West" is afraid of an attack from the "East" any more, except some worst-case thinking militarists. Some political analysts, therefore, fear a return of the interwar period with its continuous struggles for hegemony and its shifting alliances.[1] Others see the survival of NATO, only in a less cohesive structure, and a turbulent East with the former socialist states -- more or less -- oriented and inclined to existing Western institutions. Therefore, in comparison to the recent past, the prevailing bipolarity is being replaced by a kind of multipolarity with a relatively stable "West" and an extremely unstable "East" in which nearly all political, military, economic, social, and ethnic structures are changing; in sum, the complexity will be greater.[2]

Although the old enemies have vanished with the end of the East-West conflict, the "deep cuts" in weapons stockpiles envisaged so far are not as deep as they could be, and not congruent with the new situation. Currently, an all-encompassing rationalization process of military apparatus on the basis of a shift from "quantity" to "quality" is under way. The dynamics of armament innovations, vested interests aiming at great armament potentials, ambitious power politics and other mainly domestic factors of armament dynamics are not at all under control. In addition, the dissolution of WTO will lead to extremely complicated arms control negotiations: up to now one had to compare the military potentials of two alliances; now the capacities of independent states potentially involved in regional arms races need to be balanced. All this severely affects security in Europe.

There are great differences amongst the new democracies in Central and Eastern Europe concerning the level of democratization, prospects of the democratization process and the realization of constitutional principles. The return to power of the old elites does not seem to be the main danger. But attempts at solving the economic and socio-political crises by chauvinism, populistic-authoritarian means or by military rule do not seem unlikely. Introducing market economies based on the principle of private property will be followed by nearly unsolvable problems of adaptation. Opening the Eastern markets for Western investments and exports initially stimulates economic growth in Western Europe, and there is no evidence that in the case of post-socialism capitalist modernization works effectively.[3] So the economic and social asymmetries between Western and Eastern Europe will increase at least during the next twenty or more years, and it is possible -- and perhaps even likely -- that the latter will be dependent on the West to such an extent that this part of Europe and the former Soviet Union will become Western Europe's backyard. The social consequences during the transition period and probably still longer, namely hunger, misery and migration will concern all European societies. This could affect European security if attempts at distracting attention from internal crises are made by pushing interstate issues such as border and minority questions with growing human rights violations.

The upheavals in Central and South Eastern Europe and in the former Soviet Union have led to a strong emphasis on the nation state and on ethno-national demarcations. One can understand this because national self-determination was suppressed during "real socialism."[4] But this emphasis is in deep contrast to the relativization of national sovereignty in Western Europe and to the ideas of a "civil society" which guided the intellectual leaders of the revolutions of autumn 1989. Not only the "system of Yalta" has come to an end, but the territorial order of the Paris peace treaties of 1919/20 seems to be in question too, just as in the interwar period.

Special problems are following the breakdown of the Soviet Union. All new states there have large minorities, populist nationalism abounds and the possibility of "wars for succession" cannot be dismissed. Also, there is the very important task of guarding against an (illegal) proliferation of the former Soviet Union's enormous nuclear arsenal.

The unification of Germany concerns European security in a special way, too. The "old" Federal Republic of Germany was integrated in the West (via NATO, WEU, and the EC). With the 2 + 4 treaty, the Soviet Union gave its consent that the same could apply to the united Germany. But all states which were concerned by the process of German unification stressed the need to "embed" Germany in more far-reaching systems of integration.[5] Without doubt, Germany will be a great power in Europe, but a revival of the past is extremely unlikely. Integration in NATO and the EC did work, does work and is going to work, thereby mitigating the danger of German hegemony which could result from its economic power.[6] But the role of Germany is not yet clearly fixed: will its "special relationship" with the states of Eastern Central Europe and its economic interests in the whole "East" lead to a weaker cohesion of NATO and the EC? How shall Germany, situated as it is in the center of Europe, and economically stronger after having solved the problems of integrating the former GDR, fit into a pan-European security architecture?

## Institutionalization, Regime-Building, Integration, and Peace

In the following, regime-building, international organizations, and integration will be considered as the best means of handling the new problems and conflicts facing Europe's societies in the next decades. But one has to warn against expecting too much: many of the problems and conflicts root deeply in history and mentality, and only integrating the post-socialist societies into existing Western organizations or into a pan-European structure can improve the conditions for security and peaceful cooperation.

The peaceful resolution of conflicts emanating from the challenges outlined above requires a complex strategy. There are three major aims such a strategy should encompass:[7] (1) promoting democratization and the rule of law (constitutionality), (2) promoting reliable expectations, (3) promoting welfare and economic progress.

(1) There is much evidence that democracies do not fight wars against each other. In general, constitutional states are more capable of solving problems by peaceful means, in both domestic and interstate relations.[8] Constitutionality and democracy are more readily taken for granted by citizens when fair distribution and equal opportunities for participation are given.

(2) Democratisation, constitutionality and the protection of human rights, of course, do not automatically lead to peaceful interstate relations. Peace has to be made on the basis of binding committals. The international scene is not characterised by an intrinsic stability of expectations; rather, nation states are confronted with a security dilemma. Scholarly debates have brought forward several proposals for how to deal with this security dilemma: deterrence, balance of power politics, etc.[9] But, in the main, they have been focused on patterns of conflict emanating from the East-West divide. Now, after the demise of this conflict, a strategy building upon a high degree of networking of both societies and states appears to be especially promising. Such a networking strategy promises to heighten the stability of expectations. By way of institutional linkages, a mutual predictability of motives and actions becomes possible. Once the networks of cooperation between states and societies have become tightly meshed, the security dilemma loses its explosive effect, because strong constraints in favour of political coordination will have come into force. The security dilemma is thus superceeded by political predictability and transparency. Embedded in a network of institutionalised cooperation, nationalist outbursts and military adventures by single states become difficult and, espe-

cially, counterproductive.[10] Networks can be constructed in different ways. They can consist of integration systems, of so-called pluralistic security communities and of so-called regimes.

*Integration* means to bind oneself and to bind others; it leads to policy networks, which overlap interstate conflicts through manifold supranational structures of communication and decision-making. Thereby it diminishes the disposition for an unconditional enforcement of particularistic interests.[11] In the same way as effective regimes, stable systems of political integration need international organizations. Good examples are Western Europe and the transatlantic area: here integration has worked as a means -- among others -- of promoting interstate peace, non-violent conflict resolution, stable democratic systems, and economic welfare.

Concerning Europe as a whole, the economic and socio-political conditions for integration have to a great extent not yet been achieved. But in theory, preliminary forms of integration -- which can be described as *pluralistic security systems* -- are already being discussed. Such systems consist of independent states; on the political, economic and socio-political level, however, they are bound together to such a degree that they do not handle their conflicts by violent means.[12]

Below the level of pluralistic security communities we have looser forms of reducing security dilemmas: *international regimes*.[13] These are -- following Stephen Krasner's famous definition -- "sets of implicit or explicit principles, norms, rules, and decision-making procedures around which actors' expectations converge in a given area of international relations."[14] They must be effective and durable. International organizations serve -- according to this theory -- as institutions for implementing, monitoring and improving regimes.[15] They perform in a twofold manner: on the one hand, the states' rivalry over power "can be mitigated by an institutional structure that provides legitimate and effective channels for reconciling conflicting interests"[16]; on the other hand, they can show a dynamic by themselves which transcends the common denominator of member states' interests. Thus, international organizations can be -- and often are -- more than only exclusively the reflex of nation-state politics.

In sum, the strategy of regime-building and institutionalization described in the following is based on the assumption that both should aim at integration or -- at least -- security communities. Both strategies are based on the "liberal" -- in contrast to the "realist" -- assumption that states calculate their interests not only in terms of the distribution of power but also act in the context of effective restrictions by regimes and international organizations. The conceptualization of a future European security structure combines elements of regime theory with others of "neo-liberal institutionalism."[17]

(3) That economic asymmetries, poverty, and mass immigration provide fertile soil for violent conflicts needs no further explication. It is also clear that the transition from a socialist command economy to a market economy is a social and economic experiment without precedence. The failure of this experiment would lead to the division of Europe and would destroy the economic basis for a security community encompassing the whole of Europe.

## *The Role of Individual European Institutions*

The future will not see an all-encompassing organization, in which all European issues will be dealt with. Rather, it can be assumed that manifold overlapping jurisdictions will continue for some time; only during the evolution of pan-European structures will we see, which functions can be best performed by which institutions.

The major concern of the following argument will lie on the CSCE. This has mainly normative reasons resulting from the concept of regime- and institution-building, but also practical political reasons, as I wish to concentrate primarily on strategies able to prevent violent methods of conflict resolution. None of the existing European institutions cover all European states, with the exception of the CSCE. Apart from the European Council, which, however, is unlikely to be consolidated into an all-encompassing security organization, this will hold true for the next two decades. The two North American states are also member to CSCE. All states involved in European issues -- especially in the field of security -- are thus formally part of the CSCE. For this reason, the CSCE is presently the only organization in which certain states with potentials for internal and/or external violent conflict hold membership.

Especially those conflicts pertaining to the protection of minorities, secessions, and dissolution and formation of states are -- as a historical rule -- particularly violent, and, at the same time, natural issues of settlement by CSCE. Interference or military intervention can be necessary, if other mechanisms of non-violent conflict resolution have failed. But, interference or intervention should in principle only take place -- here a normative argument -- by an organization, to whom both conflicting parties belong and whose norms and rules they have submitted to. Such a collective security system currently exists only in the form of the United Nations. The CSCE rudimentarily shows such characteristics; the EC and NATO, however, do not. What emerges from these theoretical-conceptional considerations is the idea, that regime-buildung and interdependence (in the form of looser security communities or the more comprehensive renunciation of sovereignty rights in favour of an international organization) is the direction in which a pan-European policy should move, if it aims at improving the conditions for a non-violent settlement of present and future conflicts.

Moreover, various network gradations can be set in relation to different institutions. With regard to regime-building, the development of norms and the monitoring and implementation of agreements in the areas of human rights, minority protection and state dissolution/formation, as well as with regard to potential (military) interventions in interstate, interethnic or intrastate conflicts, the main responsibility will lie in the hands of the CSCE; in certain areas -- such as the codification of human rights and the rights of minorities -- the European Council will have important powers too.

Integration will be easiest in the economic realm; here, the EC will be charged with the main task of contributing to the gradual reduction and elimination of economic asymmetries between Eastern and Western Europe. In this context, the question of EC extension as well as the question of overlapping spheres of responsibility between CSCE, NATO, WEU and an EC with stronger characteristics of political union -- issues covered more extensively below -- will arise. NATO could, for instance, become a pluralistic Euro-Atlantic security community, if its membership would be extended to include Eastern European nations. The following deliberations will point to some basic elements of a future security arrangement in Europe, in which the CSCE plays a central role.

## The Future of the CSCE

The CSCE is a regime-building negotiating process[18] which was developed to a rudimentary international organization in 1990. As mentioned above, regimes consist of norms, rules, procedures, and decision-making processes. If one wishes to improve the CSCE's capacity to perform better in helping solve current and future conflicts in Europe, it would be useful to enlarge the -- heretofore -- embryonic regime structure of the CSCE to a full international organization, i.e. giving it the power to create, monitor, and implement pan-European security and cooperation regimes. The possibilities for developing the CSCE to such an institution are treated with respect to four issues:

(1) the institutionalization of the CSCE,
(2) the reform of CSCE procedures and decision-making processes,
(3) the norm-building processes concerning human rights (including minority protection),
(4) norms and procedures for the "peaceful settlement of disputes."

*Institutionalizing the CSCE Process:*
*The 1990 "Charter of Paris for a New Europe"*

The Paris summit meeting in November 1990 ended with a first outline of a new CSCE designed to meet future challenges in post-Cold War Europe. The most important agreements reached there concern the institutionalization of the CSCE process: Meetings of the Heads of State or Government on the occasion of follow-on conferences are to be held every two years; the Ministers of Foreign Affairs (the CSCE Council) will hold meetings regularly and at least once a year; a Committee of Senior Officials was established; a Secretariat in Prague will provide administrative support to the Council and to the Committee of Senior Officials; a Conflict Prevention Center in Vienna will, during its initial stage of operations, give support to the implementation of confidence- and security-building measures; an Office for Free Elections in Warsaw was mandated to facilitate the exchange of information on elections; and, finally, a CSCE Parliamentary Assembly was set up to hold its first session in July 1992 in Budapest.

In the Charter, the institutionalization is seen as the beginning of a process: the CSCE Council and the 1992 Follow-on Conference in Helsinki are requested to discuss proposals for possible next steps. The establishment of new institutions by the CSCE member states directly evolved from an analysis of the new situation after the end of the East-West conflict. The previous CSCE was a vague, flexible process accomodated to an antagonistic conflict; an earlier institutionalization would have been counterproductive on the background of the Cold-War structure of East-West relations up to the mid-80s.[19] Now, the declared aim was to establish a pan-European structure to "embed" Eastern Europe and the USSR, and to develop (more binding) procedures aimed at promoting democracy and the respect for human rights in the countries of former "real socialism."

Although these objectives were verbally accepted by all CSCE states, the start to institutionalization had to be put through against manifold opposition. The United States and Great Britain, but also -- to a lesser degree -- the Netherlands, were afraid of weakening NATO and loosening the transatlantic links by institutionalizing CSCE. France was cautious of first steps potentially leading to constraints on its national sovereignty. Some neutral and non-aligned states, like Switzerland, had reservations against any sign of supranational institution-building. The initiatives to institutionalize the CSCE came from Germany, the CSFR, Poland, Hungary, and the Soviet Union. Germany, especially, felt a special responsibility to complete its unification process by establishing a pan-European network and thus acted in favour of Eastern European expectations.

Currently, the countries earlier sceptical about CSCE institutions are getting more ready to accept further steps towards institutionalization. The CSFR, Poland and Hungary are knocking at NATO's door, but the Anglo-Saxon states are afraid of watering-down the Alliance by admitting new members. Therefore, the much looser organized CSCE is seen as a compensation which NATO offers to applicants for its membership. Thus, the development of the CSCE to an international organization -- parallel to NATO and the European Community -- does not seem an unrealistic perspective. It will depend on the answer to two questions: will the member states perceive the necessity of having institutions and mechanisms to deal with the emerging conflicts in the Balkans as well as in and between the former USSR; and will the institutionalization of CSCE serve as an addendum to NATO and not as its replacement?

Under these circumstances, the consent of the United States and the other "Atlantic-oriented" countries to an enhancement of CSCE institutions seems possible. The long-term goal should be to upgrade the Secretariat to a General Secretariat, in analogy to the UN.[20] In a parallel move, the powers of the Conflict Prevention Centre should be enlarged to include conflict prevention in a broader sense (including an early warning system), not restricted solely to military confidence-building measures; and it should be subordinated directly to the Secretariat. In this way, the CSCE would develop to become a "normal" international organization. The Secretariat with its sub-institutions must have the right to act by itself, e.g. to decide on fact-finding missions, to initiate the peaceful settlement of disputes or to convene the Council of Foreign Ministers. Based on sufficient CSCE institutions, Europe would have been better prepared to react earlier and quicker to conflicts like in Yugoslavia, in order to make the conflicting parties better understand the consequences violent behavior can have.

*Reform of CSCE Procedures
and Decision-Making Processes*

Upgrading the CSCE to a full international organization entails imbueing procedures and decision-making processes with greater flexibility and putting them in a position to react quickly and effectively -- more than in the past -- to challenges to peace and security. Until now, CSCE procedures and decision-making needed unanimity. At its first meeting, the Council of Foreign Ministers decided to modify this consensus rule: initiatives to start the mechanism for the peaceful settlement of disputes or to convene emergency meetings of Senior Officials or of the Consultative Committee of the Conflict Prevention Center no longer need the consent of all CSCE member states. For decisions, however, unanimity is still necessary.

Several proposals for the improvement of decision-making procedures are under discussion. Some, already agreed upon, e.g. in Moscow at the Conference on the Human Dimension (September 10, to October 4, 1991) aim at the provision of more possibilities to initiate actions of monitoring and control with respect to human rights. Others tend to call for the establishment of a CSCE Security Council (in analogy to the UN) or at least weighted votes in the Council of Foreign Ministers (in analogy, for example, to the German *Bundesrat*). They have as a final objective a kind of collective security system, in which the Security Council, supported by a General Secretary, disposes of peace-keeping forces or even peace enforcement capabilities.[21] It has also been discussed, as to whether the CSCE Security Council should consist of standing and non-standing members without any right of veto, but with weighted votes and majority decisions.

Of course, these are dreams for the future. The debate about the development of the EC to a Political Union, responsible for a common foreign and security policy, shows the deep differences between the governments of only 12 EC members and the reluctance of many states to abandon sovereignty rights. But, nevertheless, a first step to more effective decision-making procedures seems achievable and is likely to be agreed upon at the next CSCE Follow-on-Conference: the establishment of a steering committee (in analogy to the EC "troika"), consisting of the former, the current, and the future president of the Council.

## Human Rights and Minority Protection

Principle VII of the Final Act and the agreements of Basket III have proved to be one of the most dynamic elements of the CSCE. They legitimized the international discussion about lacking respect for human rights and fundamental freedoms and confirmed by this, that internal affairs could become issues of international diplomacy. Even after the end of the East-West conflict, democracy and respect for human rights have not yet been comprehensively realized, especially if one takes into consideration minority or social rights. Norm-building and the establishment of monitoring procedures -- potentially with sanctionary mechanisms -- will therefore be the main theme of human rights discussions in the future.

A monitoring mechanism was agreed upon in Vienna in 1989; it allows a signatory state to raise an issue pertaining to the human dimension, if it considers another state has not implemented its CSCE commitments. This can be done either publicly or discreetly, depending on the complaining state's wishes. If no result is forthcoming, the state has the right to officially inform all the CSCE member states, as well as the right to have the matter discussed at one of the three meetings of the CSCE Conference on the Human Dimension (held previously in Paris in 1989, Copenhagen in 1990, and Moscow in 1991). Many states have already made use of this opportunity. If the issue is still not resolved to the satisfaction of the complaining state, it has the right to raise the matter as an official agenda item at the next CSCE Follow-on Conference (to take place in Helsinki in 1992). In other words, state monitoring is now formalised under CSCE rules. In addition, the monitoring mechanism was improved at the last Moscow conference. This mechanism has a value in itself. But the debates on the respect of "classical" human rights will be of minor importance in the future, unless the process of democratization suffers setbacks and social unrest in the post-socialist countries leads to new dictatorships. Rather, minority protection will be the main task within the framework of general human rights.

As mentioned above, minority rights and conflicts between nationalities or ethnic groups need special consideration. The breakdown of Yugoslavia and the breakup of the USSR into independent states show the war-pregnancy of such conflicts. The main problem is whether the right to self-determination includes a right of secession or not. The dominant position in International Law denies such a right.[22] But, nevertheless, protection of minorities within existing states could settle many problems, so that minorities or ethnic groups do not become interested in achieving their own state. Therefore, norm-building in the CSCE context -- for example, an enlargement of human rights and monitoring rules for minority and ethnic group protection -- could help prevent or at least diminish the violence inherent in ethnic conflicts too.

In CSCE documents up until the Copenhagen Meeting on the Human Dimension (June 5-29, 1990), minority protection was only mentioned in the context of non-discrimination and individual rights. This followed the traditional understanding that minority rights are safeguarded if human rights are respected. In addition to this assessment, the Concluding Document of the Copenhagen Meeting noted that the participating states declare they "will protect the ethnic, cultural, linguistic, and religious identity of national minorities on their territories and create conditions for the promotion of that identity" (Section 33). This means that the CSCE states have recognized minority rights as individual as well as collective rights. The chapter in the Copenhagen document is the most far-reaching international statement on this subject to date.

The Geneva Meeting of Experts on National Minorities (June 1-19, 1991), however, achieved only little progress in specifying the Copenhagen agreements. It is not surprising that the member states could not reach a consensus on how to treat the tension between the right of self-determination of peoples and the sovereignty of existing states. Therefore, the problem was excluded from the final report. There was also a debate between delegations with a traditional understanding of minority rights (especially France, Great Britain, Spain and, to a lesser degree, the United States) and those who pushed for collective minority rights, which could inter alia lead to a preferential treatment of minorities, thus injuring the principle of equality, for example, through an ethnically disproportionate parliamentary representation of an ethnic minority. This position was put forward especially by Germany, Austria, Switzerland and most of the Central and Eastern European states.

The report speaks only of "persons belonging to national minorities." In the same way, only the traditional catalogue of minority rights was enlarged and specified. Thus, no disadvantage is to arise from the exercise of minority rights including social and cultural rights, and minorities are not to be hindered in preserving their identity. It was also declared that "issues concerning national minorities, as well as compliance with international obligations and commitments concerning the rights of persons belonging to them, are matters of legitimate international concern and consequently do not constitute exclusively an internal affair of the respective State" (Section II). But one could not agree upon a monitoring procedure -- such as fact-finding missions -- enforcable without the consensus of the state concerned because of the reluctance of France, Great Britain and the Soviet Union, which feared that their own minority conflicts could be internationalized. However, if ethnic and minority conflicts in Eastern Europe lead to civil wars, genocide and waves of mass migration, the opponents of massive interference into internal affairs could well change their stance.

Norm-building could help moderate violence in cases of secession or the dissolution of states. One could refer to UN documents and debates as well as to draft conventions in the context of the Council of Europe. In the long run it will become necessary to reach an agreement on a "Convention for the Collective Rights of National or Ethnic Minorities" containing guidelines on how minorities should be treated and, in case they want, how they can gain autonomy or independence in a non-violent process. Such a convention would require rules of conduct for the dissolution and formation of states. In this connection it could also be sensible to establish a "European Court of Minority Rights." But when a conflict has escalated to violence and war, all this does not work effectively if it is not backed by an institution capable of imposing sanctions against rule-breakers.

## CSCE Procedures for a Peaceful Settlement of Disputes

The decisive value of CSCE diplomacy has been the gradual process of "civilization," through which East-West conflicts were mitigated by compromises and by the obligation of vindicating non-cooperation or violations of CSCE norms. The primary technique of achieving consensual declarations has been a comprehensive negotiation agenda and "package dealing." Because the fundamental systemic conflict has come to an end, both approaches will have less weight in the future. There will be less demand for largely declaratory documents and more for concrete conflict management and conflict resolution. This seems to be both more important and more likely to be achieved than before, even though conflicting interests will naturally remain.

One technique -- well known, but seldom used -- is the "peaceful settlement of disputes."[23] It was already mentioned in the CSCE Final Act of 1975. Since that time three "Meetings of Experts" were held; the last one (in La Valletta, January 15 - February 8, 1991) adopted a CSCE dispute settlement mechanism. This mechanism provides only for the non-binding advice of a "third party," consisting of a body of independent persons. If one party requests action by the CSCE dispute settlement mechanism, the other one is not allowed to reject it. The mechanism, however, is not to be established in cases where one party considers the dispute as having arisen due to "issues concerning its territorial integrity, or national defence, title to sovereignty over land territory, or competing claims with regard to the jurisdiction over other areas" (Section XII, Art. 1). Moreover, the mechanism is restricted to interstate conflicts. The mechanism's scope is fairly limited, a fact which is in some respect compensated by the arrangement that the procedure can be initiated unilaterally and any dispute of importance to peace, security, or stability among the CSCE states may be brought before the Committee of Senior Officials. But the Valletta report does not spell out which CSCE institution is to initiate the dispute settlement mechanism. According to my explications above, this institution should be the proposed General Secretariat of the CSCE.

The very restrictive agreements of the Valletta meeting can be seen as the first step in new territory, after two failed attempts during the East-West conflict. Improved measures depend on the willingness of states to move to a kind of supranational institutionalization. Then a mechanism for the peaceful settlement of disputes could help to render possible resolutions in conflicts which are neither highly politicized nor carried out militarily. One might envisage such conflicts in transitional periods in which states engage in a conflict over specific issues, but the general long-term trend points to interstate cooperation and integration. However, one restiction needs to be made: conceptionally, every mechanism requires the existence of functioning states, which resolve conflicts of interest with one another. Things become more difficult with non-state actors, or those in the process of demanding statehood.

Despite these qualifications, the mechanism should be enhanced in the following years. It would be possible to begin with disputes concerning minor issues while later advancing to more politicized conflicts. Conflicting parties are unlikely to accept the advice of a third party as binding. But the obligatory character of such advice would be greater if it came from a strong and effective international organization. Therefore, the effectiveness of a peaceful settlement of disputes is closely connected with CSCE institutionalization.

Proposals to develop the CSCE into an international organization with similar structures to the UN are in many aspects far beyond short-term realization. As stated earlier, opposition by many states continues to be strong. However, the need to react appropriately to possible turmoil in post-socialist countries is obvious. All in all, one can only hope that the long-term trend will encourage interdependence, leading -- in a continuing interplay between cooperation and conflict -- to more coordination, harmonization and integration.

## Conclusions

The war in Yugoslawia has clearly shown the lack of instruments with which the European nations having only just escaped from the East-West conflict can adequately react to those (military) confrontations that are for one at odds with CSCE agreements and for another in danger of widening to international conflicts. Mechanisms that would enable interference at an early stage, when conflicts have not yet escalated militarily, as well as mechanisms for intervention after bloodshed has occurred are both missing. Of course, any mediation first of all depends upon the willingness of conflicting parties to make use of it. But, as I have mentioned above, willingness for a peaceful resolution of conflicts can be underpinned if the mediating body has sanctionary measures at its disposal. The body -- to whom conflicting parties must belong -- needs to be an institution of collective security, and not an institution that intervenes on the basis of its own definitons of interest, i.e. interests that do not properly belong to its obligations and fields of action. Obviously, the CSCE will never have at its disposal the military and economic potential of a truly supranational institution; this potential, however, can be made available to the body by member states and member alliances for the purpose of concrete actions of conflict prevention or conflict regulation, or these members can act on the basis of a CSCE mandate.

The following design for a European security structure evolves from this:

The CSCE would be the primary forum in which all European states as well as the United States and Canada would be integrated on the basis of a common code with regard to human rights, basic freedoms, democracy, constitutionality, security and the market economy. The CSCE would be the central controlling agent regarding intervention in intrastate and interstate conflicts in Europe when violations of norms, rules, and procedures laid down by the CSCE occur.

Other institutions with limited membership would not thereby be devalued. To the contrary: they would obtain new, additional functions contributing to the pan-European security system. This is valid for NATO, too, enhancing its ability to provide military security to its core members, while at the same time also serving as a coordinating organ for arms control and disarmament of its (possibly enlarged) membership. The EC's main task would be solving the economic problems of Europe; it would be -- if developed to a Political Union with the WEU as a sub-organization -- *the* European center of power. For reasons mentioned above, however, not all European states will be able to hold

EC membership in the forseeable future. The European Council, as the last pillar of European architecture, would play an important role mainly with respect to conventions bound to international law. Finally, I will sketch the functions of these organizations in a future Europe. I wish only to point to the direction in which these institutions should develop, without going into depth concerning the problems this may raise.

## Other European Organizations and Their Relationship to the CSCE

### *From NATO to EATO*

The main task of the Atlantic Alliance is the continued warrant of its members' security by military means, as a "last resort" against uncertainties. All neighbors of the united Germany regard its membership in NATO as a guarantee against a German *Sonderweg* in military and security affairs. The nearly total integration of German troops into the alliance and the renunciation of a German general staff and military supreme command is the guarantee of American and Western European control over the German military potential. The hegemonic role of the United States ensures that the economically and militarily weaker members of the alliance are not dominated by Germany or any other state. These functions -- as well as the linkage of the United States to European military and security affairs -- cannot be substituted by another organization.

It will be decisive for the future of NATO whether it can survive as an organization without having clearly identifiable enemies. After the failed *coup d'état* and the dismembering of the USSR, maintaining a highly integrated military apparatus equipped with a variety of nuclear weapons makes little sense, and public support in member states will continue to decrease. NATO will therefore play a lesser role in security matters than before, because the former task of preventing a massive nuclear and/or conventional attack by the Soviet Union has ceased to exist. NATO will subsequently assume more "political" tasks, such as linking the United States to European affairs and coordinating pan-European military affairs in general. Besides the "liaison"-links between NATO and the former WTO states this task could be carried out by enlarging the Alliance. This aspect is dealt with in the following.

The integration of new members would be in accordance with the integration concept underlying the assumptions and proposals I have put forward in this chapter. Europe faces the problem of a kind of "security vacuum" in Central and Eastern Central Europe, emanating from the desintegration of the Warsaw Treaty Organization. The Polish, Czecho-Slovak, Hungarian and even the Rumanian and Bulgarian governments seek NATO membership in line with the Spanish example, i.e. without military integration and without the stationing of foreign nuclear weapons on their own soil.

Until now NATO has been very reluctant to admit new members, originally anxious not to weaken Gorbachev's power in the USSR. Since August 1991 the situation has changed, and some successor states of the USSR have also declared their interest in applying for NATO membership. In the longer run, one might therefore envisage NATO becoming a European-American Treaty Organization (EATO), which would include North America and also parts of the former Soviet Union.[24] EATO would have nothing in common with the old alliance. Its main task would be to prepare for CSCE peace-keeping or -- if necessary -- peace-enforcement missions, thus acting as a deterrent against potential rule-breakers in internal European and international affairs. Another task would be to coordinate and harmonize the national military and armament policies of its members. EATO could then take up an additional function for Europe as a whole, a function which NATO has already played in the past as a -- partly integrated -- security community *among* its members.

All this would not make the CSCE superfluous. For one, not all European states will demand NATO membership in the forseeable future. Second, as a military alliance, NATO is not the right organ for agreements on regimes aimed at stabilizing and controlling developments toward democracy and the respect for human and minority rights. Third -- as mentioned above -- what is required is an organ for pan-European conflict regulation. The value of a NATO extension would, however, lie in bringing about additional impediments to regional arms races and war by binding the military potential of its members into a larger military alliance structure. On the other hand, extending membership to states in potential conflict zones contains the risk of involving "old" members in conflicts they would otherwise not be directly affected by.

## An Enlarged European Community

So far, the impact of the CSCE on East-West economic relations has been very low. Even after the full introduction of a capitalist market economy in Eastern Europe, the CSCE would not play a major economic role, because it lacks the instruments for helping to develop the former COMECON economies. The economic pole of growth for Europe will remain with the European Community. According to the concept of institutionalization and integration, enlarging the EC to include the former COMECON members would -- in the long run -- contribute to the economic and political stabilization of the post-socialist countries.[25]

The European Community is characterized by a non-hegemonic political structure. Germany, however, has the quasi-hegemonic function of a dominant economy, but its political consequences are mitigated by the mechanisms of integration, the supranational EC bureaucracy and its inherent self-dynamics. Until now, the EC has solved conflicts peacefully and has been successful to some extent in reducing the asymmetries between poor and rich member states.

Two main obstacles have to be eliminated if the Community is to be enlarged. First, the current process of deepening economic integration and aiming at a political union in Western Europe must not be hindered through an eastward extension. Only a consolidated European Community can be an anchor of stability in the new Europe and can help make the democratization of Eastern Central Europe irrevocable. Therefore, one should envisage a "Community of different speeds" in which only the twelve would move to economic and political union in the coming years. Second, the eastward extension should not overburden the former centrally planned economies. A premature full membership would be desastrous to them and could not be coped with by the Community, which is currently fully occupied with "1993." An enlarged Community -- whatever its concrete shape will be -- needs a reform of its decision-making procedures. And it could mean discarding the original idea of a "United States of Europe" as envisaged in the Rome treaties of 1957. Even if the twelve form a closer political union, the Community as a whole will be more of an association of states centred around the old EC core, a community of "concentric circles."

## The Council of Europe

So far, the Council of Europe has played only a marginal role. In present circumstances, its mission is to facilitate the post-socialist countries' path to pluralism, constitutionalism, and democracy. Full membership has served as a demonstration of a country's international recognition, implying that its government is democratically elected, and human, political, and civil rights are being respected. It is an "admission ticket" raising hopes for membership in other European institutions.

Until now, the Council of Europe's concern has been the ratification of conventions over social, cultural, scientific, and economic issues. Its crucial working themes have been human rights, social problems, culture and education, youth, health, environment, regional and urban planning and the establishment of a common, united legal space.[26] It has passed conventions like the "European Convention on Human Rights" which regulates inter alia the powers of the "European Court of Human Rights." The Council of Europe can be used -- as previously -- as a "think tank" and a "creative training center," in which one can consider and debate new ideas and proposals for a pan-European peace order.[27] It could prepare further drafts for conventions, especially concerning minority rights.

In contrast to the CSCE, the Council of Europe passes conventions as international law. Although their character is legally more binding than CSCE agreements (which are only political obligations), they are not necessarily more effective. The permanent monitoring process during follow-on conferences and meetings of experts in the CSCE context has only led to rules of conduct, but these might have restricted state behaviour more profoundly than legal conventions. The latter are usually less concrete, because states prefer more general wordings if and when they enter into legally binding commitments. This assessment should not discredit the Council of Europe; both institutions have to be regarded as complementary. In the CSCE framework, regimes would be negotiated with a more comprehensive and far-reaching effect than conventions, which would be further on the agenda of the Council of Europe.

## Concluding Remarks

The scenario for the future of Europe is very optimistic. Its underlying assumption is that the behavior of nation states can be civilized by integration and international organizations, and that a stable peace order is based on democracy and pluralism. The different circles of integration, cooperation and consultation described above relate to different political issues and have different degrees of obligations and commitments. All should be deepened with the aim of integrating national policies, and in order to prevent the return of nationalism, bloody conflicts, and war. In practical terms, the idea of having a number of institutional frameworks with partly overlapping powers seems more and more appropriate and politically acceptable -- at least for the intermediate future.

The CSCE could become a regional organization according to Articles 52 and 53 of the Charter of the United Nations which encourage regional arrangements or agencies in order to relieve the Security Council. That would show the world that Europeans are able to handle their conflicts autonomously.

## Notes

1. Cf. John G. Mearsheimer, "Back to the Future. Instability in Europe after the Cold War," *International Security*, Vol. 15, No. 1, Summer 1990, pp. 5-56.

2. For a comprehensive analysis of different futures of Europe see Barry Buzan et al., *The European Security Order Recast. Scenarios for the Post-Cold War Era* (London-New York: Pinter, 1990).

3. Klaus Müller, "Nachholende Modernisierung? Die Konjunkturen der Modernisierungstheorie und ihre Anwendung auf die Transformation der osteuropäischen Gesellschaften," *Leviathan*, Vol. 19, No. 2, 1991, pp. 261-91.

4. Cf. Zbigniew Brzezinski, "Post-Communist Nationalism," *Foreign Affairs*, Vol. 68, No. 5, Winter 1989/90, pp. 1-25, and F. Stephan Larrabee, "Long Memories and Short Fuses. Change and Instability in the Balkans," *International Security*, Vol. 15, No. 3, Winter 1990/91, pp. 58-91.

5. Peter Schlotter, "Die Einhegung einer Großmacht? Deutschland und die zukünftige Architektur Europas," in: Bruno Schoch (ed.) *Deutschlands Einheit und Europas Zukunft, Friedensanalysen No. 26* (Frankfurt: Suhrkamp, 1992), pp.280-300.

6. Reinhard Rode, "Deutschland: Weltwirtschaftsmacht oder überforderter Euro-Hegemon?," *Leviathan*, Vol. 19, No. 2, 1991, pp. 229-46.

7. Dieter Senghaas, "Peace Theory and the Restructuring of Europe," *Alternatives*, Vol. 16, No. 4, 1991, pp. 353-66.

8. Volker Rittberger, "Zur Friedensfähigkeit von Demokratien. Betrachtungen zur politischen Theorie des Friedens," *Aus Politik und Zeitgeschichte*, No. B 44, 1987, pp. 3-12.

9. See especially the debate between "neo-realists" and "neoliberals;" as an example see Robert O. Keohane (ed.), *Neorealism and its Critics* (New York: Columbia University Press, 1986).

10. Senghaas (*op.cit.* in note 7), p. 357.

11. Lothar Brock, "Frieden. Überlegungen zur Theoriebildung," in: Volker Rittberger (ed.), *Theorien der Internationalen Beziehungen. Bestandsaufnahme und Forschungsperspektiven* (Special issue No. 21 of *Politische*

*Vierteljahresschrift*), (Opladen: Westdeutscher Verlag, 1990), pp. 71-89; see also Jürgen Bellers, Erwin Häckel, "Theorien internationaler Integration und internationaler Organisationen," *ibid.*, pp. 286-310.

12. Cf. Karl W. Deutsch, *Political Community and the North Atlantic Area* (Princeton: Princeton University Press, 1957); Peter Schlotter, "Die Ost-West-Beziehungen als pluralistisches Sicherheitssystem," in: Hessische Stiftung Friedens- und Konfliktforschung (ed.), *Europa zwischen Konfrontation und Kooperation. Entspannungspolitik für die 80er Jahre* (Frankfurt: Campus, 1982), pp. 37-61.

13. See Volker Rittberger (ed.), *East-West Regimes. Conflict Management in International Relations* (London: Pinter, 1990), and also Beate Kohler-Koch (ed.), *Regime in den internationalen Beziehungen* (Baden-Baden: Nomos, 1989).

14. Stephen D. Krasner, "Structural Causes and Regime Consequences: Regimes as Intervening Variables," *International Organization*, Vol. 36, 1982, p. 186.

15. Volker Rittberger, "Theorie der internationalen Organisationen," in: Rüdiger Wolfrum (ed.), *Handbuch Vereinte Nationen*, 2nd. edition, (München: Beck, 1991), pp. 363-73.

16. Jack Snyder, "Averting Anarchy in the New Europe," *International Security*, Vol. 14, No. 4, Spring 1990, p. 15.

17. For the concept of "neo-liberal institutionalism" see Robert O. Keohane, *International Institutions and State Power. Essays in International Relations Theory* (Boulder: Westview, 1989), pp. 1-20.

18. Norbert Ropers, Peter Schlotter, *Regime Analysis and the CSCE Process* (Frankfurt: PRIF Reports No. 13, 1990).

19. See for this argument Norbert Ropers, Peter Schlotter, "Die Institutionalisierung des KSZE-Prozesses. Perspektiven und ihre Bewertung," *Aus Politik und Zeitgeschichte*, No. B 1-2, 1987, pp. 16-28.

20. Gregory Flynn, David J. Scheffer, "Limited Collective Security," *Foreign Policy*, No. 80, Fall 1990, pp. 77-101.

21. Charles A. Kupchan, Clifford A. Kupchan, "Concerts, Collective Security, and the Future of Europe," *International Security*, Vol. 16, No. 1, Summer 1991, pp. 114-61.

22. Cf. Hurst Hannum, *Autonomy, Sovereignty, and Self-Determination. The Accomodation of Conflicting Rights* (Philadelphia: University of Pennsylvania Press, 1990), pp. 3-118.

23. See Richard B. Bilder, "International Third-Party Dispute Settlement," in: W. Scott Thompson, Kenneth M. Jensen (eds.), *Approaches to Peace. An Intellectual Map* (Washington: United States Institute of Peace, 1991), pp. 191-226.

24. See Malcolm Chalmers, "Beyond the Alliance System," *World Policy Journal*, Vol. 7, No. 2, Spring 1990, pp. 215-250.

25. Hans Arnold, "Die Europäische Gemeinschaft zwischen Vertiefung und Erweiterung," *Europa-Archiv*, Vol. 46, No.10, 1991, pp. 318-326, and John Pinder, "1992 and Beyond: European Community and Eastern Europe," *The International Spectator*, Vol. 25, No. 3, 1990, pp. 172-183.

26. Otto Schmuck (ed.), *Vierzig Jahre Europarat. Renaissance in gesamt-europäischer Perspektive?* (Bonn: Europa Union Verlag, 1990).

27. Per Fischer, "40 Jahre Europarat -- Vom gescheiterten Föderator zum "kreativen Trainingscenter"," *Integration*, Vol. 12, No. 3, 1989, pp. 119-126, and Michael R. Lucas, Birgit Kreikemeyer, "Der Europarat und der gesamteuropäische Integrationsprozeß," *Wissenschaft und Frieden*, No. 4, 1990, pp. 1-9.

# 4

---

# The Role of NATO in the Emerging
# European Security System

*Harald Müller*

### Theoretical Considerations:
### The Origins and Dynamics of Alliances

The sizable body of alliance theory and empirical research gives us some important hints regarding the origins, dynamics, and typical conflicts of alliances, all of which apply to a greater or lesser degree to NATO and its future.[1]

Alliances are formed to balance a threat. Classical "realist" theory has hypothesized that balancing is directed, in the first place, against accumulated power, that is, against the capabilities of a potential enemy. Recent empirical research, however, gives evidence that this is not true: alliances are more likely to emerge if there is a visible and percieved urgent threat against the core interests of several nations. They are less likely to emerge when only an "abstract" potential for becoming a target is perceived, if the policy of the state(s) in question does not hint to a veiled or open intention to use these capabilities for aggressive purposes. In addition to past policies and statements of the leadership of a suspect state, the deployment of its forces and its military strategy (offensive versus defensive) is the most frequent indicator of "threat" used by neighbouring states. In comparison to the motivation of balancing a threat, ideological affinity has less often been a motivating force for states to ally, and quite often it has been a reason for division and conflict, as several states adhering to the same ideology competed for ideological leadership.[2]

States allied to each other have to live with the dilemma of entrapment and abandonment fears. They are afraid of being "entrapped" in conflicts in which they have no interest of their own, by allies who abuse alliance ties for fostering national ambitions. In Western Europe, for instance, the fifties and sixties were marked by a concern that a revanchist West German foreign policy could entangle the allies in a violent struggle for reunification -- and some of the organizational and decision-making features of NATO have their origin in the aim of preventing just such a scenario from unfolding.

Conversely, allies fear that their friends may defect to the enemy and thereby weaken one's own side fatally. This dilemma is all the more acute whenever power asymmetries in an alliance are large, and geographical interests diverge -- both characteristics easily applicable to NATO. When tension mounted between the US and the Soviet Union -- particularly when driven by conflict in the Third World -- the Western Europeans hurried to convince Washington that a more forthcoming policy towards Moscow was appropriate; the continued support of arms control by West Germany at the beginning of the eighties was a case in point. On the other hand, when the US and the Soviet Union embarked on an amicable dialogue, the allies would demur that a "condominium," at the expense of their own interests, was imminent.[3]

In all alliances, quarrels over sharing the costs of common security abound. In asymmetric alliances, the characteristic debate is about the overproportional share of the "hegemon" and the "free ride" of the smaller allies. In NATO, this subject has been perennial, and it has been revived in the eighties with increasing perseverance by the US Congress.[4]

However, there are two factors that may be more supportive for the longevity of alliances. The first is the emergence of a normative framework based on the faith that an existing alliance is "good," irrespective of its original rational legitimization. Such norms, inbuilt into the decision-making systems of allies and leading to the quasi-automatic considerations of allies' opinions and repercussions for the alliance whenever a more important foreign or security policy decision is on the agenda in a given state, should not be underrated. In this sense, the alliance is more than a physical organization, it is a social institution, integrated into the "nerves of government,"[5] and capable of surviving the demise of the original international constellation that caused its installation in the first place. Alliances may thus be more survivable than purely rational-utilitaristic analysis would conclude.[6] The second factor is bureaucratic inertia, that is, the vested interests by those bureaucratic actors whose careers depend on the continuation of the alliance. Of course, this factor of perseverance is stronger the older, and the more differentiated and expanded the alliance's organization becomes.

These findings present some puzzles for the continuation of NATO in new and altered circumstances. First, the disappearance of a manifest threat, as contrasted to the theoretical possibility of a "risk" posed by remaining Russo-Soviet capabilities, presents a more serious risk to NATO's perceived legitimacy than many of its proponents like to admit. This problem has been exacerbated by the failure of the August 1991 coup and the political underpinnings of the quick dissolution of Soviet military power in favor of the republics, many of which were poised to seek some sort of independent armed forces. Second, while the fear of becoming "entrapped" -- in particular by the alliance's nuclear component -- has eased with the end of the East-West conflict, the "glue" provided by the fear of abandonment has dried up as well. As a consequence of both developments, the need to engage in an endless framework of interconnected consultation within the West will be far less felt than in the past, while the necessity to engage the Central and Eastern European countries and the Soviet Union in a constructive and regular dialogue is all too obvious.

There are thus very manifest and powerful trends that will make it more difficult for NATO to survive the end of the East-West conflict even if all its members are inclined to continue. It will require a special effort at legitimizing the alliance, at defining an iron-clad and convincing mission, and at maintaining the necessary diplomatic efforts to provide for the survival of the organization. The vested interests of bureaucracy are only a partial answer to these troubles. While this factor provides for some perseverance, it might also lead to increasing public opposition, if this body is perceived as consuming public ressources for self-serving interests without real justification in the general security situation. The normative allegiance to alliance values provides a somewhat more solid basis; but even here, it appears that without a well-argued and morally justified mission, a normative framework may not be able to persist. The "chemistry" among the allies will come under increasing strain if the requests put forward to each other are no longer seen as valid. In other words, if the alliance norms are in manifest conflict with other recognized norms (e.g. peace, international cooperation), alliance norms will be contested, and support for alliance cohesion will dwindle. In the end, then, NATO's survival, and the length of its continuation, depend on a morally justifiable mission.

### Historical Considerations:
### NATO's Mission in the Past

NATO has often been credited, by the Warsaw Treaty Organisation's (WTO) leadership and by speakers of Western peace movements, with underlying or aggressive intentions and strategies. This picture, however, does not capture the historical truth.[7] By its very nature, NATO is and was very much a defensive alliance. The North Atlantic Treaty only establishes an obligation of support for defense (in reply to an attack on one member state) in times of war, and it does not even contain an automatic obligation to take arms in support of an ally, but only the duty to take action as deemed necessary -- a rather loose wording. Moreover, Art. 1 of the Treaty obliges the parties to settle their disputes peacefully and to refrain from the use or threat of force; by implication this means that parties deviating from the behavior prescribed by Art. 1 will be deprived of the entitlement to aid by the other parties as stipulated in Art. 5.

Beyond this legal argument, the organization and decision-making of NATO are not conducive to preparing and starting an attack. NATO is basically governed by "committees," with the Council at the top, the Defense Planning Committee and the Nuclear Planning Group as important groups, and with the Military Planning Committee as the main military body, composed of the chiefs of staff of the member states' armed forces. An international staff, in which, again, all member states participate, serves to prepare and to execute the decisions of these bodies.[8] To prepare intentionally a premeditated attack in this decentralized and multinational organization which is by no means void of leaks is virtually impossible. An open preparation would always meet the resistance of some of the members. The situation might have been slightly more complicated in a situation of crisis and high tension when an attack from the WTO appeared to be imminent and a preemptive (particularly air) attack promised some military advantage. Yet even then, it would have been difficult to achieve a consensus in the Council. Anyhow, this issue has now fortunately been relegated to history.

NATO's strategy, too, was defensive. Its most critizised aspect, the readiness to use nuclear weapons first in a conflict, was the direct result of the sheer unwillingness of the Western welfare states to put up sufficient conventional power to achieve a satisfactory defense posture vis à vis a perceived superiority of an offensively deployed and trained WTO. The difficulties of flexible response where compounded by the different interpretations afforded to this strategy by the Europeans and the US. The Europeans viewed flexible response as a seamless web of automatic escalation that would very soon involve the strategic weapons of the United States. In other words, for the Europeans flexible response was the means to render any war unthinkable. For the United States, flexible response was seen as a tool for maintaining firebreaks between a conventional war (which might break out among the "crazy" Europeans) and strategic nuclear war. It was never seen as a tool to make Europe safe for either conventional or tactical nuclear war -- Americans were never that naive, and they were quite capable to see the risks that any war in Europe would entail.

Each partner, thus, tried to interpret flexible response in a way serving best the special, geographically-motivated immediate security interests, but both shared the conviction that any war contained unacceptable nuclear risks. Flexible response was basically a political tool to maintain this basic consensus while papering over the substantial differences in interpretation.[9] The political character of NATO's strategy was demonstrated by almost twenty years of ineptitude to agree on a more detailed deployment concept for nuclear weapons; and apart from a very crude first use, no agreement was reached on follow-on use. When, in 1986, new guidelines were finally issued, they lost their validity in about a year when the INF treaty was signed. So much for the strategic consistency of the Western Alliance.

Beyond this, NATO has espoused a panoply of rather ironic features not consistent with the image of an organization grimly preparing for starting and winning a war. Force and spending goals were mainly set only to be neglected by a considerable number of member states a short time later. Troops in West Germany were maldeployed in the most grotesque way, and the Dutch and Belgian corps were relying on Russian friendlyness to grant time enough to mobilize, assemble, and move forward through a country in which frantic north- south and east-west movements would cross each other. NATO's defense industrialists could never agree on standardization or even interoperability of their equipment. The main concern was jobs for domestic workers and money for domestic industry. For all its splendid organization, high-tech weaponry and well-trained soldiers, the organization was certainly not a war machinery poised to jump forward at a moment's notice.

One fear has always been that NATO was the instrument of "US imperialism," a drive by the most powerful capitalist nation to conquer and reign the world. But this imagination, again, was not in line with basic facts. NATO was never the willful poodle of the United States. It is true that most -- though not all -- initiatives within the Western Alliance originated in Washington. Some of these initiatives, however, were refused, and others where changed, modified, or supplemented.

The Europeans, in many cases (and for better or worse) extracted compromises or even stalled US initiatives. Particularly in arms control, their influence was considerable and, during the last decade, highly positive.[10]

All this does not mean, however, that NATO was or is unequivocally a "force of light." NATO is a big politico-military organization with all the symptoms of "Parkinson's law": bureaucratic self-preservation and -expansion. NATO has accumulated a largely oversized nuclear arsenal, has indulged in a lot of unrealistic and stratheological considerations how it would be used in the hour of catastrophy, has cultivated an exaggerated enemy image and has had, after all, some difficulties to say goodby to the past happily and without regrets. The last five years have seen fervent attempts by the military and political bureaucracy to emphasize old threats, maintain old answers, preserve traditions, and embark on peacemeal change only. NATO is anxiously defending its monopoly as a security supplier for the West and has extreme problems in abandoning a nuclear strategy whose days have passed.

### NATO's Future Under Scrutiny

It is obvious that the immediate reason for NATO's formation -- the fear of an imminent Soviet attack (either through overwhelming threat or by military action) -- whatever its merits at the time may have been, does not exist anymore. Nor does the substitute reason -- that of a permanent confrontation with a strong militarily and politically hostile bloc -- exist anymore. For this reason, a fundamental review of the Western alliance is in order. Its continued existence is by no means self-evident.

On the European left, people draw the conclusion that NATO should dissolve. This argument is somewhat weakened by the fact that the same people put forward this request long before the fundamental changes in Europe took place, and the suspicion is not completely unfounded that old preferences have only been adapted to new circumstances. However, in the absence of manifest threats, the promotion of a complete demilitarization of Europe has gained far more plausibility than ever before. On the right, we find a mirror image of leftist preferences: "risks" have replaced "threats," and NATO should stay as it is. In a version that has lost credibility since the fall of the wall and German unification, all the changes in the Soviet Union and Eastern Europe had been described as a particularly vicious variation of communist *maskirovka*, as a deceptive ploy to lull the West into complacency, only to repeat the assault after restoration of Soviet strength.

The political center pursues more sophisticated considerations. Very soon after the fall of the wall, NATO adopted "risks" instead of "threats" as its rationale for continued military vigilance. The meaning of "risks," and the measures to be taken, though, were and are by no means agreed upon. One version sees NATO slowly fading, as new all-European security institutions step by step assume basic security functions. Another version believes that NATO will continue well into the distant future, but as a subsidiary body to the CSCE (Conference on Security and Cooperation in Europe). Then, some see NATO and CSCE as complementary, with NATO working on strictly military and CSCE on political aspects of security. This is in some contrast to the proposal to make NATO a more political body than it is now. Last (and in combination with one of the other versions), NATO is perceived to take over important tasks for European security in extra-European crises.[11]

At NATO headquarters, it is projected that NATO will be there in permanence, as the dominant military-political organization for European security. Its strategy will contain a nuclear element, with the continuing deployment of a small number of nuclear weapons in non-nuclear weapon states on the continent, if politically feasible. NATO's tasks are the stabilization of European peace, the prevention of the re-emergence of a "Soviet threat," a reassurance against conflicts in Eastern Europe, and a body to coordinate and implement policies and activities out of area, that is, in conflicts south of the Tropic of Cancer. CSCE is not perceived as being able to take over these NATO functions, because of its heterogeneous membership and the unit-veto presently characterizing its decision-making structure.[12] What the "complementary" relation between both organizations would mean in practice is never precisely elaborated. Nor do we learn how European states not members to the Western alliance will be satisfied with entrusting an essential part of their security to an organization they have no say in.

The United States sees NATO as its essential anchor in Europe, and as the indispensable instrument of its leadership within the West. EC member states coordinate their positions in CSCE and present them through their presidency. It is thus harder for the United States to get its interests accepted than within NATO, where the American representative deals with his colleagues from fifteen individual states. If CSCE were the pivotal security organization for Europe, the US would also encounter increasing pressures from non-NATO countries to accept more and stronger legally binding commitments and obligations in the area of security policy. This prospect satisfies neither the US interest in continued leadership nor its attempts in preserving for itself maximum freedom of action. Washington is thus inclined to see CSCE as a "forum," and NATO as an operational organization; only in reaction to the stubborn prodding by Germany and other European nations has the US -- particularly its State Department -- discovered some merits in giving CSCE a greater role as a European security organization. This has not, however, detracted from the overwhelming importance Washington places in NATO.[13]

The United Kingdom (UK) has been following the US position. For London, NATO is the essential instrument to keep the United States a European power, and to preserve its own special relationship as well as its political identity in world politics after the decay of the Empire. If NATO disappeared, the UK's security policy would be mediated by a stronger European Community, and its special ties to the United States could well be lost. This explains Britain's position in the current debate: one of insistence on keeping the "European pillar" firmly integrated into, and subordinated to, NATO. Last, there has been a more fundamental scepticism in the British security establishment as to where Soviet developments might lead, and a greater readiness to stick to old arrangements as an insurance against policy reversals in other European countries.[14]

In France, the political class has been virtually shaken by the disappearance of the whole framework on which French political identity and security policy was based; nuclear weapons have lost their importance, Germany has become reunited and the Soviet threat has disappeared. The reconsideration of policy has not yet led to clear results. On the one hand, there appears to be an interest in a somewhat closer coordination with NATO -- this is expressed in the willingness of French participants to discuss military matters with less shyness than in the past in the NATO council. A second route, however, is the transfer of responsibility to Western European organizations, as expressed in the plan to make the Western European Union (WEU) an operational organization with an independent military structure. The Mitterrand-Kohl initiative of October 1991 went into this direction, but was mitigated by the German desire to uphold the close relationship such a "European pillar" should keep to NATO.[15] A third strategy is to entrust the CSCE with more security functions, or to create a "European Confederation," whatever this means. And the last possibility -- apparently preferred in certain sections of the Defense Ministry -- is to go back to national security policies rather than to embark on a more multilateral path. Presently, a combination of West European/CSCE emphasis slowly appears to be gaining ground.[16]

As for Germany, the Defense Ministry has an understandable inclination to align itself with NATO headquarters in Brussels. For the Foreign Office, and presumably also for the Chancellor's Office, a stronger role for CSCE than envisaged by the Paris summit, and a corresponding reduction of NATO's centrality for European security is the preferred policy. By the same token, a strengthening of Western European defense collaboration is desired, first, to please and to reintegrate France into a common security framework, and second, to be able to make a stronger stand towards the United States on issues where American and European views may diverge. This does not mean that Mr. Genscher wants to emasculate NATO. The Foreign Office has a realistic understanding of the remaining risks that make it advisable to preserve the functioning military alliance. Rather, the strategic vision deviates from the Brussels approach in that the necessity to include the Soviet Union in an all-European security system, and to give this system more competence and power, is understood with greater clarity than elsewhere.

Among the other European countries, the Netherlands, Denmark and Portugal are more inclined to follow the British preference for keeping as closely to existing arrangements as possible so as not to lend support to US isolationist voices. Belgium, Spain, and Italy are more prone to look favourably on closer Western European security integration. For the whole Southern flank, however, continued US security support remains indispensable because of the concern about possible security threats emerging from militarization and advanced weapons proliferation in the Middle East and North Africa. In this context, strengthening the European pillar is certainly not interpreted by Madrid or Rome as a substitution for the reassuring presence of the 6. US fleet in the Mediterranean. Given the alternatives and the discussion going on in and between NATO capitals, it is useful to explore at first the security functions that NATO could usefully perform in the future.

### Functional Considerations: What Is NATO Good For?

NATO has served three classical functions: to counterbalance the power of the Soviet Union, to commit the Germans, thereby preventing them from starting a replay of 1914 or 1939, and to bind the United States to Europe. In a far less dramatic way, and presumably only for a transitory period (the limits of which, however, cannot be defined at present), some of these residual functions remain valid. We should face the fact that Germany and the Soviet Union (or Russia), for geopolitical as well as for historical reasons, are still seen by many of their neighbours as potential threats to stability in Europe. It is not necessary to discuss whether this fear is justified; most likely it is not. Yet the fear is real, and it has to be dealt with until it finally disappears. This will happen some day, but it will take a while even if we create effective institutions to deal with security on an all-European level. The same applies to increasing discomfort with nationalism and mutual territorial claims that is springing up in Eastern Europe and among the Soviet republics.

As long as CSCE has no credible enforcement branch, it is believed that a well-functioning military organization, under due procedure and with the consent of the countries involved, might be a useful instrument for peacekeeping purposes in circumstances comparable to the bloodshed in Yugoslavia. For this reason it is prudent to maintain NATO parallel to the construction of effective all-European institutions. This is the most convenient and cheapest way to fulfill the old residual as well as new security functions, without the claim to an entitlement to decide upon these functions unilaterally. Of particular importance is the integrated military structure, which by its very existence prevents Germany from setting up a Grand General Staff of the old kind, and makes it impossible to plan and conduct large-scale military operations nationally because of the international composition of the command structure. This structural feature would be strengthened if, as presently considered, multinational units would be created at corps or even divisional level.[17]

However, NATO developments since the summer of 1990 give reasons for hope that the alliance might manage to adapt to new circumstances. Already, the renouncement by the 1990 NATO summit of both the follow-on to Lance and the further modernization of nuclear artillery was important not for the numbers involved, but because NATO therewith gave up its principle of a highly diversified nuclear arsenal. The decision by NATO's Nuclear Planning Group (following US leadership) to unilaterallly shred nuclear artillery, short-range missile warheads, and nuclear weapons aboard general purpose navy ships deployed in European waters was a decisive step to scrap the heretofore central doctrine of flexible response. With the halving of nuclear gravity bombs in Europe -- the remaining tactical nuclear weapons in NATO's arsenal -- flexibility has been drastically reduced down to about 700 warheads from a high of 7000 at the end of the seventies.[18]

The replacement for these bombs, the Tactical Air-to-Surface Missile, may never be procured, and even if it is, might not be deployed on the European continent, thus effectively denuclearising the territory of NATO's non-nuclear weapons states.

A transition to a no-first-use doctrine can no longer be excluded. NATO intends to accord arms control a more central position in its overall policy and to create a major permanent staff group for verification purposes. It is now ready to accept a more prominent role for CSCE in the security structure as a supplement to NATO's functions. The 1990 summit extended a "hand of friendship" to Eastern Europe and the Soviet Union. After the failed coup in Moscow, NATO has become even clearer about its willingness to abolish the old "enemy image,"[19] this intention being strengthened by the Baker-Genscher initiative in late 1991, calling for a "cooperation council" including all former WTO members.[20] Furthermore, NATO leaders have made it clear that its readiness for closer association applies to Central and Eastern Europe as well as to the successor states to the Soviet Union.[21] However, there is no intention at present to admit the former allies of the Soviet Union as members and to include the political entities on Soviet territory. The recognition of Soviet and subsequently of Russian security interests and political sensitivities is the main motivation for this policy.[22]

There is something strange, however, about the repeated calls for NATO to become a "political organization." First, the NATO Council has always been a political organization, meeting at the levels of heads of state and government (rarely), of foreign ministers (twice a year) and at ambassadorial level as representatives of the foreign ministries (regularly). The consultative process has regularly and primarily been concerned with political issues, military issues being on the agenda only in as much as they were connected to basic political purposes. Every time NATO endeavoured to discuss non-security issues, it approached caricature. Even NATO's economic department was largely born out of the need to afford France a senior post in the organization without compromising the French refusal to associate itself with the military organization. In the same way, the existence of the "Committee on the Challenges of Modern Society" was challenged mainly because of its difficulties to define appropriate subjects not addressed by other organizations more competently and efficiently.

The talk on "politization" conceals another, more far-reaching claim, namely a monopoly for NATO as the European security institution. In this capacity, NATO would have to widen its political consultation process considerably. The CSCE would be degraded to a useful forum of exchange among all European states, while the "real" operational thinking on political and military security issues would take place under the auspices of NATO.[23] In this claim lies the unacceptable core of some Western positions. NATO is an exclusive organization, to which only a part of the CSCE membership belongs. Admitting Russia or any other CIS member state is not possible for the time being. As long as some countries feel that there may be a need to counterbalance the inherited Soviet power (just in case), there will be insuperable resistance their entry into the Western Alliance. If, under these circumstances, NATO would take the center stage of a European security system, it would be the governance by some over all; the eastern part of the continent, whose consent to a new arrangement of European security is indispensable, would not be part of the superior organization for security. This could hardly be a healthy security system.

The point becomes obvious when the geographical limits of the present alliance are compared to the regions within Europe most likely to suffer violent conflicts in the next two decades. These regions presumably lie east of NATO's frontier. NATO has no legitimate claim, on its own, to contribute to peacekeeping there. It could do so if requested, with the consent of all parties concerned, by a pan-European security organization. NATO posseses quickly deployable forces such as the Allied Mobile Force and the two highly mobile multinational corps that will be formed under current restructuring plans.[24] NATO also possesses functioning political consultation and operational planning systems that are useful in contingency situations. The crux of the matter is, however, that there is a tendency to claim the security function in these areas for NATO on its own merits, not at all mediated through another system. This is not likely to be acceptable to Russia or the Ukraine, and maybe not to all smaller countries in the region concerned.[25] As mentioned above, NATO has recognized this fact itself by refusing consideratons of extending membership to Eastern Europe.[26]

The same applies with equal force to the claims that NATO will have to fulfill global security roles, claims that have been fueled by the 1990/91 Persian Gulf war. If NATO would come to see itself as the global policeman, it would be disastrous for domestic legitimacy of alliance membership in quite a few European countries, in the Third World, and presumably in some European countries without NATO membership. The only organization with a legitimate claim to be an actor in global conflicts is the United Nations. NATO -- within the framework of a pan-European security organization -- may lend its services to the UN Security Council in acute crises. To act on its own in areas not immediately concerning the self-defense of its members would be outrightly illegal, according to its own Charter as well as the Charter of the United Nations. Extra-European security threats, as far as they directly concern European countries, should be addressed by the annual meeting of foreign ministers at CSCE level as envisaged by the Paris Charter for a New Europe (and, of course, by their political directors who are in charge of daily business). If such crises threaten violent conflict, they must be referred to the United Nations. Again, in the course of the last twelve months, some sobering appears to have taken place in the Western Alliance's thinking. While out of area missions continue to be discussed, NATO staff has explicitly refuted the claim of becoming a "world policeman."[27]

## Prospects for a Pan-European Security System

At this point, it is useful to remember what the new security system is all about. A system based on nation-states only is not promising, as history has shown. The persistent security dilemma forces states to arm, to ally and, eventually, to fight even if no bad intentions may initially exist. A collective security system in the classical sense is no way out. It leaves the states in a status of complete sovereignty with no accountability for their peacetime armament behavior; security is granted by a "conditional alliance," not directed against a particular state but against any possible aggressor. The crucial point is that one basic reason for insecurity, namely unfettered sovereignty, is permitted to persist in a collective security system. A supranational security system in which supreme power, including superior arms, rests with a supranational body is not realistic; it is also questionable whether it is wise to invest that much power in any body.

What Europe needs is a new type of security system which I would call transnational.[28] Nation states retain important but not all attributes of their sovereignty: they are not completely free to act as they wish in the realm of security. They are subject to a universal principle of accountability for their foreign and domestic actions concerning security issues. This accountability may mean strict compliance with agreed legal rules, it may mean sufficient transparency or the obligation to justify actions in areas not covered by treaties, in the light of the overall norms guiding the security system (e.g. the Helsinki Act). Supplementing this basic structure of transnationality, elements of national as well as supranational security systems may exist.

An alliance, in this perspective, is a possibly useful but not sufficient structure for the security of all its members. Alliances are useful as they educate member states to learn to live with a somewhat constrained sovereignty. They are insufficient as they reestablish the sovereignty, i.e. non-accountability principle at a collective level: alliances are not obliged to account for their precautions against non-alliance members. Alliances thus cannot serve as a superior security structure, but they may fulfill useful functions as substructures in such a broader system if they are properly integrated and if their decisions are constrained by a framework of common rules to which non-members have consented. It is exactly this role -- a substructure within a broader CSCE framework -- which NATO could usefully play in the coming period.

The solution, in my view, thus lies in getting the hierarchies right: CSCE must be established as the superior body of European security to which all member states are accountable for all aspects of their military policies. Member states would be free to seek their security either individually or through voluntary association -- NATO would thus acquire legitimacy under future CSCE rules regulating, inter alia, the size of armed forces, reporting requirements on military planning, limits on troop movements, procedures to identify military contingencies etc., but only if it accepts these rules explicitly. The North Atlantic Treaty would have to be amended: Art. 1 would have to mention obligations derived from the Paris Charter and other future CSCE agreements as well as from the UN Charter, hence accepting CSCE as the superior order. Alliances would be instrumental in reporting for their members on all their obligations under present and future arms control and disarmament treaties. Member states or alliances would be obliged to answer questions, and to justify activities, concerning their military planning, budgets, research and development etc. The principle of accountability would thus be superimposed over the principle of individual or collective self-defense.

CSCE would assume some specific tasks for pan-European security:
(1)   multilateral central verification and the settlement of compliance disputes,
(2)   the settlement of political disputes,
(3)   crisis management, conflict prevention, and peacekeeping,
(4)   consultation on "out of area" issues,
(5)   coordination of joint efforts to prevent terrorism, particularly terrorist actions involving weapons of mass destruction,
(6)   coordination of export policies for arms and dual-use item exports.

The proper implementation of these tasks requires a stronger permanent structure for preparing and administering decisions. It is thus indispensable to install an effective secretariat for CSCE. The CSCE secretariat would also assume the right to initiate new arms control proposals. Alliances and member states would be obliged to assign national contingents to CSCE missions. For practical purposes, the command may then devolve in actual contingencies to the NATO structure by CSCE decision. NATO's planned multinational units would be ideal for this purpose, and one could even imagine that multinational units would comprise NATO as well as non-NATO troops.

True, this would be a dual system in which two types of security structures would coexist: national (or alliance) structures and a CSCE superstructure. But this dualism corresponds very much to the transitory character of the present historical period, in which old security problems still persist while a new approach to security is already desired but only partially possible. The pan-European structure would be the first and superior line of security; the alliance structure would provide a fall-back position should this line break due to unfortunate political circumstances. Within the alliance, it may be desirable to strengthen the Western European security identity in order to better balance the political weight of the United States. For the European security system this may offer another welcome vehicle for closer association and integration, but it is of second-rate importance compared to the need of strengthening the institutions that encompass from the outset all members of the CSCE.

This arrangement would make non-membership in the Western alliance acceptable to Russia, as all European states would be part of a legally and politically superior institution. NATO could play its politically useful role within an overall European framework for a transitional period without any necessity to define the particular duration of this transition. After a while, security and military functions may be taken over, step by step, by the emerging CSCE framework. In this case, NATO would lose much of its role, and a complete integration into CSCE institutions would become a possibility. Alternatively, NATO's membership could be extended stepwise, first by way of institutionalized dialogue and discussion as in the case of the North Atlantic Cooperation Council, then by common exercises, force planning, procurement, staff training and joint doctrine, and finally by full membership for all countries in the CSCE region, at which point NATO's and CSCE's bodies would merge.[29] This, however, is something to be achieved through unlearning of fears and learning of opportunities -- coming about only at the end of a new period, not at its beginning.

**Conclusion**

Measured by the evidence derived from past alliance research, NATO is confronted with an extraordinary task. It can no longer derive its legitimacy from the classical function of alliances, to balance a threat. Its further existence will be based on a far more abstract objective, namely to serve as a residual insurance against remote risks. Moreover, it will face increasing demands of domestic publics for a "peace dividend." For the Western alliance, the legitimacy needed to survive future "burden sharing" debates in the absence of a threat must be derived from principles and norms not borne of the alliance itself, but of the commonly agreed European security system of which NATO should become an integral part. The irony is that Russia's consent is required to achieve such legitimacy. However, on a closer look, this is not too unusual: the consent of Germany was also needed to maintain the alliance for the last decades, and balancing Germany was also a purpose of the alliance. The difficulty is that the Germans were always in, while Russia will continue to be out of NATO.

This points, again, to the overwhelming importance of a pan-European security order. NATO is no substitute for such a system nor is it this system by itself. It was a major step when NATO's London summit in mid-1990 extended the "hand of friendship" to its former Eastern enemies and -- even before the final German settlement and the conclusion of the CFE Treaty -- embarked on moves to deemphasize the role of nuclear weapons, to discard "forward defense" and to assign (much on German prodding) some limited security responsibilities to CSCE.[30] It is encouraging that major NATO states now appear willing to invest somewhat greater responsibility in CSCE -- a procedure for the settlement of interstate and ethnic disputes, for example -- than the US and the UK were willing to consider before the 1990 Paris Conference.[31] But from there it is still a long way to go to establish a healthy place for NATO in the greater European security system.

**Notes**

1. George Liska, *Nations in Alliance: The Limits of Interdependence* (Baltimore, Maryland: Johns Hopkins University Press, 1962); Ole R. Holsti, P. Terence Hopmann, John D. Sullivan, *Unity and Disintegration in International Alliances: Comparative Studies* (New York: Wiley, 1973); William H. Riker, *The Theory of Political Coalitions* (New Haven, Connecticut: Yale University Press, 1962); Glenn H. Snyder, "Alliance Theory: A Neorealist First

93

Cut," *Journal of International Affairs*, Vol. 44, Spring/Summer 1990, pp. 103-25; idem, "Alliances, Balance and Stability," *International Organization*, Vol. 45, No. 1, Winter 1991, pp. 121-42.

2. Stephen M. Walt, *The Origins of Alliances* (Ithaca, New York: Cornell University Press, 1987).

3. Glenn H. Snyder, "The Security Dilemma in Alliance Politics," *World Politics*, Vol. 36, July 1984, pp. 461-96.

4. Mancur Olson, Richard Zeckhauser, "An Economic Theory of Alliances," *Review of Economics and Statistics*, Vol. 48, August 1966, pp. 266-79; Bruce M. Russett, Harvey Starr, "Alliances and the Price of Primacy," in: Bruce M. Russett (ed.), *What Price Vigilance? The Burdens of National Defense* (New Haven, Connecticut: Yale University Press, 1970), pp. 91-127.

5. Karl W. Deutsch, *The Nerves of Government. Models of Political Communication and Control* ( New York: The Free Press, 1966).

6. Based on unpublished papers by Thomas Risse-Kappen.

7. Good overviews are Stanley R. Sloan, *NATO's Future. Toward a New Transatlantic Bargain* (Washington, D.C.: National Defense University Press, 1985); Lawrence S. Kaplan, *NATO and the United States* (Boston: Twayne Publishers, 1988), and James R. Golden, Daniel J. Kaufman, Asa A. Clark, David H. Petraeus (eds.), *NATO at Forty. Change, Continuity and Prospects* (Boulder, Colorado: Westview, 1989).

8. Cf. *NATO Handbook*, Brussels, NATO, 1989.

9. Lawrence Freedman, *The Evolution of Nuclear Strategy* (Second Edition, New York: St. Martin's Press, 1989), Section 7; Leon V. Sigal, *Nuclear Forces in Europe. Enduring Dilemmas, Present Prospects*, (Washington, D.C.: Brookings, 1984).

10. Robert O. Keohane, "The Big Influence of Small Allies," *Foreign Policy*, No. 2, Spring 1971, pp. 161-82.

11. Cf. Stanley R. Sloan, "NATO`s Future in a New Europe: An American Perspective," *International Affairs*, Vol. 63, No. 3, 1990, pp. 495-511; Ernst-Otto Czempiel, "Die Modernisierung der Atlantischen Gemeinschaft," *Europa-Archiv*, Vol. 45, No. 8, 1990, pp. 275-86; Joseph S. Nye, *Bound to Lead. The Changing Nature of American Power* (New York: Basic Books, 1990).

12. Vernon A. Walters, "Die Vereinigten Staaten und die europäische Sicherheit nach der Vereinigung Deutschlands," *Europa-Archiv*, Vol. 45, No. 22, pp. 655-62.

13. Cf. Harald Müller, "Primat Europas? Europapolitische Konzeptionen in den USA," in: Bernd W. Kubbig (ed.) *Transatlantische Unsicherheit. Die amerikanisch-europäischen Beziehungen im Umbruch* (Frankfurt: Fischer, 1991), pp. 233-50.

14. Cf. Philip A.G. Sabin, *British Strategic Priorities in the 1990s, Adelphi Papers No. 254* (London: IISS, 1990), pp. 16-23.

15. *Atlantic News*, Vol. 25, No. 2350 (October 18, 1991), p. 1.

16. cf. Diego A. Ruiz Palmer, *French Strategic Options in the 1990s, Adelphi Papers No. 260* (London: IISS, 1991), Part III.

17. Cf. *Atlantic News*, Vol. 25, No. 2316 (April 24, 1991), p. 3; Karl Lowe, Thomas-Durell Young, "Multinational Corps in NATO," *Survival*, Vol. 33, No. 1, 1991, pp. 66-77. A thorough discussion of the future missions of NATO from a strategic studies perspective is Uwe Nerlich, *The Atlantic Alliance at the Crossroads. Possible Political and Military Functions in a Changing Europe* (Paris: European Strategic Studies Group, 1990).

18. *Atlantic News*, Vol. 25, No. 2361 (October 19, 1991), p. 1.

19. *Atlantic News*, Vol. 25, No. 2348 (September 6, 1991), pp. 1, 2.

20. *Atlantic News*, Vol. 25, No. 2356 (October 4, 1991), p. 2.

21. Mr. Woerner's speech in Washington, D.C., *NATO Press Service*, Brussels (October 9, 1991), p. 7.

22. *Atlantic News*, Vol. 25, No. 2317 (April 26, 1991), pp. 2, 3; No. 2356 (October 4, 1991), p. 1.

23. This position was most pointedly articulated by the former US ambassador to Germany, Vernon A. Walters (*op. cit.*, in note 12).

24. Cf. Lowe, Young (*op. cit.* in note 17).

25. For a careful analysis of Eastern European security problems see Curt Gasteyger, "The Remaking of Eastern Europe's Security," *Survival*, Vol. 33, No. 2, 1991, pp. 111-24.

26. *Atlantic News*, Vol. 25, No. 2306 (March 15, 1991), pp. 1-2 and No. 2311 (April 4, 1991), p. 3; see also Mr. Wörner's speech in Prague, *NATO Press Service*, Brussels (April 25, 1991).

27. *Atlantic News*, Vol. 25, No. 2311 (April 4, 1991) pp. 1, 2.

28. I have elaborated on such a security system in *Arms Control Today*, Vol. 21, No. 1, Feb. 1991; see also Dieter Senghaas, *Europa 2000. Ein Friedensplan* (Frankfurt: Suhrkamp, 1990), Chapter 4; Barry Buzan et al., *The European Security Order Recast: Scenarios for the Post Cold War Era* (London: Pinter, 1990).

29. Such considerations even exist within NATO circles; see *Atlantic News*, Vol. 25, No. 2356 (October 4, 1991), p. 1.

30. For the London summit, see *Survival*, Vol. 32, No. 5, 1990, pp. 469-72.

31. *Atlantic News*, Vol. 25, No. 2313 (April 12, 1991), pp. 1, 2.

# 5

## Back to Europe? The Old Continent and the New Policy in Moscow

*Vladimir Baranovsky*

### *Perestroika* and Foreign Policy

Soon after 1985, the notion of "new political thinking" became the centerpiece of the fundamental change in Soviet behavior on the international scene. It was to a pragmatic foreign policy what *perestroika* was to the internal development of the USSR. A number of novel ideas had to be injected into Soviet foreign-policy thinking in order to do away with traditional dogmas and define new criteria for assessing international realities and the place of the country in the world arena. But starting the process proved fairly difficult, for at least two obvious reasons.

First of all, the initial incentives for *perestroika* were primarily internal. It was the poor economic performance and an increasingly inefficient management of the transformation of Soviet society that underlay the search for modernization. It is true that this interpretation of events is far from being accepted by all politicians and analysts. Some of them explain the reforms in the Soviet Union as the result of external military and technological challenges. "All those shifts in the party leadership after the death of Brezhnev, all those attempts to find a new type of leader (first Andropov, then Gorbachev) were primarily a reaction to the Euromissiles and then to SDI," wrote the political commentator Igor Kliamkin.[1] The same idea was expressed by Aleksander

Obolensky, the unexpected and desperate challenger to Mikhail Gorbachev when he was elected Soviet head of state at the First Congress of People's Deputies in 1988, and now one of the leaders of the emerging social democratic movement in the country.[2] It is difficult to deny, however, that the enthusiasm for reform was initially inwardly oriented. The increasing shortcomings of the economic system were of much greater concern to the Soviet people in their everyday lives than were the country's "exclusively" peace-loving international activities. These were met with some skepticism and in fact constituted a relatively low-profile political issue.

Secondly, the "subjective factor" (which had always been of prime importance in the Soviet political tradition) was also responsible for a relatively high degree of continuity in foreign policy during *perestroika's* initial stages. Since 1957 this field had been the "domain" of Andrei Gromyko, who not only played a key role in Mikhail Gorbachev's rise to power but also ensured the necessary support to the new CPSU general secretary in his struggle with the old guard. Awarded the then largely ceremonial but symbolically important post of Chairman of the Presidium of the Supreme Soviet, Gromyko became even more invulnerable to direct and indirect criticism of his previous activities.

Nevertheless, a "spillover" of the reform movement into the sphere of foreign policy was inevitable. The very logic of the process, based on the aspiration to a rational reassessment of social reality, precluded "blank spots." These were not filled in for some time, especially when of a sensitive nature, but they had, sooner or later, also to be addressed. At the same time, the readjustment of foreign-policy thinking was not a tabula-rasa exercise. The roots of the "new thinking" with respect to Soviet perceptions of the external environment (and, accordingly, of the requirements for a pragmatic foreign policy) go back as far as the early postwar period.[3] For example, the idea of "peaceful coexistence" with the West was launched by Georgy Malenkov -- i.e. at a very high political level -- as early as the beginning of the 1950s, in other words, even before the Khrushchev era. And intellectual debate in academic circles (though with a relatively small number of participants) did go on during the whole period of stagnation -- though remaining within the confines of the official doctrine, but also influencing it to a certain degree.

With the coming to power of Mikhail Gorbachev, however, a qualitatively new development began to take shape. Rather slow and cautious to begin with, and often painful, it nevertheless produced real breakthroughs and a radical reconsideration of all the major elements of the country's thinking on foreign policy. Three of these deserve special mention.

The first concerns the traditional, dogmatic, "black and white" stereotype of international realities. In this vision, the "contemporary epoch" was defined as the age of transition from capitalism to socialism, with international relations being shaped by the so-called class struggle. This resulted in special emphasis being placed on "solidarity with the forces of progress, peace, and socialism." Clearly, such an outlook could not but have a confrontational impact on the definition of the interests and goals of Soviet foreign policy. It was a zero-sum-game interpretation of world developments. Any difficulties experienced by the capitalist world redounded to "our" advantage: the more numerous those difficulties became, the better the prospects for "world socialism." Conversely, any problems inside the "socialist world" were either the result of "imperialist conspiracy" or at least liable to be exploited by the West for hostile ends. Dialogue with the "class enemy" was either impossible or to be used to undermine its position.

This basic model might have more rigid or more flexible versions, depending on practical needs or on the internal balance of forces between its old-style and its more open-minded proponents -- hence the policy modifications that occurred with regard to various international problems. For example, the attitude toward the outside world might oscillate between two extremes: "those who are not with us are against us" (as in the case of Yugoslavia in the late 1940s and Czechoslovakia in 1968); or "those who are not with them are with us" (viz. the initial romanticism about the West's former colonies). These variations were by no means unimportant in terms of practical policy. Nevertheless, all of them (including the most flexible and "liberal") fitted into the basic concept of antagonism and irreconcilable contradictions between the two social systems. All were potentially expansionist (because at any moment the "revolutionary values" might become predominant, as was the case to a great extent with Afghanistan). And all lacked credibility in terms of stability, predictability, and acceptability to foreign partners. The latter became particularly skeptical of the Soviet Union, following the bankruptcy of detente at the very end of the 1970s.

Mikhail Gorbachev chose the idea of "human civilization" (and the related notion of "universal human values") as the main point of reference for all considerations about overall international developments and foreign policy.[4] Although this approach was open to question for its rather vague (if not arbitrary) character in terms of implementation, it became a useful instrument in several respects. First of all, its chief focus was not a critique of the past but the introduction of additional paradigms for the future. In other words, it did not insist on an immediate renunciation of traditional policy, and so it made the transition less painful in ideological terms and left scope for compromises between the "old" and the "new" thinking. The trend was set by Gorbachev himself when he insisted that ideological differences "should not be translated into the sphere of foreign policy," but at the same time argued that ideological, economic, and political competition between capitalist and socialist states "is inevitable."[5] The new approach proved more acceptable to the Soviet Union's Western partners as well. Despite initial doubts about the practical consequences of the "new political thinking," its "preachy" elements proved attractive to public opinion (which was exhausted by the renewed confrontation at the beginning of the 1980s and thus sympathized with appeals for a new morality), and this had a marked effect on the international climate.

But the most important aspect of the new approach was its dynamic and unorthodox potential. It opened the way for more radical reassessments and for new themes to be introduced into further debates. Although the radicals in the Soviet Union were initially somewhat skeptical about the new rhetoric, they understood very quickly that it could be used to good effect to influence the Kremlin's new practical policy, by reducing its megalomanic inclinations (as in the case of the "comprehensive system of international security")[6] and by reorienting it toward more practical issues (e.g. military imbalances).[7] Of special importance was the argument that, in a civilized society, force can no longer be an instrument of foreign policy. It should not be used in support of ideological allies: so withdrawal from Afghanistan became a Soviet priority. It should not be used to settle international or internal disputes: so Moscow adopted a much more cooperative approach to regional conflicts. It should not be the main element in ensuring the international status of the country: so the USSR reconsidered its policy on arms control and defense. By and large, the basic assumptions on foreign policy, and the means of implementing it, became a matter of fundamental revision.

Closely related to the aforementioned ideological view of foreign-policy thinking was an unrealistic (if not illusory) assessment of the economic, political, social, and military situation in the outside world, as well as of the existing Soviet potential that might be "projected" onto the international arena. In this respect, Soviet thinking throughout its history was characterized by a traditional set of ideas or "credo:" the capitalist system was in its death throes and doomed to failure, and the struggle against monopolies and "political reaction" was the major axis of internal development in "imperialist states;" the contradictions between these states were sharpening, making any coherent strategy for dealing with the problems of the contemporary world impossible; at the same time, these contradictions were put aside whenever the West wanted to undermine the achievements of socialism and control the developing countries; the "socialist community," meanwhile, (this embraced the Soviet Union and its closest political and ideological allies), was constantly increasing its influence in the international arena; and the main objective of "Third World countries," representing the most important strategic reserve of "world socialism," was to get rid of the imperialist dictate. Actually, this list was much longer and included a lot of other exotic (but ideologically irreproachable) evaluations.

Such a distorted picture of the world was not particularly conducive to the development of an effective foreign policy. The latter had to operate within false parameters: waiting for the further development of the "general crisis of capitalism" (if not for capitalism's collapse in the immediate future); hoping for manifestations of solidarity on the part of the developing countries; considering as natural (and thus not requiring any special efforts) the support given by "fraternal socialist countries." The price for such self-imposed ignorance was the dramatic inefficiency of Soviet foreign policy, and its remarkable lack of vision. Moscow had convinced itself (and intimidated itself in the process) of an ill-intentioned desire on the part of "international imperialism" to acquire military superiority in order to impose its will on the whole world. This perception could not but lead to a massive arms build-up, with the illusory goal of being able to stand up to any coalition of states that might arise. By the mid-1980s, the USSR had achieved the unprecedented foreign-policy feat of having encircled itself almost completely with unfriendly states -- in the West, East, and South, all at the same time.

Meanwhile, Soviet pretensions to the status of economic superpower had proved absolutely unfounded (not to mention that the kind of foreign policy then pursued by the USSR would have required resources still beyond the capabilities of any state). Not only had the Soviet Union lost the "peaceful competition" with the United States; its living-standards, compared with those in practically all developed countries, had dropped dramatically. As for the military contest with Washington, that had become a heavy burden -- not only because of Moscow's attempt to gain the upper hand, but also because of the growing gap in respect of the new technologies, and the need to compensate by primitive quantitative superiority. Finally, support for ideologically or politically "close" regimes in the Third World had become increasingly expensive, at a time when the ideology itself was no longer an effective foreign-policy instrument, since the idea of communism had lost much of its previous attraction.

In fact, the expansionism of the late Brezhnev era proved a real disaster for the Soviet Union. Thus, one of the key elements of *perestroika* in foreign policy was a more appropriate perception of the world and of the place of the USSR in it. The economic dynamic of the West was now regarded as what it had been all along: a major stabilizing factor in the world. Moscow also recognized that military power was no longer the main source of influence in international relations, and would become less and less so. Although the Soviet Union retained global interests, this did not necessarily justify its direct presence all over the world. In addition -- and this was not the least consideration -- its limited economic resources had to be taken into account, inevitably limiting the scope of its international activities, or at least changing their character. By and large, the main internal message of the "new political thinking" may be summed up as follows: foreign policy should be less ambitious in scope and more realistic in terms of cost-effectiveness.

Seemingly paradoxically, Soviet thinking on foreign policy had been marked by both Messianism and xenophobia. The ideologically based pretensions of the "first socialist state" to a unique status (not only in the world arena, but in human civilization) had resulted in overwhelming arrogance *vis-à-vis* the economic, social, and political achievements of other countries. Looking for some miraculous path to "social progress," and even pretending to have found such a path, the Soviet Union had actually cut itself off from the outside world. Any external influence was rigorously rejected as undermining the integrity of the very idea of socialism and communism. Autarky, not only in economics but also in a more general sense, had become a way of life and a way of thinking. It was only natural that such self-isolation should gradually reduce the viability of Soviet society, its competitiveness and capacity for innovation. Even if not deliberately, the USSR's foreign policy had contributed to this development by exercising a "protectionist" function in the most conservative and primitive way, preventing a constructive interaction with potential foreign partners.

The logic of the "new political thinking" challenged the idea of the country's axiomatic uniqueness. The dominant idea in its new perception of itself was that of being just one component (among many others) of world civilization. The notion of "interdependence," severely criticized only a few years earlier, became a key word in the new foreign-policy philosophy.[8] More important still, set against world civilization, the Soviet Union lost its superiority complex. The other extreme, a feeling of inferiority, was becoming more and more apparent. Even if psychologically and ideologically painful (at least for some segments of public opinion), this made the country's foreign policy much more open and responsive to the West. The very logic of this reversed perception required that the country's main international ambition be defined as follows: to become a full member of world society and to achieve reintegration into the community of civilized nations.

The Soviet Union had not only overcome the confrontational image of the traditional "enemy;" it had adopted a number of that enemy's values, and these in turn became one of the motors of the country's foreign policy. Although by no means openly acknowledged (especially in the early years of *perestroika*), this fact assumed increasing importance as the country moved steadily toward democratization and its elites became more westernized, but also as its economic difficulties worsened. The whole spectrum of the Soviet Union's international activities was increasingly marked by all these changes in its thinking on foreign policy. This was especially visible in Europe.

## Soviet Policy on Europe After 1985

Europe was a focus of special attention as Soviet goals and priorities were redefined in the spirit of the "new political thinking." There are several reasons for this. The most important has to do with geopolitics. The territorial proximity of the Soviet Union to the countries of Europe made the former sensitive to any problems (whether security-related or ecological) in relations with the latter. At the same time, however, this proximity opened up various possibilities for actively developing mutual cooperation. It is no accident that, of all the developed countries, those of Western Europe enjoyed a huge preponderance as trade partners of the USSR. Even in the era of East-West confrontation, Soviet cooperation with the West was much greater with the countries of Western Europe than with any others. In addition, a number of long-term factors (such as historical background, a common civilization, etc.) were perceived as conducive to *rapprochement* in Europe. This is why the Soviet Union considered that climbing "through the European window" was the easiest and most natural way to achieve reintegration in the world community. The expected West European responsiveness also played a role: the West European's vulnerability to Soviet hostility has always helped make them flexible. Moreover, the USSR was always able to bank on upgrading its ties with the West Europeans to the detriment of the latter's relations with the United States. In other words, it was an indirect way for the Soviet Union to score additional points in the superpower "competition."

Initially, Soviet policy after 1985 accorded symbolic priority to improving relations with Western Europe. This was clearly demonstrated by Gorbachev's first visit abroad as Soviet leader, which took him to Paris. It is even possible that Moscow's initial intention was to launch an updated version of Charles de Gaulle's Franco-Soviet *entente cordiale* of the 1960s. This time, however, there was no real breakthrough in Soviet relations with Western Europe. This was due partly to the very general character of Moscow's new ideas, partly to their being perceived as predominantly rhetorical. Nevertheless, the message was clear: the Soviet Union was ready to open a new era on the European continent. Such "preemption" proved very useful later, however, as Soviet-American cooperation began to gain momentum. It was important for the Soviet Union not to antagonize the West European countries, and to be particularly careful in regard both to their suspicion concerning Moscow's alleged desire to exploit transatlantic contradictions, and to the "condominium syndrome" in their own political mentality.

The reshaping of Soviet behavior in Europe had been initiated even before the new ideological principles were "sanctified" in full and in their radical interpretation. In other words, new approaches became possible even within the traditional, bipolar vision of Europe. These were presented as part of the attempt to make the peaceful coexistence of the two opposing groups of states not only more secure and "more civilized" but also more efficient from the point of view of Soviet interests. There were indeed major grounds for dissatisfaction with East-West relations on the continent. The international regime in Europe, which had existed for four decades, had proved only relatively stable. It had failed to neutralize the arms race (or even to reduce its scale), and it was only theoretically reliable in terms of war prevention (having never actually been tested). The division of Europe was the source of numerous economic, political, and even ideological shortcomings. The perceived security-interests of the USSR were seriously challenged by the deployment of US intermediate-range nuclear missiles, and the deadlock at the INF talks in Geneva had not given much cause for optimism in the field of arms control. By the mid-1980s, the whole political atmosphere in Europe had grown substantially worse, creating an extremely unfavorable external environment for the Soviet Union.

The new approach inaugurated by the new Soviet leadership in 1985 was expressed in the idea of the "common European home." It was initiated not as an elaborate political concept but as a general appeal to a certain pan-European identity based on geographic proximity, common history, cultural similarities, economic ties, political experience, and so on. Although the substance of this formula, and the ways it might be put into practice, were not very clear, its launch did create additional possibilities for the Soviet diplomacy. Despite all the initial (quite comprehensible) skepticism it encountered in the West, the notion of a "common European home" could not be rejected out of hand -- precisely because of its rather general character and of its positive and constructive nature. What was more, the Soviet Union's claim to be an organic part of the continent could easily be challenged by being set against the values and behavioral norms generally accepted in "Europe." In other words, even if the notion of a "common European home" had been mere propaganda from the outset, Moscow could easily become a hostage to its own rhetoric, thereby exposing itself to external pressure. However, Soviet adherence to new ideas in regard to Europe had to be tested at the level of practical policy. The field of arms control provided the setting for the first serious test of that policy.

In fact, a number of important new elements were introduced into Soviet security and arms-control policy quite early on. Starting with the reassessment of traditional perceptions of threat[9] and leading to practical decisions that produced some real breakthroughs (such as the 1986 Stockholm agreement, the 1987 INF treaty, and the 1988 Gorbachev announcement of deep unilateral cuts in conventional forces), they focused primarily on Europe.[10] After several rounds of discussion (at first in academic circles, and later amongst "civilian strategists," journalists, military experts, and diplomats in the media), the Soviet Union declared its endorsement of a new defensive military doctrine and of the principle of "reasonable sufficiency." Both these concepts remained open to broad interpretation, however. Whatever Moscow considered "defensive" and "sufficient" might be viewed differently in Washington and other Western capitals. Hence new basic political approaches and their content seemed more important than modified military terminology.

Moscow actually rejected certain simplistic, though traditional and deep-rooted, assumptions governing its security policy on Europe. This policy no longer proceeded from the axiomatic thesis that the "enemy" had deliberate plans to invade the country. Much more importance was attached to political means than to military instruments. The arms race was identified as a serious burden for the national economy, and this was highlighted by the poor economic performance of the country, which was sometimes described as "Burkina Faso with nuclear weapons." The military balance in Europe was reassessed on the basis of much more realistic criteria. The huge numerical superiority of Soviet and Warsaw Pact ground forces over those of NATO was acknowledged. Accordingly, the traditional "arithmetical" approach to arms control, which required equal reductions of armed forces and weaponry on both sides, was no longer considered the *sine qua non* of any agreement. The idea of asymmetrical reductions (i.e. much more substantial on the Soviet side) was endorsed and later implemented. The Soviet Union radically changed its approach to verification, which had been a stumbling-block in many arms-control negotiations. No arms-control agreement could have been concluded in recent years unless stringent provisions for intrusive verification procedures had been written into them. The internal transformation of the USSR into a much more open society also played a key role here.

Another important dimension of the revolution in Soviet foreign policy was that relating to the military alliances in Europe. The traditional call for a simultaneous elimination of NATO and the Warsaw Pact had never been perceived as a serious proposal by the West, and it does seem as if propaganda considerations had really been the first (and only?) concern of the old-style Soviet policy in this regard. The "new thinking" introduced an important new emphasis: overcoming the bloc structure in Europe was still declared a valid goal, but only in the long term. For immediate practical reasons, it was recognized that the military and political alliances (together and separately) could play a constructive role in creating greater stability on the continent. For example, they could be used as vehicles to launch an effective dialogue on the vital problems of security and arms reduction; they could set up joint bodies (as, for instance, for verification of arms-control agreements); and they could help to establish cooperative security-structures for the whole of Europe.

This approach was undoubtedly a practical one, but one should not underestimate the obvious political considerations involved here. On the one hand, such a move constituted an attempt to have the Warsaw Pact recognized as an equal partner, thereby increasing its viability and creating additional possibilities for the Soviet Union to increase its control over its allies. On the other hand, the idea of a "partnership" with NATO could not but legitimize the opposing alliance in the eyes of the Soviet public and political elite. Ironically, the readiness of the Soviet Union's move to put the Warsaw Pact on an equal footing with NATO more or less coincided with the former's collapse. Meanwhile, Soviet recognition of NATO's legitimacy, the other by-product of the reassessment of both alliances, took on added importance. At the end of the 1980s, the official Soviet image of NATO's role as the traditional "enemy" started to change. Contacts between official representatives of both sides, high-level visits (Eduard Shevardnadze at NATO headquarters in Brussels, Manfred Wörner in Moscow), diplomatic accreditation to NATO of the Soviet ambassador to Belgium -- these were visible and impressive signs of the emergence, in the Soviet Union, of a new mood in regard to a military bloc which until recently had been seen as a symbol of the "evil capitalist empire."

The relative ease with which Moscow accepted NATO's legitimacy may be explained by the simultaneous emergence of a potentially much more explosive issue -- that of Eastern Europe. Dramatic events in this region, which until recently had been a secure sphere of Soviet influence, radically transformed what used to be called "the socialist world." The role of the USSR in this development was twofold. First of all, there are good reasons to suppose that without the advent of *perestroika* in the Soviet Union, the East European countries could not have made fundamental changes in their social and political structures. It is true that, for two decades, gradual changes had been taking place in Hungary, but it is unlikely that the climactic phase leading to democracy in that country could have been successfully completed without the additional impulses emanating from the Soviet Union, which created an atmosphere conducive to decisive breakthroughs. It is also true that, for ten years, Poland, had been experiencing a kind of "underground *perestroika*," though at the price of martial law, which was imposed in the winter of 1981 to forestall a Soviet-led armed intervention. It is also highly significant that, prior to the largely peaceful revolutions of late 1989 in Czechoslovakia, Bulgaria, Rumania, and the former GDR, public expectations in those countries were closely associated with what was going on in the Soviet Union, and their rulers turned rather cautious and reticent in regard to Big Brother in Moscow.

Secondly, the USSR refrained from exerting any pressure on these countries, even when internal developments had gone far beyond the limits that were politically and ideologically acceptable to the Soviet leadership of the time. This provided the most convincing evidence yet that the so-called Brezhnev doctrine had ceased to be part of Soviet foreign policy. One could argue that it is an open question whether such unprecedented Soviet behavior resulted from a new political ethics (the right of countries to self-determination) or was just a manifestation of political realism, since Moscow had lost physical control over events in Eastern Europe. Nevertheless, the Soviet reaction could have been different, even if not an exact repeat of its intervention in Czechoslovakia in 1968.

At the same time, any actual enthusiasm about Soviet policy in Eastern Europe would seem to be misplaced. The Soviet Union could have acted much more effectively to prepare itself for the fundamental changes in relations with the new East European governments. Instead, Moscow was very benevolent, even paternalistic, toward the old "friendly" political elites, thereby jeopardizing Soviet prospects for an "organic relationship" with the new authorities (and diminishing its chances of enjoying much greater prestige among, and support from, the public in those countries). However, such retrospective criticism fails to take into account a number of important features of political developments in the USSR itself. Toward the end of the 1980s, the opponents of economic and political reform (the conservative hard-liners), recovered from the shocks they had suffered during the early years of *perestroika*, and began stirring again, offering increasingly active resistance to further changes. In addition, there was the danger that a "second front" might be opened up by the military establishment, which was increasingly nervous about the character and pace of arms-control negotiations and agreements. Under these conditions, it may be that "disengagement" from such East European leaders as Gustav Husak, Todor Zhivkov, and Nicolae Ceausescu was perceived by the Soviet leadership as bringing with it the danger of an even more threatening "third front."

Assuming this is a plausible explanation, Moscow's first concern would have been to avoid additional problems with the old allied rulers and political elites, even at the price of disappointing the populations under their sway. Not a single political gesture was made that could have been interpreted as encouragement by those East Europeans who initially pinned their hopes on Mikhail Gorbachev. The official Soviet reassessment of the "fraternal help" to Czechoslovakia in 1968, for example, was made only after the Velvet Revolution there. Had such a reassessment been made a few months earlier, it could have had an enormous impact. At the time it was carried out, however, it had practically no effect. But could the Soviet Union in fact have acted otherwise? One can argue that, as the wave of peaceful revolutions washed over Eastern Europe, the prospect of "losing" that Soviet glacis, even if already accepted (at least theoretically) in Moscow, consolidated all the anti-democratic forces in the Soviet Union, thereby forcing Mikhail Gorbachev to take a more aggressive foreign-policy stance. According to this argument, treating the epoch-making change in Eastern Europe as a non-issue would seem to be the most rational strategy the Kremlin could have pursued at the time. In fact, there was no strategy at all, only a reactive policy prompted by entirely unexpected developments in

Eastern Europe. However, the same was true of all the other members of the international community. Almost no one had anticipated the kinds of upheavals that occurred in Eastern Europe, producing such radical results in such a short period of time. Moscow's policy of non-interference (and its renunciation of the option to exert pressure) no doubt contributed to Soviet prestige in the international arena. However, this cannot conceal the fact that the Kremlin was unable to provide a rational definition of its interests and aims, let alone of the means to defend and pursue them.

The same can be said of Soviet policy regarding the "German question." This provided the most important test of the "new political thinking," and the greatest challenge to Moscow's chosen path to the "new Europe." In the final analysis, the Soviet leadership can be said to have passed this test, having given evidence of realism in assessing the situation and of readiness to overcome its traditional foreign-policy stereotypes. One could argue that the issue of German reunification was closely connected with the very logic of the "new political thinking" (the right of nations to self-determination) and the idea of the "common European home" (overcoming the division of the continent). It is true that, to a degree, Moscow became a hostage of its own rhetoric: an open and active opposition to reunification might have discredited its attempts at a radical renewal of its foreign policy. But it is also clear that the international community recognized the historical, political, and legal rights of the Soviet Union to participate in any deliberations and decisions on this problem. A more rigid approach would not necessarily have been perceived as totally unjustified, especially taking into account the hidden hopes in some other quarters that reunification could be prevented with a helping hand from Moscow.

In this case too, however, diplomatic tactics replaced diplomatic strategy. More often than not, Soviet diplomacy followed events rather than initiated them. Sometimes it was too hesitant, and lagged behind political developments. Also, its moves were not always sufficiently well thought out. For instance, to begin with, the possibility of German reunification was regarded as a matter to be dealt with only in the relatively distant future, not as a matter that could be tackled straight away by means of a practical policy. When the process began, the Soviet Union tried to slow it down, initiating the rather exotic idea of a pan-European referendum on the issue. Later, Moscow declared categorically that neutrality was the *sine qua non* of a reunified Germany. The Soviet Defense Minister, Marshal Dmitri Yazov, was unequivocal: "The participation of a united Germany in NATO would undermine the strategic balance and destabilize the situation."[11] This traditional strategic consideration was soon abandoned, however, and the idea of dual membership (in NATO and the Warsaw Pact) was floated. As any foreign-policy expert could have predicted from the outset, this idea also proved unacceptable to the West. Only after the process had actually passed the point of no return did Moscow recognize the German right to define its international status independently -- including the question of its participation in the Atlantic alliance.

Such zigzagging can be explained in part by concerns within the Soviet leadership about threatened domestic reactions to "withdrawal from the center of Europe." Another obvious reason for such a course was that the Kremlin inevitably found it difficult to accept an agenda which, from the outset and in its entirety, had been set by the West. The same was true of all the formulas for settlement of the "German question." However, Moscow's meandering course in negotiations shows little trace of any convincing policy-line that could have been effectively and consistently defended in the international arena. This had negative consequences -- not primarily in terms of concessions in the negotiations, but with respect to the credibility of Soviet foreign policy in general, insofar as it was becoming more and more open to influence by both internal and external criticism.

By the beginning of the 1990s, Soviet foreign policy on Europe had changed substantially in most respects. Moscow had renounced the fundamentals of its pre-1985 behavior and had become much more cooperative in its relations with the rest of Europe. The positive potential of the "new political thinking" was being clearly demonstrated in the way issues of key importance to Europe were addressed. But the most spectacular part of this potential, which proved relatively easy to mobilize (like skimming cream off milk) seemed to be exhausted. The Soviet Union's European policy was facing qualitatively new and, in many respects, more serious problems.

### The Soviet Union Approaching Its End

As the Soviet Union entered the 1990s, a number of factors which had traditionally secured it a high political status and considerable influence on both the world stage and on the European continent were losing their importance, or had already lost it. In the field of foreign policy, Moscow could no longer reap the fat dividends that accrued from the mere possession of nuclear weapons, the relevance of which was steadily declining. The Soviet military presence in Eastern Europe was coming to an end, and the demise of COMECON and the Warsaw

Pact meant that the Soviet Union could no longer act as the leader of a group of states that, until recently, had almost automatically fallen in with whatever decision it made.

In circumstances such as these, there was a need to reassess the very substance of the Soviet Union's European policy. Its initial ambition -- ensuring that East-West relations were "civilized", had to be jettisoned, simply because "East-West" relations in the traditional sense were about to disappear. With the Cold War over, the West European countries no longer felt compelled to treat the Soviet Union as a permanent adversary. And for a while, the emergent international system in Europe -- non-confrontational and cooperative -- seemed indeed to reflect "the end of history," as predicted by Francis Fukuyama in 1989.[12] However, the outlook for the Soviet Union in terms of European affairs did not by any means become totally unproblematic, either conceptually or in terms of practical policy. In the first place, problems inherited from the past continued to play a role; second, the emerging international system was (and still is) far from being the embodiment of harmony; and thirdly, the Soviet Union itself represented the most uncertain variable.

The most serious of the "traditional" problems affecting the Soviet-European interaction were those related to defense and arms control. The prospect of the minimization, or indeed disappearance, of the "Soviet military threat" was one of the main bargaining strengths of the new policy initiated by Moscow. There is no doubt this line had to be preserved, otherwise the credibility of the "new thinking" would have been dramatically undermined. The danger in this regard was far from being merely theoretical. For instance, lack of cooperation in some important aspects of the implementation of the CFE treaty jeopardized its ratification by Western countries and increased uncertainties about future Soviet policy. Particulary worrying was the (increasingly less) tacit opposition of the bodies in charge of the country's military security. They had monopolized policy-making in this field and were extremely reluctant to concede reductions in either the size or funding of military potential.

The changes that occurred in some aspects of traditional military thinking were rather slow, and were also superficial. When, for instance, the Warsaw Pact published its first official document on military doctrine in 1987, the Soviet defense minister declared "we have revealed" its defensive character -- as if it had always been defensive.[13] According to the logic of this approach, no doctrinal changes at all were needed, and this could not but undermine the credibility of the Soviet position. The INF and CFE treaties required that the Soviet

Union make much greater cuts in its weapons arsenals than the West. Though such a requirement was fully justified in terms of establishing a military balance, it could easily be criticized by those internal opponents of Mikhail Gorbachev intent on accusing him of undermining Soviet security interests. The fact that NATO seemed to be in no particular hurry to reduce its own military potential was also used as an argument against further disarmament and for a renewed campaign against the "imperialist aggression." On the other hand, the growing concern among military professionals about the demobilization of tens of thousands of their own, with no secure prospects in civilian life (housing, jobs etc.) also appeared justified. The most serious problem, however, was the absence of a coherent political strategy specifying the future role of military forces. What kind of forces were necessary, for what purposes, and in what configuration? These questions were in fact not addressed in the public debate, and this cast doubt on the legitimacy of the official defense and arms-control policy, and the legitimacy of Soviet policy on Europe as well.

At the same time it is clear that there could hardly have been clear-cut answers to these questions, in particular because of the accelerating changes outside the Soviet Union. In fact, international processes initiated by Moscow were getting more and more out of control and were going far beyond what Moscow might consider desirable or even acceptable. The most important factor in this regard was the dramatic developments in Eastern Europe, creating both opportunities and new problems for Soviet foreign policy.

On the one hand, the rejection of the "Brezhnev doctrine" paved the way for an improvement in relations with neighboring countries. By renouncing its established paternalism, Moscow could hope for healthy, non-discriminatory, mutually beneficial relations, cleansed of the old inferiority/superiority complex and thereby realizing the idea of an "organic relationship" with its European neighbors, as suggested by Helmut Sonnenfeld. These countries' geopolitical concerns, and their high degree of economic interdependence with the Soviet Union, no doubt pointed in the same direction. On the other hand, the legacy of post-war history undermined these prospects. Relations between the East European countries and the USSR were increasingly affected by their internal shifts. Moscow could hardly have any illusions about the future in this respect: the economic crisis, an underdeveloped political culture, and centuries-old ethnic problems provided a fertile ground for radicalism in these societies, with the obvious consequence that former "Big Brother" became an ideal candidate for the role of "external evil." Moreover, the East European countries, were (or at least seemed to be) becoming "westernized" in a more dynamic way and with more far-reaching results than the Soviet Union. They were looking for an "organic relationship" with the EC and with other Western organizations rather than with their former ally, thereby moving the "dividing-line" from the center of Europe to the western borders of the Soviet Union. As a result, the latter was in danger of being gradually marginalized in European affairs, and of seeing its foreign-policy options greatly reduced.

Some very real problems were thus emerging as a natural (though painful) consequence of the ongoing changes, and they were forcing a thorough reassessment of the substance and priorities of Soviet foreign policy. This served as pretext for increasing attacks on the part of the conservative forces. The hard-liners were becoming bolder in their attempts to put their own spin on the events in Europe and to influence future developments there. Colonel Victor Alksnis, one of Mikhail Gorbachev's fiercest opponents in the Supreme Soviet, went as far as to incriminate the foreign ministry, the KGB, and the central comittee of the CPSU in the organization and financing of the "velvet revolutions" in Eastern Europe.[14] Even those who did not support such a radical interpretation of recent history considered the results disastrous for the Soviet Union. One of the leading representatives of conservative thinking, Yegor Ligachev, said: "The events of 1989 in Eastern Europe mean a defeat for socialism, a victory for imperialism, and a strengthening of NATO . . . There is no doubt that our position in the world has been weakened and the security of the USSR reduced."[15]

A more sophisticated version of Soviet traditionalism stressed the objective difference between the national interests of the USSR and those of the West, strongly criticizing the euphoria generated by "foreign policy romanticism." It was argued that, for a merely symbolic recompense, the Soviet Union had surrendered all its trump-cards (armed forces, Germany, Eastern Europe) and that it should try to find some new ones in the east.[16] Such an approach, however, would have exacted a very high price: it would have discredited the "new political thinking" and undermined the prospects for cooperation with the European countries, in return for uncertain (if not illusory) benefits. Nevertheless, the "anti-Western" (and *ipso facto* anti-European) considerations became a popular theme, especially after the resignation of Eduard Shevardnadze as Soviet foreign minister in December 1990, and the launching of a large-scale conservative counteroffensive in the country. The impact of this offensive was considerable, and Soviet foreign policy's room for maneouver was markedly reduced. Mikhail Gorbachev's misgivings about German participation in NATO (the possibility of "certain marshals" taking his place in the Kremlin was reportedly mentioned during the meeting with French President François Mitterrand) are only one, albeit significant, example of this problem. Another was Moscow's failure to initiate a radical reform of the Warsaw Pact before it was too late, presumably because of opposition from the military establishment.

By late 1990 it was becoming clear that the leadership was in dire straits; it lacked legitimacy and was losing control over the country. To many observers, the prospect of force being used to "maintain internal stability and the integrity of the country" seemed increasingly likely. But recourse to authoritarian methods inevitably harbored the risk of a new totalitarianism. A well-known Soviet political analyst had good reason to ask: "To what extent was the totalitarian monster gathering its strength for a regeneration of old-style foreign policy?"[17] Eduard Shevardnadze's answer was pellucid: "If the country continues to be destablized, and the process of democratization stops, it will be impossible to continue on the present foreign-policy course."[18]

The short but dramatic episode of the abortive *coup d'état* in August 1991 certainly corroborated this forecast. If Yanaev and the other plotters had gained the upper hand, Soviet foreign policy would have undergone a profound change. Although chiefly symbolical, one of the few international actions of the leaders of the putsch was to write to Saddam Hussein stating that their aim was reestablish the USSR as a counterweight to the United States.[19] Clearly, if such an approach had been implemented, little would have been left of the positive results of the "new political thinking." From this point of view, the decision of Aleksander Bessmertnikh, the successor to Eduard Shevardnadze as head of Soviet diplomacy, to decline the "invitation" of the putschists to become a member of their team, may be attributed not only to his political loyalty and political values, but also to professional considerations that precluded the resurgence of a confrontational foreign policy.

Even before the coup, the uncertain nature of the trends toward democracy within the Soviet Union had become a matter of special concern to the Western states, thus damaging Soviet foreign-policy interests. The threat of dictatorship, the dissolution of newly formed legislative bodies, a ban on the activities of political parties, and so on would inevitably have scuttled the incipient democratization process in the Soviet Union and raised the question whether the country had really opted for democracy. And it was precisely the belief that the USSR had indeed so opted that made the country more acceptable to Europe. Not surprisingly, the West reacted very strongly to the events in the Baltic republics in January 1991; equally negative (if not even more so) was the reaction to Moscow's attempts to limit freedom of the press and to have security forces supervise business activities.

As late as 1991 the West still regarded Mikhail Gorbachev as the most viable political figure in the Soviet Union; but "Gorbymania" was gradually disappearing, and in any case it did not really prevent the European countries from raising serious objections to any possible erosion of democracy in the Soviet Union. Some experts went as far as to predict extremely negative consequences for the country if such a scenario emerged, namely the establishment of "the last military coalition in history: the United Nations against the Soviet Union."[20] Whether these kinds of apprehensions were important in preventing the advent to power of the conservative forces is now a theoretical question. The problem was overtaken by the disintegration of the Soviet Union, brought about both by the republics' emerging national self-confidence and by the inability of the "center" to preserve the integrity of the country. Desperate attempts by Mikhail Gorbachev to ensure some kind of continuation of the USSR failed, despite clear support from the West, which was keen to minimize uncertainties and avoid unpredictability in the foreign policies of the successors to the Soviet Union. However, following the official decision to discontinue the USSR in December 1991, a new political reality has emerged in place of the former superpower. Its fragmented political heritage has transformed interaction with Europe into a multidimensional problem with specific (and often different) parameters for each of the new independent states.

All these states have to define their own priorities in foreign and security policy. But Russia has a special status in facing this challenge. It played the most important part in destroying the USSR (or, more appropriately, in finalizing its self-destruction). It is the largest and most powerful of the former Soviet republics and, although for the time being its status in the world arena has been substantially reduced by its deep internal crisis, in the long run it will inevitably assume the role of one of the major actors on the international scene (even if without global ambitions). Last but not least, Russia is acknowledged *de facto* by the international community (including the other former Soviet republics) as having the right and the obligation to assume the lion's share of the legacy of the USSR. In all these capacities, Russia faces a number of uncertainties in regard to its European agenda.

## Approaching Europe or Moving Away?

One of the main reasons for the collapse of the former Soviet Union was a dramatic lack of effective political and economic reforms. The crisis which the Gorbachev leadership experienced in regard to legitimacy resulted primarily from its inability to carry out a radical transformation of society. However, the fact that power in Moscow is now in the hands of more radically oriented political forces in itself represents a real breakthrough in terms of a "westernization" of society, or at least of the political line pursued by the country. The same is true for the policy on Europe of the new political elite in Russia, which is by far more radical and substantial. It is no longer a question of managing East-West relations, since one of the two sides of this equation has definitively and irreversibly disappeared with the collapse of the USSR. For the same reason, it is no longer a question of preserving a certain balance of forces in the international arena, even if delicately renamed "balance of interests." It is not a question, either, of searching for face-saving solutions; the Russian leadership has every reason to reject any kind of continuity with the previous occupants of the Kremlin.

It is precisely the collapse of "real socialism" as a political and economic system based on the communist ideology that has dispelled all the ambiguity associated with the former Soviet Union's proclaimed "Europeanization." When it comes to the reduction of military forces, Russia is no longer constrained by traditional considerations: it need no longer be suspicious of NATO, which is now perceived not as the arch-enemy but as a partner. In trying to introduce a market economy, Russia has chosen the only possible way of overcoming its fundamental incompatibility with the West. By renouncing deeply rooted pretensions to political primogeniture, by overcoming illusions of (and temptations to) Messianism, and by recognizing the major values of parliamentary democracy, the Russian political consciousness is becoming much more "European-oriented" than ever before. The process is certainly painful and fraught with controversy. The price of this kind of "Europeanization" is extremely high, and immediate success is by no means guaranteed. Serious difficulties in regard not only to the national economy and to living-standards, but also to the political infrastructure, seem inevitable. The national spirit is frustrated both by the collapse of traditional values and by the uncertainties of the future. Yet this is the only way out of the deadlock resulting from a giant social and political experiment.

Yet Russia is emerging from the Soviet drama as an entity that will not necessarily be any closer to Europe. Politically it has undoubtedly become much more "pro-European" (i.e. pro-Western), even to the extent of declaring that "the West is the natural ally of the new Russia."[21] But the overall context in which its renaissance is taking place is far from being conducive to this kind of *rapprochement* with the "other Europe." Ironically, in defining a new *raison d'être* for state and society in Russia, reference can no longer be made -- or at least can be made to a much lesser degree -- to inherent difficulties in overcoming the Soviet legacy within the confines of the USSR. The definition has become an end in itself. In the USSR the setting of a new course with respect to the major aspects of social life (economic system, political institutions, security policy, basic relations with the outside world, etc.) was tantamount to a peaceful revolution. This in itself constituted a dramatic challenge to the traditional "anti-Western" values and patterns of political behavior, and was thus one of the reformist leaders' major bargaining strengths in the country's relations with Europe. This is no longer the case for the "new Russia," precisely because it has emerged as a kind of alternative to the "old" USSR, with its own values and political foundations. What would once have been a dramatic breakthrough in society -- i.e. getting rid of the totalitarian legacy -- should now simply be the normal pattern for a society that claims to be normal. What used to fascinate the political classes (and public opinion in general) both inside and outside the country should now not even be a matter for discussion, since the "old regime" is over.

Paradoxically, access to Europe has become relatively more problematic. Since the "choice" as such is much less important than it was until recently, it is the quality of the above-mentioned attributes that is regarded as the main test. In the light of this, it becomes clear that democracy is not functioning, and may indeed remain purely declaratory in the absence of real political parties; that the market is merely symbolic, given the continuation of state-owned monopolies and the lack of adequate legislation; and that "human rights" could prove an empty phrase if such rights are not efficiently protected by an appropriate judiciary. In other words, good intentions do not count any more. One of Russia's great assets is the readiness of its present leadership to go beyond these intentions and initiate real changes. But the price of admission to Europe has substantially increased. To mobilize all the economic and political resources to pay this bill is the basic challenge facing Russia as it searches for a way into Europe.

Another complicating factor for Moscow also derives directly from the collapse of the Soviet Union. Geographically speaking, the latter was much closer to Europe than Russia is today: that country is now separated from the West by two territorial belts comprising the former socialist countries and the former republics of the USSR.[22] Having suddenly become the most remote territory of Europe, Russia is having radically to reassess its foreign-policy priorities. Hence another *entente cordiale* between Moscow and Paris, or some kind of "special relationship" with Germany, such as was cultivated (or at least hinted at) right up to the recent past, will hardly rank at the top of Russia's current agenda in international relations. Instead, the prime concern is now the immediate vicinity. This seems more than justified with respect to practically all the country's old and new European neighbors. Russia's responsibility for the withdrawal of the former Soviet troops from the Baltic states and Poland, territorial claims by Latvia and Estonia, a possible "finlandization" of Karelia, with some doubt as to the official stance in Helsinki, the "great schism" with the Ukraine -- these are just some of the problems that are inevitably attracting most attention in Moscow.

In addition, Russia is in some respects more vulnerable to external pressure than was the former Soviet Union. This is not only because of the reduced size and military-cum-political weight of the country, but also because of a greater readiness to compromise now being introduced into Russian foreign policy by the new leadership. Greater flexibility, however, does not mean being able to avoid difficult choices. For example, any future arrangement with Japan on the question of the Kurile Islands (regardless of its form and time-scale) could have a great impact on the whole problem of territorial claims against Russia, including its European part. This would result in a kind of "domino effect," damaging the interests of the country and reducing its flexibility in the international arena.

One important challenge to Moscow's foreign policy is the problem of the so-called Russian-speaking populations in the former Soviet republics. Although this issue is much more explosive in the Central Asian states, Russia's new European neighbors will most probably be affected as well. In fact, the problem has already led to a worsening of relations with the Baltic states, thus destroying much of the positive potential resulting from the active support given to their move to independence by the democratic forces in Russia (including President Yeltsin). In a sense, Russia is a victim of the short-sighted and obstinate policy of the former Soviet leadership, which provided the strongest incentive to the extreme nationalist tendencies on the periphery of the empire. As a result, even in the most developed civil societies in the Baltics, political practice still does not satisfy all the requirements of democracy and human rights. This in turn encourages further nationalist feeling in Russia, giving some justification for a great-power and revanchist mood *à la Zhirinovsky*. Russian foreign policy could become a hostage to both external and internal nationalisms, each reinforcing the other. Although such a development is not unique in history, the scale of the challenge seems unprecedented, and enormously complicates the European agenda for Russia. A striking illustration is what has happened in the Trans-Dnestr region. Rational considerations in favor of non-interference, including the obvious fact of an absence of common borders, would seem to militate against directing the attention of the political classes and the public at large to this explosive issue,[23] which of itself places additional pressure on Russia's foreign policy. The cumulative effect, incidentally, extends even further, causing nervousness in Rumania and hardly contributing to good relations between Bucharest and Moscow or, in wider terms, to stability in this part of Europe.[24]

These kinds of issues could emerge in Russia's relations with practically any of its neighbors. The case of the Ukraine, however, is undoubtedly of special importance, both because of the objective potential of this state, and because of a number of particularly serious unresolved problems. The dispute over the Black Sea fleet is probably the least important of these: Russia's sensitivity is apparently prompted by symbolic considerations rather than being the result of rational deliberations (though it is quite clear that the Mediterranean will become virtually inaccessible to the Russian navy). The question of the Crimea, on the other hand, has every chance of becoming a real apple of discord, given the questionable tradition of its belonging to the Ukraine and the fairly strong support for a revisionist line in Russia. Such revisionism, however, could damage Moscow's "Europeanism" and make its position even more vulnerable with respect to existing or potential territorial claims against Russia. Another issue that has brought Russia into controversy with the Ukraine is the latter's nuclear status. Here, however, the international community undoubtedly has much more convincing arguments, and Moscow may have some difficulty explaining to Kiev why Russia's going nuclear should be justified, but the Ukraine's claim that it should do the same is not. In this case, the interests of Europe in preventing nuclear proliferation seem to tally exactly with those of Russia, who will hardly feel more secure with an independent nuclear force close to its borders.

There is another reason why it seems important for Russia to avoid antagonizing the Ukraine. The latter will almost certainly act as a kind of challenger to Moscow's European policy. The two major successors to the Soviet Union will compete with each other for the political and economic "attention" of the West. Moreover, the Ukraine's claim that it should be considered a "genuine" European country are not likely to be based merely on ephemeral considerations invoking a deep-rooted historical legacy or the exclusive heritage of "Kiev Russia" (9th to 13th century). A more important argument is that relating to the country's geopolitical status and cultural characteristics, as contrasted with those of Russia, which extends far beyond the Urals and has strong connections with Kazakhstan, Central Asia, and the Transcaucasian states. In fact, Russia's problem here is not confined to its relations with the Ukraine. For several obvious reasons, Russia cannot permit itself the luxury of not being involved in events in Asia. Indeed, lack of attention in this quarter has already provoked criticism: Russian diplomacy has been accused of "sleeping through" events in Central Asia and allowing a kind of power vacuum to develop there. Whether an alternative policy would necessarily "divert" Russia from Europe remains an open question. At the same time, the problem should be addressed not only in terms of Russia's interests: trends of a more global nature are involved here. Debates focusing on the danger of Islamic fundamentalism, even if they exaggerate the prospects for its expected (or ongoing?) offensive, are certainly germane to the future development of Central Asia, and in this context to the future role of Russia in the region.

However, this role will also depend on the more general image which Russia has of itself. Stated simply, the question is to what extent Russia is going to ally itself with the West or adopt an alternative approach which stresses the need to be either a leader of the less developed countries or a "bridge" between North and South (or perhaps between Europe and Asia). A purely ideological answer to this question is probably inadequate, because it does not resolve the issue of Russia's "dual geopolitical identity". In fact, the problem is not a new one for the country; it has been actively discussed since at least the time of Peter the Great. The Soviet Union also had to confront these basic foreign-policy options as it strove to overcome its ideological alienation from the external world. (The subject was widely discussed in political and academic circles from both a liberal and a conservative perspective.)[25] With the disappearance of the USSR, it is chiefly Russia that has inherited this fundamental problem as well -- though it has undoubtedly become more "European" ideologically and politically.

Russia's "Europeanism" is also expressed in a greatly modified attitude to different multilateral mechanisms operating or based in Europe. In the past, the political hesitations of the Soviet Union *vis à vis* the European Community reflected a fear that the community could seriously threaten Moscow's international influence, particularly in Europe. Since the problem has been removed from the agenda, the EC is no longer perceived as a challenger but as the most reliable partner in Europe. Not only is the important (and positive) role of the EC fully recognized, but all the traditional concerns with respect to its possible "expansion," "politicization," or "militarization" have been resolutely jettisoned. The main reason for this is apparently the ability of the "twelve" to provide Russia with economic assistance on a scale that far exceeds anything being provided by the other members of the "rich men's club." In addition, the results of the centripetal development in Western Europe in general, and the breakthrough in Maastricht in particular, are perceived as especially impressive in the light of the disintegration of the Soviet Union. Last but not least, Moscow has good reason to appreciate the EC's role as a "peacemaker" in the general disorder prevailing in the eastern part of the continent.

If there is any uneasiness in Moscow with regard to the community, this can be only due to the realization that full membership by Russia is not really possible. When the EC signed associate agreements with Poland, Czecho-Slovakia, and Hungary in December 1991, signalling the possibility of eventual admission to the community, it became clear that the "concentric circle" model was the most likely to prevail in Europe, with Russia remaining either in the outermost circle or outside the whole structure. This means that Russia has no realistic prospect either of full memberhip or of equal partnership in the most viable emergent economic and political structure in Europe. Even if not stated openly, such a situation may be rather painful. Here again all the fundamental ideological and political changes that have taken place in the country might prove to be of no help; recognizing the right of Finland to participate in the EC, for example, does not necessarily imply accepting the border between Russia and Finland as that between Russia and Europe.

NATO has been the subject of an even more radical reassessment. Only two years ago the efforts of Soviet diplomacy were focused on preventing the participation of united Germany in this structure, and this in itself clearly reflected the perceptions prevailing in Moscow at that time. Only a year ago the argument was being convincingly stated that it was essential that NATO refrain from extending its zone of responsibility to the former Warsaw Pact countries, in order not to provoke Moscow. Since then, not only have these considerations lost their validity; NATO itself has actively been trying to play down its ex-enemies' excessive enthusiasm in seeking its guarantees.[26] In principle, security cooperation with NATO could become one of the most important channels of interaction with Europe. As one of the major military powers on the continent, Russia has a good case for insisting on a more respectable status than in other fields where its position is much weaker. However, given the prevailing uncertainties in regard to its internal development (with particular reference here to the reorganization of ex-Soviet military forces) any conclusions about the scope and forms of such cooperation seem premature for the time being.[27]

The dramatic developments in Eastern Europe and in the former Soviet Union have created strong incentives for a "new start" for the CSCE mechanism. The Russian agenda has undergone substantial change in this respect as well. Whereas in the past there was a permanent (and not always unjustified) suspicion that the West wanted to use the CSCE as a means of interfering in the internal affairs of the East, this is now precisely the role that Russia seems anxious to impose on the "Helsinki process." It is significant that the proposal to create CSCE special military forces for use in Nagorny-Karabakh was made by the Russian Foreign Minister Andrei Kosyrev.[28] The aim is obvious: to involve the international community in conflict-management in the immediate vicinity of the country, and to make those new neighbors whose behavior is or could become a matter of concern for Russia internationally accountable. Such an approach, however, entails a number of hypothetical risks: for example, in the case where Russia got involved in serious external conflicts, or where, in a worst-case scenario, forces were used inside the country to preserve its integrity. For the time being, however, it seems probable that Russia will remain a strong supporter of any proposals for measures that might increase the efficiency of the CSCE and its role in ensuring stability.

Turning the CSCE into a cornerstone of the "new European structure" has another advantage for Russia. As one of the chief successors to the Soviet Union, it can be considered (or at least consider itself) not as a newcomer in this structure, but as one of the founders of the CSCE process -- a not insignificant asset for Russian diplomacy. For this reason, as *Nezavisimaya Gazeta* puts it, the orientation toward the CSCE (rather than toward NATO) would advance the task of increasing the political weight of the country much more than would the "persistent quest for second-class membership of the first class Western club."[29] Even more important is the participation of the USA in the CSCE, which justifies the participation of Russia as well, and nullifies concerns about its size and "non-Europeanness." By and large, the activation of the CSCE fits in well with Russia's specific interests, and has undoubtedly been fostered by them. One other outcome seems ambivalent from the point of view of the future role of the CSCE mechanism, namely the admission of the Asian republics of the former Soviet Union as full members. Although the logic of this hasty expansion is quite understandable, its consequences may have not been sufficiently well thought through. It remains to be seen whether it will bring about the "Europeanization" of the new independent states or a "de-Europeanization" of the CSCE. At any rate, one cannot exclude the possibility that an increase in its efficiency has now become less likely.

Against this background, the Council of Europe, even if less ambitious in its scope, has the great advantage of remaining a truly continental structure. It is within this body that Russia could operate above all as a European country, rather than as a former superpower which has to be counterbalanced by the remaining superpower, or as a junior partner trying to find its place in the backyard of the "common European home." The very substance of the problems that the Council of Europe deals with is of utmost importance for Russia precisely in terms of its "Europeanization." At the same time, participation in the structure will make Russia internationally accountable on a non-discriminatory basis, thus avoiding real or even perceived damages to the country's political prestige and to its reemerging national self-confidence.

Throughout Russian and Soviet history, Europe has always been an area of special importance in the country's foreign policy. The "window to Europe" opened up by Peter the Great, and the idea of the "common European home" initiated by Mikhail Gorbachev are just two expressions of the importance attached to this dimension of Moscow's external activity. A special (even if unintentional) role was played by Europe in the rise and fall of *perestroika*, and in the breakup of the Soviet Union. Europe provided a point of reference for the major transformations inside the country, beginning with democratization and working up to the transition to a market economy. It was with respect to Europe that the most important breakthroughs were achieved in the field of arms control, first with the INF treaty and later with the CFE agreement. And it was in Europe that Moscow's "new political thinking" underwent its most striking test, beginning with the renunciation of the Brezhnev doctrine and working up to the dismantling of "real socialism" in the Warsaw Pact's *cordon sanitaire*, which in its turn proved to be only the prelude to the collapse of real socialism in the "cradle of the world revolution".

The new independent states emerging in the geopolitical space occupied by the former USSR will most probably have a "variable-geometry" pattern of relations with Europe. But Europe will undoubtedly have a great impact on post-Soviet developments -- by providing economic assistance and by minimizing the potential for conflict between the former superpower's successors, thus working to prevent an explosion that would certainly have extremely negative international implications. Russia's European agenda is influenced by the legacy of the past and by the new political realities inside and outside the country. Moscow is facing a new challenge -- that of finding a place in Europe that will correspond to Russia's changing perception of itself, to its new domestic priorities, and to its new international status.

## Notes

1. J. Kliamkin, "Strasti vokrug vlasti (Passions of Power)," *Vek XX i mir*, No. 11, 1990, p. 9.

2. *Demokraticheskaya Rossiya*, No. 1, 1990.

3. Neil Malcolm, "De-Stalinization and Soviet Foreign Policy: The Roots of "New Thinking," in: Tsuyoshi Hasegawa and Alex Pravda (eds.), *Perestroika: Soviet Domestic and Foreign Policies* (London: SAGE Publications, 1990), pp. 178-205.

4. M.S. Gorbachev, *Perestroika i novoye myshleniye dlya nashey' strany i dlya vsego mira* (*Perestroika* and New Thinking for Our Country and for the Whole World), (Moscow: Politizdat, 1987), p. 149.

5. *Ibid.*, pp. 146, 151.

6. L. Gotsev, "Kontseptsiya vseobyemlushchey sistemy mezhdunarodnoy bezopasnosti i eyo istoricheskoye znachenie (The Concept of a Comprehensive System of International Security and its Historical Significance)," *Mezhdunarodnaya zhizn*, No. 1, 1987, pp. 63-69; P. Vladimirsky, "Bezopasnost -- vseobyemlushaya ravnaya dlya bsekh (Security -- Comprehensive and Equal for the Whole World)," *Mezhdunarodnaya zhizn*, No. 9, 1987, pp. 3-14.

7. A.G. Arbatov, "Glubokoye sokrashcheniye strategicheskikh vooruzheny (Deep Cuts in Strategic Weapons)," *Mirovaya ekonomika i mezhdunarodnye otnosheniya*, No. 5, 1988, pp. 18-30.

8. R.L. Garthoff, "Soviet "New Thinking" on the World and Foreign Policy," in: Klaus Gottstein (ed.), Western Perceptions of Soviet Goals: Is Trust Possible? (Boulder: Westview Press, 1989), pp. 397-406.

9. V. Zhurkin, S. Karaganov, A. Kortunov, "Vyzovy bezopasnosti -- starye i novye (Challenges of Security -- Old and New)," *Kommunist*, No. 1, 1988, p. 42.

10. *Razoruzheniye i bezopasnost, Ezhegodnik IMEMO 1987* (Disarmament and Security. IMEMO Yearbook 1987), (Moscow: Izdatelstvo APN, 1988), pp. 39-62, 331, 345; *Ibid.*, 1988-1989 (Moscow: Izdatelstvo APN, 1990), pp. 131-78, 277-374.

11. *Izvestia*, May 13, 1990.

12. F. Fukuyama, "The End of History?," *The National Interest*, No. 16, Summer 1989, pp. 3-18.

*123*

13. *Pravda*, July 27, 1987.

14. *Literaturnaya Gazeta*, February 6, 1991, p. 1.

15. "Rozhdeniye i smert' perestroiki (Birth and Death of *Perestroika*)," *Kuranty*, January 17, 1991, p. 5.

16. S. Lunev, "Vneshnepoliticheskiye uspekhi SSSR ne obchevidny (International Political Successes of the USSR are not Obvious)," *Nezavisimaya Gazeta*, December 21, 1990, pp. 1, 4.

17. M. Pavlova-Silvanskaya, "Otstupleniye nachinayetsa? (Is the Retreat Beginning?)," *Literaturnaya Gazeta*, January 9, 1991, p. 4.

18. *Moskovskie Novosti*, January 6, 1991, p. 11.

19. "Saddama postiglo razocharovaniye (Saddam is Disappointed)," *Izvestia*, August 23, 1991, p. 5.

20. B. Kochubey, "Uderzhat li bolsheviki gosudarstvennuyu vlast'? Vospominaniye o budushchem (Will the Bolsheviks Stay in Power? Remembering the Future)," *Nezavisimaya Gazeta*, February 2, 1991, p. 2.

21. *Izvestia*, January 16, 1992, pp. 1, 5.

22. Cf. A. Sorokin, "Sanitarniy bar'yer ot Baltii do Chernogo morya (From the Baltics to the Black Sea)," *Nezavisimaya Gazeta*, February 13, 1992, p. 1.

23. Cf. V. Portnikov, "Komu nuzhna yedinaya Moldova? (Who Needs Indivisible Moldova?)," *Nezavisimaya Gazeta*, March 20, 1992, p. 3.

24. Cf. L. Bereznitskaya, "Strasti po Moldove ( Moldovan Passion)," *Nezavisimaya Gazeta*, March 20, 1992, p. 1.

25. A. Kortunov, "Krizis v Zalive i podkhod SSSR (Crisis in the Gulf and the Approach of the USSR)," *Moskovskie Novosti*, January 13, 1991, p. 3; "Nasha bezopasnost' i Parizhskiy dogovor (Our Security and the Paris Treaty)," *Sovetskaya Rossiya*, January 9, 1991; E. Volodin, "Irakskaya tragediya (The Tragedy of Iraq)," *Sovetskaya Rossiya*, January 31, 1991; Yegor Ligachev, "Segodnya i zavtra (Today and Tomorrow)," *Sovetskaya Rossiya*, February 6, 1991; V. Borisov, "Ni dukh, ni bukva (Neither Spirit, Nor Letter)," *Sovetskaya Rossiya*, February 16, 1991; V. Tiksin, "Podobno danaytsam (Like the Danaens)," *Sovetskaya Rossiya*, February 22, 1991; Yu. Gvozdev, "Dovol'no polupravdy (Only the Half-Truth)," *Sovetskaya Rossiya*, February 27, 1991.

26. S. Blagovolin, "NATO mozhet stat' garantom nezavisimosti Rossii (NATO Could Become a Security Guarantor For Russia)," *Izvestia*, January 22, 1992, p. 3.

27. A. Arbatov, "Rossiya i NATO: nuzhny li my drug drugu? (Russia and NATO: Do We Need Each Other?)," *Nezavisimaya Gazeta*, March 11, 1992, p. 2.

28. *Izvestia*, March 27, 1992, p. 7.

29. V. Razuvayev, "Bumerang dlya Vernera. Luchshe byt' ravnym v CBCE chem "meneye ravnym" v NATO (Boomerang for Woerner. Better to Be Equal in CSCE Than "Less Equal" in NATO)," *Nezavisimaya Gazeta*, March 20, 1992, p. 1.

# 6

---

# From Internationalism to
# Nationalism: The Soviet Armed Forces
# and the Winds of Change

*Yuri Streltsov*

The shift in the tectonic plates under the eastern part of the continent, which could already be felt in the mid-eighties, triggered the political earthquake of the winter of 1989-90, the aftershocks are still rocking the former Soviet Union and have fundamentally recast Europe's strategic landscape. New security regimes have emerged, the brainchild of concerted efforts by the former enemies. Actually, by the end of the 1980s, the security system built on the reality of two antagonistic blocks had ceased to exist, and we now witness developments which up to the mid-eighties would have been perceived as most threatening to the former Soviet Union. What are the threat perceptions like at the beginning of the 1990s? What are their political implications? What is the impact of the politico-economic developments in the now-defunct internal Soviet empire on its armed forces? How and to what degree have they influenced the process of military reform that, according to the highest military authorities, began four to six years ago? And finally, what will be the future shape of armed forces originally based on internationalism and now being converted into purely national symbols of sovereignty? These are the questions we will seek to answer here. The staggering pace of change in a mosaic of republics once called the Soviet Union, and the high degree of uncertainty about the future there make it rather difficult, however, to come to definite conclusions.

## Perestroika and the First Debates on Security

Compared to what they were at the beginning of the 1980s, threat perceptions in Europe have changed just as dramatically as has the strategic situation there. *Glasnost* and *perestroika* split public opinion into a wide spectrum of divergent views in the ex-Soviet Union. This in itself was encouraging, both as a reflection and a result of the process of de-ideologization and democratization that began in 1985. To be sure, there were numerous groups in Soviet society with quite different, sometimes even opposite, views on the military threat to, and military reform in, the country. For systematization' sake, however, we will focus on three main groups.

The first such group was (and still is) made up of the so-called conservatives and other advocates of the "old thinking." It recruits its members overwhelmingly from among the military leadership and the officer corps, in the military-industrial complex, among veterans of the now-forbidden Communist party, and in the armed forces. For them the ideas of an "imperialist encirclement" and of the "inherent aggressiveness" of the capitalist system were psychologically comforting and materially beneficial. A manifesto of this group was published in March 1991 in the newspaper *Den*, under the title "Are There Any Patriots in the Foreign Ministry of the USSR?"[1] The "fourteen questions to the foreign ministry" put forward in the article encapsulate the key arguments of these advocates of an entrenched philosophy. The "retreat" of the Soviet Union and the loss of its strategic buffer zone, the "destruction" of the Warsaw Treaty Organization, the "strengthening" of NATO and of the United States, the "betrayal" of our allies and the "one-sided" disarmament of the Soviet Union -- these are but a few of the grievances of those who call themselves "patriots."

Such issues were at the heart of a heated debate that raged in the former Soviet Union between late 1989, as mostly peaceful revolutions did away with communism in Eastern Europe, and August 1991, when the Moscow hard-liners staged their putsch. Two fundamental questions underlay this debate: Who is a patriot? What interests of which fatherland (the term commonly used here being "national interests") does he defend? According to those self-styled Soviet "patriots", the security of the country could be ensured only if the fighting capability of the armed forces proved at least equal to that of all its "potential enemies" taken together (i.e., the United States, the Atlantic alliance, China and Japan). Such an approach to security, however, can only be bought at the expense of what ought to be the overriding interest of any state: the well-being of its citizens. Only this can ensure both the internal stability and the internal security of the state -- a lesson the former Soviet Union had to learn the hard way.

As history has shown, the main threat to the integrity and the security of the defunct USSR emanated from within, not from without. It was the threat stemming from the inherent weakness of an economy geared primarily toward satisfying the voracious appetite of the military-industrial complex. In this respect, the last of the "fourteen questions" in the *Den* article (Where do that 250 billion rubles Eduard Shevardnadze claims to be a direct result of the new Soviet foreign policy come from?) rings hollow. The answer is clear: It was the money saved by renouncing both the use of force and the production of yet more weapons, as security was achieved through diplomacy.

The top military brass used to describe the military threat in most general terms such as it "exists," it "is still present," or, in a somewhat more conciliatory vein, it "has receded but provides no guarantees of irreversible changes." Army General Vladimir Lobov, the Warsaw Pact's last commander in chief, was more explicit: "The XXVIII Congress (of the CPSU), having noted the presence of a military threat, did not indicate whence or from whom it comes or might come. But these facts are crucial for building up and training the armed forces. The source of the military threat determines how fast and how effectively it can be neutralized and war prevented, as well as how high the level of defensive sufficiency should be. Quantitatively and qualitatively, the state must have the necessary armed forces to rebuff an aggression, and no more."[2] Professor and Major General Ivan Vorobeyev, specially knew where the military threat came from. He pointed to the foreign bases ringing the Soviet Union and to Operation Desert Storm, and was sure that "some" aggressor would attack the Soviet Union in a surprise and massive mode.[3] As for Army General Ivan Tretyak, then the air defense chief, he stated that the military threat was embodied in the military capabilities of the United States and NATO, and added that these existed in reality and were directed against the Soviet Union and its allies.[4] Marshal Sergei Akhromeyev, in all of his latest publications stated that the danger existed and specifically pointed to NATO (which "is being preserved while the analogous Eastern alliance has ceased to exist"), to Western military superiority on the high seas and to attempts by the Atlantic alliance to negotiate "from a position of strength." All this was somehow connected with the notion of a military danger to the Soviet Union.

In the draft military-reform concept submitted by the ministry of defense at the beginning of 1990, the "external military threat" was subdivided into a "direct threat of war" and a "more general threat" in a distant future. According to the ministry, the "direct threat of a global nuclear conflict" had been reduced and a military conflict between East and West was "of very low probability" now. And it went on to say: "The "general threat" of war will exist as long as large nuclear arsenals and massive concentrations of armed forces of potential rivals continue to exist." Up to the beginning of 1991, these potential rivals were, in order of importance, the United States, the Atlantic alliance and some developing countries deemed dangerous as "proxies."[5]

One must admit that the former Soviet territory is still ringed by Western military bases, that NATO strategy has not yet been fundamentally revised, and that new military technologies are still high on the Western agenda. All this corresponds to reality, though it is not the whole picture. The paradox of the contemporary strategic situation in Europe is evident. Up to now stability rested on two pillars. Today, one of these has collapsed while the other has been reinforced. Time and again, the Soviet military leadership stated that the armed forces of the USSR were getting no more than what was necessary for ensuring the country's security. Even though beginning in 1989 and until the official breakup of the country on December 31, 1991, Soviet military power had been substantially pared, military authorities confirmed that up to that point the security of the former state had been guaranteed. But this is the kind of argument that can only play into the hands of the "appeasers," who are convinced that there is no military threat from the West. The basic question in this context is for what kind of war and against what enemy the Soviet military leadership had been training the armed forces during all the years of the Cold War. Which could be regarded as the most likely war scenario? One along the lines of 1914? Or along those of 1941? Or would it be some war by proxy? If the military threats are not clearly defined, the "worst-case scenario" wins out, and the political and economic results of this are clear. Naturally, irresponsible and unrealistic pacifism, rightfully condemned as it was by some Soviet generals, should be ruled out determinedly. But no less determination is needed to exclude the alarmist worst-case assessments of a military threat, for, in the final analysis, they are a far greater danger to the state.

Another stratum of society subscribed to quite contrary views. This group predominantly comprised young people of pre-draft age and parts of the radical intelligentsia. They asserted that for a democratized Soviet Union the danger of war was negligible, and that the illusion of a military threat is needed only by those who are concerned about their well-being as part of the military-scientific-industrial complex. The members of this group viewed the arms race (as well as arms control and disarmament) as managed mainly by the interest of the military-industrial complexes of the United States and the ex-Soviet Union. Their conclusion dovetailed with Shakespeare's "plague on both your houses." They also stated that any dangers for the Soviet Union from Third World countries were grossly exaggerated and that democracy goes hand in hand with the "nonuse" of force.

To be sure, all these arguments are true, but again, this is only part of the truth. The military-industrial complexes would never have become that strong if their interests had not coincided with those of the state (as they are understood by those who are in power). "National interests," whether right or wrong, form the basis of international politics. And up to the time when nations (or at least the main international players) learn how to reconcile contradictory national interests by solely peaceful means, armies and deterrence should be preserved. The new European security regime the CSCE countries are trying to work out presupposes that the former ideological rivals learn the art of compromise and become partners in order to survive in an interdependent world packed with quite new global threats.

As for the third group of those concerned with issues of military threats and military reform, it comprised democrats in the Supreme Soviets of the USSR and of Russia, most members of the academic community (not from the military-scientific-industrial complex), as well as some former military men and veterans in general. Their perception of probable threats can be summarized as follows: The end of the WTO should not be dramatized. The withdrawal from it of the East European countries, which were seen by some military strategists mainly as a sort of bridgehead close to NATO, might turn out to be a significant strategic loss only if NATO were to unleash a war against the USSR. The Soviet Union, however, is not to be considered a loser, for a belt of democratic and rather weak states is being created along its western borders. A situation in which the East European countries are really sovereign states -- without a superpower on their eastern borders limiting their right to self-determination -- serves our correctly understood vital interests much more than the previous state of affairs did. It has now become clear that the ideological linkage was very weak. A common security space in Europe presupposes mutual, equal and voluntary cooperation -- the only way to create real stability in the interaction of the countries involved. Moreover, the changes in Eastern Europe decisively brought to a close the post-World War II history of the continent, doing away with the consequences of the Cold War. This will be instrumental in overcoming the division of Europe and creating a common European economic, legal, and humanitarian space. However, in the months and perhaps even years ahead, Eastern Europe will remain a zone of instability, beset by numerous political and social crises. As a result, totalitarian and radical nationalistic regimes may appear in some of the countries there. One may add that the WTO lid, which for decades had kept the long-simmering ethnic tensions in the Balkan cauldron from boiling over, has now been taken off, with all the negative consequences this might have for the fledgling Commonwealth of Independent States and the continent as a whole.

Considering their grievous experience with the Germans during World War II, one can easily understand the uneasiness of the Soviet people after the old Federal Republic "swallowed" the second strongest member of the former Warsaw Pact, the German Democratic Republic. And yet the new situation has at least two positive aspects. First, democracies are very reluctant to prepare for war, let alone wage it. And this is the all the more difficult since Germany is embedded into a community of democratic states. Second, reunification bestowed a key "linking" role in East-West cooperation upon the new Federal Republic. The fact that the Atlantic alliance is still thriving while the Warsaw Pact has ceased to exist should not be overdramatized. The WTO can only blame itself for not having developed the political structures necessary to maintain its existence. As for NATO, its highly developed political structures of NATO might just make it the core of a future pan-European security system. Should NATO prove unable to seize this opportunity its "victory" over the WTO will be a short-lived one. For a NATO that would be unable or unwilling to shake off the Cold-War mentality, could not but once again lead the Europeans onto the dark path of confrontation.

In these circumstances, those regions where the new political philosophy has not yet taken root assume ever-greater importance. For a belt of potentially dangerous areas beginning in the Balkans and running south- and eastward stands in sharp relief. Unfortunately this outer zone of potential conflict borders on the highly unstable peripheral republics of the former Soviet Union. At first blush, the negative developments in the former Soviet Union seemed unrelated to the problem of Soviet threat-perception. In fact they were interrelated for so long as clear-cut decisions within the country remained pending. Thus Western threat-perception (a new totalitarian regime or a violent breakup of the country) and corresponding actions on the part of the West would have been perceived by the then- Soviet Union as a mounting threat.

## The "Symmetrical" Versus the "Asymmetrical" Approach in Changing the Strategic Landscape

The most important problem of the European process in the late 1980s and at the very beginning of the 1990s was seemingly that of politico-military stability in the midst of the momentous changes sweeping the continent. In an effort to ensure the kind of stability that might contribute to establishing some common European security regime, the Atlantic alliance and the then-Soviet Union initially put forward different political strategies. Evidently, the ambitious task of transforming the bipolar security system into a pan-European system of common security and cooperation needed political will, time and an agreed-upon strategy. Absent the last two prerequisites, two competing strategies were suggested in 1990, both based on quite different assessments of the possible future role of NATO and the WTO in the period of transition to a Europe without blocs.

The Soviet strategy (which may be labeled "symmetrical") deemed it necessary to draw the military-political alliances closer to each other in conjunction with the process of German reunification. In addition, a reform of the blocs "in an organic linkage" with the Vienna talks and the CSCE process was suggested. A reunited Germany, according to one much-publicized scheme, would have acquired for a transitional period the special status of an "associated member" of both alliances, up to the time when the blocs were dissolved. In other words, both alliances would have been preserved for the transitional period and then dissolved simultaneously. In the meantime, they would have regulated, controlled and verified the process of transition to a pan-European security system on the basis of CSCE institutions.

The other ("asymmetrical") strategy proposed by NATO envisaged the preservation of the Atlantic alliance while at the same time taking into consideration the security interests of all European states, including those of the Soviet Union. Thus, NATO was ready to develop political contacts with the WTO at all levels. A reunited Germany was to be included in NATO's political and military structures. At the same time, NATO was ready to give some security guarantees to the WTO and the Soviet Union (among them: no NATO troops in the eastern part of Germany, continued stationing of Soviet troops on the territory of the ex-GDR for an agreed period of time, reduction of German armed forces, etc.). In other words, it was the Atlantic alliance that, according to the "asymmetrical" strategy, would have formed the nucleus of a new European security system. Nonmilitary aspects of the new security system would have been dealt with by CSCE institutions. NATO even considered preserving the WTO for a certain period of time for the sake of military stability in Europe.

Obviously there have been other security models as well as other scenarios and strategies of transition from the bloc-to-bloc security to common security. But since the two strategies outlined above were official, they deserve closer analysis. Assessing the two strategies in retrospect, it is possible to say that the symmetrical model was theoretically preferable for preserving stability in Europe while the asymmetrical one (which ultimately won out) was much closer to reality. In early 1991, the WTO had virtually ceased to exist as a military organization, and later in the year it was officially disbanded. The "common enemy" was gone, and so was the common ideology. As a result, the common political basis of the WTO military doctrine crumbled, too. With the withdrawal of Soviet troops from Hungary and Czecho-Slovakia, the Warsaw Pact's military infrastructure in Eastern Europe was shattered and became inoperative. Moreover, some of the former allies started to pin their security hopes on NATO.

Of the two main functions of NATO (defense and détente) that have retained their conceptual significance in terms of relations with the Commonwealth of Independent States and the other former Soviet republics, it is clear that the second function has become predominant. At the same time, the first one, i.e., defense against "the threat from the East," has undergone (and is still undergoing) significant changes. First of all, its main thrust is now aimed at providing a kind of insurance against such risks as a failure of Boris Yeltsin's program of radical economic change (the offshoot of Mikhail Gorbachev's *perestroika*), unrest and violent conflicts in adjacent zones of instability, and a potential German threat.[6] Control and verification after implementation of the CFE treaty may also, to a certain extent, be included in such a "risk-insurance package." Second, the Gulf war vividly demonstrated the significance of a threat from outside Europe to NATO governments and the greater part of the public.[7] All in all, this allows the alliance to retain its role in the foreseeable future, not only as a political but also as a military organization.

"Out of area" probably has become NATO's greatest concern in light of the new situation. During the Gulf war, pressure increased to spread NATO's responsibility to regions adjacent to NATO territory and to the Middle East in particular. Also, there is the interest expressed by Japanese officials in developing a full trilateral relationship involving the United States and Western Europe to ensure near-global stability.[8] Obviously, there are some very valid reasons for considering an expansion of NATO's theater of operations: economics (securing the oil lifeline), terrorism and drugs, and an enormous conflict potential close to the southern and south-eastern edge of Europe. It is doubtful, however, that NATO military capabilities are sufficient to cope with these new threats . And still more doubtful is that an organization based for the most part in Western Europe will be capable and ready to protect the security of the entire continent and its neighborhood.

## The Impact of German Reunification

There is also a "German aspect" to NATO's role and place in Europe. It was widely discussed in the course of the so-called Two-plus-Four talks. Its essence is that NATO be given a latent "insurance" function in the interests of Western as well as Eastern Europe -- including the former USSR -- to contain united Germany in both a military and a political sense. As far as Western Europe is concerned, this role was never officially declared but rather "implanted" in the NATO concept from the very beginning. New aspects of this NATO reassurance concern Eastern Europe and the former Soviet Union.

Three main versions of the German question are known to have been put forward and discussed in 1989-90. The first version provided for a neutralization (on the Austrian model) of a reunited Germany, with the FRG and the GDR withdrawing from NATO and the WTO, respectively. The advantages of this proposal were also its shortcomings: outside a military alliance, Germany, no doubt economically the most powerful nation in Europe could not have been constrained in its military buildup. This would have been all the more problematic in a Europe without alliances (which were to lose their *raison d'être* or disintegrate with the departure of their members) and lacking a new overarching security structure, hence "vulnerable" under conditions of growing instability. An independent German power center endowed with an overwhelming economic and political potential would then have emerged in Europe. In all likelihood, such a giant would have become an apple of discord, the focus of mutual suspicion for the United States and the former Soviet Union as well as for its immediate neighbors. A neutral Germany would hardly have been suitable for the development of the envisaged security system of a new Europe.

According to the second approach, the so-called twin-anchor concept, the western part of a reunited Germany would have retained its membership both in the European Community and the Atlantic alliance, while its eastern part would have remained a member of both the Warsaw Pact and Comecon. In this case, German territory might have become a zone of constructive interaction between the alliances, a sort of testing ground for future pan-European structures. This scenario would have been very constructive if the two states that were to unite had been equal, and the alliances that were supposed to interact, equally powerful. In neither case was this true. The starting position of the trio FRG, NATO and EC was incomparably better than that of its eastern counterpart GDR, WTO and COMECON. This meant that the attractive "twin-anchor concept" could not be realized.

The third approach envisaged the inclusion of a reunited Germany into NATO. Initially, the Soviet side decisively rejected the very idea of it. The reasons for this were clear: the NATO front lines would have been much closer to the Soviet borders, the results of World War II as good as annulled, and the security of the USSR substantially reduced. In order to reach a compromise, no-reduction-of-security guarantees were required from NATO and the FRG, as well as guarantees of a NATO "transformation" that would turn the original enemy of the Soviet Union and the Warsaw Pact into a partner in a new pan-European security system. The first issue was resolved on the basis of the "Treaty on the Final Settlement on Germany," and the second one by a forthcoming NATO attitude as well as by major international legal acts, namely, the Charter of Paris for a New Europe and the Joint Declaration of 22 States, both of November 21, 1990.

Many Soviet experts acknowledged that this latter approach to the settlement of the German question, contrary to the former two, contained a substantial potential for overcoming the division of Europe, accelerating the process of European unification and setting up a system of pan-European security. Thus, NATO remained a stable alliance of democratic states sharing common values. Although the alliance has its problems, it has developed a political structure that could prove very helpful in the current period of transition. In light of this, it might be worthwhile for the successor states to the Soviet Union to consider seriously an application for membership in the Atlantic alliance -- a step already taken by Russia on December 20, 1991. As for CSCE process and yet-to-be-created institutions and mechanisms, they should play three major roles: to ensure transparency in the European security space, to organize arms-control efforts in Europe and to guarantee security of every single state. These tasks may constitute a useful "frame," which would ensure greater stability on the continent. Much, however, will depend on developments in the former Soviet Union. This is true with regard to the (still uncertain) political future of the country beyond the mere transformation of Soviet republics into sovereign states. But, from the outset, both the problem of threat perceptions and the corresponding arms buildup were closely linked to progress in the efforts at military reform.

## The Difficult Task of Initiating Military Reform in the USSR

The task to "intensify, expand and deepen" *perestroika* in the Soviet armed forces was announced in Communist Party documents and in the military press as early as 1985. The notion of "military *perestroika*" remained just that, a notion. The conservatism of the Soviet military administration first became apparent in a rejection of military *perestroika* as such ("Everything is OK in the armed forces"), and then in attempts to reduce it to mere changes in the military doctrine of the Soviet Union and the Warsaw Treaty Organization. It was not until 1990, when the former ideological and military adversaries declared that they were no longer enemies and ready for cooperation, that the way was finally cleared for a true military reform, meaning a radical remaking of the existing military machine.

Meanwhile, public dissatisfaction with the lack of reforms in the military was growing. Military officials countered this criticism by pretending that they had actually initiated reforms in 1987, concurrently with the changes in Soviet military doctrine. Some military leaders dated the start of the reform process back even further -- to the spring of 1985 (which marks the beginning of *perestroika* ), when "the general direction military reform should take was set."[9] They argued that a number of practical steps on the way to an overall reform of the military had been taken. They were: the new defensive military doctrine; changes in training; the unilateral cuts in the Soviet armed forces announced by Mikhail Gorbachev before the UN General Assembly in December 1988; and the decision to withdraw some Soviet troops from Czechoslovakia, Hungary and Mongolia. Seen in that light, what passed as military reform seemed more like the sum of individual measures imposed on the military by the very course of events and in no way reflecting a comprehensive concept. At best, they represented separate components of a possible military reform.

This conclusion, which contradicts the statements issued by the Ministry of Defense was supported by a number of commanders in chief of Soviet military districts. For example, Colonel General Boris Gromov, at the time (August 1990) commander in chief of the Kiev military district, asserted that there was no comprehensive concept for military reform and that the changes that actually did take place in the armed forces (cuts in equipment and personnel, withdrawal of Soviet troops from Eastern Europe, structural changes) were the result of the new defensive military doctrine and not of reforms in the Soviet military.[10] The nonsystematic approach resulting from the absence of a comprehensive military-reform concept was also noted by Colonel General Yevgeni Vorobeyev, then commander in chief of the central group of forces, who stated that the changes taking place followed the practice-to-theory path though it should have been the other way around.[11] Others again argued that military reform should be envisioned as a "wide and complex program aimed at transforming national military policy, the structures controlling the military sphere, as well as all material and moral factors affecting national defense capabilities and the combat readiness of both army and navy."[12] This much more comprehensive understanding of military reform was supplemented by the conclusion that "military reform should embrace not only the military buildup per se but also the development of military theory and Soviet military science."[13] Such a comprehensive approach, however, had the practical effect of consigning any realistic military reform to a fairly distant future.

The very notion of military reform calls for specific criteria and excludes expanded interpretations. And it is these prerequisites that, from the very inception of the idea of military reform, determine the pace of its implementation. As to the reform of the Soviet military, it was officially defined as a "substantial reconstruction of the national military system carried out by decisions of the highest state organs."[14] It was to be based on appropriate legal acts as well as on revised military laws and service manuals. These laws were drafted in 1990 and 1991. The suggested package of legal acts included, among others, laws on defense, military service and the service members' legal status. As long as those laws were not enacted, there was no ground to assert that the military reform had been realized as was claimed by the Soviet military authorities.[15] (All such legal acts and concomitant regulations, however, should be derived from a comprehensive concept of military reform. Obviously, it is not laws that are to determine military reform, but the concept approved by the relevant national authorities.)

That is why it is very important to underline that the very concept of military reform in the former Soviet Union could not have been formulated, let alone adopted, without prior resolution by the legislative and the executive of vital problems of national and social development. Indeed, how could structural changes in the Soviet armed forces have been decided upon, let alone implemented, without prior knowledge of the shape of what one then thought would be a new union? The degree of "military sovereignty" delegated by the republics to the central government (or vice versa) could not have been clearly determined until the possible members of the putative union had come to terms with one another. Just as vague was the principle of military service, whether national/territorial, all-union (i.e, exterritorial), or mixed. In addition, one would have been unable to determine the role and tasks of the armed forces absent a law on defense. Even after the breakup of the country, this latter point remains the subject of an intense debate among different political forces in society. Various political groups (even those of a radical, i.e., democratic, orientation) believe, for instance, that the armed forces must ensure the internal stability of the state under "extreme conditions,"[16] while others reject that very idea outright. Finally, it was also clear that a successful reform of the military could only have gone hand in hand with a successful reform of the economy.

All this means that the necessary prerequisites for a meaningful military reform in the USSR were lacking. It seems appropriate, however, to look somewhat more closely into some of the problems that military reform, as initiated and discussed by military authorities, people's deputies and various academics, faced in the former Soviet Union. The original concept of the Soviet ministry of defense referred to a reform of the Soviet armed forces as the "nucleus of a complete military reform." The armed forces must be made "to conform with the level of real military threat and new political, economic and social conditions."[17] Of all the problems of organizing the armed forces of the defunct Soviet Union in accordance with this concept, it seems reasonable to look at those that caused the most heated discussions nationwide.[18]

Up to the putsch of August 1991, they concerned primarily the issue of creating so-called national-territorial formations. The two most elaborate concepts, submitted to the Supreme Soviet of the USSR in 1990 (one by the ministry of defense, the other by a group of deputies), treat this issue differently. While the defense ministry advocated maintaining and ensuring the exterritorial principle of the Soviet armed forces,[19] the latter called for "the right of sovereign states to have their armed formations and military reserves, delegating to the central administration the right to employ these in order to ensure the union security against external military threats."[20]

The position of the ministry was substantiated by reasonable arguments. Apart from those derived from the postwar tradition,[21] there were, among others, those pointing to the risk of a weakening of the armed forces' combat capability; to the danger of losing control over the troops in case of war due to an expanded system of command; and to the inevitability of increased expenditures (by a factor of 1.8, as estimated by Colonel General Dmitri Volkogonov, deputy-chairman of the Soviet of Nationalities in the Russian Supreme Soviet) to finance newly created armies in the republics.[22] One more argument in favor of this approach should be added. As the higher military authorities and some experts have stated, it was feared that territorial military formations might have instigated or intensified local conflicts within what was then the USSR. This was indeed a relevant argument, for one of the chief aims of Soviet military reform was to stabilize the internal situation. In any case, we ought to consider some of the counterarguments tossed about at the time (and, to a degree, still valid after the official breakup of the Soviet Union): internal stability depends not so much on the creation of military formations in the republics as on the resolution of economic, political, national contradictions. The best way to put an end to internal military conflicts consists of removing contradictions by political and economic means; under the present conditions, the process of creating territorial military formations is taking place largely uncontrolled. The eventual conclusion of an agreement between the republics might at least make it possible to regulate the process; and finally, territorial defense is not entirely new to the Soviet Union. Such a system existed in the country in the 1920s and 1930s. It was then replaced by the exterritorial system, not because the former intensified local conflicts, but because the latter was much more appropriate in view of the imminence of World War II. Nowadays both systems exist side by side in many Western countries, and it might be useful to study their experience in light of the new international situation.

Arguments of the opposition (the aforementioned group of deputies headed by Vladimir Lopatin) were just as weighty. The right to have their own military formations and to participate in decision making on a joint defense policy, they argued, could be seen as reflecting the sovereignty of those republics that were ready to join the kind of union Mikhail Gorbachev was then striving for. This right may not necessarily have had to be implemented, but it would have had to be recognized. The deputies assumed that the territorial armies, which would have included both land forces and professional reserves, would have been subordinated to both the individual republics and the central authorities. The apportionment of the strategic forces and chemical weapons among various republics was totally ruled out at the time. The most powerful argument in favor of the parliamentary group, however, is current events. Ukraine, Belarus and Georgia were among the first republics to declare a right to their own armed forces, and a number of other republics and regions have already started to exercise that right. Since 1990, de facto military formations have been put together in Armenia and Azerbaijan, and in the autonomous regions of Abhazia and South Ossetia. Since the August putsch, the process of military disintegration has accelerated greatly, with Ukraine, Azerbaijan and Moldova among the first to seize control over the Soviet forces deployed on their territory. Thus, it has become even more imperative to find a compromise taking realities into account instead of just closing one's eyes to them. Such a compromise may look like this: a combination of the territorial principle (setting up formations of dual subordination intended primarily to cope with disasters and disorders as stipulated by law) and of the exterritorial principle (volunteers who would receive appropriate financial compensation and benefits).

The problem of army professionalism is no less acute -- and remains so even after the final collapse of the Soviet Union at the very end of 1991. Improving the level of professionalism in the armed forces has thus become an urgent necessity. But recruiting personnel with adequate technical skills and an acceptable educational level under the current system of conscription has become increasingly difficult. The restructuring of the armed forces in accordance with the doctrine of reasonable defense sufficiency, when the quality of weaponry and the concomitant skills of personnel take on added importance, poses a challenge to the very idea of compulsory military service. In this context, one has to be aware of the widening gap between an increasingly complex military technology and the time needed to master it on the one hand, and the insufficient qualitative level of recruits together with too short a training for mastery and maintenance of advanced weapons systems on the other. Thus, the problem of the transition to a largely professional army has become more challenging in theory and, even more important, in the day-to-day practice of the armed forces. Initially the ministry of defense rejected these ideas until it came round and recognized their validity -- though with reservations and doubts as expressed in the draft concept of military reform. These reservations and doubts can be summarized as follows:

(1) The idea of a professional army was imposed on society by self-styled advocates of mercenary troops[23] and by those "who are pursuing their selfish interests in relieving parts of the population of the sacred duty and honorable obligation to defend the motherland."[24]

(2) The renunciation of compulsory military service would lead to the loss of skilled reserves. "Military experience shows, claimed a document prepared by the ministry of defense, that a state without militarily-skilled human resources is unable to

rapidly ensure combat readiness of its armed forces and provide qualitative replacements of losses."[25]

(3) A fast transition to a professional army would also be dangerous to the cohesiveness of society, which would have to absorb hundreds of thousands of senior military personnel (and their families), which would be retired with only meager, if any, social benefits.

(4) In conclusion, the defense ministry argued that a professional army would be economically unfeasible: "The argument that a professional army is economically efficient to maintain is ungrounded and based on emotions only."[26]

All these doubts and reservations deserve careful consideration. Turning to the "mercenary" argument, it is necessary to point to the principal difference between a mercenary army and a professional army. The notion of mercenariness stems from antiquity and consisted in recruiting citizens of other states, principalities and cities. Of course, they were professionals, but the main incentive for a mercenary was to go to war for money. A professional army, on the other hand, is an army recruited on a voluntary basis from citizens of the state they belong to. So, the attempt to equate the notion of professional army with that of mercenary troops is nothing but propaganda aimed at creating negative stereotypes. Today, what used to be the Soviet armed forces has in its ranks about a million officers, volunteers and reenlisted servicemen who, unlike the bulk of the draftees, are real professionals, though not paid as such.

The statement that professionalism would undermine army morale is also dubious. Army morale, as Russian and Soviet history demonstrates, depends much more on conditions within the army and in the country, on people's attitudes toward the army, and on general public acceptance of the necessity of a military. Here, it is worth noting that, compared to the draft, a system based on the recruitment of volunteers would have fewer negative effects on the national economy and would not interfere with the private life and plans of the young generation. Albeit intangible, such a gain would be large enough, provided it stirred general interest in an otherwise intellectually and morally healthy society. As far as the argument of a "loss of combat-ready reserves" is concerned, it causes one to think that the military leadership of the ex-Soviet Union was preparing to fight a war along the lines of World War II. The probability of a global conventional war with the West, however, has all but disappeared. And the regular army could be reinforced by much smaller but more skilled reserves, undergoing regular training and receiving adequate pay and certain socioeconomic benefits.

The toughest problem is of the cost of a professional army. It is striking that cost estimates by the ministry of defense were altered several times in 1990-91. Once the very idea of a professional army had been recognized (in the spring of 1989), it was said that an all-volunteer force would be eight times as expensive as a conscript army. In December 1989, experts of the general staff revised this factor down to five. And in April 1990 the Center for Social and Psychological Studies, which is part of the Main Political Directorate of the Soviet Army and Navy, determined that military spending probably would not rise by a factor of more than 1.8.[27] As for the experts of the Military Financial and Economic Department of the Moscow Financial Institute, they believed (in December 1990) that, taking already scheduled reductions into account, the total increase in expenditures would amount to 15 billion rubles, whereas the overall total positive effect was estimated at 11 to 12 billion rubles.[28] In the end, the official concept of military reform submitted by the ministry of defense provided for annual increases in spending from 3.3 percent to 4.2 percent.[29]

On the other hand, various dissenting estimates were put forward by experts from what was then known as the Academy of Sciences of the Soviet Union. Thus, retired Major General Vadim Makarevsky believed that one of the cornerstones of Soviet military reform was the reduction of quantitative in favor of qualitative parameters. The process of unilateral cuts (500,000), which began in 1990, was intended to bring the armed forces down to a level of defensive sufficiency. The CFE treaty, which mandates troop cuts of one million in the ex-Soviet Union (an obligation the independent republics have pledged to honor), thus will contribute to bringing the overall reductions in the former Red Army to 1.5 million out of a total of more than 4.2 million personnel in early 1989. Given a total remaining strength of roughly 3 million, the Soviet armed forces would have had about one million skilled professionals (officers, volunteers, reenlisted service members) and circa two million draftees (the ranks, including noncommissioned officers). It was on this basis that a professional Soviet army would have been built. The annual number of draftees would then have been reduced by half, to one million. The remaining million would all have been reenlisted personnel or volunteers, which would have greatly improved the overall situation in the armed forces. This ratio of draftees to reenlisted personnel/volunteers would have been optimal and have permitted to differentiate between personnel in accordance with skill requirements. According to General Makarevsky, 4 to 5 billion rubles would have been required annually to keep that million of reenlisted personnel/volunteers in the Soviet armed forces (in addition to the 5.7 billion still allocated for service members' salaries today). General Makarevsky believed that these additional funds could have been obtained through further cuts in army personnel. Furthermore, the overall allocation of funds was to be revised. For instance, the funds allocated for research, development and procurement of new military technology exceeded those reserved for army personnel by a factor of 1.5 to 2.0.[30] According to estimates by Aleksei Arbatov, a largely professional army would have cost an additional 13.7 billion rubles a year. He also considered that this amount could have been deducted from funds intended for weapons procurement and R & D, and channeled to the troops. In his view, there were (and still are) enormous possibilities for saving money in the area of weapons production as a result of the switch from extensive to intensive economic growth.[31]

The experience of other countries with their recruitment systems (conscript armies, all-volunteer forces, or a combination of both) is worth looking into. Many European countries have a mostly professional officer corps whereas most enlisted personnel are draftees. Countries like the United States, India, Pakistan, Britain, Japan and Canada have all-volunteer forces. In others with compulsory military service, the share of conscripts does not exceed 50 percent (France and Germany) or is slightly over 30 percent (Belgium). Even in the People's Republic of China, where the total strength of the armed forces is 3.2 million (all technically skilled), 58 percent are volunteers. In a number of nations, owing to fairly small size of their armed forces relative to the total population, opportunities for a fastidious selection of service people are greater. In 1989 the strength of the armed forces in all WTO countries was 1.6 percent of the total population, whereas in most NATO countries it ranged from 0.35 percent to 0.7 percent. For this reason alone, the selection process in NATO countries is stricter. But just as important is a sufficient educational level of the draftees, a homogeneous national composition, an absence of language problems and good physical training. Furthermore, NATO units undergo sophisticated technical training and have an extensive material basis (for example, simulators and electronic equipment) at their disposal. And finally, enlisted personnel enjoy much better financial and living conditions than their counterparts in the former Soviet Union. All this creates a different environment for conscripts, allowing them to go through basic and advanced training fairly rapidly (typically in three months) before completing their term of active duty, which usually lasts 12 to 15 months. Service efficiency in NATO countries is two to two-and-a-half times greater than it was in the former Soviet Union.[32]

Of course, a switch to voluntary military service may be effected in various ways, starting with the most technology-intensive components (strategic rocket forces, navy and air force) while the army retains the draft (with a better pay) a while longer. (It must be reemphasized here that this switch also applies to the national armed forces being set up in the new independent republics following the collapse of the Soviet Union.) Originally, higher military authorities in the ex-Soviet Union rejected the idea of a professional army for a number of reasons. First of all, they had gotten used to an inexpensive labor force (often employed in fields totally unrelated to military service). They also rejected cuts in army personnel because this would have shrunk the administrative apparatus and the number of command posts as well. Also, they were eager to preserve the strategy of protracted wars since this necessitated a huge number of reservists as well as a giant industrial mobilization potential, and justified maintaining the largest army in the world. Finally, there were (and still are) large regional and urban recruiting offices staffed with senior military officers. An all-volunteer force would hardly need such an extensive infrastructure. Evidently, the times of an army more often than not used as a cheap labor force are over. Poor living conditions and a low morale were the primary causes of weakened Soviet capabilities. Neither political indoctrination nor giant military arsenals were able to remedy that state of affairs. The national-defense needs that prevailed up to the putsch of August 1991 had made it imperative to reject most decisively the approaches adopted at the time of World War II. This obviously was the *sine qua non* for a sensible military reform.

Even a brief analysis of the draft concept of military reform proposed by the former defense ministry shows that the highest military authorities wanted to change but some minor aspects of the organization and structure of the armed forces, not the substance. But, as has now become clear, not only was the very magnitude and structure of Soviet defense expenditures totally out of proportion to any conceivable military threat the West might have posed to the USSR but it had also become one of the main sources of the further destabilization (if not ruin) of the country's economy. The military reform was to have been debated at the fourth session of the Supreme Soviet in December 1990. There were two alternative drafts: one prepared by the ministry of defense, the other one by a group in the Congress of People's Deputies. They were not, however, given equal chances for discussion. Instead, the Committee for Defense and State Security, where both drafts had been under consideration, recommended that the ministerial draft be adopted as a basis for further debate and asked the government to revise the document. But during 1991, no practical results were achieved. This was hardly surprising as the dominant role in elaborating the reform was delegated by the political leadership to the top echelon of the old defense establishment, which had no real interest in a radical restructuring of the military. This was just another manifestation of the reversal of Mikhail Gorbachev's reformist policy (initiated in late 1990) and of its drastic shift to the right in order to retain control and power in the face of democratic movements in Russia and other republics. In this respect, the condition of military *perestroika* was but a reflection of the state of the economic, political and constitutional reforms as a whole.

Despite the fact that many problems connected with the armed forces still need thorough analysis, one conclusion after the coup attempt of August 1991 seems indisputable: the absence of a radical and far-reaching military reform in the USSR was the direct result of conscious attempts on the part of the former military authorities to sabotage the policy of reforms. This, in turn, became one of the main preconditions for the attempted coup, as its leaders felt confident they could count on a broad dissatisfaction within the armed forces that had not yet adopted to the new situation within the country and abroad. Thus, it was only logical that a rapid and thorough reform of the military had to be carried out in order to make further coup attempts, if not impossible, at the least highly unlikely.

## More Courageous Efforts at Military Reform

The most important period in the evolution of Soviet military reform began right after the failure of the August coup. Within a month, a committee (attached to the Supreme Soviet of the USSR) had been set up to elaborate and implement military reforms. And just two weeks after the attempted coup, the new military leadership was ready to publish the main points of the revised official concept. Marshal Yevgeni Shaposhnikov, the new defense minister, summarized it a follows: "The army should be preserved as one of the attributes of a single system of defense. But this system should be transformed in conformity with the new political realities, the gaining of sovereignty by the republics, and it should be based on the principles of collective security and defense, quality and sufficiency."[33] The new approach was purposeful, practical and, in at least five points, drastically different from the original concept of military reform.

First, the ouster of the Communist Party from, and the depoliticiza-
tion of, the armed forces were to be carried out fully and in the shortest
possible period of time. The army was never again to become an instrument of any party and never to be used against its own people.

Second, taking into account the emergence of sovereign republics,
territorial (or national) military formations -- to be called national (or
republican territorial) guards -- were to be created. They were to number several thousand men and be subordinated to the political leaders of
the sovereign member states within the collective defense system. In
wartime these national guards were possibly to become a reserve of
single and joint armed forces. At the same time, the new official concept of the ministry of defense preserved in full the idea of unified
armed forces of the new state that was to succeed the Soviet Union (be
it a federation, confederation, association or a commonwealth). Command and control of nuclear forces were to remain under central control of the supreme command of the then-planned "union." As Defense
Minister Yevgeni Shaposhnikov and General Valdimir Lobov, the new
army chief of staff, pointed out, joint forces were necessary for historical, economical, political, geopolitical, and military reasons. The central authorities considered this the key starting point of the planned reform of the military. Prior to the official breakup of the Soviet Union
on December 31, 1991, however, both the shape and scope of this reform were seen as hinging on whether the idea of collective defense
(and hence collective armed forces under a unified command) would
prove acceptable to the former Soviet republics.[34]

Third, a completely new command and control structure was to be
developed. The prospective "Union of Sovereign States" was to have a
civilian defense minister subordinated to the president, who himself
was to be the supreme commander of the joint armed forces.
Correspondingly, committees on defense and security were to be created in the sovereign republics and subordinated to their respective
presidents. The central ministry of defense was to comprise various departments to deal with issues of military personnel, defense policy,
R & D, weapons procurement, military legislation and social security,
and military infrastructure. The committees on defense and security in
the member states were to have analogous structures if necessary. But
they alone were to be in charge of their national guards. The joint
armed forces were also to be placed under the authority of a military
commander in chief, who at the same time would assume the responsibility of chief of the general staff. Likewise, the national guards were
to have their own military commanders in chief (i.e., the heads of the
military departments in the respective republican committees on defense

and security), who would have be subordinated to their presidents. Because the members of these departments and committees were to be represented in the corresponding union bodies, any secret preparations for some future military coup would have become barely imaginable. An additional safety lock against possible military coups was provided by the combination of political (by the defense ministry headed by a civilian) and military (by the military committee of the defense ministry headed by a military commander in chief) control.

Fourth, the reform provided for partly professional armed forces within the next few years and fully professional with soldiers and sailors serving on a contractual basis before the year 2000. The first components to have been made fully professional were the strategic rocket forces, the strategic air force and the navy. (This might still come to fruition under the "unified nuclear command" of some of the successor states to the USSR).

Fifth, the system of recruitment was to have evolved from general conscription to a contractual system for professionals. In the coming years the recruitment system was to have become a hybrid one, combining the two approaches. In addition to this, a conscript was to have been given the choice between 18 months of military service or an alternative civilian service with a longer duration (such as, for example, nursing in hospitals and invalid homes). Presumably by 1993 the armed forces were to have been reduced to three million men.[35]

It should be borne in mind that these five points refer only to the main differences between the earlier and the later draft concepts of the military reform as presented by the ministry of defense under Yevgeni Shaposhnikov and its predecessor Dmitri Yazov. Needless to say that the later variant corresponded to a much greater degree to the notion of reform while the earlier merely reflected "cosmetic repair," as the Chief of the General Staff, General Vladimir Lobov, has said.[36] Actually, the main features of the concept put forward by the military authorities after the August putsch coincided with the proposals submitted by those experts who opposed the Yazov draft in 1990-91.

The task of restructuring the former Soviet armed forces has become much more complex since the Commonwealth of Independent States (CIS) was founded in December 1991. The creation of the CIS came about as a result of two major opposing tendencies: a centrifugal and a centripetal one. To a certain extent theses tendencies both contradicted and complemented each other. The CIS was thus a case of "marriage after divorce," and the problem was to divorce in a civilized manner, in order to be able to live side by side after the new marriage.

This problem was extremely important for the armed forces, since they represented the crucial portion of the heritage of the departing sides.

Unfortunately, because of nationalistic ambitions on the part of a number of leaders, the creation of the CIS was soon followed up by attempts to "nationalize" the armed forces deployed on the various national territories. The Ukraine was in the most favourable position in this regard since the USSR's best and most powerful military formations were deployed in the western part of the former empire. Thus it was the "nationalization *à la Ukraine*" which made a civilized divorce impossible after all. By mid-1992 practically all CIS member-states had started to create their own national armed forces. In the end, Russia, which has lagging behind in this process, was forced to act accordingly. "We held on to the principle of the unity of the army. This was our main idea. It was impossible to cut the armed forces into pieces... But when other states (of the CIS) one after another proclaimed the creation of national armies we realized that we must defend the interests of Russia by ourselves."[37] This statement by President Boris Yeltsin reflects the way in which Russian thinking on the problem evolved. The law on defense adopted on June 3, 1992, opened the way to the setting up of Russian armed forces. Russia also pledged to extend its jurisdiction to the groups of forces in Germany, Poland, and the former Baltic Republics, as well as to the Transcaucasian military district and other "hot spots" of the former empire.

The process of dismembering the single, interconnected body of the former Soviet armed forces was hindered to a certain extent by the centripetal tendency finally formalized in the Treaty on Collective Security signed in Tashkent on May 15, 1992. With respect to this treaty, two points deserve special attention. The Ukraine categorically rejected any such treaty, and this was only a logical continuation of its policy of becoming "completely independent" and "non-aligned". Russia's position, on the other hand, was no less logical. It initiated the treaty, and, immediately after extending its jurisdiction to the groups of forces beyond the Russian borders, placed them under the operational control of the commander in chief of the unified armed forces, in order "to defend the sovereignty and territorial integrity of all the CIS member-states".[38] Thus Russia and the Russian armed forces became the nucleus of the collective security-system proclaimed in Tashkent by the 6 signatories, namely Russia, Kazakhstan, Armenia, Kirgistan, Uzbekistan, and Tajikistan.

Given that only one month has elapsed since Tashkent, no member-state of this collective security-system has, of course, as yet worked out any comprehensive military doctrine or programs of military reform.

The case of Russia is a different one, and the central role of the Russian armed forces within the security system makes it necessary briefly to characterize the official approaches of the Russian political and military leaders to these problems. Essentially, the principles of the military doctrine and military reform developed after the August 1991 *coup d'etat* remained unaltered and formed a solid basis for the program to restructure the Russian armed forces. Only a few weeks after the nomination, on May 17, 1992, of Army General Pavel Grachov as Russian minister of defense, the major elements of the official concept on military reform were unveiled. As regards military doctrine, this began with a drastic reevaluation of military threat following the end of the cold war. The cardinal point in this reevaluation is that Russia now perceives the West no longer as an enemy but as a partner and potential ally. The primary security-concern is the preservation of peace, and Russia is ready to ally itself with any peaceful state in order to prevent war and to strengthen international security. However, potential military threats to Russia are regarded as having multiplied, and as likely to originate in the form of small-scale conflicts within Russia or along its south-eastern perimeter. In order to counter these emerging threats, Russia does not need extremely costly armed forces, but small, highly mobile, professionally trained and well-equipped military formations. Nuclear forces must be drastically reduced and kept for deterrence only.

The program on military reform unveiled by the new Russian defense minister tallies exactly with the points mentioned above. It is envisaged that it will be implemented in three stages.[39] In 1992 (the first stage) it is planned to create the higher echelon of Russian command and control (the defense ministry and the general staff) and to pass the laws that will regulate the functioning of the armed forces. In 1993-4 (the second stage) the existing armed forces will be reorganized and the transition to the new system of recruitment will be partially effected. By 1995 the personnel of the armed forces will be reduced by 700,000 men, to no more than 2.1 million. In 1995-9 (the third stage) a further restructuring and more reductions are envisaged, resulting in armed forces with an overall strength of 1.5 million by the year 2000.

Of course, these plans accord with the situation as it stands at the beginning of June 1992. Other concepts and plans for military reform may well emerge, depending on political developments in the country. However, a general trend toward armed forces tailored to the principles of non-aggression and reasonable sufficiency in defense may clearly be observed, and the process of transition is now well under way.

# Notes

1. *Den'*, No. 2, 1991.
2. Army General Vladimir Lobov. "Voennaya reforma: Tseli printsipi, soderzhanie (Military Reform: aims, principles and essence)," *Kommunist*, No. 13, 1990, p. 18.
3. *Krasnaya Zvezda*, February 21, 1991.
4. Army General I. Tretyak. "Oboronnaya dostatochnost i protivivazdushnaya oborona (Defensive sufficiency and air defense)," *Voennaya Mysl'*, No. 12, 1990, pp. 3-4.
5. *Pravitelstvenny Vestnik*, No. 48, 1990, pp. 6-7.
6. Interview with General John Galvin, Supreme Allied Commander Europe, and General W. Eyrie, Chairman of the NATO Military Committee, *Krasnaya Zvezda*, November 20, 1990.
7. NATO Secretary-General Manfred Wörner said on November 13, 1990, that future military threats to the alliance would originate on NATO's southern flank, coming from the Balkans, North Africa and the Middle East.
8. See *Pravda*, September 27, 1990; *Independent*, May 14, 1990; *International Herald Tribune*, May 15, 1990.
9. *Voennaya Mysl'*, No. 4, 1990, pp. 31-4; *Krasnaya Zvezda*, June 3, 1990.
10. *Krasnaya Zvezda*, August 3, 1990.
11. *Krasnaya Zvezda*, July 29, 1990.
12. Lobov (*op. cit.* in note 2), pp. 17-8.
13. *Voennaya Mysl'*, No. 4, 1990, p. 39.
14. *Voenno entsiklopedichesky slovar'* (Military Encyclopedic Dictionary), (Moscow, 1986), p. 633.
15. *Krasnaya Zvezda*, June 3, 1990.
16. V. Lopatin, *O podgotovke i provedenii voennoi reformi v SSSR* (On Preparation and Realization of Military Reform in the USSR) Draft Paper, 1990, p. 9.
17. "Konsteptsia voennoi reformi (The Concept of Military Reform)," *Voennaya Mysl'*, Special Edition 1990, p. 6.
18. *Ibid.*, p. 7.
19. *Pravitelstvenny Vestnik*, No. 48, 1990, pp.8, 10.
20. *Ibid.*, p. 7.
21. *Krasnaya Zvezda*, August 19, 1990.
22. *Krasnaya Zvezda*, November 3, 1990.
23. Kontseptsia (*op. cit.* in note 14).
24. *Pravitelstvenny Vestnik*, No. 48, 1990, pp. 8, 10.
25. *Ibid.*
26. *Ibid.*

27. *Izvestia*, April 10, 1990.
28. *Krasnaya Zvezda*, December 5, 1990.
29. *Pravitelstvenny Vestnik*, No. 48, 1990, p. 8.
30. *Novoe Vremya*, No. 46, 1989, pp. 23-4.
31. A. Arbatov, "Oboronitelnaya dostatochnost i bezopasnost (Defense Sufficiency and Security)," *Znaniye*, 1990, pp. 61-2.
32. *Novoe Vremya*, No. 46, 1989, pp. 23-4.
33. *Sovietskaya Rossiya*, September 20, 1991.
34. *Ibid.*; also: *Krasnaya Zvezda*, September 10, 1991.
35. *Nezavisimaya Gazeta*, September 19, 1991.
36. *Pravda*, September 9, 1991.
37. *Izvestia*, June 11, 1992.
38. *Krasnaya Zvezda*, May 22, 1992.
39. *Krasnaya Zvezda*, May 26, 1992.

# 7

---

# An Unfinished Agenda:
# Arms Control and
# Disarmament in Europe

*Matthias Dembinski and Hans-Joachim Schmidt*

For thirty years, arms control has been closely connected with the East-West conflict. The concept of arms control in its modern form was created in the early 1960s as an answer to the specific problems concerning confrontation and arms races in the nuclear age. Yet although arms control was broader and wider in practice, only few attempts were undertaken to use this instrument outside the context of the East-West conflict; and only one or two of these might be called successful, the most important being the Non-Proliferation Treaty.

At the end of the East-West conflict, and with the disappearance of one of the former antagonists, the question naturally arises whether arms control, tailored to manage this conflict, is still good for anything or how one should adapt it to the new situation. Influential voices from the left and the right have contended for some time that arms control is too cumbersome and time-consuming to deal with the changing situation. Worse, it is too artificial, could even delay unilateral disarmament which might otherwise take place, and should therefore be abandoned altogether.[1] We do not share this pessimism. Instead, we present the argument that arms control still has an important role to play, though a fundamentally different one. Our defense of arms control begins with a brief review of its objectives and achievements, outlines in a second step the functions arms control should pursue in the new, fundamentally changed political situation and eventually develops some recommendations for the future of nuclear and conventional arms control in Europe.

## The Changing Context of Arms Control

The critics' strongest argument refers to the famous arms control dilemma, whereby arms control must necessarily remain meaningless in a high tension environment, whereas, in a low tension environment, it becomes superfluous. These critics are right by stressing the relationship between arms control and the overall conflict figuration.[2] But, nevertheless, they miss the point because the world is rarely either black or white. When political relations are somewhere between these extremes (as they normally are), arms control can perform important functions.

In the original mainstream Western understanding, arms control was seen as a strategy for dealing only with additional tensions which resulted from the interaction of attempts by both sides to create security by unilateral means. Arms control was aimed at the prevention of war by reducing crisis instabilities and tensions resulting from the very existence of weapons and the arms race itself.[3] In practice, however, arms control pursued a second, more far-reaching aim, as its proponents hoped to transform the political relationship itself. This aim, which could be labelled peace promotion, becomes the more promising, the more compatible the political interests of the parties involved are.[4]

Still controversial and difficult to assess is the question what arms control really has accomplished. Taking into account the recent literature, one has to conclude that the record is at best mixed. However, the accusations articulated against arms control from the right and the left were exaggerated. Neither did arms control deceive or delude the public with respect to the dangers of the arms race, accelerate the arms race through the alleged buying-off or levelling-up mechanisms, or prevent unilateral reductions by complicating the disarmament process with the well-known verification and definition problems. Nor did arms control ever prevent the formulation and execution of a sound and stabilizing defense policy or, even worse, worked into the hands of the enemy.[5] Of course, the general assumption that arms control accomplished only little to improve stability and save money is surely true for the years before 1987. But some of its measures taken before 1987 -- especially the ABM and the never ratified SALT-II treaty -- did enhance arms race and crisis stability and therefore helped in preventing war. Unilateral or bilaterally agreed measures establishing rules of engagement, created a dialogue on force employment, and induced the establishment of secure communication and control mechanisms which also contributed in stabilizing the military confrontation.

To a certain degree, arms control was also successful in changing the conflict structure itself by influencing the long-term interests of the participants. The record shows that it was precisely cooperation in the security field which produced a redefinition of national interests on both sides. Arms control alleviated the dangerous consequences of the security dilemma, initiated learning effects,[6] created more openness, enhanced the possibility of "democratic control," and led to the formation of bureaucracies and pressure groups with an interest in arms control.

Even more important for a conceptual fresh start of arms control is the question why arms control did not accomplish more. As the record clearly proves, the lack of success, even with regard to the traditional aim of war prevention, was not due to technical problems or verification demands, but to the perception, prevalent on both sides, that the conflict was fundamentally antagonistic. Arms control suddenly worked -- enabling agreements which were thought to be impossible to be arranged within the shortest period of time -- after the Soviet Union had redefined its traditional foreign policy goals. Now that the traditional conflict is over and the interests of the states in Europe are quite parallel, the chances and possibilities for arms control should be viewed much more optimistically.

### The Future of Arms Control

#### *Political Conditions and Prospects in Europe*

The East-West conflict in its traditional form is definitely over. Its underlying foundation, the ideological conflict between liberalism and communism, has vanished with the collapse of the communist ideology. The traditional power and territorial conflict began to disappear even earlier with the *de facto* renunciation of the Soviet claim to be a global superpower, on equal footing with the United States. With the USSR abandoning its "outposts" in Latin America, Africa and Asia, it removed the main cause for the breakdown of detente and rendered possible solutions for originally hotly debated regional conflicts. The dissolution of the Soviet Union and the region-wide recognition of Western values and principles has created necessary preconditions for the establishment of a European peace order. But the creation of a peace order is not a foregone conclusion. There are numerous impediments on the way to such an order, which have to be removed by careful and imaginative management. The following discussion of worst cases refers to these obstacles.

What remains of the old conflict are the instruments of warfare, vast armies and arsenals full of conventional and nuclear weapons. In addition, the end of the East-West conflict has created new problems and unleashed older conflict formations previously suppressed by the former tight superstructure. The now independent states in Eastern Europe and the former USSR are almost inevitably experiencing a resurrection of patterns of national identification and the importance of ethnic affiliation. The potential for conflict is further reinforced by the fact that with the dissolution of the Warsaw Pact, self-help might again become the main feature of this region. Also, there are the old ethnic and territorial conflicts in Eastern Europe. And there is the possibility of a further disintegration of multi-ethnic states or the crumbling of central authority in whole countries, something familiar to us from European history. Quite new, on the other hand, is the prospect of hostile developments outside the region which could threaten security in Europe.

While the probability of a large-scale, deliberate military aggression against Western Europe has diminished to the point of non-existence, uncertainty and a new *Unübersichtlichkeit* have increased in Eastern Europe. It is quite probable that the new security policies and military structures within the Eastern European sub-system, if permitted to take place on a national basis, will result in competing attempts to create security against one another, unleashing complex arms races and creating intractable instabilities. Worse still, there is a growing likelihood for civil wars, ethnic clashes across borders at the many places where national and ethnic boundaries are not identical, foreign intervention in those conflicts and the possibility of widespread anarchy. Also not unimaginable is the emergence of dictatorial regimes and with them the possibility of deliberate aggression. The special volatility of the situation, however, is created by the combination of vast arsenals of weapons, especially weapons of mass destruction, inherited from the previous era of stable bipolarity, and the variety of instabilities and conflict formations mentioned above. Especially critical in the short-run is the preservation of peace and rudimentary stability within and between the four nuclear-armed states on the territory of the former Soviet Union.

*The Future Role of Arms Control*

Given the variety of tensions and potential conflicts, arms control is of utmost importance in helping to avoid worst cases and build a European peace order. Military relations in Europe should be influenced with the aim of: (1) enhancing peace, i.e. providing stable structures for the security dimension of a European peace order; (2) preventing war within the new political environment, and (3) providing precautionary measures against worst cases. Although unilateral steps can play a role in abolishing the old Cold War structures, we believe that negotiated arms control has many advantages unilateral disarmament lacks: (1) it can lock in reductions and make reversal less likely; (2) negotiated reductions are much more specific, call for verification, and can therefore increase confidence; (3) negotiated reductions are better suited for fostering stability (According to all experience, unilateral reductions follow the logic of cost savings and are not necessarily stability oriented); (4) it can establish norms and principles and can thereby enhance peace.

Parallel to removing the still vastly over-sized armaments and old structures of the East-West conflict, more far-reaching and innovative measures are appropriate. The formerly second-rank goal of enhancing peace will problably become the main interest of arms control. Arms control will no longer be preoccupied with stabilizing an antagonistic relationship. Instead, it will deal with building a cooperative security structure in Europe. Its immediate goal in this respect is threefold. Arms control should: (1) guarantee that the construction of a European peace order is not hampered by negative effects emanating from the security sphere, (2) symbolize and codify the changed nature of the military, (3) lay the ground-work for a regional collective security system.

Alleviating the consequences of the security dilemma by over-arching the European state system with security regimes is a pressing aim. The near-term challenge is, in other words, the organization of the remaining reassurance requirements of all participants in a coordinated way, confining unilateral room of manoeuver by multilateral consent. Ideally, forces would be structured in a way that no state gets the feeling that its security is threatened by the armament of others. Arms control would thereby confirm the changed nature of military power. It would express that military force is no longer exclusively a unilateral instrument directed against an enemy state, but an instrument with which states try to provide common security. All this is especially important for the Eastern European states and for the new sovereign republics on the territory of the former USSR. Appropriate measures in this context are formal agreements covering all important segments of armaments which limit not only the numbers but also the quality of weapons, as well as formal and informal steps aimed at increasing transparency, creating confidence, and making the future more predictable. Future principles of arms control should therefore include:

(1) sufficiency and defensive defense (The principle of sufficiency means that security should be created at the lowest possible level of armament. Exceptions to the principle of defensive defense will become necessary in the longer term, when the creation of a system of collective security will necessitate the existence of at least some highly mobile units, preferably under international command);

(2) transparency (Transparency is important in avoiding misperceptions and overstated worst-case planning);

(3) comprehensiveness (The arms control regime should cover all important segments or armaments of all participants);

(4) accountability (By obliging to this principle, states accept that national sovereignty is restricted by common European norms);

(5) information and consultation duty (This principle means that states oblige themselves to inform and consult the other participants before introducing new or modernizing existing weapons systems. It is necessary in order to protect the emerging arms control regime against the technological dynamic).

A situation of military stability in which every participant feels secure is, of course, an ideal construction. It will be extremely difficult to accomplish in a multipolar structure with actors of vastly different size and power. Providing military security will be an especially troublesome endeavor when it comes to the states in Eastern Europe. Striking a military balance between individual Eastern European states, or between the new small republics on the territory of the former USSR and Russia or the Ukraine will be impossible. Offering explicit security guarantees, like NATO membership, would not be an appropriate solution either, at least for the time being. This would create severe problems for Russia, just because Russia would feel excluded from the most important security framework in Europe. Therefore, one should try to alleviate the concerns in Eastern Europe by framing specific political and arms control measures. One might imagine the conclusion of non-intervention treaties or arms control agreements which oblige the great powers to reduce more than the small ones.

More important, enhancing peace should aim at building a common European code of conduct for military organizations. One initiative in this regard should aim at the creation of common norms concerning the function and role of the military in society, especially the principle of democratic control. A military which is guided by civic norms and which is democratically controlled would be an impediment against aggression, could dampen the violence of domestic conflicts, and could make an international solution of such conflicts easier. The time to take measures in this regard is ripe, because military professionals in the West, and all the more so in the East, have lost at least parts of their identity and are looking for role-models. Contacts between the military of different countries could be an important tool to foster a pan-European, civic military identity. Practical steps which could be taken in this respect are discussed below.

A second string of this common code of conduct for military organizations should, with different speed in East and West, lay the groundwork for a collective security system. Without discussing the pivotal political prerequisites, we will only deal with the military side of such an order. On the one hand, a collective security system has to deal with intra-system violence, which could take the form of civil wars or deliberate aggression. Deliberate aggression, if it cannot be prevented, should be dealt with collectively. Preventing civil wars from spreading could be one approach to deal with intra-system violence. The European Community (EC), *de facto*, chose this strategy after its mediation and peace-keeping efforts in Yugoslavia failed. This example shows that the containment strategy is not a satisfactory solution. A European peace order should therefore be entrusted with the task of mediating, controlling and policing, and -- in the longer run -- even stopping or suppressing domestic violence with military means. Arms control could lay the ground-work for such a system by creating binding norms which govern the relations between states and those internal affairs that might have violent transnational effects.

To win recognition for these norms and their execution, the progressive creation of supranational institutions in the security field would be extremely helpful. This process could start with the establishment of widespread officer exchange programs, multinational units, joint manoeuvers, a pan-European intelligence-gathering and verification agency and end up with the creation of a military arm of a collective security system. By transferring some sovereign rights to supranational institutions in the security field, states can learn that integration is actually beneficial to their interests. Again, this is of great importance for Eastern Europe. On the other hand, a collective security system has to organize security with regard to the outside world. Ideally, adjacent regions would be guarded by the same principles prevalent in Europe, and would be coupled by various mechanisms with the system.

Otherwise a collective security sub-system would have to engage adjacent regions into a dialogue on security or, if this dialogue fails, provide functions of a military alliance against the hostile outer world. It would have to provide security for the members located at the fringe of the system in order to prevent those states from gaining security with national means, thereby violating the norms and shaking the balance of the system.

Europe is firmly coupled to the North American region through a number of economic, political and security treaties and through a close net of interdependence. Relations with the East-Asian democracies and with Australia are becoming close too, even if they are not as regulated. If one includes the whole of Russia into the European system, it becomes obvious that the Northern Hemisphere plus the OECD countries in the South and maybe the emerging democracies in East Asia and Latin America are governed by similar political principles. That would leave the countries at the southern fringe of Europe as regions where a threat toward Europe might develop.

A European strategy for global arms control should consist of three elements: (1) promotion of arms control and disarmament treaties with global range, (2) fostering of regional arms control measures in regions adjacent to Europe, (3) active participation in supplier cartels to prevent the spread of weapons of mass destruction and conventional armaments. Prospects for the adoption of meaningful measures in all categories have improved in the recent one or two years. Talks on the Chemical Weapons Convention have picked up steam after US President Bush announced on May 13, 1991, that the US would drop two US positions, which had blocked such a convention.[7] The United States formally forswore the use of CWs for any reason, including retaliation, agreed to the elimination of all CWs within 10 years, and revised its position on anytime-anywhere inspection in favor of a more elastic approach which would delay, in some places even restrict, access to sensitive facilities.[8] This approach is well suited to accommodate reservations by Third World countries, especially China and India. Since the military potential of chemical weapons is somehow limited, adequate verification of a CW ban does not depend on 100% certainty that no member state possesses them any longer.[9] Therefore, the European states should abandon their opposition against a modification of the original inspection scheme and should support the compromise formula which Australia had introduced in the spring of 1992.[10]

The growing danger that progress in bio-technologies could make biological weapons more efficient and widespread has so far not led to a substantial improvement of the Biological Weapons Convention. The

Third Review Conference did not, as experts had hoped and demanded,[11] close the major loophole of the convention, the missing verification regime. Instead, the conference charged an ad hoc group with conducting a study on the feasibility of verifying the convention. The European states should use this possibility to try to convince the US that a verification regime, even if not capable of detecting violations with 100% certainty, would be a major improvement of the convention.

The nuclear non-proliferation regime, too, has been strengthened in spite or because of the revelation that Iraq was able to pursue a secret nuclear weapons program for almost ten years. The last nuclear weapons states outside the treaty -- France and China -- have signed up; South Africa, Brazil and Argentina which had pursued clandestine nuclear weapons programs for several years, acceded to the regime and arranged safeguard agreements with the IAEA; all important supplier nations and even some of the emerging suppliers have agreed to a policy of full-scope safeguards, banning the flow of nuclear technology to non-trustworthy members or countries outside the treaty; and, last but not least, the IAEA is determined to use its special inspection rights and to utilize intelligence provided by third parties to check undeclared and uncover clandestine nuclear facilities. In 1992, with North Korea, the Indian subcontinent and the Middle East, only three problem regions remain. And even in these regions, positive developments are underway.

Even more promising developments have taken place in the field of supplier cartels. The London Suppliers Group and the Zangger Committee, responsible for the control of the flow of nuclear technology, have significantly increased the number of nuclear and nuclear related dual-use items that are controlled, and have won new members even from the ranks of emerging suppliers. The Australia Group which now controls 50 precursors for chemical weapons, has agreed to include hardware necessary for the production of CWs to the list of controlled items and is discussing new lists for biological weapons precursors. The Missile Technology Control Regime has been successful insofar as it was one factor among others which slowed down dramatically the pace of the spread of ballistic missiles and ballistic missile technology. In 1992, it became more and more obvious that the alarming predictions which were uttered at the end of the 1980s and during the second Gulf War, were grossly exaggerated. The area however, where no substantial progress is visible, is the Five Power Talks on the control of conventional weapons sales to the Middle East.

If efforts to foster regional approaches and global arms control should fail, it would become necessary to shield the countries on the

European periphery which are most threatened by hostile outside developments. A link of pivotal importance in this regard is Turkey, which is closely connected to the European sub-system and which feels itself directly confronted with the extremely volatile Middle Eastern and the Caucasian regions. If a significant threat toward Turkey should arise and if Turkey is willing to live up to European standards of human rights and democratic government, then Europe would be well advised to associate Turkey closely with European institutions and to buttress its security.

## The Future of Nuclear Arms Control

The end of the East-West conflict and the disintegration of the USSR have fundamentally changed the character of nuclear deterrence and the dangers associated with nuclear weapons. During the East-West conflict the majority of political experts and academic observers perceived nuclear weapons as instrumental. The nuclear weapons of the other side were seen as a dangerous expression of a hostile political will; the own arsenal was described as a guarantor of stability and peace. After the East-West conflict, and deprived of their political setting, the nuclear arsenals -- still consisting of over 20 000 nuclear weapons on both sides -- appear as superfluous and as a peril in themselves. The first task of nuclear arms control after the end of the East-West conflict should therefore be the removal of the nuclear legacy. With the disintegration of the USSR, the former Soviet arsenal is becoming especially hazardous. If the originally tight central control over the nuclear complex crumbles, nuclear know-how, material or even entire weapons could trickle to other countries, seriously jeopardizing non-proliferation efforts. Furthermore, if the arsenal remains to be spread over several republics and if conflicts within the Commenwealth of Independent States (CIS) escalate, one could not exclude the possibility that nuclear weapons might be used in these conflicts. And even a safe transfer of all nuclear weapons to Russia would not solve the longer term problems. Possession of an uncontrolled and large arsenal by Russia would at best create untractable security problems for the neighboring republics and in the worst case create a serious threat if the reform process in Russia should fail and a totalitarian regime takes over.

The safe reconstruction of the former Soviet arsenal should therefore be at the top of the current nuclear arms control agenda. Contrary to the operational wisdom of some political scientists, we join the widespread consensus that the best outcome of the current succession-crisis would be the emergence of only a single nuclear heir. However, possession of nuclear weapons is only justifiable if it is coupled to responsibilities, the most important being the creation of credible precautions against nuclear use, so that neighbors of nuclear weapons states do not feel threatened but can accept the unequal status. Safe reconstruction of the former Soviet arsenal has therefore a broader meaning than just taking care of the safety of the nuclear weapons themselves and the prevention of a funneling of nuclear material to other destinations. The same criteria certainly apply to the other nuclear weapons states as well. Removal of the nuclear legacies should not stop with the reconstruction of the former Soviet arsenal. On the agenda is the minimization of the American nuclear complex and the inclusion of third nuclear powers into the disarmament process.

The second task of nuclear arms control after the East-West conflict is finding a long-term solution to the nuclear question. The first -- and so far last -- attempt in this regard was launched in 1946 within the UN Atomic Energy Commission. There was at that time general agreement that a solution had to be found on a global scale, that the answer should be the complete elimination of all major weapons of mass destruction, especially nuclear weapons, and that this outcome could be reached through one treaty, which would slash the Gordian knot of ideological and political conflicts, mutual mistrust and the possibility of a military application of nuclear technology. We believe that a solution to the nuclear question must indeed be found on a global scale, but argue that the solution will probably not be the complete disarmament of all nuclear weapons according to a fixed scheme and time schedule. Rather, we anticipate a process of continuous devaluation of nuclear weapons and increasing confinement of atomic power, restricting both the quantity and quality of nuclear deterrence and replacing its political and military functions. Toward the end of this process, nuclear weapons will probably continue to exist in small numbers, but they would fulfill no operational function, would not be integrated into military planning, but be kept in secure storage only for unanticipated contingencies.

## The Removal of the Nuclear
## Legacy of the East-West Conflict

Although the East-West conflict had already begun to crumble when George Bush assumed office, in its first three years, his administration pursued a very cautious and reactive arms control policy. The first year was wasted on a review of the US arms control policy, which was motivated by concerns about a resurrection of the old conflict pattern, and not by an interest in speeding up the disarmament process. And even as the crumbling of the Warsaw Pact and pressure by some of its European allies convinced Washington that initiatives were necessary, the American arms control policy continued to codify political developments which had already taken place rather then fostering or spearheading political change.

After the failure of the 1991 August *coup d'état* in the USSR, and confronted with the possibility of a loss of control over the Soviet nuclear complex, Bush for the first time showed some willingness to adjust the American nuclear policy to the radically changed political environment. Because short-range nuclear forces (TNF) were widespread and thought to represent the gravest security problem, initiatives were concentrated on those forces. On September 27, 1991, Bush confirmed the prior decision to remove all American land-based tactical nuclear weapons (TNW) from European soil. In addition, he canceled the development of an air-borne nuclear stand-off weapon (TASM) and announced the withdrawal of all tactical nuclear weapons from American naval vessels. The modern weapons, including nuclear sea-launched cruise missiles will be put into storage, the older ones will be destroyed. Bush did not specifically mention the 1 400 nuclear bombs deployed in Europe, but NATO announced in October 1991 that one half of these bombs would be brought back to the United States for dismantling.

Then Soviet President Mikhail Gorbachev responded positively. In October 1991 he announced that the USSR would remove and dismantle its nuclear artillery shells and warheads for short-range nuclear missiles. Tactical nuclear weapons from the ships of the Red Fleet would be removed and destroyed, making all surface vessels of both the American and the Soviet navy nuclear weapons free. In addition, Gorbachev announced that all nuclear weapons of the tactical air forces (frontal aviation) would be put in storage. In addition, the Soviet president demanded an early ratification of the START treaty and proposed more substantial follow-on talks to begin immediately after ratification of START. To underline the credibility of his offer, he added some unilateral measures, reducing the Soviet nuclear arsenal further.

The START treaty, although outdated at the time of its signature in July 1991, nevertheless fulfilled important functions during the disintegration of the Soviet Union. At the end of 1991, the strategic nuclear forces and the majority of TNWs were still deployed in four republics (Russia, Ukraine, Belarus and Kazakhstan), the greatest part of it in Russia.[12] Some TNWs were said to be also deployed in other republics.[13] The Ukraine alone would have been the third strongest nuclear power in the world with at that time more than 4 300 nuclear warheads. After the failed August coup, the Ukraine and Belarus announced that they would become non-nuclear weapons states; Kazakhstan also declared its intention to get rid of nuclear weapons, but constantly coupled this willingness to several conditions. In December 1991, agreement in principal was reached during meetings of the presidents of the republics in Alma Ata and Minsk, that all nuclear weapons would be concentrated in Russia under the command of the Russian president. The political responsibility for these weapons was to be shared between four republics (Kazakhstan, Russia, Ukraine, Belarus). During the interim period, nuclear weapons would be controlled by the joint command of the CIS. According to the agreed schedule, all TNF would be moved to central storage in Russia by June 1992; the strategic nuclear weapons from the Ukraine and Belarus would be transferred by the end of 1994 and those from Kazakhstan by 1996. All these nuclear weapons would be destroyed. To prevent nuclear weapons from the other republics ending up in the Russian arsenal, the Ukraine insisted on a verified destruction of the transferred nuclear weapons. It furthermore demanded a say over the use of nuclear weapons but settled for *de facto* voluntary consultations, the weakest instrument of participation.

However, the agreements of Minsk and Alma Ata were vague and fragile and the future of these agreements seems questionable. Only Belarus stuck firmly to the understanding. Kazakhstan, after sending contradictory signals for over six months declared only in May 1992 that it, too, would join the NPT as a non-nuclear weapons state. Beginning in early 1992, the Ukraine hesitated to fulfill its promise, partly because of a perceived Russian dominance, partly because Russia would not guarantee the verification of the withdrawal and destruction of TNW by the Ukraine. Second thoughts on the part of its leaders and discernable voices by the opposition in support of a nuclear status had increased the uncertainty over the future course of the Ukraine. In the spring of 1992, the Ukraine even temporarily stopped the transport of tactical nuclear weapons.

Western involvement was of utmost importance to produce the Minsk and Alma Ata agreements and to keep them alive. The reciprocal unilateral initiatives in the sub-strategic area and the 30% reductions envisaged under START were a critical tool in this regard. Because the nuclear weapons deployed in the republics outside of Russia were earmarked for destruction by START and by unilateral initiatives, the other republics had no reason to fear that they would end up in the Russian arsenal. In addition, these agreements provided the West with additional leverage to press for the removal of these weapons. Western pressure and the fact that the nuclear weapons were tightly controlled by CIS troops loyal to the Russian republic ensured that the transfer proceeded smoothly, efficiently and rapidly despite the above-mentioned interruption. By May 1992, all tactical nuclear weapons, including those from the Black Sea Fleet, had been moved back to Russia. While the situation seems to be under control for sub-strategic nuclear forces, the future of the strategic forces is still in limbo. Distressing is the extended interim time-period over which strategic nuclear weapons would be deployed in the Ukraine and Kazakhstan.

The question of safety and security of the nuclear weapons and the possible leaking of the nuclear complex has been tackled, too. The United States Congress has authorized the spending of $400 million to guarantee the safety of transport and storage of the former Soviet nuclear weapons. More important is the creation of an internationally sponsored center which will finance civil projects and employ Soviet nuclear scientists, providing them with an alternative to unemployment or emmigration to countries interested in the production of weapons of mass destruction. These measures might very well be successful in stemming the flow of nuclear know-how and material to other destinations.[14]

The immediately necessary steps to remove the nuclear legacy have been taken. For the time being, the security of the former Soviet weapons complex and the creation of a single nuclear heir have been assured. What remains to be done is the dismantling of the transferred nuclear weapons in a safe and verifiable manner. This process should include several steps: immediate inventorying and tagging of the weapons involved, dismantling of the weapons and long-term storage of the fissionable material, preferably under international control.[15] Accounting of the weapons in terms of a complete and reliable data base and verification of their destruction is of utmost importance in order to (1) provide credible information on the weapons complex and assurances that weapons are not ending up in the wrong hands, (2) alleviate fears of Russia's neighbors and (3) provide a favorable starting position for a long-term solution. The agreed unilateral initiatives lack those assurances. Accounting of the weapons should be undertaken internationally. International assistance during the destruction phase would be equally important. Russia can only dismantle 1500 warheads per year.[16] Western aid could help upgrade this capacity. Storage of the fissionable material under international control, even if the storage would take place on Russian territory, would symbolize that this material is no longer at Russia's disposal and not available for military purposes. The highly enriched uranium generated through the destruction could be diluted to low-enriched uranium, usable in civilian reactors. The plutonium itself should be stored indefinitely.

Additional measures necessary to remove the nuclear legacy are a continuation of disarmament in the strategic realm and an integration of third nuclear countries into the disarmament process. First steps in this regard have already been taken, but crucial decisions, allowing a more substantial disarmament, are still pending. In his State of the Union address on January 28, 1992, President Bush announced that the production of the B-2 would be stopped after 20 bombers had been built. He declared that strategic bombers would be used mainly for conventional purposes and terminated the "Advanced Cruise Missile" program. Additionally, he canceled further production of the W-88 counterforce warhead for the Trident II submarine-launched ballistic missiles (SLBM) and ended the Seawolf submarine program. In the area of land-based strategic missiles, he cut off production of the MX-ICBM test missiles and decided that the Midgetman-ICBM will be neither produced nor deployed. In addition to these unilateral measures, Bush proposed a new strategic nuclear arms control initiative. He repeated the older American demand for a ban of all MIRVed land-based missiles but added a new element consisting of an offer to cut sea-based MIRVed missiles by about one third. This modification made the US proposal more balanced since the American advantage is with sea-based forces while Russia is superior in land-based missiles. Bush's new approach would reduce the American arsenal from 9 500 warheads, planned under START, to some 4 700 warheads. President Yeltsin responded only hours later with similar unilateral initiatives plus a counter-proposal aimed at reductions of both arsenals to 2 000-2 500 warheads. In June 1992, after only brief negotiations, an agreement was reached. Both sides will reduce their strategic arsenal to an overall ceiling of 3 000 (for Russia) and of 3 500 warheads (for the US). At the same time, Russia gave its consent to dismantle the MIRVed land-based missiles, whereas the US is ready to destroy 50 per cent of its sea-based warheads.

Another contentious issue is the future of strategic defense. Boris Yeltsin, obviously remembering Ronald Reagan's rhetoric, has suggested sharing of defensive technologies and the creation of a joint missile defense system. So far, the United States has been very reluctant to discuss the sharing of technology. The US $5.4 billion provided for SDI in Bush's proposal for the 1993 defense budget clearly indicates that the administration is still determined to deploy a defensive system early and probably on a unilateral basis. The other "left-over" from the nuclear legacy of the East-West conflict, the inclusion of third nuclear powers into the disarmament process, proves even more pugnacious. Despite the fact that Great Britain, France and China welcomed the American-Soviet/Russian initiatives on short and long-range nuclear weapons, they seem not willing to participate in these measures at present.[17] Quite to the contrary, all three still pursue plans for a quantitative and qualitative augmentation of their forces. Nevertheless, France decided to cancel the development of a follow-on to its land-based medium-range missiles. Production of the new French nuclear short-range Hades missile will be stopped and the units responsible for the use of these missiles will be dissolved.[18] And Britain has announced that it will destroy its small stock of tactical land and sea-based nuclear weapons.

## *Laying the Groundwork for a Long-Term Solution of the Nuclear Question*

Two impediments are in the way of a long-term solution of the nuclear question. One is the still missing willingness on the part of existing nuclear weapons states to accept the total disfunctionality of nuclear weapons and to overcome the concept of nuclear deterrence. The other is the possibility of the emergence of new nuclear powers. The examples cited above indicate that the nuclear weapons states, including the US and Russia, have not yet made vital decisions concerning the role of their nuclear forces after the East-West conflict. The United States is still considering whether it should continue the way toward a further denuclearization of its foreign and security policy or whether it should instead try to regain and preserve offensive nuclear superiority or rely on a system of defense superiority.[19] Attempts to regain superiority would create tensions and consume scarce resources. Worse, a superiority strategy, even if successful, could ensure American security only as long as potential competitors have not equalized the technological advantage. Such a strategy runs the risk of creating more insecurity in the long term. As long as there are prospects for a viable solution of the nuclear question, the nuclear weapons states are well advised to make use of this opportunity.

The United States and Russia should restructure their remaining nuclear forces along the lines of a minimized flexible counter-value posture. They should articulate the strictly reduced function of nuclear weapons by announcing that they would under no circumstances use nuclear weapons first, by taking nuclear weapons off of alert status and by de-targeting the forces. Forces governed by such a doctrine could comprise a small number of securely deployed single-warhead missiles, preferably based on sea. Both sides should immediatly enter into a dialogue on the minimization of their forces. Although a future modernization, meaning the development of more stable, non-provocative forces, should not be excluded, advanced arms control measures can be taken. Important steps are a cut-off of the production of fissionable material and a comprehensive test ban. The dialogue on the minimization of deterrence would have to tackle the future of strategic defense as well. A unilateral SDI system is clearly incompatible with a long-term solution of the nuclear question. A multilateral system providing protection against the danger of an accidental launch is clearly not worth the costs, would quite to the contrary be the most expensive method of making the existence of nuclear weapons safe. And since a meaningful missile threat against the United States or Western Europe is not yet in sight, a multilateral system directed against third countries is also not worth the investment. It might be prudent to continue research and development of defensive technologies as a fall-back option, but plans for an early deployment of SDI should definitely be abandoned.

The small nuclear weapons states should enter the disarmament process. The least they should do is forsake their modernization plans. Britain and France have special responsibilities since their example could put pressure on China, making the "wild card" of the new world order more predictable. The European nuclear powers should relinquish plans for the introduction of air-launched nuclear stand-off missiles, dismantle under international verification their air-borne and land-based weapons and declare their willingness to cut back the number of warheads on their sea-launched missiles. These steps plus the prospect of political and economic isolation might create incentives for China to enter the disarmament process and abandon the planned augmentation of its forces as well.

Yet it is not only the growing British, French and Chinese forces that create obstacles for further disarmament, but also the emerging potentials of politically unstable and unpredictable threshold countries. Fortunately, the prospect of hostile nations appearing on Europe's southern fringe and possessing both the means of mass destruction and long-range delivery vehicles is not really imminent even if a future possibility. There is still enough time for efforts at preventing the full materialization of this danger by the above-mentioned instruments: stricter export control regimes, regional arms control and new global arms control agreements banning weapons of mass destruction. A global nuclear denial regime, at present consisting of the NPT and supplier restrictions, is indispensable in the short term. Europe should take care that attention toward non-proliferation, currently at a high point, does not fade away as alarming incidents abate. Also the EC has to develop a common export control regime to accomplish the Common Market. This regime should be as comprehensive as the currently strongest national export control regime. Even more important is the development of satisfactory export control mechanisms in Eastern Europe and the CIS. The EC should feel obliged to help these countries in setting up an efficient export control administration.

In the long run, however, supplier cartels are bound to fail if proliferators remain determined to acquire weapons of mass destruction. Regional regimes fostering cooperation and reducing tensions, which would change the motivation of proliferators, are essential. Europe will have to play a much more active role in encouraging regional cooperation. North Africa and Central Asia are regions where developments could have severe ramifications for European security and where internationally orchestrated negotiations are insufficient. Italy, Spain and France have started a dialogue with the Maghreb states of the western Mediterranean on economic and security affairs and Italy has invited the countries bordering the eastern Mediterranean to emulate this example. The EC and the CSCE should step up efforts to intensify these dialogues.

Regional regimes should be supplemented by global arms control measures. An initiative whose time has come, is a Comprehensive Test Ban Treaty (CTBT). A CTBT, while not positively preventing threshold countries from developing a nuclear warhead, would make weaponization efforts more difficult and could slow down the diversification of evolving arsenals like India's. Russia has announced that it would stop the testing of nuclear weapons; so has France. A similar declaration by the United States would leave China as the only country pursuing tests, and might create enough pressure for a global CTBT.

A third element of a global regime would aim at the strengthening of norms governing the non-possession and non-utilization of nuclear weapons. Nuclear weapons states should reiterate their promise not to threaten non-nuclear weapons states with nuclear attack. That means that studies like those recently commissioned in the USA by an advisory panel under General Lee Butler, calling for options to threaten Third World countries with nuclear attack, should be renounced.[20] Such a promise would have a rather symbolic meaning since nuclear threats against non-nuclear weapons states are almost never credible and since the motivation of nuclear proliferators with regard to nuclear weapons states is not fear of nuclear attack but the inability to overcome the conventional superiority of the five nuclear weapons states.

Since symbols are nevertheless important to strengthen norms, the nuclear weapons states should fulfill their part of the equation.

## The Future of Conventional
## Arms Control in Europe

The change in Soviet foreign policy, the democratic revolutions in Eastern Europe, the first results in conventional arms control and finally the disintegration of the Soviet Union in the wake of the failed *coup d'état* have created a fundamentally new situation for security in Europe. Since 1990, the WTO has been inoperable as a military alliance[21]; and the former Soviet troops are now in the process of withdrawing from the territory of their erstwhile allies.[22] In contrast to the past, the former Soviet Union was forced to accept inferior conventional forces in Europe as compared to NATO.[23] The Soviet republics have emerged as sovereign states and are establishing their own forces and defense organizations.[24] Germany was united and has accepted as the first country in Europe a limit on its personnel of 370 000 men and an almost 50% cut in the military potential of both former states combined. The forces stationed in Germany will be reduced by more than 50 % in the coming years.

The possibility of a great war in Europe and especially a conventional attack on short warning has largely disappeared. This was a major goal of the CFE negotiations. However, political developments in Europe may have contributed more to this goal than the CFE treaty itself. Nevertheless, the CFE treaty did codify and stabilize the revolutionary changes in Europe to some extent, and the agreements on a detailed data exchange as well as the verification regime of CFE I represent major steps toward a future security system in Europe. NATO adopted a new strategy, giving up forward defense and the high readiness of forces particularly in Central Europe.[25] But, not least due to the rapid changes and developments in Eastern Europe and beyond, a new security system will hardly be created in the short term. In the meantime, conventional arms control could help to bridge the security gap.

Because of these developments, the context of conventional arms control has changed significantly and is faced with new challenges. In the past, the major goal of conventional arms control was to stabilize the antagonistic military structure in Europe without changing the whole East-West context. NATO's basic elements of attaining this goal were the *alliance approach* for reductions and the *principle of parity*, both reflected in the mandate for the CFE negotiations. It was an important step when the WTO countries accepted these basic elements in the second half of the 80s. But during the last year of the CFE I negotiations, both elements became increasingly obsolete, in spite of the fact that no participant wanted to abandon them for fear of jeopardizing the basis of the ongoing negotiations.[26] However, both the principle of parity and the alliance approach are no longer applicable with regard to the follow-on negotiations (CFE IA) which are to find a solution for the "left overs" of CFE I in limiting military manpower.

### *The Impact of the Soviet Legacy*

Most pressing, however, is another problem: the rapid disintegration of the former Soviet Union after the failed *coup d'état* in August 1991 and the establishment of the CIS in December 1991 have caused fears that the CFE I treaty may become obsolete before it can even take effect. Clearly, an early ratification would be very important for solving the question of legal succession of the Soviet Union, and in forcing the new European republics -- with the exception of the Baltic states[27] -- to adhere to the treaty obligations. Otherwise, the danger of an arms race between several republics (e.g. Armenia and Azerbaijan or Russia and the Ukraine) might easily increase as would the risk of an uncontrolled proliferation of conventional weapons in other areas of the world. One can reasonably assume that an early ratification of the CFE I treaty together with a number of necessary adjustments to the new situation within the former Soviet Union would establish a higher threshold against these dangers.

Therefore, the results of the CIS summit in Tashkent in May 1992 concerning the distribution of CFE holdings between the eight concerned republics was an important step toward ratification as was the signing of the Final Document in Oslo in June 1992.[28] The agreement in Tashkent shows that Russian negotiators reduced their initial demands to get two thirds of the equipment of the land forces and 75 percent of attack helicopters and combat aircraft. In the end, Russia obtained about 50 percent of tanks and artillery, 60 percent of armored combat vehicles and attack helicopters and 67 percent of combat aircraft, while the three Caucasian republics, Armenia, Azerbaijan and Georgia, share small but equal weapon allotments. In particular for Armenia this was an important precondition to ratify CFE I.

The solution in Tashkent is also an example for the future function of arms control in this region. Because Russia gave the impression of using conventional arms control as an instrument for hegemonial ambitions, the other republics wished to control and narrow down Russian options in that area. At the present stage of disintegration, however, the question arises as to whether the republics concerned, in particular Belarus, the Ukraine, Russia, Armenia, and Azerbaijan, are really willing to ratify CFE I in time for the CSCE summit in July 1992 without a clear understanding on how much equipment should be reduced by each republic and what the costs of those reductions are. And even if they are willing to come to terms with one another, it is still an open question whether the treaty can be implemented in the following forty months without special regional or temporal exceptions because of domestic or interstate conflicts. In such cases, Western participants might use economic assistance as an incentive for treaty compliance.

The Tashkent agreement also cleared the way for CFE IA. After national holdings were distributed among the relevant CIS states, the problem of manpower ceilings could be settled. The initial aim of CFE IA was not only to establish national manpower ceilings, but also to introduce an inspection regime in the area of application. The latter became unnecessary after the signing of the Open Sky treaty in March 1992. The agreement on manpower ceilings, however, shows that most of the countries concerned succeeded in maintaining their military strength at existing higher levels (in particular Spain, Portugal, Russia, Ukraine, Canada, United Kingdom and USA). Only a few states, such as Germany and France, were willing to reduce their forces. CFE IA is therefore virtually meaningless in military terms. Its major achievement lies in the constraints it places on manpower and in the data exchange.

The decision of late January 1992 to include all members of the Commonwealth in the CSCE creates a new situation for the CSBM negotiations.[29] The Mandate of Madrid does not provide for the inclusion of the Asian part of the former Soviet Union. Also, full CSCE membership gives the Asian CIS member states all rights (e.g. for on-site inspection) without forcing them to meet any obligations. For the time being, the new members accepted all CSCE obligations in order to clear the way for their admission.[30] But the details of implementation, like the extension of the area of application with possible exclusion zones for several southern republics, must be determined as early as possible. And because of the unresolved military problems they will need time to meet their obligations.

*New Approaches to Conventional Arms Control*

Apart from the break-up of the Soviet Union, conventional arms control faces a number of challenging problems. In principle, the implementation of CFE I and CFE IA is the major precondition for further progress in conventional arms control. After the Cold War and in light of the new relationship between Eastern and Western Europe, conventional arms control in most general terms should aim at organizing the military in such a way that no country feels threatened by the conventional forces of its neighbors within the area of application. A *continuous dialogue, transparency* and *growing cooperation* in military affairs together with *measures to enhance conflict prevention and crisis management* are the constituent elements of this process. On the basis of *national ceilings*, the principle of parity can no longer be used because the differences in the size and power of the participating states are simply too large. Thus, and in contrast to the past, there will be no clear criterion which can be used as a political principle for conventional arms control. Only the term *unusual military measure(s)* could serve as a substitute, but it should not be defined by a single criterion. Different criteria could constitute unusual military measures, such as an unfounded increase of the defense budget or in the production of major military equipment, unprovoked mobilization and an unusual frequency and size of manoeuvers. It seems difficult or even impossible to unanimously determine these criteria in advance. Thus, the main question is whether it will be possible to establish a sufficiently broad and common consensus on specific criteria applicable to special cases in order to provide legitimate reasons for joint action.

The difficulties of future conventional arms control will be compounded by the large number of participants. In the past, 22 or 23 members of both alliances were involved in the CFE negotiations and 34 (or 35) in the CSBM-negotiations. In the future and following the merger of CSBM and CFE, Europe is faced with 52 participants or more.[31] The integration and "harmonization" of CSBM and CFE will therefore at the same time be a major challenge as well as a precondition for further conventional arms control measures. It is difficult to imagine how, under these conditions, every arms control measure can be applied to all participants in the same way. Why, for instance, should a country accept constraints on its sovereignty with, at the same time, only little relevance for its security, while the same constraints may be very important to stabilize a conflict in another region? Regional arms control could be helpful in such cases.[32] However, regional approaches only work with the consent of the countries involved; this means that any regional regime of conventional arms control must be linked to pan-European arms control in order to enhance European security.

On the pan-European level we are faced with different and sometimes even conflicting developments. Whereas Western Europe is heading toward a political union with a common foreign and defense policy, various Eastern European countries face the challenge of separatism and disintegration. Thus, arms control measures should also be used to help manage such a process of transition in a peaceful way. As to Western Europe, the growing military capabilities of the emerging political union should be constrained by arms control and should be made available for peace-keeping missions under UN auspices or within a future legal system of the CSCE. On the other hand, an increased US movement toward unilateralism in order to strengthen its hegemonic position together with a growing unilaterlism by new nationalistic leaderships in Eastern Europe could seriously hamper or block the above-mentioned function of arms control.

Most challenging in Eastern Europe are domestic conflicts as opposed to inter-state wars. But traditional arms control regimes work only at the inter-state level. It is not easy to imagine to what extent new arms control measures could really reduce the risk of civil wars. Main conventional weapons systems are not so important in fighting a civil war, whereas the small arms frequently used cannot be controlled in a reliable way. Nevertheless, in addition to traditional means of political interference and mediation, there are potential instruments at our disposal that could influence or even control such conflicts based on an effective CSCE conflict prevention centre. Fact-finding missions or peace-keeping forces, for instance, can be used to prevent a war or to guarantee an armistice, provided the conflicting parties accept these. The Open Sky treaty, signed in March 1992, can also be extended to tasks in this direction.[33] Sanctions such as a ban on arms trade and other forms of military assistance or on raw material needed for the war-fighting capabilities of the parties involved can also support a peaceful solution. Measures of such a kind must be organized on a CSCE level. In any case, traditional arms control needs to be complemented by effective crisis management in order to prepare for the conflicts looming on the Eastern European horizon or for those already visible in the Balkans.

Because of the current instability and potential spill-over effects of conflicts, many countries in Eastern Europe will be interested in very low ceilings for the forces of their respective neighbors. On the other hand, due to obvious risks, the same countries are interested in high limits for their own forces in order to be prepared for any conceivable contingency irrespective of economic constraints. In such circumstances, the prospects for further deep treaty-based cuts in the next five to ten years seem rather bleak. But in cases where the effective numerical strength of forces has fallen much below the CFE treaty ceilings (for reasons of unilateral reductions due to temporary economic constraints), one might consider the introduction of a notification procedure (on unit or percentage level) in order to enhance stability if one country wants to increase its forces up to the legal ceilings.

In Western Europe, however, the question of constraints seems much less relevant because of the absence of domestic or inter-state conflicts and due to NATO. Only the conflict between Greece and Turkey (and, possibly, Bulgaria) may be an exception. Therefore, the Western Europeans favour force limitations and reductions particularly with regard to Eastern and South-Eastern Europe, in order to control the political and military dynamics there. And it is because of the instability in Eastern Europe that, for the time being at least, many countries in Western Europe are not willing to accept further legally binding reductions.[34] Instability in the Middle East and in North Africa contributes to this stance.

Furthermore, it is still doubtful as to whether the area of application for confidence-building and arms control can be extended, because especially the US does not accept any treaty-mandated limitations on its conventional forces at home in spite of the fact that it will cut its forces unilaterally for economic and financial reasons. Even a global information exchange is becoming less likely. Whereas the US has indicated that in principle it is still ready to join such a system, Turkey is eager to keep its southern CFE I exclusion-zone out of any transparency measures. At the beginning of the talks on a new Security Forum Mandate in Helsinki, NATO proposed to extend the area of application for any kind of constraining measures to all participating states in Eurasia from the Atlantic to 90 degrees east of Greenwich.[35] This proposal includes all successors to the former Soviet Union with the exception of the eastern part of Siberia, which belongs to the Russian Federation. First, Russia rejected this NATO proposal and suggested to include the territory of all CSCE member-states completely. But later on it gave the impression of being ready to accept the Western formula, because it will guarantee Russia a similarly exceptional position *vis-à-vis* the US in the coming negotiations.

The US together with other European participants (i.e. France and Great Britain) is also not yet ready to include naval forces into negotiations. At present only some confidence-building measures (e.g. information exchange) seem possible. This is all the more surprising since, after the principle of parity and the alliance approach were given up, there is no longer any rationale for excluding Western naval forces from conventional arms control. They will be reduced unilaterally anyway. Thus, in the long run, it seems inconceivable that the European countries will accept a situation where only they will have limits on all their forces and on their whole territory whereas the US, Turkey and Russia are only faced with minor or partial constraints while at the same time maintaining an equal right of control. France in particular observes developments in this direction very critically. A cooperative security structure either in Europe or in the Northern hemisphere (from Vladivostok to Vancouver) can hardly be set up in a credible way if some members want to exclude their territory or major parts of it together with a sizeable part of their forces. Therefore, the real question will be at what time and under what circumstances these countries will give up their restrictive attitudes toward traditional conventional arms control measures.

All in all, prospects for transparency, openness and confidence-building measures seem brighter at present. A continuous dialogue should be established on military doctrines and strategies. This could result in a harmonization of doctrinal thinking and could create a better understanding of the reasons for differences. Transparency in military budgets, military planning and research and development is a precondition for a more cooperative security system. The data exchange on military budgets should concentrate on the specific structures and the methods of comparison. Regular discussions on military planning, or research and development might be important to create a common feeling for which military technologies and tactics should be abandoned or constrained to enhance stability and accountability.

Some adjustments in establishing CSBMs should also be considered. For instance, thresholds for the invitation of observers to military manoeuvers should be reduced to the level of divisions or in some cases to the level of brigades in a CFE II agreement because of the increased use of computer simulations for manoeuvers and the integration of the neutral and non-aligned countries with very small forces. Otherwise, this instrument will affect only states with strong forces and cannot be used on a regular basis. Similarly, the size, frequency, and duration of (large) manoeuvers should be constrained. The Vienna Document on CSBMs signed in March 1992 is a first step in this direction.[36] Military cooperation could be increased through implementation of the liaison concept as proposed at the NATO foreign ministers meeting in Copenhagen in mid-1991. The aim of this concept is to facilitate an exchange of senior military personnel of, for example, military academies or training centers among all members of the CSCE process on a bilateral and multilateral basis. In this context, the recently established North Atlantic Cooperation Council (NACC) could be an adequate institution for creating a joint system of military cooperation and training for civil emergencies, also deployable in cases such as the Western food aid program for the former Soviet Union.

Verification, too, needs a fresh start, as the verification regime of CFE I, being mainly based on the old system of confrontation and the alliance approach, cannot be adopted for the follow-on negotiations. However, under a new arms control agreement based on national ceilings, it will be impossible for one nation to control all the other members of the security regime. Therefore, a new inter-governmental agency will be needed to coordinate verification and to provide free access to all verification reports of other nations or groups of nations. This will also be a further step toward institutionalizing European security.

Similarly, increased cooperation and Western assistance seems necessary for the conversion of closed military facilities and the build-down of the military industry in Eastern Europe and in particular in the former Soviet Union. In the former USSR alone there are between ten and twenty million people directly dependent on the military. The assistance for conversion will be necessary to reduce the danger of uncontrolled arms transfers in other areas of the world. Successful programs of conversion supported by the West will also enhance the readiness for arms control and reduce the influence of conservatism and desperate moods within the military industrial complex.

In the end, this raises the question what conventional arms control can really contribute to enhancing peace and security in Europe. Arms control can codify the political changes in Europe. It can contribute to managing instability and crisis in Eastern Europe, in the former Soviet Union, and in the Balkans in a peaceful way. And it can be an important instrument for regulating and managing security relationships in the Northern hemisphere with the aim of creating a new inter-state code of conduct for military forces thereby facilitating a new cooperative security system. On the other hand, the possible results of arms control should not be overestimated. As long as the fundamental economic and political problems in the eastern part of the European continent are not overcome and as long as the US and others are not willing to refrain from unilateralism, the prospects for negotiated arms control are less optimistic.

## Global Aspects

Obviously, conflicts outside of Europe can influence European security too. The Gulf War of 1991 is a recent case in point. In particular the countries on the Southern flank and those with extra-European security ties are concerned with conflicts outside of Europe. This causes additional problems for a stable defensive posture and for lower limits specifically in Southern Europe. Thus, a cooperative security system creates the need to develop a common arms control approach for regions outside Europe in order to reduce the risks emanating from these areas. Especially in the Middle East and in Asia, regional conventional arms control initiatives could enhance stability and security.

A first step could be to set up a European monitoring system for exports and imports of conventional arms and their technology. The decision of the CSCE Council of Foreign Ministers in Prague in January 1992 to firmly support the United Nations Register of Conventional Arms strengthens efforts in this direction.[37] In December 1991, the UN General Assembly decided to create a register of arms transfers on a voluntary basis. It consists of seven major weapon categories: tanks, armored combat vehicles, artillery, attack helicopters, combat aircraft and vessels.[38] Experience will show how far other UN members will participate in this register and how reliable their data will be. Since the second half of 1991 the five permanent members of the UN Security Council (USA, Russia, China, France and the United Kingdom) have negotiated a prior notification of conventional arms transfers and, specifically, Guidelines for Conventional Arms Transfers in the Middle East.[39] This initiative aims at constraining transfers if stability in the region is in danger. Up to now an agreement was not possible because these five nations are responsible for 90 percent of the arms transfers to the Middle East and their interests in that region differ too much.[40]

Since May 1992 first steps toward confidence-building measures have also been discussed in the Middle East.[41] The success of these talks depends mainly on political detente between Israel and its Arab neighbors and a satisfactory solution to the Palestinian question. Finally, based on an intiative of the G-7 industrialized states, there is a drive to supplement the NPT Treaty by way of the Missile Technology Control Regime, which was installed to prevent the proliferation of missiles with a range of 300 kms and above and a throw-weight of 500 kgs or more.[42] It is a discriminatory regime and China and Russia accepted large parts of the regime's code although they have not acceded. Despite the fact that it has prevented the transfer of missiles and missile technology in several cases, its range is limited: non-member countries such as Argentine, Brazil, Israel, India or North Korea possess the capability to develop, produce, and export missiles of that category. Iraq's efforts also proved that the regime has certain gaps, and that the dual-use issue with civil missile technology has not yet been adequately solved.[43] In the long term, regional arms control efforts could be more important in helping solve this problem while at the same time reducing its discriminatory character.

Conventional arms control measures on a global or regional scale outside the CSCE are still rather limited and mainly oriented toward confidence-building and transparency. Only the Missile Technolgy Control Regime includes constraints. Although at present the record of global or regional conventional arms control is meager, one should not underestimate these efforts remembering the example of the fairly slow progress in the initial stages of the CSCE process.

## Notes

1. See, for instance, John Mueller, "A New Concept of Europe," *Foreign Policy*, No. 77 (Winter 1989/90), pp. 3-16.

2. See in greater detail Gert Krell, "Zur Theorie und Praxis der Rüstungskontrolle," in: Hessische Stiftung Friedens- und Konfliktforschung (ed.), *Europa zwischen Konfrontation und Kooperation. Entspannungspolitik für die achtziger Jahre* (Frankfurt: Campus 1982), pp. 105-42, here p. 110.

3. John H. Barton, Lawrence D. Weiler, *International Arms Control. Issues and Agreements* (Stanford: Stanford University Press, 1976), pp. 335-44.

4. See Ivo Daalder, "The Future of Arms Control," *Survival*, Vol. 34, No. 1, pp. 51-73; here p. 52. Daalder uses the terms "competitive arms control" versus "cooperative arms control" but refers to the same facts.

5. April Carter, *Success and Failure in Arms Control Negotiations* (Oxford: Oxford University Press, 1989), p. 257-68.

6. Joseph S. Nye, "Nuclear Learning and U.S.-Soviet Security Regimes," *International Organization*, Vol. 41, No. 3, 1987, pp. 371-402; see also the results of the "World Policy Study" in: Robert Axelrod, Robert O. Keohane, "Achieving Cooperation under Anarchy: Strategies and Institutions," *World Policy*, Vol. 38, No. 1, 1985, pp. 226-53.

7. On the proliferation of chemical weapons and efforts to curb their spread see Gordon M. Burck and Charles G. Flowerree: *International Handbook on Chemical Weapons Proliferation* (New York: Greenwood Press, 1991).

8. *Arms Control Today*, Vol. 21, No. 5, 1991, p. 29.

9. For the potential of chemical weapons see Matthew Meselson, "The Myth of Chemical Superpowers," *Bulletin of the Atomic Scientists*, Vol. 47, No. 3, 1991, p. 12-5.

10. Lee Feinstein, "Australia Offers New Draft Treaty at Chemical Weapons Negotiations," *Arms Control Today*, Vol. 22, No. 3, 1992, p. 20.

11. Erhard Geissler, "Strengthening the Biological Weapons Convention," *Disarmament*, Vol. 14, No. 2, 1991, pp. 104-18; Barbara Hatch Rosenberg, "The Next Step: A Biological Verification Regime," *ibid.*, pp. 119-46.

12. According to the Arms Control Association and Natural Resources Defense Council, 17 500 nuclear weapons could be deployed in Russia, 4 360 in the Ukraine, nearly 1 700 in Kazakhstan and 1 200 in Belarus, see: *Der Spiegel*, No. 51, 1991, p. 136. Recent reports indicate that presumably all strategic nuclear weapons in the Ukraine, Belarus and Kazakhstan were deactivated by Russia, see *Frankfurter Rundschau*, January 21, 1992, p. 2.

13. See *Der Spiegel*, No. 51, 1991, p. 136. TNWs were reported to be deployed in the following republics: Armenia (200), Azerbaijan (300), Georgia (320), Kyrgyzstan (75), Moldova (90), Tajikistan (75), Turkmenistan (125) and Uzbekistan (105).

14. See Kurt M. Campbell, Ashton B. Carter, Steven E. Miller, Charles A. Zratek, *Soviet Nuclear Fission. Control of the Nuclear Arsenal in a Disintegrating Soviet Union, CSIA Studies in International Security, No. 1*, (Cambridge: Center for Science and International Affairs, 1991).

15. Ashton Carter, "Reducing the Nuclear Dangers from the Former Soviet Union," *Arms Control Today*, Vol. 22, No. 1, 1992, p. 10-5. On international storage see Lawrence Scheinman and David A. V. Fischer, "Managing the Coming Glut of Nuclear Weapon Materials," *Arms Control Today*, Vol. 22, No. 2, 1992, pp. 7-12.

16. Robert S. Norris, "The Soviet Nuclear Archipelago," *Arms Control Today*, Vol. 22, No. 1, 1992, pp. 24-31, here p. 27.

17. See the reaction of the speaker of the Chinese Foreign Ministry to the disarmanent initiative of Gorbachev in: *Radio Bejing*, October 7, 1991. For the UK see *Frankfurter Allgemeine Zeitung*, October 1, 1991, p. 1. For France see *Frankfurter Rundschau*, October 1, 1991, p. 2.

18. See *Frankfurter Allgemeine Zeitung*, June 13, 1992, p. 5.

19. Charles A. Glaser, "Nuclear Policy without an Adversary. U.S. Planning for the Post-Soviet Era," *International Security*, Vol. 16, No. 4, 1992, pp. 34-78.

20. See *Arms Control Today*, Vol. 22, No. 1, 1992, p. 43.

21. In reality, the Eastern European revolutions put an end to the WTO as an effective military alliance in late 1989. The formal decision, however, to dissolve its military organs took place on April 1, 1991, while the alliance as such was dissolved in June 1991.

22. Through bilateral agreements, the Soviet forces stationed in Hungary and the CSFR had left these countries completely by June 1991. They will be withdrawn from Poland by the end of 1993. The withdrawal from the territory of the former GDR started before the 2+4-treaty was ratified; it is to be com-

pleted by the end of 1994. Still an open question is the withdrawal of the former Soviet troops from the three Baltic states.

23. This may be one reason why in 1990 the Soviet military decided to move 57,300 pieces of Treaty Limited Equipment (TLE) (16,400 tanks, 15,900 ACVs, 25,000 arillery pieces) beyond the Urals prior to the completion of the CFE I treaty.

24. Moldova, the Ukraine, Azerbaijan, Belarus, Russia and Georgia have decided to set up their own forces. Moldova wants to assemble a force of 12 500 men, the Ukraine of 220 000-450 000 men. In Belarus, there are proposals for a force of 35 000-50 000 or 90 000 men. Russia plans to establish a force of 1.5 million. See *The Arms Control Reporter*, No. 10, 1991, pp. 407.E.1.45-49; No. 12, 1991, p. 407.E.1.54; *Frankfurter Rundschau*, February 5, 1992, pp. 1-2; *Frankfurter Allgemeine Zeitung*, May 8, 1992, p. 8.

25. See the NATO Declaration of Rome on November 7-8, 1991, Presse und Informationsamt der Bundesregierung (ed.), *Stichworte zur Sicherheitspolitik*, No. 11, 1991, pp. 11-20.

26. See in greater detail Pal Dunay, *The CFE Treaty: History, Achievements and Shortcomings, PRIF Reports No. 24* (Frankfurt: Peace Research Institute, October 1991), pp. 81-2.

27. On October 18, 1991, the Joint Consultative Group decided that the three Baltic republics (as they had wished) will not be a part of the CFE I treaty with the exception of the Soviet forces stationed there. See *The Arms Control Reporter*, No. 12, 1991, p. 407.D.83.

28. See Institute for Defense & Disarmament Studies (ed.), "Agreed Weapon Allocation Removes Major CFE Hurdle," *Vienna Fax*, May 20, 1992, pp. 2-3; *Frankfurter Allgemeine Zeitung*, June 6, 1992, p. 5.

29. *Frankfurter Rundschau*, January 28, 1991, p. 2.

30. See *Bulletin* des Presse und Informationsamtes der Bundesregierung, No. 12, February 4, 1992, p. 86.

31. This number is based on current CSCE membership after the accession of all successors to the former Soviet Union. If the break-up of Yugoslavia gives rise to more than just the three new states, the figure can easily rise. Also, a separation of Czecho-Slovakia cannot be excluded.

32. Possible solutions for such regional approaches could be seperate negotiations between the republics of the former Soviet Union (with the exception of the Baltics); the Nordic countries including the Baltics; Greece, Italy, Hungary, Austria, Albania and, last but not least, the successors to Yugoslavia. In several cases (like between Rumania and Hungary), bilateral talks could be helpful, too.

33. See *Vertrag über den Offenen Himmel* (Bonn: Auswärtiges Amt, 1992), p. 1. The Treaty was signed by all NATO members and former allies of

the USSR together with Russia, the Ukraine, Belorussia and Georgia. Because of financial and technical problems the treaty will not enter into force before 1993. The preamble of the treaty specifically mentions an extension with regard to measures of conflict prevention and conflict management. However, it seems doubtful to what extent Open Sky can really be used for such purposes because it could be extremly difficult to guarantee flight safety for open skies missions in a hostile environment.

34. At present, only Germany and Italy are willing to reduce their forces further for domestic reasons. But during the talks about the future structure of CFE II within NATO's High Level Task Force, all other participants strongly rejected any call for further reductions.

35. See *Basic Reports*, No. 21, April 10, 1992, pp. 4-7. France, insisted on defining respective "areas of application" in a way that would not prejudice subsequent negotiations.

36. See *Bulletin* des Presse und Informationsamtes der Bundesregierung, No. 31, March 21, 1992. The new document contains obligations to notify the mobilization of non-active units, the lowering of the thresholds for notification and observation of military activities (notification above 9 000 men or 250 tanks down from 13 000 men or 300 tanks, observation above 13 000 men or 300 tanks down from 17 000 men), and certain constraints on the size and frequency of large manoeuvers.

37. See *Bulletin* des Presse und Informationsamtes der Bundesregierung, No. 12, February 4, 1992, p. 88.

38. The definition of five of the seven weapon categories is based on the CFE treaty. The first data exchange will take place in April 1993 and is to contain every transfer since the beginning of 1992.

39. See *Basis Reports*, No. 20, February 19, 1992, pp. 1-5.

40. *Frankfurter Rundschau*, May 30, 1992, p. 1; *Frankfurter Allgemeine Zeitung*, June 1, 1992, p. 5.

41. *Frankfurter Allgemeine Zeitung*, May 12, 1992, p. 2.

42. See *The Arms Control Reporter*, No. 1, 1991, pp. 706.A.1-2.

43. *Aviation Week & Space Technology*, May 18, 1992, p. 21.

# PART THREE

# Germany -- A European Problem?

# 8

# Germany Assumes a Dominant Position in the "European House"

*Bruno Schoch*

*The new Germany . . . has acquired the power and scope to free itself of most of the restrictions placed on it up to now. Only now is the real statesman's task becoming apparent, namely determining how the Federal Republic will handle its new power. . . Something quite extraordinary has happened to Germany: it has been given a second chance. This century is ending as it began, with a great thrust ahead by Germany, founded on economics, technology and human industry. Germany and Europe now have a second chance to assure their true values in peace and freedom, and to do so under much more propitious conditions than in the age of crude nationalism prior to 1914.*
*Fritz Stern[1]*

It is in Germany that the disintegration of real existing socialism and the end of the East-West conflict have produced what is, to date, their most striking effect. That conflict, besides effecting a Manichean friend-foe split into two highly armed antagonistic political camps, had effectively acquired the function of a shaper of states. In Germany, therefore, its dissolution in the historic year of 1989 not only brought about the downfall of the SED regime but deprived the GDR as such of its *raison d'être* and removed the justification for the division of Germany into separate states. However, the return to a German nation-state, effected initially through currency union and then generally through constitutional union, aroused ambivalent feelings in many quarters.

On the other hand, there was delight that the dictum that "The French Revolution is the Russians' future,"[2] coined as early as autumn 1988 by François Furet, the renowned historian of the French Revolution, should have been fulfilled precisely in the year of the *bicentennaire*. Indeed, the triumph of the ideas of 1789 over those of 1917 could hardly have been more emphatic. The Soviet leadership had scarcely issued its definitive revocation of the Brezhnev doctrine when the call for *glasnost* and *perestroika* in the "popular democracies" began to take on a more radical tone. The upshot was a desire to see the dictatorship of the party and the real-socialist command economy replaced by individual freedom, political democracy, and a constitutional state based on the rule of law, as well as forms of social interchange and styles of life typical of advanced capitalism -- what is generally termed a "social market economy." In Germany, there was also the satisfaction felt at the first successful -- and peaceful -- political "revolution" in German history.[3] Once the conflict between the systems had been deprived of its basis by the "new thinking" and by the demise of the social and governmental systems of state socialism, most people believed they were witnessing nothing less than the dawning of "a new age of democracy, peace, and unity."[4]

The obverse of this delight was the unmistakable anxiety that was expressed in many quarters about the breathtaking speed at which power politics was shifting in Europe. The seemingly unstoppable fragmentation of the erstwhile real-socialist camp -- a fragmentation which eventually also affected the Soviet Union itself -- together with the astonishing political dynamic that led to the unification of the two German states, catching most of those involved unawares, reawakened old anxieties about balance and stability in European power-politics. One fear that emerged particularly prominently was the historically grounded one that a unified and sovereign Germany might once again abuse its hegemonial power.[5] Certainly, all the evidence indicates -- particularly in retrospect -- that the rapid collapse of power in the GDR left no alternative open but swift union with the Federal Republic. However, in a moment of decision preponderance of the executive -- which, following the fall of the Berlin Wall, saw the much-talked-of "mantle of history" briefly flutter past -- the chancellor, despite all protestations to the effect that the era of the nation-state was long since past, and despite all the relevant multilateral treaties, chose to go out on his own and push for national unification. This, like the nature-related metaphors that were repeatedly used by the political class and published opinion, was hardly likely to dispel the fear of a return of nationalist thinking in Germany. Germany has too often kept the Europe of the twentieth century in suspense with its national aspirations for all doubts to be overcome in one fell swoop.

Abroad, there was, from the outset, no dispute about the fact that Germany had acquired increased power as a result of the end of bipolarism and the unification of the country on 3 October 1990. On the other hand, it is glaringly obvious from the internal political debate that within Germany itself there was for a long time a refusal to acknowledge this increase. It was doggedly asserted that, after 40 years of the Federal Republic, the Germans had learnt their historical lesson once and for all: it was inconceivable that, as a model -- post-1945 -- of an extremely successful trading state (in the sense of Richard Rosecrance's distinction between the "trading world" and the "military-political world"[6]), with its typical predominance of civilian technological production, the Germans should be thirsting for a return to that fatal tradition of national power-politics that had driven Europe into two wars and had ultimately also reduced Germany to rubble. And even if, contrary to expectation, they should at some point be tempted by such an option, to realize it had now become "objectively" impossible. This was because -- so it was claimed by the politicians of Bonn, by prevailing opinion, and by countless political scientists, in a constantly rehearsed credo that had become almost second nature to them -- the extent of international interdependence and supranational integration was such that it precluded any return to earlier nation-state politics and thus also to old *incertitudes allemandes*. The irreversible embedding of the Federal Republic in the institutional structures of the West -- NATO and the EC -- and in the CSCE agreements precluded any doubt on this matter; anyone who intimated anything to the contrary merely revealed to what degree he himself was still bound up in national -- i.e. antiquated -- ways of thinking.

Now there is certainly little to support the assumption common to adherents of a crude kind of Marxism and to functionalist theoreticians that economic power, expanded territory, or an increase in population automatically translate into power-projection and great-power politics -- indeed, military great-power politics. Nor is there any historical law that dictates that the same things always recur, as is insinuated by the precipitate and unreflecting talk of a "Fourth *Reich*."[7] Yet the stubbornness with which people deny even the simple fact that the Germany that has resulted from the unification of FRG and GDR is evolving into a position of new strength, cannot fail to astonish. (Moreover, this

188

evolution is taking place at a time when the international context is itself undergoing radical change -- dissolution of the Eastern bloc, ending of the antagonism between the two systems, the disarmament process, etc.) It is striking that "people in Germany do not like to talk
about the reality of this kind of strength. People react to it as if it were
a taboo subject. The prevailing attitude is one of "me-no-understand,"
and people incredulously shake their heads and admit to being completely unable even to unravel the political signs of power."[8]

It seems as if there is a desire to keep at bay the unpleasant fact that
the East-West conflict brought about the end not only of the GDR but
also of the Federal Republic in its old familiar form. This widespread
rejection of reality may be taken to indicate that the Federal Republic,
taken unawares by unification, will need some time to absorb the fact
that it has lost its role as a genial "political dwarf" and as everybody's
darling -- a role of which it had grown rather fond. The rejection may,
however, also be an intimation that Federal German self-confidence
about the future is not as strong as is widely claimed. The extent to
which the co-ordinates of Federal German politics have changed is most
clearly revealed in the dramatic developments that are taking place in
the states belonging to the erstwhile socialist camp. In view of the economic and social difficulties that are piling up as a result of unification,
the argument that was constantly reiterated during 1990 as a kind of
calmative is now beginning to lose its force. That argument claimed
that sixteen million GDR citizens shaped by decades spent under two
totalitarian systems that rewarded "authoritarian personalities," were
not capable of altering the Federal Republic or the substance of its political culture, since their number was no greater than that of the inhabitants of Nordrhein-Westfalen.

## The Growth in Germany's Power

Two years after the fall of the Berlin Wall, on 9 November 1989,
and eighteen months after the currency union of 1 July 1990, the realization is gradually beginning to sink into the west German consciousness that the momentous events of 1989/90 have radically altered the
realities of power politics, and that the demise of the two front-line
German states -- on which the seal was set by unification -- have
brought a fundamental change to Germany's own position within Europe. Whereas immediately after unification, there was a significant gap
between the Germans' new international standing and their own appraisal of themselves, one now increasingly encounters the following

kind of diagnosis of the situation: "On 3 October 1990 Germany re-entered European politics as a great power;"[9] or even: "Germany is now one of the great powers; it is now, as Rudolf Augstein writes, one of the three most potent countries in the world. . . Germany belongs . . . in the great-power category; indeed, in Europe it is the only real superpower."[10]

Although Germany's self-image following unification oscillates between denial of reality and trumpet-blowing, it is generally accepted that the majority of the Germans, though they were in favour of unification, in no way linked this, as had happened previously, with a desire for greater international weight. On the contrary, "At the end of 1990/ beginning of 1991 an *Infratest* poll conducted for the *Süddeutsche Zeitung* showed that, in the context of the Gulf War, three-quarters of all Germans wanted the Federal Republic to assume no international responsibility, and preferred to keep out of international crises, with 40 per cent wishing to live *à la Suisse* -- i.e. "prosperously and independently" -- and a further 20 per cent wanting a life patterned on the supposed "Swedish model." What these answers reflect above all is the old perspectives and models of behaviour resulting from decades of comfortable habituation"[11] -- habituation, that is, to Germany's own international position within the context of the East-West conflict and under the aegis of the two world-powers, and habituation to "parochial existence with restricted sovereignty," as this conservative writer mockingly terms it.

I propose to begin by drawing together the various factors of the shift in power-politics in the Federal Republic which have, willy-nilly, called into question both the Federal Republic's view of itself and its low-profile foreign policy. The factors, in other words, that have put an end to the "comfortable parochial outlook" or "oblivion to power"[12] -- another common catchword from the conservative spectrum -- that were produced by Germany's firm implantation into East-West antagonism.

The first and most salient aspect of the changed state of affairs is the ending of the restrictions on sovereignty applied by the victors of the Second World War to Berlin and to Germany as a whole. The "Treaty on the Final Settlement on Germany," signed in Moscow on 12 September 1990 by the two German states and the four victorious powers -- the "two-plus-four" formula -- regulates the external aspects of German unity. With the formal and definitive termination of all the rights and duties pursuant on the defeat of Germany and on its occupation, Germany has regained its full sovereignty in international law.[13] In place of the two German states which formed the pivot on which the precariously balanced and potentially globalizing confrontation between the blocs rested, we see the return to the international stage of a figure not seen for the last 45 years: Germany. From a peripheral position as two front-line states "bracketing off" their respective leading powers, united Germany has shifted to a central position between wealthy western Europe and an eastern Europe endeavouring to make up ground. What appears to many in the east to be an opportunity could also bring a resumption of the specific ideologizations associated with this centre, and could loosen the political and cultural ties that anchor Germany into the West.[14]

Since the Soviet Union renounced its claim to military parity with the United States and began to pursue the goal of "self-sufficiency" -- i.e. possession of sufficient military potential for self-defense -- economic condition has begun to replace military resources as the currency of international power. As a result, the FRG's self-image -- partially imposed by its curtailed sovereignty and partially a matter of choice, and succinctly expressed by Helmut Schmidt in the phrase "an economic giant and a political dwarf" -- has begun to lose some of its previous certainty. The efficiency of the former FRG's economy secured it a position of dominance in Europe. The Federal Republic produces more than a quarter of the gross national product of the EC and thus occupies fourth place behind the United States, Japan, and the former USSR. Even without European currency union, the DM already *de facto* plays the role of leading currency in Europe; moreover, it is, after the dollar, the second most important reserve currency in the world. Since 1986, the Federal Republic has been in most years the "world export champion," ahead of the United States and Japan; in 1990 it exported goods to the value of $421 billion -- more than France ($216 billion) and Britain ($185 billion) put together.

In regard to economics in particular, the effects of unification are disputed and the prognoses contradictory. In the short term, unity will bring considerable costs and risks. The former GDR's crash-landing into the market economy will initially have to be financed by west Germany. This will mean a massive increase in state loans and a rise in taxation, bringing the risk of inflation; the welfare system, which was not designed to take on millions of people, seems about to be subjected to the ultimate test. As against this, we have a booming economy in the former West German *Länder* and predictions of an upturn in the erstwhile GDR, which leads most experts to conclude that Germany's position as the leading economic power in Europe has, in the medium term, been strengthened.[15]

The third aspect is the fact that the Federal Republic has become larger. Its territory has increased by almost one third; Germany is now the third largest territorial state in the European Community, after France and Spain. In addition, next to Russia it is the most populous country in Europe: with almost 79 million inhabitants, it makes up almost a quarter of the total population of the EC; the gap between Germany and the other big three of the EC -- Italy and France with 57 million inhabitants each, and Britain with 56 million -- has shifted greatly. Even today, there is no lack of conventional theories -- they like to describe themselves as realist -- which continue to view the territorial extent and demographic potential of a state as the bases of its power.[16]

Fourthly, the unity of Germany and the disintegration of the Eastern bloc are two facets of one and the same historic event. The unification of Germany was paralleled by a collapse of the "socialist camp" -- the formal break-up of the Warsaw Treaty Organization and of the Council for Mutual Economic Assistance merely set the seal on a process of erosion that had become apparent some time before. It is not merely that the GDR, once the Soviet Union's pawn in its claim to power in central Europe, has now become part of the Federal Republic, and thus also of NATO's sphere of activity; the collapse of all Eastern European alliance-structures means that to the east, Germany now borders not on what was once perceived as the fearsome Eastern bloc but on a set of states that are economically and militarily weaker. The fragmentation does not stop at national boundaries: national secession not only in Yugoslavia but also in the erstwhile Soviet Union, from the Baltic to the Trans-Caucasus, has proven unstoppable. The same principle that led to the unification of Germany -- namely the right to national self-determination -- harbours a dynamic which, for multiethnic communities such as Yugoslavia, the USSR, and possibly also Czechoslovakia, led to fragmentation. Not least for this reason, the shift in power politics brought about by the ending of the East-West conflict and the unification of Germany have been compared to the situation that obtained after the First World War, when Poland reemerged, Finland regained its independence, and three independent Baltic republics were formed -- not to mention the states that were born out of the former Habsburg monarchy.

Fifthly, because of its increased economic power, the Federal Republic has become the most important political partner of the United States and the Soviet Union as well as its major successor states in Europe. As early as May 1989, President Bush, speaking in Mainz, coined the term "partner in leadership" to describe the FRG, a term that rapidly became a catchword in Germany. [17] At the same time, Mikhail Gorbachev, during his official visit to Bonn, talked of the "two great European states"[18] who would play a decisive role in the construction of the "common European home," that is to say the Soviet Union and the Federal Republic. Since then he has repeatedly stressed the "key role" to be played by Germany in the future of Europe. One need hardly point out that that importance has increased yet further since 3 October 1990. Anxiety about a powerful Soviet Union has given way to anxiety about the collapsing Soviet Union. At the same time, the victory of the West in the East-West conflict, and the consequent reduction in European military dependence on the USA, have brought a loss by the latter of its unrestricted hegemonial role and an ongoing debate about the "decline of America."[19]

In addition, there is the fact that with the formation of a sovereign Germany, France and Britain have lost their militarily based advantages as victorious powers charged with the keeping a watchful eye on Germany. As the disarmament process continues and economic performance tends to replace nuclear capabilities as the crucial ingredients of international power, the importance of the French and British nuclear weapons is, in any case, being diminished.[20] The unification of Germany put an end to the policy on Germany pursued by the two victorious powers of Western Europe. France's purpose from the outset had been to anchor the FRG in the West, as a means of perpetuating the political status quo -- a policy of integration "with ulterior motives."[21] The same applies to Britain, whose policy on Germany was once summed up by the Prime Minister Edward Heath as follows: "Of course we said we believed in German reunification because we knew it wouldn't happen."[22] In the minutes which I have already mentioned of the expert meeting organized by Margaret Thatcher at Chequers, these anxieties are set out quite bluntly: It is reported that even the optimists amongst the participants were unable to suppress certain fears in regard to the effects which unification would have on the behaviour of the Germans in Europe. The wish was expressed that Germany be tied into some sort of security framework and that there should continue to be an American presence, as a counterweight to German military power. There was support for the idea that the participation of the Soviet Union in discussions about Europe's future security-system be institutionalized within the CSCE -- not least because, in the long term, the Soviet Union, it was felt, was the only power in Europe capable of acting as a counterweight to Germany.[23] This list of requirements reveals the need that is felt for guarantees in regard to a now sovereign and expanded Germany.

For the former COMECON states, confronted as they are with massive problems as they tackle the historically unprecedented task of transition to a market economy, the "German economic miracle" of the post-war period exercises a magical fascination. The East thus has great expectations in regard to the "German model" and German economic aid. In the capitals of eastern Europe one constantly hears the refrain that the path back to Europe leads through Germany. This applies not least to the Soviet Union and its European heirs, to whose acquiescence Germany ultimately owes its unity. Nikolai Portugalov, a renowned expert on Germany, has talked of the "new reconciliation between Russians and Germans ... the expectation of a process of osmosis which will allow our return to Europe." Seen from this point of view, the Soviets' relinquishing of the GDR and of their rights as victors may be viewed as something offered in exchange for the prospect of economic aid and comprehensive co-operation with Germany: German help was to assure the establishment of a market economy in the Soviet Union -- "and for a united Germany this means acquiring great-power status through this co-operation." In the eyes of the leaders of Soviet reform this was that much easier to accept in that the Soviet Union itself had been seeking to base its international power on something other than mere military might:

> The regaining of unity signifies the return of Germany to world politics, and its return as a modern power whose importance is determined not by excessive armament but by a huge economic potential, by one of the most stable currencies in the world, by an almost watertight social-welfare system, and, last but not least, by dependable democratic institutions. From now on Germany will acquire an international political dimension through its bridging function between eastern and western Europe and through its contribution to the development of fully fledged market structures in the East. . . We hope that the partnership -- indeed friendship -- with united Germany, that the German economy, and German private investments will save us from the catastrophe that threatens us.[24]

This is a colossal, scarcely realizable expectation. At any rate it sets the previous power-relationship between Bonn and Moscow on its head.

### The Unification of 1990: A New Beginning

One advantage of the East-West conflict as far as the European community of states was concerned was that by bringing about the division of Germany it seemed to put an end to one of the fundamental problems of modern European history, namely the expansionary great-power policy pursued by Germany.[25] That policy led to the excesses committed as part of the biologically racist, rapacious, and exterminatory imperialism of the Third *Reich*. Coming after this, the East-West conflict made it possible for the Germans to return to the international community of states. And during the 40 years of existence of the FRG and GDR as states within their respective alliances, this status quo seemed -- in line with the French saying "C'est le provisoire qui dure" -- to have become a settled *modus vivendi*. This was so not only in the European community of nations and, at an early stage, in the GDR, but also to an increasing extent in the economically and politically successful FRG -- despite all the national rhetoric. The official welcome extended by the Kohl Government to the East German Head of the State and Secretary of the SED, Erich Honecker, in autumn 1987 was, in a symbolic sense, the West German seal to the prior recognition of national borders via the CSCE.[26] Hence, the remark made by a well-informed observer of European affairs in the fortieth-anniversary year of the FRG and GDR reflects a widely held belief: because "everyone agrees with the division of Germany, with the exception of one or two Germans -- though even many Germans accept it --, it will in all probability prove to be an irreversible judgement, at least as far as one can assess the future."[27] We now know that the future cannot be assessed. The irony is that unity fell into the Germans' lap just at the time when they had largely come to terms with dual statehood.

If one compares the unification of 1990 with earlier attempts to solve the "German question" -- in other words to reconcile a unitary German state with European security -- one is immediately struck by a number of important differences. Certainly, up to now, the periods at which Germany was a nation-state were not the happiest experienced by Europe. But this should not blind one to the fact that the unity of 1990 is different, and came about under radically changed conditions, so that optimistic prognoses claiming that the nightmare of history has now been banished are not at all outlandish.

The foundation of the *Reich* by Bismarck was part of a trend in which the idea of the powerful nation-state was accorded absolute status. This absolutism was something which continued to bind together the neo-Rankian national historiography and the political élites until 1945. The unification of 1990 did not form part of any such trend. This time, national unity was achieved not through war, but by peaceful means -- which makes all the difference, if one only thinks what fateful effects France's humiliation and the annexation of Alsace-Lorraine had on Franco-German relations. Bismarck's famous, or infamous, maxim at the time of the foundation of the *Reich* -- "The great questions of the day will not be settled by speeches or majority decisions -- that was the great error of 1848 and 1849 -- but by blood and iron" -- is not applicable to the conduct of the federal chancellor in autumn 1989. This time, unification came about in concert with the other powers and with Germany's neighbours, even though the Federal Republic was the key actor, and even though it was ultimately the Soviet leadership's change of course at the bilateral summit in Zheleznovodsk that tipped the scales. The international concert took concrete form in the "two-plus-four" process, and Poland, which was particularly affected on account of its western border, also took a symbolic part in the final phase of this process. It was also reflected in the formal resolutions of the EC and NATO, where eastern Germany received unique treatment. Finally, unification also slotted into the CSCE process. The confirmation of the Germans' renunciation of the production and possession of ABC weapons, and their undertaking to reduce the number of forces in united Germany to 370,000 within a maximum of four years undoubtedly also contributed to European acceptance. They, more than anything else, reveal the historical difference between the most recent events and the foundation of the second *Reich* "by blood and iron."

Unlike in 1918, the unconditional capitulation and total military, political, and moral defeat of 1945 had brought the German *Reich* to an end and broken the continuity of German great-power politics. The utter defeat delivered the Germans from their special path -- "a turning-point in German history that was more abrupt and more decisive than any earlier break in modern times."[28] The "German catastrophe" precluded any link back to national traditions -- instead, in the period immediately following the war, such traditions were held to be directly responsible for the triumph of National Socialism.[29] Identification with the respective victors and the dismissal of the idea of a "special path," delimited from both East and West, provided the only way forward. Most importantly, after 1945, not only was the old pernicious authoritarian-cum-military ideology of Prussian/German tradition regarded as a major cause of the catastrophe: the military as such was severely delegitimized. Despite the rearmament of the two German states during the Cold War, both the *Bundeswehr* and the *Nationale Volksarmee* continued to be viewed as rather disagreeable institutions by the majority of the population in both German states. The fact that the churches were never willing to give them their unreserved approval is an indication of this, as is the number of conscientious objectors in Germany, which is comparatively high in international terms. If one compares this with

German tradition, where military and warlike values always set the tone amongst the political élite, and where the reserve officer was the ideal in terms of social advancement, the contrast is striking.

Territorially, the Germany established in 1990 is about one third smaller than Bismarck's *Reich*. Specifically, it lacks the eastern regions lost by the Third *Reich*. This situation was definitively acknowledged by Germany in the "Treaty on the Final Settlement on Germany" and in the border-treaty which was finally concluded with Poland in September 1990, following a long *chronique scandaleuse* in which the legal fiction of the "1937 borders" was maintained for electoral reasons. This has put an end to German possession of a region in which feudal agrarian attitudes were long entrenched -- one need only think of the decisive influence wielded on the leadership of the *Reich*, and above all on the army, by the Prussian *Junker*-caste, with its conservative, anti-bourgeois, war-like code based on power, honour, and the duel; or of the consequences on the other social strata of the tardy removal of paternalistic rule. The part which these traditions played in the downfall of the Weimar Republic is well known.

Over 40 years, the Federal Republic has come to terms with parliamentary democracy. Its opening-up to the influences of liberal-republican civilization closed that earlier chapter of ideological-cum-cultural anti-western reservations associated with the "German character" and the "German mission" -- reservations symptomatically and seismographically recorded by the early Thomas Mann. To all those individuals who have undergone political-cultural socialization within West German democracy, Mann's "Betrachtungen eines Unpolitischen" written during the First World War, and later retracted by him, are bound to seem thoroughly antiquated.

The racist war waged by National Socialism had a paradoxical outcome. It aimed, through its policy of suppression, resettlement, and extermination, to achieve ethnic homogenization, and therefore helped to eliminate the *mêlée* of national minorities whose well-nigh insoluble problems had already spoiled the 1848 *Paulskirche* parliament in Frankfurt. Since then, the territories that lay at the eastern edge of the German *Reich* have repeatedly constituted a bone of contention that has destabilized the European system of states. This has been true from the expansionary projects of Wilhelminism, through the memoranda on the aims of the war and the ideas on *Mitteleuropa* propounded during the First World War, to the general revisionism of the inter-war period, and the annexations and war of plunder carried out by Hitler's Germany. Alongside with the shifts in boundaries effected by power-politics, the national rebirth in eastern Europe following the total defeat of

the Third *Reich* completed the ethnic homogenization begun by the latter and implemented through expulsion and naturalization. The well-
known result of this was that in eastern Europe -- i.e. in the region that
borders on Germany to the east -- nation-states re-emerged which for
the first time in their history had (relatively) homogenous populations
and in which German minorities no longer played any significant role.
There is no indication that united Germany could produce a Weimar-
type national revisionism; such revisionism was inescapable for most
parties, not least because of the strength of the German minorities.

## Hegemony and Containment of Germany: Future Opportunities and Risks

Having compared the unification of 1990 with the history of the
German *Reich* from Bismarck to Hitler, it seems reasonable to conclude
that the chances that the old dream of a united Germany will not this
time become a nightmare for Europe are better than ever before. Although the venerable Norbert Elias concluded, in 1985, that the continuity of national behavioural traditions was "much more fragmented" in
the case of the Germans "than in that of most other nation-states,"[30]
there is, of course, no guarantee that this will remain so in the future.
At that time, the Federal Republic was not a nation-state but a state
with partial sovereignty, occupying the front-line in the conflict between East and West. In what follows, an attempt will be made to
assess the potential political effects of the changes and shifts that have
resulted from the epoch-making turning-point in 1989/90. Since no one
can foresee the future, it goes without saying that the following
judgements are hypothetical in character. But the inevitability of this
has to be accepted by anyone venturing more in the way of concrete
analysis than is demanded by all those who confidently believe they can
simply extend the FRG into the future, or insinuate that there will be a
definite return to the "Faustian soul" and thus also to the *incertitudes
allemandes*, or indeed to a "Fourth *Reich*."

The history of the Federal Republic is unquestionably one of the
happiest periods of German history. The parliamentary democracy imposed by the occupation powers after Germany's unconditional capitulation gradually won wide acceptance amongst the German population -
- not least because the "economic miracle" brought a marked improvement in their standard of living. The anti-democratic and anti-western
reservations that prevailed amongst Germany's social and political
élites and had smoothed the way for National Socialism in 1933 were

no longer a handicap in the case of the Bonn democracy. It has more to rely on than on the compulsory, as it were, republicans of the Weimar democracy -- at that time dubbed *Vernunftrepublikaner* or "rational republicans."

Yet 40 years is but a short period in history. The Bonn democracy has never been shaken by a profound economic and political crisis -- a fact which in itself precludes comparison with Weimar. With unification, however, this may change. The process of unification is burdened from the outset with the problematic legacy of the GDR. What I mean by this is not so much the dire economic situation or the catastrophic ecological state but the almost incalculable socio-psychological effects of an authoritarian state socialism which, despite certain differences -- and they were considerable ones -- none the less promoted and rewarded established behavioural attitudes based on a long tradition of obedience to state authority: integration of the individual into collective bodies regulated by the state, omnipresent surveillance, the tendency to kow-tow or to go along with the crowd. Republican virtues such as individualism, standing up for one's beliefs, and spirited defence of one's own opinion were frowned upon, or indeed were regarded as suspect. The economic and constitutional integration of the GDR into the Federal Republic is one thing; the democratization and republicanization of the east Germans is another. The latter will no doubt take decades to complete. Tendencies to nationalist populism and authoritarianism in the other states previously belonging to the real-socialist camp at any rate point to a number of potential imponderables in the development of eastern Germany as well.

Federal Republican foreign policy is characterized by a high degree of effort and skill at holding together divergent, or indeed contradictory, interests. Thus, despite conflicting pretensions on the French side, Franco-German co-operation has never called into question the close Atlantic ties of the FRG to the United States; similarly, the renowned *Ostpolitik* initiated by Willy Brandt took meticulous pains to ensure its anchorage in the West. What is, comparatively, a strikingly high degree of willingness to engage in multilateralism and supranationalism -- grounded to a considerable extent in the international sensitivity to the "German question" -- has been dubbed "the German vision."[31] It did a lot also to propel the development of the European Community -- a fact reflected in the popular metaphor which has the FRG as an economic and political engine driving the process of integration.

All this is uncontentious. What is questionable, however, is the claim, often encountered in German politics and political science, that the foreign policy pursued by united Germany share the same basic characteristics as Federal German foreign policy. It has been said that "out of the *shadows* of an expansionist past" the FRG had "seized the *chance* of rehabilitation through integration and was transformed from a power-oriented *Saul* to an interdependence-oriented *Paul.*"[32] How far this observation, apposite to the Federal Republic, will remain true in the future has yet to be revealed. Wishful thinking is no substitute for analysis and reflection. The fact of the FRG's acting as a motor to integration, and of Franco-German co-operation's functioning somewhat like a two-headed Western European *fédérateur* was part of a specific set of conditions. There have been frequent analyses of how the European idea managed to become a substitute for the ruined nation in Western Germany. For the defeated, nationally divided, and only partially sovereign West Germans, the handing-over of competencies was no great feat. It was bound to be more difficult for the European nation-states who had not destroyed their own sovereignty: as is well known, even the anti-Fascist resistance movements who contributed to the restitution of the states subjugated by the Axis powers almost always assumed a national form.

In addition, other -- external -- circumstances had favoured European integration. For one thing, East-West confrontation disciplined the Europeans. The iron bipolarity that prevailed under the nuclear sword of Damocles superimposed itself on, and tended to level out, old European rivalries. The perceived threat presented by a Soviet power that had advanced as far as Berlin welded the Europeans together, and the undisputed hegemony of the United States after 1945 resulted in the Western Europeans' making the leap beyond the long historical shadow of their old national conflicts. The world war unleashed by the Third *Reich*, and the resultant rise of the two semi-European peripheral powers to the status of superpowers had, after all, diminished the importance of all the European states. That Britain and France -- not to mention Portugal, Belgium, and others -- were still great colonial empires in 1945 in no way belies this state of affairs: indeed, it found fulfilment in the rapid process of decolonization. Finally, the approximate balance -- if not military, then at least demographic, territorial, and, given the "economic miracles" experienced by the two vanquished states, economic -- between France, Britain, Italy, and the FRG also acted as an aid to integration.

But all the factors cited here -- Europe as a substitute identity in divided Germany, the antagonism between East and West, the fear of the Soviet Union, the hegemony of the United States, and the approximate balance between the four great Western European nations -- were thrown into disarray by the political earthquake that occurred in 1989/90.

It is conceivable that the enlarged Federal Republic will continue to be the driving force of the European Community, as is the declared aim of the Kohl Government. However, there are a number of indications that, following the disintegration of the frame of reference within which European politics had operated for decades, the proposed, but by no means fully realized, process of political integration will bring with it a re-emergence of differences in national interest. The differences that arose during the Gulf War, and the publicly conducted disputes about the right policy to adopt in regard to Yugoslavia, are not the only indications that particular interests and interpretations of history are acquiring greater significance. There is also great variation in western European readiness to give assistance to, and co-operate with, those states that formerly made up "Eastern Europe" -- let alone accept these states into the Community. Should these dissonances and controversies intensify, they could put the EC to the test as never before. As far as the EC countries are concerned, the task of squaring the circle consists in themselves having to forgo national competencies in favour of integration, in order to keep the German giant firmly bound into the Community. Even if one assumes that the mass of integration achieved to date is hardly reversible, one can none the less imagine scenarios in which the economic predominance of the German economy and the DM[33] might reinforce the desire elsewhere to slow down the dynamic of integration or to offset German economic hegemony with military counterweights -- something that would severely shake German euphoria and support for the EC.

These are admittedly scenarios, nothing more. Yet although the European nation-states are no longer able, in the nuclear age, to fulfil their classical functions, they are nevertheless "still strong enough," under certain circumstances, to "thwart the development of an effective supranational European policy."[34] Viewed from this angle, the widespread optimism about integration takes as much of a knock as does the alleged definitive transformation from "Saul" to "Paul."

With the end of military bipolarism, NATO, though not perhaps necessarily losing its *raison d'être*, has none the less undoubtedly lost some of its internal cohesion, given that the threat which it addressed -- whether real or imagined, this is of no relevance here -- has now disappeared. According to a much-quoted *bon mot* of Lord Ismay's, NATO's first Secretary-General, the organization initially had a threefold task: "to keep the Americans in, to keep the Russians out and to keep the Germans down." Little by little, the ever-present but seldom so bluntly expressed goal of keeping the Germans under control militarily disappeared behind that of containing the Soviet Union. But now it is re-emerging. If, despite all the upheavals in Europe, not one of the sixteen member-states wishes to alter the North Atlantic Treaty, it is because that treaty is the only means of guaranteeing that the United States continues to be politically and militarily involved in Europe and that German hegemony is kept under control.

It was on this concern -- present in equal measure in Western and Eastern Europe -- that all the proposals that Germany be neutralized which the Soviet Union made at the time of the 1989/90 turning-point ultimately foundered. Unification and a pan-German army in a sovereign Germany were only acceptable internationally because Germany remains contained by NATO, with its international command-structure. However, the more candidly the nub of the matter is laid bare, as efforts are made to transform NATO from a military into a political alliance, following the demise of its counterpart, the more easily a mood of rejection of this "singularization," and above all of the stationing of foreign troops on German soil, may start to spread. Approval of the Atlantic Alliance is in any case naturally much less strong in eastern Germany.[35] But even in the west -- and by no means in dissident circles, but at the political centre -- NATO is declared to be a "moribund model," and people openly voice their dream that it might be replaced by a "classical alliance" -- in other words "with no large-scale troop-deployments on foreign territory."[36]

To have overcome not so much the "special path" but the long tradition of German ideologies that propounded a special anti-western consciousness was one of the greatest achievements of the Federal Republic. The FRG was in the process of evolving something in the nature of a post-national "constitutional patriotism" (the term was coined by Dolf Sternberger but has been widely adopted) as a self-image for Federal Germany. Although the desire for reunification used to crop up in all the polls, with time it lost a good deal of its intensity and priority, whilst the West Germans' awareness of their identity became increasingly firmly established.[37]

In assessing whether the constitutionally based German *Staatsbürgernation* (in the Western sense) will be able, even after unification, to oppose the renaissance of a pre-political, ethnically based nation, one has to consider the radically changed conditions that now prevail. Whereas the dominant self-image of two German front-line states was defined in socio-political and ideological terms -- namely as a negative demarcation from National Socialism as well as from each other -- the restitution of a German nation-state will bring with it a tendency for the

German self-image to pick up national threads. And this will happen not just because Germany is once again in possession, and legitimately so, of something of which it was so long deprived, namely the "normality" of a nation-state; to put it thoroughly prosaically, it will also happen because the unification of two systems which were like "fire and water" -- as the former GDR leader was fond of remarking -- constitutes a completely novel experiment and will of necessity turn the attention of the Germans inwards. Official unification has, of course, already taken place. But the moulding of a nation has not even really begun, be it in respect of the equalization of living-conditions or in regard to mentalities or forms of behaviour. For the time being, Germany remains split into *Wessis* and *Ossis*. Overcoming this divide also implies a change in the Federal Germans' image of themselves.

There are numerous indications that unification will bring with it an increase in national allusions. The Brandenburg Gate, the monument to Prussian-German national history, which for years was a symbol of German division, seemed to become the navel of the world for whole months during 1989/90: it was at their feet that the seal was set on the collapse of the GDR and thus also on the restitution of the nation. There is no question but that the connection between the world war unleashed by Germany and the division of that country was not a simple one; but "German acceptance of the division of Germany had a lot to do with a widespread feeling of guilt and expiation."[38] In Germany, the Wall was a scar from the past, at its most visible in Berlin. It has now healed over. As a result, collective consciousness of the significance of 1933 will recede. Despite the jubilation of the mass media in particular, there was little national euphoria in the Federal Republic; nevertheless, it was possible to detect some subcutaneous shifts in attitude. After the hypostatization of the German nation by the National Socialists, the national and all its symbols were delegitimized and discredited. They were tabooed and scorned to a much greater extent in Germany than elsewhere -- despite the activities of football fans and the efforts of the SED to create a national basis for the GDR's existence as a state. That attitude has now been broken. The T-shirts that were hastily brought on to the market on the day after the Wall was opened up, and which bore the legend "9 November -- I was there" may have been no more than a peripheral phenomenon, but they were a significant one: the unexpected and joyful events of 1989 superimposed themselves on the indelible historical fact which had up to then been associated with the 9 November: the so-called *Kristallnacht*.

The debate about the location of the German capital also acquired a symbolic character, causing a remarkable churning-up of passions. The

fact that Bonn, village-like heart of Adenauer's state and nub of political modesty, lost the contest, brought about a general realization, in
west Germany as well, that the old FRG was a thing of the past. Willy
Brandt summed up the decision as a "national signal": since Germany
was no longer "the eastern edge of the West" but had become "the new
centre of Europe," Berlin, he said, was a good location. Then he said:
"In France, incidentally, no one would have thought of staying on in
the idyllic location of Vichy when there was no longer any foreign
force blocking the return to the capital city on the Seine."[39] That an experienced and historically sensitive statesman like Willy Brandt --
whose act of going down on his knees in the Warsaw Ghetto is regarded to this day as a token of the credibility of a morally reformed
Germany -- should have lighted upon such a tasteless comparison points
to certain shifts in the German public self-image. Up to now, public
appearances by representatives of the state were inevitably dominated
by references to the "twelve brown years;" attempts to get out of this --
such as Helmut Kohl's Bitburg appearance in 1985, or Philip Jen-
ninger's bungled commemorative speech on 9 November 1988 -- provoked violent debates about the past, a past which can never fade. This
is now beginning to change; the historical and political perspective is
shifting away from the question of how 1933 was possible, towards
1945. How else could one explain Brandt's comparison other than by
assuming that from the standpoint of recovered unity, the two German
states, GDR and FRG, sink, *post festum*, to the status of mere political
constructs of the victorious powers -- "licensee states," as it were, or
even, like Vichy, collaborationist regimes. A fatal trend, since it threatens, precisely, to play down both the historic break in German continuity and the greatest achievements of the Federal Republic.

Germany's conduct in the Gulf War has also been interpreted as a
historic break, in the (often unconscious) sense of a return of national
experiences and models of interpretation of reality:[40] the relentless re-
petition of the view that war must no longer be an instrument of politics
determined the behaviour of both the political class and the public in
Germany. Under the pressure of the widespread antipathy to a war,
Bonn behaved in a strikingly ambivalent manner in regard to the troop-
deployments and ultimately also the counter-offensive initiated by the
alliance of twenty-eight states empowered by the United Nations and
clustered around the United States. On the one hand, Germany provided logistical -- and financial -- assistance without which operation
"Desert Shield" would scarcely have been possible, and thus made a
more significant contribution than many other participants. On the other
hand, however, the Federal Government shrank for a long time from

justifying this involvement in public. The Federal Government's equivocal attitude to the collective UN-sanctioned defence against Saddam Hussein's aggression was bound to cause that much more confusion in that it was accompanied by a passionate, emotional rejection of the US-led military coalition by a protesting public that encompassed broad sections of the population.

Yet this "war is war" equation, which in Germany reached far beyond this particular milieu, right into the centre of politics and public opinion, overlooks -- or belies -- two things: first, the profound difference that obtains here, in that the wars conducted by Germany during this century were the extreme expression of an uncontrollably aggressive policy aimed solely at expansion and the extension of national power, whereas in 1991, the United States had precisely the opposite aim, namely to prove by way of example that the unscrupulous invasion and immediate annexation of a state cannot be accepted at any price if the international system of states, now no longer dominated by bipolarism, is to be controlled and tamed, and is not to fall back into Hobbes's "natural state." Secondly, we do also after all owe our liberation from the German *Herrenrasse* mania for world power to a war, about the justness of which there is little room for doubt. Taken together with anti-American feelings and identification with the victim -- who was in reality the perpetrator -- this widespread equation of the Gulf War with Germany's own experiences of war -- an equation involving the repression of historical fact -- is apt, if not to perturb previous certainties in regard to the westernization of political culture in the Federal Republic, then at least to play down their importance.

The restoration of a Germany constituted as a nation-state, and the tendency once again to revert to a context of national tradition is in line with the renaissance of the national that is taking place all over the East, and which, in many places, has long since mutated into militant nationalism. Ralf Dahrendorf has recently bemoaned the collapse of "heterogeneous nation-states" as a retrograde step and has noted a "curious and disquieting process . . . which one would have to describe as a reversion to type." However, Dahrendorf, like that pope of anti-totalitarianism, Karl Popper, reminds us that the tribalistic ideal has never led to freedom but more to "inquisition, secret police, and a romanticized gangsterism."[41] Indeed, indications of a flare-up of nationalism at the right-hand edge of the political spectrum are on the increase in the new Germany as well. The stream of bloody attacks on refugee centres that have taken place since October 1991 are the writing on the wall.

If one is to draw an interim conclusion from all these considerations, then it can only be this: despite all the profound and promising differences between the German unification that took place in 1990 and earlier events, it is by no means a foregone conclusion that Germany will actually prove to be that stable, predictable contributing factor to peace in Europe that it is made out to be in official rhetoric and in the analyses of many political scientists, who have all too rashly extrapolated the experiences of the old FRG. As I have tried to show here, considerable doubt may justifiably be cast on the reality and predictive value of this picture of the now more powerful Germany as basically no more than an extension of the old FRG -- a picture reassuring both to those who project it and to others. The truth is rather that the situation is a historically open one. The end of the East-West conflict has given Europe -- of which Germany, as is well known, considers itself to be the heart -- a new chance. At the same time, it has opened up the *Pandora's* box of old European problems and diseases.

## Notes

1. Fritz Stern, "Die zweite Chance. Die Wege der Deutschen.," *Frankfurter Allgemeine Zeitung (FAZ)*, July 26, 1990.
2. As quoted in Wolf Lepenies, "Erinnerung an einen Glücksfall. Das neue Selbstbewußtsein der Deutschen könnte die bewährte Aufgabenteilung mit Frankreich im Prozeß der Einigung Europas gefährden," *FAZ*, February 24, 1990.
3. According to Ulrich Wickert, the talk of a "revolution" in the GDR slots into the traditional repression of history: "The Germans are once again beginning to lie their way out of their history: they are declaring something to be a revolution that was the result of a collapse of the Eastern bloc, a collapse of which the Germans took advantage without really having made any revolutionary contribution to it -- though people in Germany would like it to have been that way, and thus provide them with an alibi." Preface to Ulrich Wickert (ed.), *Angst vor Deutschland* (Hamburg: Hoffmann und Campe, 1990), p. 18.
4. The words of the *Charter for a New Europe*, agreed at the grandiose CSCE summit held in Paris in November 1990; reproduced in *FAZ*, November 22, 1990.
5. In September 1990, the blunt remarks made by the British Secretary of State for Industry, Nicholas Ridley, cost him his job. On this, see also the minutes -- not intended for publication -- of the meeting of experts on Germany called by the British Prime Minister at Chequers, as published in *Der Spiegel*, July 16, 1990; see also Wilhelm von Sternburg (ed.), *Geteilte Ansichten über*

*eine vereinigte Nation. Ein Buch über Deutschland* (Frankfurt/M: Anton Hain, 1990).

6. Richard Rosecrance, *Der neue Handelsstaat: Herausforderungen für Politik und Wirtschaft* (Frankfurt/M.: Campus 1987). This much-discussed theory would appear not to be entirely new: "The consolidation of the absolutist princely state meant that, from the mid seventeenth century, a sharper distinction began to be made between the internal and external power of the state, and that in political calculations, as much importance -- indeed greater importance during the relatively peaceful eighteenth century -- was attached to the latter as to the development of external power." Karl-Georg Faber, "Macht, Gewalt," in: O. Brunner, W. Conze, R. Koselleck (eds.), *Geschichtliche Grundbegriffe. Historisches Lexikon zur politisch-sozialen Sprache in Deutschland*, Vol.3 (Stuttgart: Klett-Cotta, 1982), p. 878.

7. On this, see, as a representative text, Heleno Sana *Das Vierte Reich. Deutschlands später Sieg* (Hamburg: Rasch und Röhring, 1990). Not only does the title play down the horrors of the Third *Reich*; Sana's argumentation is influenced in the crudest fashion by ethno-psychological stereotypes devoid of any relation to concrete social realities and changes.

8. Dan Diner, *Der Krieg der Erinnerungen und die Ordnung der Welt* (Berlin: Rotbuch, 1991), p. 56. Symptomatic of this sort of denial of reality is the fact that at the preparatory conference for the present work, held in February 1991, certain colleagues from the PRIF hotly disputed the evidence of an "increase in power" for Germany as a result of unification; symptomatic too is Volker Rittberger's explicit tabooing of the term "power" *per se*: "Therefore, in the context of western European integration, to raise the Federal Republic as an individual state to the rank of a "power" -- of whatever size -- must increasingly appear an anachronism, an example of "outdated thinking" ("Die Bundesrepublik Deutschland -- eine Weltmacht?," *Aus Politik und Zeitgeschichte*, No. 4-5, January 19, 1990, p. 17). The author intends this as a counter to advocates of a new German power-politics but is misled into supposing that potential harm can be warded off by means of a little terminological magic.

9. Eberhard Schulz, "Die Doppelkrise im Baltikum und am Golf," *Europa-Archiv*, Vol. 46, No. 3, 1991, p. 78.

10. As stated by Christoph Bertram, "Der Riese, der ein Zwerg sein möchte," *Die Zeit*, April 26, 1991.

11. Hans-Joachim Veen, "Die Westbindung der Deutschen in der Neuorientierung," *Europa-Archiv*, Vol. 46, No. 2, 1991, p. 34; the same polemical approach was adopted by the pugnacious editor of *Merkur*, Karl-Heinz Bohrer, in a noted series of articles directed at the increasing tendency in Germany to "take refuge from international politics in the fairy-tale forest where no one will ever find us again except the good fairy come to tell us that world

peace has broken out." ("Provinzialismus," *Merkur*, No. 501, December 1990, p. 1100.)

12. From the title of a book by Hans-Peter Schwarz, Adenauer's biographer, *Die gezähmten Deutschen. Von der Machtbesessenheit zur Machtvergessenheit* (Stuttgart: Deutsche Verlagsanstalt, 1985). According to Schwarz, every tentative, power-politcs-eschewing endeavour, within foreign policy, to achieve harmonization is a reaction to Hitler's bloody but unsuccessful attempt to seize world power, and a reaction to the precarious security-situation in divided Germany; at the same time he believes such endeavours are consonant with the "wide-ranging interests of a global trading-power" (p. 33).

13. On this, see the brochure published by the Press and Information Service of the Federal Government entitled *Vertrag über die abschließende Regelung in bezug auf Deutschland* (Bonn, 1990).

14. On this, see my essay "Renaissance der Mitte -- ein fragwürdiger Bestandteil deutscher Ideologie kehrt wieder," in: Bruno Schoch (ed.), *Deutschlands Einheit und Europas Zukunft, Friedensanalysen No. 26*, (Frankfurt: Suhrkamp, 1992), pp. 118-27.

15. On this, see Reinhard Rode, *Deutschland: Weltwirtschaftsmacht oder überforderter Euro-Hegemon?* HSFK-Report No. 1, 1991; also Reinhard Büscher and Jochen Homann, Japan und Deutschland. Die späten Sieger? (Zürich: Interfromm, 1990).

16. Thus in 1989 Alain Minc argued, in an almost naïvely traditionalist way, that "In comparison with the Federal Republic, with a birth-rate of 1.1 or 1.2. children per woman, France, with a rate between 1.8 and 1.9, will appear almost to have a prolific birth-rate. At the beginning of the twenty-first century France will, demographically, be the strongest European power -- a position which it lost during the eighteenth century. Its economic importance will also increase accordingly." *Die deutsche Herausforderung. Wird die Bundesrepublik den europäischen Binnenmarkt beherrschen?* (Hamburg: Hoffmann und Campe, 1989), p. 177. One need scarcely add that the 3 October 1990 must have come as a shock to anyone with this point of view.

17. The speech was reproduced in *FAZ*, May 31, 1989. President Bush's term "partner in leadership" was quoted, not without a degree of pride, by the Federal Chancellor during a parliamentary debate as early as 16 June 1989.

18. See the special issue of *Sowjetunion heute*, June 1989, p. 9.

19. On this, see the informative survey by Rudolf Witzel, "Der Niedergang Amerikas -- Mythos oder Realität? Zur Selbstverständnisdebatte in den USA," in Bernd W. Kubbig (ed.), *Transatlantische Unsicherheit. Die amerikanisch-europäischen Beziehungen im Umbruch* (Frankfurt: Fischer, 1991), pp. 105-24.

20. On this, see Alfred Grosser in Ulrich Wickert, (*op. cit.* in note 3), p. 151; also Walther Stützle, "Auf dem Weg zu einer neuen europäisch-ameri-

kanischen Sicherheitsstruktur," in: W. Weidenfeld and W. Stützle, *Abschied von der alten Ordnung* (Working paper 5, Gütersloh: Bertelsmann Stiftung, 1990), p. 21.

21. Ingo Kolboom, "Die Vertreibung der Dämonen: Frankreich und das vereinte Deutschland," *Europa-Archiv*, Vol. 46, No. 15-16, 1991, p. 471. As late as the end of 1989, François Mitterrand, when visiting Leipzig and Kiev, had stressed, with regard to Germany, that German unity was not a matter that concerned the Germans only; it also concerned the guarantor powers, who had to assure European equilibrium.

22. As quoted in Thomas Schmid, *Staatsbegräbnis. Von ziviler Gesellschaft* (Berlin: Rotbuch, 1990), p. 79. Alfred Grosser has always said almost the same thing about France's attitude, see the article by him in Ulrich Wickert (ed.), (*op. cit.* in note 3), p. 142.

23. *Der Spiegel*, July 16, 1990.

24. Nikolai Portugalov, "Der Dornenweg zur Weltmacht," *Der Spiegel*, October 8, 1990, pp. 187-90.

25. First-rate information on the continuity of this from Wilhelminism to Hitler's *Lebensraum*-inspired imperialism is provided in Bernd Martin's most recent work *Weltmacht oder Niedergang? Deutschlands Großmachtpolitik im 20. Jahrhundert* (Darmstadt: Wissenschaftliche Buchgesellschaft, 1989).

26. Information on the gradual transition from Federal German revisionism to acceptance of the GDR may be found in Gert Krell, "Die Ostpolitik der Bundesrepublik Deutschland und die deutsche Frage," *Aus Politik und Zeitgeschichte*, No. 29, July 13, 1990; and in Hans-Joachim Spanger, *The GDR in East-West Relations*, Adelphi Papers No. 240, (London: IISS, 1989).

27. William Pfaff, *Die Gefühle der Barbaren. Über das Ende des amerikanischen Zeitalters* (Frankfurt: Eichborn, 1989), p. 148.

28. Gordon A. Craig, *Über die Deutschen* (München: Beck, 1982), p. 15.

29. To cite only a few examples: Alexander Abusch, *Der Irrweg einer Nation* (Berlin: Aufbau-Verlag, 1946); Friedrich Meinecke, *Die deutsche Katastrophe. Bemerkungen und Erinnerungen* (Wiesbaden: Brockhaus, 1946); and Ernst Niekisch, *Deutsche Daseinsverfehlung* (Berlin: Aufbau-Verlag, 1946).

30. Norbert Elias, *Humana conditio. Beobachtungen zur Entwicklung der Menschheit am 40. Jahrestag eines Kriegsendes (8. Mai 1985)* (Frankfurt/M.: Suhrkamp, 1985), p. 58.

31. On this, see the chapter by Mary Hampton in: Bruno Schoch (ed.) (*op.cit.* in note 14), pp. 301-24.

32. Thus Volker Rittberger (*op. cit.* in note 8), p. 17; (italics in original).

33. "According to a prominent British currency-expert, national sovereignty consists in the British national bank's being able to wait five minutes before it falls in line with the decisions of the Bundesbank." Klaus Hänsch, "Erweiterung und Vertiefung sind nicht vereinbar. Die EG in einer gesamteu-

ropäischen *géometrie variable*," *Blätter für deutsche und internationale Politik*, Vol. 36, No. 6, 1991, p. 688.

34. Aptly summed up by Peter Glotz, *Der Irrweg des Nationalstaats. Europäische Reden an ein deutsches Publikum* (Stuttgart: Deutsche Verlagsanstalt, 1990), p. 169.

35. On this, see the poll-findings in Hans-Joachim Veen, "Die Westbindung der Deutschen in der Neuorientierung," *Europa-Archiv*, Vol. 46, No. 2, 1991, pp. 31-40.

36. This was the view expressed by *Die Zeit's* chief editor Theo Sommer, in a leader: "Zapfenstreich für den Atlantikpakt?," *Die Zeit*, October 25, 1991; another interesting feature is the difference between support for NATO, which showed no significant decline up to autumn 1990, standing at almost 60 per cent (cf. Hans-Joachim Veen, *op. cit.* in note 11, p. 32) and the growing support for a withdrawal of American troops, see Ronald D. Asmus, *German Unification and its Ramifications* (Santa Monica, Ca.: Rand, 1991), p. 75.

37. Cf. the cautious interpretation by Irma Hanke: "Experiment Deutschland oder: Ein neues deutsches Nationalgefühl?," *Deutschland Archiv*, Vol. 24, No. 2, 1991, p. 157.

38. Heinrich August Winkler, "Das Ende der Nachkriegszeit," in Wilhelm von Sternburg (*op. cit.* in note 5), p. 271.

39. Willy Brandt speaking in the Bundestag, during the debate on the location of the German capital; as quoted in *Das Parlament*, June 18, 1991.

40. On this, see Dan Diner (*op. cit.* in note 8), pp. 37-80; see also his polemical article "Den Westen verstehen. Der Golfkrieg als deutsches Lehrstück," *Kursbuch*, No. 104, June 1991, pp. 143-53.

41. Ralf Dahrendorf, "Politik. Eine Kolumne. Europa der Regionen?," *Merkur*, Vol. 45, No. 509, August 1991, p. 704.

# 9

# Moscow and Bonn: From Confrontation to Partnership

*Aleksandr Kokeev*

From the end of World War II to the collapse of the USSR in December 1991, Soviet-German relations played a key role in Moscow's foreign policy. And Russia, the dominant member in the new Commonwealth of Independent States, seems intent on nurturing this special relationship. Not only has this to do with a rather complex historical legacy but also with the increasing economic and political weight of the new Federal Republic of Germany in European affairs, in the EC and NATO. And not least it also has to do with the mutual and highly specific interests stemming from German reunification.

It is hardly possible to exaggerate the significance of the peaceful settlement of the German question at the end of 1990 and the resulting qualitatively new dimension of bilateral relations. This was one of the most sensitive issues in modern European and world politics, and, had it not been successfully resolved, all reflections on a new European peace order would have remained pure theory. German reunification is bound to have a great impact on international relations. No doubt, the impact of German reunification on European and world affairs can already be felt, and, in the coming years, it is expected to shape the policy toward Germany of the successor states to the former Soviet Union. This is all the more true since the definitive collapse of the erstwhile Eurasian superpower called the Soviet Union and its succession by a (probably ephemeral) Commonwealth of Independent States has not only left a vacuum but has also increased the relative weight of unified Germany in European affairs.

The last obstacles on the road to German unity were removed during the difficult and intensive but fairly rapid "Two-plus-Four" talks, which concluded on September 12, 1990, in Moscow with the signing of the Treaty on the Final Settlement on Germany by the foreign ministers of the United States, the Soviet Union, Britain, France, and West and East Germany. The mutual interests of the direct participants in these talks, as well as those of other states, formed the basis of this document, which opened a new era in both German and European history. The decisive breakthrough, however, had been reached two months earlier during talks between President Mikhail Gorbachev and Chancellor Helmut Kohl in Moscow and in Zheleznovodsk, a spa in the Caucasus Mountains. In a Europe that had undergone cardinal changes, the complex Soviet-German relations had found a new quality. It was expressed in agreements putting an end to what will go down in history as the Cold War: "On the eve of the day when 45 years earlier the Potsdam conference had begun, Mikhail Gorbachev finally renounced the Yalta settlement. The Second World War has really ended, at last. The Soviet Union has made peace with Germany."[1]

## Soviet Relations with Divided Germany

The stormy process of German reunification and its formal completion have revived the argument about who was responsible for the division of Germany, "missed chances," and "retribution for mistakes of the past." Without going into all the details of this admittedly important discussion, it should be noted that, in the early stage of post-war German history (1949-52), the Soviet Union did not proceed from the assumption (which took root only later) that the division of Germany into two states corresponded to the best interests of the USSR and ensured security in Europe. At the time, the Soviet Union advocated the preservation of German unity, and it was only later that it called for an official seal to the division of the country. The best-known example of this is the Soviet diplomatic note of March 10, 1952, to its Western partners, in which the reunification of Germany was proposed on conditions of its not becoming a member of any coalitions or military alliances.

It is quite possible that, having strengthened Soviet influence over Eastern Europe, Stalin was also conscious of the inherent danger of a long-term division of Europe resulting from a sundered Germany, and of the concomitant isolation of the USSR in its confrontation with the West. Stalin's German policy (e.g., the "Sovietization" of East Germany and the Berlin blockade of 1948) was in no way farsighted, however. It only triggered fierce reactions on the part of the Western powers. Besides, even if the Soviet dictator's diplomatic note had not been mere tactics, "unification on such conditions and under those circumstances would have been a risky option for the Soviet Union, for the West and even for the Germans themselves."[2] For obvious reasons, the creation of two German states at the end of the 1940s was inevitable because, at the time, Germany "had been a function of relations between the occupation powers, a function of the Cold War between them."[3]

In the opinion of many observers, one of the main blunders of Adenauer's policy of reunification in the 1950s was his overestimation of German possibilities and the attitude of the NATO allies. While officially supporting the aim of German reunification, they were not exactly striving for its realization. According to two German authors, F.W. Hanrieder and H. Rühle, "the Adenauer policy of dealing from a position of strength actually resulted in the exact opposite of what it was meant to achieve: Instead of becoming more pliable, the position of the Soviets had become more inflexible"[4] and as history has shown, it was to remain so for quite a while.

Toward the end of the first half of the 1950s, the Soviet Union embarked on its "two German states" policy, which, among other things, was reflected in its readiness to establish diplomatic relations with Bonn. From that time on, the USSR began to advocate both the definite recognition of the territorial status quo in Europe and its political and contractual formulation -- a process that would not be completed until the early 1970s when the so-called *Ostverträge* and the Helsinki Final Act were signed. By then, as a result of major changes in the international political climate (especially on the continent), Bonn's foreign strategy, most particularly its Eastern component, had been substantially modified, and the place of the Soviet Union in it considerably enhanced.

On the question of reunification, the new *Ostpolitik* of the left-of-center coalition of Social Democrats and Free Democrats, inherited and developed to a considerable extent by the subsequent right-of-center government of Christian Democrats, Social Christians and Free Democrats, was based on the premise that German unity could be achieved only after the division of Europe had been ended. This explains the efforts undertaken at the time by West Germany to reduce as much as possible military and political tensions between the two blocs on the one hand, and to strengthen East-West détente on the other. One of the most consistent advocates of this course, the German foreign minister,

Hans-Dietrich Genscher, stressed in 1975: "We can only benefit if we contribute to the process of détente and reach such a situation of peace in Europe that the German people will achieve unity by self-determination."[5] Soviet-West German cooperation became the most important element of détente in the 1970s. In a comparatively short period of time, relations between the two countries acquired a solid foundation, and a high level of mutual confidence and understanding was achieved. Regular high-level meetings and consultations took place. They dealt not only with problems of bilateral relations but also with important international questions, primarily those connected with solving European problems. The volume of trade between the two nations also increased rapidly in the 1970s.

In the early 1980s, as a result of an overall deterioration in East-West relations and of the growing awareness among both East and West Germans that their respective territory might become the nuclear battlefield of the superpowers, Bonn began to reconsider many aspects of its traditional security policy. This was most clearly reflected in an active search for alternative strategies, including deep cuts in nuclear and conventional armaments, and in increasing public calls for a restructuring of the NATO and WTO armed forces on a defensive basis. West Germany, partly in cooperation with East Germany, became one of the most determined advocates of arms control and of extended East-West cooperation. The many outstanding differences in approach between the Federal Republic and the Soviet Union notwithstanding, more common points of view emerged than had ever been the case before. This applied in particular to admitting the necessity of negotiations and taking urgent and extensive measures on arms limitation. Among the many reasons for the serious obstacles on the road to concrete action in that realm was the deeply ingrained Soviet belief that security could be achieved by military means only. In addition, its "superpower attitude" toward its opponents in Western Europe (especially toward the Federal Republic), insufficiently acknowledging their standpoints and specific problems (and thus often justifying their misgivings), also played an important role in blocking progress.

It was not until 1985 and Mikhail Gorbachev, however, that the process of radical reforms in the political and social life of the Soviet Union, together with its "new thinking" in foreign policy, cleared the way for significantly closer and warmer relations between the two countries. In this process most of the dogmatic stereotypes such as the inevitable ideological confrontation or the international class struggle between the two antagonistic systems, gradually gave way to the principle of freedom of choice, to a recognition that in the modern world all countries are interdependent, and to a reappraisal of the role of military force in security matters.

The emerging "new thinking" in Soviet foreign policy considerably expanded the possibilities of West Germany's *Ostpolitik*, opening up new prospects for cooperation with the USSR in different fields. Besides, it came close to the views of a great many West German politicians on the desirable politico-military configuration of Europe and on a solution to the German question. This is why Mikhail Gorbachev's *perestroika* and "new thinking" were both met with close attention and an increasingly favorable response in Bonn. The opposition Social Democrats, however, were the first to realize which new vistas Mikhail Gorbachev's novel policies opened. Initially, the Bonn government, and particularly Chancellor Helmut Kohl, showed great caution and restraint. The chancellor even went so far as to compare Mikhail Gorbachev's new political thinking to Joseph Goebbel's propaganda efforts, thus relegating himself to the back of the line of those Western leaders then eager to meet with the new Kremlin chief.

Egon Bahr, then a member of the governing council of the Social Democratic Party, starkly demonstrated the Bonn political establishment's change in attitude when, as early as 1986, he noted in response to practical Soviet proposals on decreasing the level of military confrontation in Europe: "Reproaches that the Soviet positions at the negotiating table do not coincide with the public declarations of Mikhail Gorbachev have come to an end. These proposals are regarded as reasonable, interesting and suitable for negotiations."[6] After the general elections of 1987, Helmut Kohl, too, in his inaugural speech to the *Bundestag*, or parliament, stressed that "the Federal Republic attaches central importance to relations with the Soviet Union" and that "their strengthening and expansion correspond to the interests and desires of both countries."[7]

As a result of the talks between then-President Gorbachev and Chancellor Kohl in October 1988 in Moscow, and in June 1989 in Bonn, relations between the Soviet Union and the Federal Republic intensified considerably and began to acquire new features. The importance of those talks was reflected in the joint declaration of June 13, 1989, which, to a certain degree, complemented the Moscow treaty of August 1970. In the joint declaration, the Soviet Union officially pledged for the first time to respect the right of individuals and all peoples and states to self-determination, and to adhere to the main principles and norms of international law.[8] A total of 23 agreements between both states were signed during the October 1988 and June 1989 talks.

Several declarations of intent were also signed on those two occasions. They were aimed at facilitating cooperation in different fields of science and technology, in environmental issues and humanitarian questions.[9] In October 1988 a consortium of German banks headed by *Deutsche Bank* signed a 3 billion Deutsche Mark credit with the Soviet Union to modernize its consumer and textile industries. This was of special significance to the USSR at that early stage of *perestroika*. More important yet, during those talks, first contacts were established between the defense ministers of both countries.

## The Road to German Unification

Despite the fundamental shifts in Soviet domestic and (especially) foreign policy, and the breakthrough in relations with the Federal Republic, the position of the USSR on the German question remained unchanged up to the beginning of 1990. In his book "Perestroika and New Thinking," Mikhail S. Gorbachev himself set forth the Soviet position most clearly: "There are two German states with different political systems. They have their own values. Both of them have derived lessons from history and each of them can contribute to European and world affairs. What will happen in a hundred years, this is for history to decide."[10] Even after the fall of the Berlin wall as a result of the peaceful revolution in the GDR, Moscow, for quite some time, continued to proceed from the assumption that, in the interest of security and stability on the continent, two German states had to be maintained, though closely cooperating and with an open border. Only their demilitarization and the overcoming of the division of Europe would make their reunification possible. But the stormy and totally unforeseen pace of events in the now-defunct GDR, coupled with the rapid movement toward German unity, made it clear that any attempt to hinder this process would not only be doomed to failure but would also not serve anyone's interest, including the Soviets'. Consequently, the USSR was to change its position more than once.

Speaking before the political commission of the European Parliament in December 1989, the Soviet foreign minister, Eduard A. Shevardnadze, touched on a series of issues that, in his view, would have to be settled before German unification could be envisaged. The recognition of existing borders by a united Germany, its membership in military and political blocs, the size of its armed forces and the deployment of foreign troops on its territory were foremost among these. In February 1990, during a visit to Moscow by Hans Modrow, then East Germany's prime minister, the Soviet Union assented to his suggestion to move on from the originally proposed contractual community to a confederation and, eventually, a federation of the two German states. President Gorbachev confirmed this to Chancellor Kohl a few days later in a meeting the two men held in the Kremlin. In that meeting, agreement was also reached that the forms and time frame of German reunification would essentially be decided by the Germans themselves.[11] This was not only a modification but "a complete U-turn in the fundamental position of Moscow on German unity."[12] And yet the Soviet Union continued to emphasize that the question of German reunification concerned not only the Germans but all the peoples of Europe. A series of factors (historic, geopolitical, military-strategic) shaped the Soviet position (in terms of its natural interests) as to the form and conditions under which German reunification would be allowed to take place. It could not come about solely as the result of the interaction of the two German states but would also have to be part of a process in the context of international obligations and European cooperation. This fairly broad formula, with its many possible options, was to be tested in the course of subsequent Two-plus-Four talks.

On May 5, 1990, the first full session of the so-called Two-plus-Four talks (comprising the foreign ministers of the two Germanys and the four Allied powers Britain, France, the United States and the Soviet Union) was held in Bonn and produced an agreement on the agenda for the subsequent meetings. This included: (1) the borders of a future Germany ("Poland's western borders"), which would encompass the current area of West Germany, East Germany, and Berlin, "no more, no less;" (2) politico-military problems, with a view to creating a European security structure; (3) ending the Four Powers' authority over Berlin (the "Berlin question"); and (4) preparing under international law a settlement under which the four World War II Allies would terminate their rights and responsibilities for Germany and Berlin as a whole.[13] Initially, only "political-military questions" were mentioned in the second item. For the USSR, however, it was of great importance to envisage in this context the creation of pan-European security structures. As a compromise, the aforementioned formula was found. Overall, however, the readiness of the Soviet Union to compromise was typical of the whole course of Two-plus-Four negotiations. This made it possible to reach agreement on problems that initially had seemed intractable.

The question of the military and political status of a united Germany was most sensitive for the USSR and turned out to be the most controversial issue on the negotiating table. Up to the final stage of negotiations, the Soviet Union regarded the membership of a united Germany in NATO as unacceptable, as this would seriously affect its security interests and disturb the balance of forces on the continent. Proceeding from this, Moscow insisted at first on a reunification of Germany on the principle of neutrality, actually reverting to the position encapsulated in the "Stalin note." It then softened its position somewhat, proposing a dual membership of a reunited Germany in both military alliances -- an offer that actually was only an interlude and, in hindsight, can hardly be regarded as serious.

The fact that it took the Soviet Union quite some time to move beyond its traditional security paradigm can be explained both by the inertia of military-bloc thinking and by domestic-policy motives. For obvious reasons, such concepts as *Lebensraum im Osten* (territory in the East for political and economic expansion) and "German militarism" caused nightmares to the Soviet people (and still do to a great many peoples of the new republics), especially to the older generation, which remembered the Great Patriotic War and retained a definite influence, notwithstanding the cardinally changed situation in Europe. Apart from historic memories, the long-standing propaganda about imperialism, German revanchism or the threat from NATO came to bear, too. Fears of a possible disturbance in the balance of power in Europe caused by the reunification of Germany were reinforced by arguments connected with the loss of Eastern Europe after the revolutions there, and the growing nationality conflicts in the Soviet Union itself. It was feared that a reunited Germany would become the dominant power on the continent and that Eastern Europe (and possibly the Baltic states) would gravitate into its sphere of influence. As a result, the notorious German threat would raise its ugly head again on the western frontiers of a weakened Soviet Union. And finally, it was felt that the USSR would be giving away its spoils of war, for which more than twenty million of its people lost their lives.

Thus, Moscow saw itself confronted with the delicate task of having to tackle what by now had become inevitable. And it had to do so fairly rapidly and in a way that could not be challenged at home, for many popular stereotypes had to be discarded and many theretofore valid concepts revised. First of all, the idea of German reunification on the basis of neutrality was abandoned. For it had become clear that, under the circumstances, not only was it unrealistic to think that it could have been implemented, but also that, had this been feasible, it might have produced the least desirable outcome for the Soviet Union -- the emergence of a large and uncontrolled power center in the middle of Europe that might have become a source of tension and instability. Besides, the very concept of neutralism was becoming less and less applicable to the winding down of the Cold War.

One had to admit that the European balance of forces (as the Soviet Union had always understood it) no longer existed after the momentous changes in Eastern Europe, the Soviet troop withdrawals from there, and the disintegration of the Warsaw Pact. Under those changed circumstances, the principle of parity itself could no longer be seen as the basis for European stability. It had become obvious that, from this time on, stability on the continent would depend increasingly on the economic and sociopolitical developments in the Soviet Union itself and in Eastern Europe, and that abandoning confrontation would mean greater interdependence, particularly economic interdependence. Also, in military terms, the inclusion of a reunited Germany into NATO could not be construed as an additional threat to the security of the Soviet Union, which retained its nuclear-power status.

Thus, the question of NATO's future role now had to be answered before the issue of the military and political status of a reunited Germany could be addressed. Washington's decision in early 1990 to cut back its forces in Europe, withdraw most of its nuclear artillery shells and renounce modernizing its tactical nuclear weapons in Western Europe (as a first step toward negotiations on eliminating that category of arms altogether) was the first sign that more profound changes in NATO were afoot. This was confirmed at the NATO summit meeting held on July 5-6, 1991, in London, which Mikhail Gorbachev dubbed "a historic landmark in the development of NATO."[14] Although alliance leaders merely pointed to a change in NATO strategy, it remains significant that, in addition to military-political issues, they also discussed, at the urging of West Germany, ways of providing Western aid to the Soviet Union.

At that meeting, the alliance indicated its readiness to abandon its strategy of forward defense and to modify its nuclear "first use" option, thereby facilitating a transition to a new strategy involving serious troop cuts in areas close to its borders and less emphasis on nuclear arms. This was in fact the most important result of the London meeting for the Soviet Union. "It is believed in Moscow that NATO really took into account the interests of Soviet security and did not just resort to political cosmetics," a Soviet commentator wrote in the magazine *Novoe Vremya* ("New Time").[15] In Soviet eyes, the NATO proposal to work out jointly with the Warsaw Pact a document on the mutual renunciation of the use of force (which would be opened for signing to all participants in the CSCE) was of special importance. Among other things, this proposal showed that, in the foreseeable future, practical questions of security might be decided within European structures, within new organs and institutions untainted by bloc-confrontation thinking.

It was in this context that Chancellor Helmut Kohl and then-Soviet President Mikhail S. Gorbachev reached a compromise on the question of a united Germany's membership in NATO during their meeting of July 16, 1990, in the Caucasus Mountains. The so-called Genscher plan formed the basis of this compromise, the essence of which was that until all Soviet troops had left what was then East Germany (no later than the end of 1994), no NATO troops could be stationed there. And in addition any German deployments should be without delivery vehicles for nuclear warheads. It is difficult not to agree with those who view the situation flowing from this compromise not only as paradoxical but as rather "unnatural and even based on the instruments of yesterday."[16] It indeed left a number of questions unanswered, stressing instead the anachronism of the division of Europe into blocs -- which has proved even more short-lived than anyone could have expected at the time this was written. Still, it will be instrumental in creating new European security structures. It is here that Russian-German harmony can play an important and positive role, with both countries acting as bridgeheads over the former East-West divide.

As mentioned above, the agreement reached in Moscow and Zheleznovodsk by Kohl and Gorbachev laid the groundwork for the successful completion of the Two-plus-Four talks, which produced the Treaty on the Final Settlement on Germany. These are the most important aspects of the Kohl-Gorbachev accords: (1) Germany renounces any territorial claims over Poland; (2) its armed forces are to be reduced to 370,000 men over a period of three to four years, concurrently with the withdrawal of Soviet forces; and (3) it pledges to forgo both production and possession of weapons of mass destruction (nuclear, chemical and biological). Two documents on the legal status of Soviet military personnel stationed in the former East Germany and a so-called "transfer agreement" on financial issues were appended to the Soviet-German agreement. Having agreed that the withdrawal of the Soviet troops from the territory of the ex-GDR would be completed by the end of 1994, Mr. Kohl pledged 12 billion DM (plus a 3 billion DM interest-free loan) to Moscow to help ease the stationing, withdrawing and rehousing costs of those troops.[17]

On September 13, 1990, in Moscow, Hans-Dietrich Genscher, then German foreign minister, and Eduard A. Shevardnadze, at the time his Soviet counterpart, initialed a 20-year treaty on good neighborliness, partnership and cooperation between their two countries.[18] Not only did this treaty call for extensive cooperation in trade and technology between the two partners, but it also stipulated the conclusion by the then-Soviet Union of similar treaties with countries such as France and Italy. Most important, however, it layed down that neither side will use force against the other (nonaggression clause) and that both will "honor without reservation the territory of all European states in their current borders."

### A New Era in Bilateral Relations

Admittedly, the Soviet-German accords negotiated in Zheleznovodsk and Moscow not only aimed at achieving progress at the Two-plus-Four talks. It is rather natural that a great many people saw in them the "growing specific weight that a united Germany as well as German-Soviet relations would assume in Europe."[19] Not surprisingly, alarms about a Rapallo redux were raised in a number of Western capitals -- a recurring reaction among some Western allies whenever Germany shows interest in drawing closer to its giant Eastern neighbor, whether the Soviet Union yesterday or Russia today. Zheleznovodsk, however, was not Rapallo, the Italian site of the 1922 German-Soviet treaty.

Rapallo was an attempt by two political outcasts to overcome their political and economic isolation by exploiting contradictions among the powers of the day -- all in all, very much within the framework of traditional European political patterns. But today, Germany, far from being isolated, is firmly committed to European integration, the successor states to the former Soviet Union (i.e., Russia and, to a degree, the other non-Asian republics) are doomed to play a constructive role in building what only yesterday went by the name of the "common European home." Against this backdrop, Germany will play a crucial role both in the foreign-policy realm, as the central connecting link between East and West in Europe, and from an economic standpoint as a major source of support for the East European countries, Russia and some of the other successor states to the former Soviet Union in their painful transition from planned to market economies. Also, not only has Germany's integration in the Western community not been questioned, on the contrary, it has been affirmed and encouraged, in the politico-economic as well as in the military sense. "We enter a period of truly new relations with Germany, noted Eduard A. Shevardnadze, the last foreign minister of the defunct Soviet Union. Soviet-German cooperation is not directed against anybody. The period of playing off some European states against others by a game of alliances and intrigues should come to an end. Our aim is a Europe based on trust, unity and cooperation."[20]

This remains valid after the final collapse of the Soviet Union, too, though its rapid disintegration initially caused great irritation in Bonn. For Chancellor Helmut Kohl and Foreign Minister Hans-Dietrich Genscher would clearly have preferred to continue to deal with a center. But the process that led to fully independent states in place of the former Soviet republics made a reorientation of German policy all but inevitable. And it was not long in coming. One of the first manifestations of this reorientation was Foreign Minister Genscher's October 1991 trip to Alma-Ata and Kiev without his bothering to stop, even briefly, in Moscow. Russian President Boris N. Yeltsin's visit to Bonn on November 21-22, 1991, ushered in a new era for Russia (which, in German eyes, had always been overshadowed by the Soviet Union) in its relations with Germany. And, to be sure, these bilateral relations, resting as they do on the solid foundation of the treaties and accords signed between Bonn and Moscow over the last two years, can be strengthened and expanded.

*Security Concerns in a New Environment*

The Two-plus-Four treaty and the series of bilateral accords signed between the ex-Soviet Union and the old Federal Republic offer all the guarantees and spell out all the obligations mandated by the current situation in Europe. The reunification of Germany, resolving one of the most painful problems in the center of Europe, can but facilitate the likely transition to a new European order, the first outlines of which came into view at the CSCE summit meeting in Paris in November 1990.

The creation of new European security structures to replace the postwar military-political blocs will become the main task in this transitional process. For the ex-Soviet Union, which lost its East European "buffer zone" and sphere of influence when the Warsaw Pact was disbanded, this was a matter of special concern -- as it is now for Russia and Ukraine. It is assumed that the foundation of a new security system can be laid within the framework of the Helsinki process. This would require substituting collective security through Europe-wide cooperation for individual (or bloc) security based on ever increasing weapons arsenals. This, in turn, can only be achieved by the institutionalization of the CSCE, the beginning of which was marked by the Paris meeting.

There can be no doubt, however, that NATO, probably for quite some time yet, will remain the most viable and stable structure for ensuring security in Europe. It also goes without saying that, the more the old bloc (or bipolar) thinking yields to pan-European security concerns, the faster NATO will have to relinquish its exclusive role as guarantor of security (even for Western Europe). This might include NATO's evolving from a military-political into an increasingly political organization. Overall, however, such a shift in security thinking would no doubt facilitate cooperative efforts with Russia (and possibly other successor states) toward establishing Europe-wide security structures. A first sign of this might be seen in NATO's decision to reject, at least for the immediate future, the request of a number of former Warsaw Pact countries to be integrated into the alliance in order not to alienate Moscow. Bearing in mind the role of united Germany in NATO and the fact that it has shown particular sensitivity to Soviet concerns, Russian-German cooperation in particular could become a significant feature of the envisaged pan-European security set-up.

For Russia, apart from everything else, still has to reappraise many of its traditional concepts and come to a more adequate assessment of the changes taking place in Europe and in the world. Though Soviet-type conservatism has largely receded after the putsch of August 1991, giving way to radical changes, it is worth looking back on the foreign-policy debates at the XXVII Communist Party congress of June 1990, in the course of which charges of "unilateral concessions" and "surrendered positions" were leveled (not only by party functionaries) at the Soviet leadership. Similarly, the negative attitude toward the German settlement in some segments of Soviet society (especially among representatives of the army leadership and in the central-power apparatus) came into sharp relief during the debates on the Soviet-German agreements at the closed-door sessions of the Supreme Soviet of the USSR in March-April 1991. On the eve of that session, Lieutenant Colonel Nikolai Petrushenko, one of the leaders of the hard-line *Soyuz* parliamentary group, demanded in *Sovetskaya Rossiya*, a conservative newspaper, the rejection of ratification and the creation of a "special commission of the Supreme Soviet of the USSR, which, together with representatives of the Ministry of Foreign Affairs, would work out new positions for new negotiations."[21] Apart from such appeals, Petrushenko claimed that the authors of the agreements had reversed the results of World War II and harmed the political-military positions and interests of the Soviet Union abroad.[22] Unfortunately, such statements reflected not only a personal point of view but also a widely held opinion in politico-military circles.

Without wanting to engage in polemicizing with those who have been talking about the "loss of the GDR and Eastern Europe" (thereby trying to play on the fear of a "German threat" and throwing into doubt the value of the agreements on the external aspects of German reunification), the following should be said: Apart from the objective reasons for that double "loss," it is necessary to point out that it has not led at all to an increased military threat to the people of the former Soviet Union. First, over all the Cold War decades, the USSR alone, not the Warsaw Pact, was NATO's counterweight -- apart from the fact that it had to expend much effort on feeding its allies and keeping them obedient. This remains true despite the so-called sufficiency rule in the CFE treaty, which mandates much greater cutbacks in the armed forces of the ex-Soviet Union than in NATO's. Second, given their nuclear capabilities, Russia as well as Ukraine and Belarus can feel safe. Third, and most importantly, it is becoming clearer all the time that nobody has any intention of attacking the Soviet Union or its successor states and is hardly likely to do so in the foreseeable future. The risk of violent clashes now comes much more from inside the now-sovereign republics of the erstwhile Soviet Union than from the outside. Much more, in the wake of the disintegration of the former Soviet giant, it is foreign powers that have extended a helping hand in order to mitigate conflicts and preserve some form of central power such as that reflected in the creation of the Commonwealth of Independent States.

It must be noted, however, that, in the process of overcoming the confrontation between East and West, new threats to security have appeared. Their names: economic decline, poverty, ecological disasters, ethnic tensions and nationality conflicts. And against such threats the traditional instruments of military might do not work. In this connection, the processes currently under way in Eastern Europe are of special relevance to the security of both Russia and Germany. For the foreseeable future, neither the Commonwealth of Independent States nor Eastern Europe can be regarded as a stable region. The point is not that, having suffered defeat, the regimes that existed in the region and relied mainly on force have left a great many seemingly intractable problems. Against the background of general destabilization inherent in any transitional period, strong nationalist tendencies are emerging in the eastern part of Europe. In conditions of a sharpening economic crisis, this could lead to a flare-up of dormant nationality conflicts and contradictions in Europe. As a result, the balance between affirmation of national identity and an orientation toward a united Europe may be upset, thereby threatening stability on the whole continent. In this connection the strengthening of the German position in Europe, coupled with that country's resulting ability to bear on the processes in Eastern Europe, can be regarded as positive. Traditionally, it has always been Germany that has shown the greatest interest in the eastern part of the continent. In the past, this did much harm to many of the countries and peoples involved. In the present circumstances, however, Germany, in view of its potential as a great economic power, will decisively contribute to the economic and political rehabilitation of the East, the fundamental prerequisite for overcoming the division of Europe.

## *How to Deal with Obsolete Armed Forces*

Deep arms cuts in Europe constitute an additional condition for progress in the pan-European direction. The curtailment of the Soviet military presence in Eastern Europe, the dissolution of the Warsaw Pact and, not least, the convincing role played by major parts of the armed forces in August 1991 greatly influenced NATO's policies in general, Germany's in particular. That country's readiness to cut the total personnel strength of its *Bundeswehr* down to 370,000 was regarded in the USSR as a substantial contribution to the success of the first stage of the CFE talks in Vienna. As for the former Soviet Union itself, its position at those talks showed considerable contradictions, as it found it hard to shake off its predilection for traditional security concepts.[23] Its successor states, however, now have ample room for further reductions in their armed forces, whose size is hardly sustainable in present circumstances of economic crisis. The reunification of Germany and the withdrawal of all Soviet troops from its eastern part by the end of 1994 have also put on the agenda the question of cutting back the NATO forces stationed in its western part. Germany's NATO allies all have declared their intention to effect deep cuts in their armed forces stationed on its territory. According to the German defense minister of the time, Gerhard Stoltenberg, the total manpower of all foreign troops on the territory of both German states in 1988 was about 1.5 million. By 1995 this will be cut back to 500,000 as a result of the ceiling of 370,000 placed on German armed forces, the implementation of the CFE treaty and unilateral measures.[24] Very soon, the time in which Europe had the highest concentration of armed forces in the world, will belong to the past.

In this situation the further deployment of a large contingent of originally 380,000 (at the end of 1991, 210,000) Soviet troops on German territory seems to make little sense. It is obvious that the return home of altogether nearly 600,000 people (with family members and civilian personnel) poses considerable logistical, human and humanitarian problems, to whose solution Germany is mightily contributing. On the other hand, it is also clear that the deployment of such a large contingent on the territory of a sovereign member state of NATO, located in the center of Europe, causes a fair amount of anxiety -- and not only among the German leadership. Significantly, this is connected with a great many uncertainties about future political developments in the successor states to the former Soviet Union. Such developments may take the form of popular uprisings, right-wing takeovers, or of a renewed authoritarian or even totalitarian rule.

Besides, it should be remembered that the living environment for the soldiers of the former Soviet Army in Germany, i.e., the money at their disposal, the political situation outside the garrisons, and the whole moral and psychological atmosphere have changed completely. An ever-greater effort will be required from the military commanders, with a view to preserving discipline and order among the troops as stipulated in the withdrawal agreement. In addition, an increase in petty crime, instances of soldiers selling their weapons, and a rising desertion rate do not help to improve contacts between the troops and the German populace. This remains a rather demanding task anyway, all the more so in view of a widespread xenophobia and hostile feelings toward the former occupation forces among ordinary people in the eastern part of Germany.

As these problems threatened to complicate relations with the former Soviet Union, educational measures were taken by the German government and social organizations in eastern Germany to curb the growth of the prevailing hostile attitude toward the then-Soviet soldiers and to create a favorable social climate around them. Meetings of state and municipal authorities with garrison commanders, contacts between members of the *Bundeswehr* and the then-Soviet forces, and invitations of the latter to German families were organized to ease the atmosphere and to get to know one another better. And these arrangements are still in force today. As for the withdrawal as such, the most urgent problem today appears to be not so much that the relevant authorities in the former Soviet Union should speed it up but how quickly it will be possible to provide, with German assistance, appropriate housing facilities on the territory of the ex-USSR for 37,000 of the officers' families still stationed in Germany. More important yet, in light of the deep cuts in military personnel currently going on in the former Soviet Union itself, are the planned efforts to educate and retrain both officers and ranks in order to make them professionally competitive in the labor market at home.

Of course, the question of a possible acceleration of the withdrawal of those troops from Germany is not simple and has many aspects. It seems, however, that these can and will be tackled:

> Our troops could conceivably come back to the motherland earlier. Alas, how prosaic, especially material problems make this difficult! During the postwar years we got used to the fact that about a million soldiers and officers were abroad, forgetting that such a situation could no last forever. Now we have to pay for that.[25]

Besides, although the agreement on the withdrawal of the former Soviet troops from Germany formally does not touch upon the mission of NATO forces there, such connection apparently exists in practice. As Yuli Kvitsinsky, then the Soviet deputy foreign minister and a former ambassador to Bonn, said:

> In itself, the withdrawal of our troops from Germany creates such conditions that the Germans might start wondering why they should keep such large allied forces on their territory. Such musings will be fed by the further development of a pan-European architecture, the creation of new security structures.[26]

This brings us to the issue of nuclear arms on the continent. On September 2, 1991, the last Soviet defense minister (and current CIS defense minister), Marshal Yevgeni I. Shaposhnikov, said that all Soviet nuclear weapons had been withdrawn from eastern Germany, thereby fulfilling the terms of the Zheleznovodsk agreement on the withdrawal of those weapons from the former East Germany. On September 27, 1991, President George Bush announced the unilateral withdrawal of all ground-based tactical nuclear weapons -- missiles and artillery shells -- from Europe. The greatest threat to Germany has thus been removed, and the country had suddenly become a zone of deep military détente.

### Shifting Concerns: The German Role in
### Reconstructing an Economy in Deep Disarray

For decades, if not longer, Germany, both because of its past role and geographical situation in the center of Europe, was regarded by its neighbors first of all as a source of danger, to be contained by dividing the country or keeping it so. Obviously, reunification will, in the medium term, increase Germany's economic and political weight in the region. And this, in turn, will stir new apprehensions. Current developments in Europe, however, shows that this need not be the case, that today's Germany has every chance of becoming the key stabilizing factor in Europe, the bridge across the economic and political divide still cleaving the continent. According to Vladimir Baranovsky, this is because the specific "instruments of Germany's expansion will be business, finances, trade; the condition of its self-assertion, an expanded economic space; and its partners, increasingly the countries of the eastern part of the continent."[27] This is why the economic aspects of Germany's future relations with its eastern neighbors take on a special importance.

For Russia and the other members of the Commonwealth of Independent States -- confronted as they are with the unprecedented task of fundamentally transforming an already crumbling economy (and to do this under conditions of political transition and instability), while at the same time trying to find an appropriate place in the European network of economic cooperation -- it is most important to have in neighboring Germany a stable and strong economic partner, ready to provide assistance ranging from emergency aid to technical and financial support. Inherent difficulties notwithstanding, new opportunities will also arise for Germany, in that it will be able to intensify its activities in the emerging markets east of the Bug River.

In principle, both bilateral trade and economic cooperation should rest on a solid foundation and sufficient experience. Of all East and West European countries, the GDR and the FRG, respectively, were the Soviet Union's main economic partners. Two-fifths of East Germany's foreign trade was conducted with the USSR. More than 140 agreements were signed and implemented between the two countries. Owing to the division of labor and specialization within COMECON, the USSR received many types of equipment and transport facilities exclusively from the GDR. Thus, it was in the mutual interest of both West Germany and the Soviet Union that, in February 1990, Chancellor Kohl declared its country's readiness to honor East Germany's obligations toward the Soviet Union in trade and industrial cooperation ("Vertrauensschutz"). This, however, could not prevent a steep decline in Soviet-German trade the following year, not least because Soviet companies lacked the hard currency needed to pay for their purchases.[28]

Besides, these efforts to prevent bilateral trade from collapsing altogether proved very costly: 15 billion DM in 1990 (the equivalent of the trade surplus in transferable rubles) and an additional 10 billion DM in 1991 as credit guarantees to firms in eastern Germany producing goods for the former Soviet Union. Bonn's willingness to shoulder such a burden is illustrative of Germany's overriding interest (greater perhaps than in other Western capitals) in the success of the economic transformation process currently going on in the former Soviet Union. This should neither be construed as purely economic self-interest nor as gratitude for Moscow's decisive contribution to bringing about German reunification. Much more, Bonn's assistance in rehabilitating Russia's and the other former Soviet republics' shattered economies corresponds to the vital interests of Germany simply because a further deterioration of the overall situation would have serious consequences not only for the neighbors of the erstwhile Soviet Union but also for European stability in general.

Obviously, the coming years will be very difficult in many respects. Both the last president of what was still the Soviet Union, Mikhail S. Gorbachev, and the president of the then-Soviet republic of Russia, Boris N. Yeltsin, have said that the country was on the brink of ruin.[29] (And Mr. Yeltsin, in his present capacity as president of an independent Russia, has not tired of reiterating this view.) This makes support of the reform process, which, at least in Russia, appears to have been put into practice, extremely desirable. Such support should entail supplying the population with food, medicine and other everyday goods, and providing technical and financial assistance for the economy's rehabilitation. And it is on the reunited Germany that a great many hopes are set. To quote Nikolai Portugalov, a venerable expert on German affairs: "I won't mince my words: We hope that the partnership -- indeed friendship -- with united Germany, that the German economy, and German private investments will save us from the catastrophe that threatens us."[30]

And it is indeed Germany that has done (and still does) the most to help the former Soviet Union in its hour of greatest need. This is particularly, albeit far from exclusively, true for food aid. From the very first, Germany has understood that not only should the supply situation be stabilized but also a huge joint effort launched to develop the infrastructure (first of all the transportation and communications networks) of the Commonwealth of Independent States and introduce modern technologies there. Without a doubt, emergency food aid must top the list of priorities if this extremely deep (and currently very acute) crisis is to be overcome. Also, German fears that Western humanitarian aid might to a very great extent contribute to a prosecution of the *modus operandi* under the old Soviet leadership -- in that grain and foodstuffs are imported while the indigenous resources are left to go to waste -- are certainly not without foundation. Therefore, a sensible course of action would consist in submitting to stringent controls delivery, storage and final distribution of all material humanitarian aid shipped to Russia and the Commonwealth of Independent States. This, in effect, means that all decisions about relief aid should be reached in consultation not only with the leadership of the new states but also with representatives of those organizations responsible for channeling such aid at the local level.

As a matter of fact, in conditions of deep economic crisis and in a state of transition, the question of assistance seems not to be so much about its amount and character (commodities, food, advanced technology, financial resources) as about whether this assistance will be effective. In this connection the period of détente in the 1970s was very significant. Back then, the Soviet Union was granted massive credits by the West to help her with the exploitation of her natural resources and the modernization and development of her basic industries, which could no longer be used effectively. By the time the Soviet Union ceased to exist, it had accumulated a foreign debt in excess of $60 billion. Although the new republics have reached an agreement among themselves as to the servicing of the foreign debt of the defunct Soviet Union, the present situation is no cause for optimism as that debt had to be rescheduled and the danger of their defaulting on it cannot be ruled out entirely. On top of that, concerns among Western partners as to whom they were to conduct business with, further restrict the prospects of expanding economic relations.[31]

On the one hand, both the reunification of Germany and the sensible approach of its leadership to the situation in the former Soviet Union create favorable conditions for a rehabilitation and qualitative expansion of its economic relations with the Commonwealth of Independent States, which should prove highly beneficial to the latter. On the other hand, however, in the more immediate future, progress in those bilateral relations will be determined mainly by the internal developments in the Commonwealth of Independent States itself, i.e., by the success of the economic reforms there and the ability of the new states to manage their most complex national and social conflicts.

## The Germans in the Commonwealth of Independent States: Doomed to Exodus?

The issue of the so-called Volga Germans, which was still pending between Germany and the former Soviet Union, could not be conclusively settled in the course of Russian President Boris N. Yeltsin's visit to Bonn in December 1991, and it remains a sticking point in relations between Germany and Russia. (During World War II, the Volga Germans were deported by Stalin to such remote areas as Kazakhstan and Siberia, and they are now striving for the restoration of their autonomous republic in the Volga region.) At the time of his Zheleznovodsk meeting with Helmut Kohl in July 1991, Mikhail Gorbachev already spoke of the necessity of reaching a consensus about "how to come to a peaceful, valid, and mutually beneficial solution" to this problem.[32]

Meanwhile, the number of ethnic Germans migrating to Germany continues to grow. So far, a total of 500,000 Germans have left the former Soviet Union, 150,000 in 1990 alone.[33] No fewer than 3 million people claiming German nationality still live there, however (actually closer to 4 million if one includes their spouses and children of other nationalities).[34] Various estimates put at over one million the number of those who have applied at the German Embassy for visas to leave the ex-Soviet Union and migrate to Germany. This is not just a great loss for the former; these people, too, are suffering, because their applying for departure "turns out to be a chain of humiliations, a cause for mockery, and just plain robbery."[35]

Of course, to a great extent, the massive migration of ethnic Germans to Germany is due to the worsening economic crisis in the former Soviet Union. It should also be added, however, that these ethnic Germans (particularly those of the older generation) have never come to terms with their forced resettlement to Kazakhstan and Siberia, always wishing they would be allowed to return to their old pre-World War II territories on the banks of the Volga in Povolzhye. Many of them do not want to go to Germany and try to obtain political rehabilitation and regain their original constitutional rights. The debate on restitution, however, was allowed to drag on inadmissibly -- even though the Supreme Soviet of the USSR had retroactively branded as criminal all repressive acts committed in the past against all the peoples in the country. The basically sound argument that it was too early to speak in greater detail about the restoration of autonomy for the Volga Germans so long as the then-planned future union had not taken shape found less and less support among the Germans because of its well-known vagueness.[36]

Having lost faith in the former central government's backing of their claims, the ethnic Germans turned for support to the Russian leadership. Boris N. Yeltsin's government has indeed shown greater willingness to meet their demands, allocating 20 million rubles for a program aimed at rebuilding German villages in the Ulyanovsk district. Because of the deepening economic crisis, however, it turned out to be almost impossible to purchase the necessary materials with those funds. The aid from Germany has been significantly more effective and is intended mainly for building schools, clubs, dairies and bakeries in regions where most Germans now live, mainly in northern Kazakhstan. Also, small businesses with German firms as partners are being set up there, and programs aimed at facilitating the rebirth of the German language and culture have been funded. But this, too, can hardly substitute for political decisions. Although official German assistance -- aimed at encouraging the ethnic Germans to remain on the territory of the former Soviet Union by helping to create appropriate living conditions -- seems justified, it has met with a number of reservations: "Will this lead to the creation of special zones in the USSR, where the members of one nationality will benefit from foreign aid and prosper while those belonging to other nationalities will get nothing and remain mired in their difficult situation?"[37] Given such suspicion, assistance should be directed not exclusively at the Germans but at all the inhabitants of those regions, irrespective of their nationality.

In mid-March 1991, despite various attempts to postpone it, the First Congress of the Soviet Germans was held in Moscow, and its radical wing prevailed. In the program adopted by the congress, it was suggested to give the authorities half a year to create a favorable social and political climate in Povolzhye and to adopt the legal acts on the restitution of their autonomy to the Volga Germans returning there. (Up to that point, only a small number of ethnic Germans had managed to get back to that region -- against the fierce opposition of the local people, stirred up by local functionaries of the now-disbanded Communist Party.) Absent any progress or results within that time frame, the moratorium was to be extended for another three months. After its expiration, i.e., by mid-December 1991, the provisional council that had been elected at the congress was to form a government in exile, whose mandate was to organize the final departure of all ethnic Germans from the territory of the former Soviet Union.[38] Although the time limit set by that quasi-ultimatum had not yet been reached, the delegates to the Second Congress of the Soviet Germans, held in Moscow in October 1991, expressed anew their desire that the ethnic Germans living in Russia and the other former Soviet republics be allowed to reunite on the territory of the former autonomous Volga republic. They called on the governments of the republics concerned and world opinion to help them establish a new autonomous republic there.[39]

During talks he held with the Russian leadership in Moscow in October 1991, Foreign Minister Hans-Dietrich Genscher of Germany received assurances that the issue of an autonomous republic for ethnic Germans would be favorably settled.[40] Since then, tensions have risen steadily between representatives of the German Autonomy Movement and the local population in the Saratov and Volgograd areas. Once again, these tensions were fomented, and are being whipped up, by members of old *nomenklatura*, in their efforts to cling to power. For example, they are deliberately spreading the rumor that, henceforth, German will either be the sole language spoken in schools or its use forbidden altogether, or that all German-language newspapers will be banned. At the same time, however, they gloss over the fact that the German government has announced its readiness to make immediately available 200 million DM (more would be forthcoming) for the construction of new factories and apartment buildings, and that such financial aid would not go exclusively to the future German population of the area but also to its present Russian, Ukrainian and Tatar inhabitants.[41]

As for the Russian government, just like its Soviet predecessor, it has consistently postponed a decision on the autonomy issue for the ethnic Germans because of the domestic problems associated with it. And as became apparent during President Boris N. Yeltsin's visit to Bonn in December 1991, Chancellor Helmut Kohl, showing his understanding for the Russian leader's predicament in the matter, has seemingly abandoned the idea of forcing from the outside the issue of a restoration of the former autonomous Volga republic.[42] (In January 1992, however, he called on Mr. Yeltsin to honor his pledge, made during the same visit, to lay down the autonomous republic's boundaries by presidential decree.) Although the German chancellor's easing out on the issue might have paved the way for a somewhat more "natural" resolution of it, it is also clear that still another postponement will do nothing to stem the flow of ethnic Germans from Russia and the other republics, quite the contrary. This, in turn, might spell the end for the German settlement called into being in the 1760s by Catherine the Great. And such an outcome would serve neither the interests of Russia nor those of Germany.

## Conclusions

In 1990, cardinal changes took place in the giant complex of Soviet-German relations. "It has been a long and hard way, and our peoples and governments have trodden it to the present stage, to the present historic decisions," Mikhail Gorbachev noted during his visit to Bonn in November 1990. And he added: "It is to our peoples' credit, peoples who have drawn the only correct conclusion from the awkward, perhaps the most awkward, period in our relations. They mustered the moral force and found the wisdom to draw closer to each other."[43]

Russia wants to deepen and intensity its relations with Germany. "Historically speaking, the transformation of the totalitarian and militaristic Third *Reich* into a modern democracy happened in a short period of time, which I would call the "second German miracle." The Germans demonstrated how it is possible to resolutely cast away obsolete institutions and to create by means of a market economy an open and rich society, acceptable to all its social classes and attractive for other peoples," Daniil Proektor wrote.[44] Not only will Russia's relations with Germany be relations with a democratic but also with a peaceful nation. This is a direct result of the postwar experience and of the obligations incurred and entered into by Germany as part of the reunification process. And these obligations serve Germany's own well-understood interests as well as those of the whole of Europe. Finally, the discussion is about an economically strong Germany, holding one of the leading places in the world community and becoming the heart of a future united Europe. This, in turn, enables Germany to extend significant assistance to Russia in its efforts to rejoin Europe.

Thus, faith in Germany corresponds to the feelings of the overwhelming majority of the Russian people, not to mention the people of Ukraine, Belarus or other parts of the former Soviet Union. Of course, both the specific feelings of veterans of the Great Patriotic War and various demagogic attempts by conservative politicians in Russia to dwell on an alleged "German threat" serving their political aims are still vivid. This might complicate the recently initiated process of reconciliation. In general, and even more so than in the case of the former Soviet Union, Russia attaches great importance to the deepening and intensification of its relations with Germany in all conceivable fields -- economic, political, cultural and scientific, etc. In addition, for the first time in the postwar history of the two nations, the discussion is not only about cooperation but about partnership and friendship.[45] And such a partnership is likely to become an important element in building the new and united Europe.

# Notes

1. Robert Leicht, "Den Frieden mit Deutschland gemacht," *Die Zeit*, No. 30, July 20, 1990, p. 1.

2. Gert Krell, "Die Ostpolitik der Bundesrepublik Deutschland und die deutsche Frage," *Aus Politik und Zeitgeschichte*, No. 29, July 13, 1990, p. 29.

3. Lev Besymenski, "Kogo nakazet istoriya (Who Will Be Punished by History)," *Novoe Vremya*, No. 38, 1990, p. 14.

4. W.F. Hanrieder, "Die westdeutsche Außenpolitik von 1949-1979: Möglichkeiten und Notwendigkeiten," in: F.W. Hanrieder, H. Rühle (eds.), *Im Spannungsfeld der Weltpolitik. Dreißig Jahre deutscher Außenpolitik. 1949-1979*, (Stuttgart: Verlag Bonn aktuell, 1981), p. 41.

5. *Das Parlament*, August 2, 1975, p. 2.

6. *Vorwärts*, June, 1986, p. 28.

7. *Bulletin des Presse- und Informationsamtes der Bundesregierung*, No. 27, March 19, 1987, pp. 217-8.

8. *Pravda*, June 14, 1989, p. 2.

9. N.W. Pavlov, *Wneschnaya politika FRG: kontseptsii i realii 80-yh godov (Foreign Policy of the Federal Republic of Germany: Concepts and Realities of the 1980s.)*, (Moscow: Mezdunarodniye otnosheniya, 1989), p. 194.

10. M.S. Gorbachev, *Perestroika i novoye myshleniye dlya nashey strany i dlya vsego mira (Perestroika and New Thinking for our Country and for the Whole World)*, (Moskow: Politisdat, 1987), p. 209.

11. *Pravda*, February 11, 1990, p. 2.

12. Reinhard Mutz, "Die deutsche Vereinigung und die europäische Sicherheit," in: *Friedensgutachten 1990*, (Münster: Lit-Verlag, 1990), p. 159.

13. See *Bulletin* des Presse- und Informationsamtes der Bundesregierung, No. 54, May 8, 1990, p. 423.

14. *Pravda*, July 17, 1990, p. 2.

15. *Novoe Vremya*, No. 30, 1990, p. 12.

16. Mutz, (*op. cit.* in note 12), p. 168.

17. *Izvestia*, September 14, 1990, p. 4.

18. It was signed in November 1990 on the occasion of President Gorbachev's visit to Bonn and, a few months later, in April 1991, ratified by the Supreme Soviet of the USSR.

19. Leicht (*op. cit.* in note 1).

20. *Izvestia*, September 21, 1990, p. 4.

21. *Sovetskaya Rossiya*, March 2, 1991, p. 4.

22. *Ibid.*

23. See S. Rogov, "Na zapadnom fronte bez peremen (All Quiet On the Western Front)," *Izvestia*, September 21, 1990, p. 4; S. Kondrachev,

"Nelogkoe rasstavaniye s tankami (Uneasy Farewell to Tanks)," *Izvestia*, September 25, 1990, p. 4.

24. *Pravda*, September 27, 1990, p. 5.

25. *Izvestia*, October 18, 1990, p. 5.

26. *Novoe Vremya*, No, 12, 1991, p. 20.

27. V. Baranovsky, "Evropa: formirovaniye novoi mezhdunarodno-politicheskoi sistemu (Europe: The Formation of a New International Political System)," *Mirovaya ekonomika i mezhdunarodnye otnosheniya*, No. 9, 1990, p. 13.

28. From January 1991 to June 1991, both the former Soviet Union's exports to Germany and its imports from that country, amounted to 88 percent and 56 percent, respectively, of what they were the previous year (*Vnesnyaya Torgovlya*, 1991, No. 9, p. 40). Current developments in the ex-USSR provide little hope that this could change soon.

29. See, for instance, the interview of Boris Yeltsin with *Die Zeit*, November 15, 1991, p. 3.

30. *Der Spiegel*, No. 41, 1990, p. 184.

31. See "Sowjetwirtschaft: Kein Eldorado für Westunternehmer," *Rheinischer Merkur*, July 27, 1990, p. 12; S. Kondratchev, "Komu my nuzhny takiye (Who Needs us Just the Way we Are?)," *Izvestia*, October 5, 1990, p.1.

32. *Izvestia*, July 18, 1990, p. 4.

33. *Izvestia*, March 12, 1991, p. 2.

34. *Izvestia*, January 3, 1992, p. 3.

35. *Novoe Vremya*, No. 7, 1991, p. 37.

36. *Moskovskie Novosti*, No. 12, 1991, p. 4.

37. *Novoe Vremya*, No. 12, 1991, p. 20.

38. *Novoe Vremya*, No. 10, 1991, p. 17.

39. *Izvestia*, January 3, 1992, p. 3.

40. *Izvestia*, October 28, 1991, p. 4.

41. *Izvestia*, January 3, 1992, p. 3; *Novoe Vremya*, No. 41, 1991, pp. 32-3.

42. *Izvestia*, November 22, 1991, p. 7.

43. *Izvestia*, November 11, 1990, p. 4.

44. *Literaturnaya Gazeta*, February 27, 1991, p. 4.

45. *Izvestia*, November 11, 1990, p. 4.

# PART FOUR

# Europe on the Way
# to Integration?

# 10

# Victims of Transition: The Failure of Economic Integration in the East and the Collapse of COMECON

*Aleksandr Nekipelov*

Economic cooperation between the countries of Central and Eastern Europe and the former Soviet Union is in a deep crisis. The slowdown in mutual trade, which began as early as 1988, is accelerating. The methods of intergovernmental exchange, which have been in effect since the foundation of the Council for Mutual Economic Assistance, or COMECON, 40 years ago, are being done away with. The process of reconsidering COMECON's role in the development of the national economies of its member states has finally resulted in a general agreement to dissolve this organization entirely. In fact, it can be said that such an outcome was by no means an accident: it had been in the making for quite some time. Negative developments became apparent in the first half of the 1970s, and in the 1980s growth rates in mutual trade declined sharply;[1] shortage of high-quality goods in the COMECON "market" increased significantly; balance-of-payment problems became very acute; and the effect of intra-COMECON cooperation upon technical and scientific progress, designed to bring about the transition from extensive to intensive growth, was lacking almost completely.

It took a very long time before it was finally understood that unfavorable developments in economic cooperation did not primarily result from some mistake made by the so-called direct executers, or were caused by some lacking "necessary political will" or by faults in determining strategic priorities in the development of the "international socialist division of labor." Before then-Soviet Prime Minister Nikolai I. Ryzhkov acknowledged at COMECON's 42nd session in 1986 that "traditional ways are now insufficient, that these ways cannot provide conditions for the intensification of the economy, and that all of us need new forms to accelerate the dynamics of economic development and co-operation," practically all conceivable measures had been tried out within the traditional mechanism of economic interaction.[2] Suffice it here to remember of the hopes pinned on the realization of long-term special programs of cooperation in the mid-1970s, on the coordination of economic policies and the homogenization of the systems of economic control at the beginning of the 1980s, or on the realization of the Complex Program for Scientific and Technical Progress in the mid-1980s.

## What Is the Cause of All These Failures?

In general, the command model of socialist economies is incompatible with an active participation in international economic relations organized on a market basis, because it is unable to adjust quickly to all the changes permanently taking place under such a system. It is no accident that, for a long time, foreign economic ties were treated as an "inevitable evil," whose main function was to acquire "deficit" commodities in exchange for the export of relatively "abundant" goods. This approach to foreign economic relations was implemented with the aid of the well-known system of state monopoly, which represented itself as a lock compartment of the command economy, eliminating "destructive" influences of external factors. This system clearly tended toward autarchic decision making: it was quite natural for it to sacrifice efficiency for the sake of maintaining stability.

The situation changed somewhat when, after World War II, socialism (to use the traditional terminology) moved beyond the borders of the Soviet Union to become a "world system." Because the development of each country within this system took place on the basis of physical planning, mutual supplies had to be coordinated in much the same way, thus robbing external ties of their role as interfering factors. That is why, in contrast to the classical market, a new type of international economic relations and the so-called world socialist economy were formed. In substance, one cannot deny that under those circumstances Stalin's thesis of a split in the single world market turned out to be quite true. Thus, the notion "world socialist economy" should not be treated as a purely ideological product. Under conditions in which there are several states with command economies, its existence is quite natural: it manifests itself in increasing mutual economic ties as compared to the volume of foreign trade with the rest of the world. In other words, a distinctive "world socialist economy" actually did exist -- which obviously does not mean that it was able to meet the demands of modern societies.

Theoretically, one can imagine that intergovernmental plan coordination could optimize the economic development of each country by using the potential of the "international socialist division of labor." This view is based on the optimistic assumption that each country is able to estimate comprehensively what it should produce itself and what is beneficial for it to get from its partners. And, as a result, the most rational distribution of productive forces within the "socialist camp" could be realized.

Such an abstraction is no worse than a pre-planned "directly social" economy on the national level. Nor is it any better. Given the degree of differentiation in modern production, any attempt to take into account external factors at the early stage of formulating economic strategies requires calculating more possibilities than any planning authority can possibly handle. Thus, the unrealistic character of this approach forced planners to choose another way: in the first stage, when compiling national economic plans, they took into account just those foreign trade flows that were based on already existing agreements. And only in the final stage, when the main parameters of economic growth had already been determined and essential corrections practically excluded, did they try to negotiate additional possibilities of economic cooperation. In practice, the traditional system of mere quantitative planning automatically reduces plan coordination to an elementary coordination of mutual supplies. As far as long-term forms of common planning are concerned, the COMECON experience showed that the joint formulation of important strategic objectives in the sphere of cooperation never entailed any real obligation for the participating countries, especially in the field of investments. Thus, it turned out that those planning programs were lacking an adequate mechanism for their realization. The failure of long-term special programs of cooperation, elaborated in the mid-1970s, is a good example of this lack.

## The Artificial Role of Prices

In conditions of just quantitative economic transactions the so-called commodity-and-money mechanism of cooperation plays an essentially passive role: it is needed only as a standard of value for those goods whose exchange has been agreed upon during plan coordination. According to the decisions made at COMECON's ninth meeting, held in Bucharest in 1958, the member states used world market prices as a basis for their contract prices. Yet, the use of world prices created some problems. The most important of these was that the efficiency of cooperation turned out to be dependent on an external factor: the price dynamics in the world market. It is quite natural that countries with rigidly planned economies were interested in some stability of their exchange parities. In practice, two ways of securing stable prices were used.

Until the mid-1970s the so-called stop-prices principle was in effect. According to it, prices for the running five-year plan period were determined on the basis of average prices on the world market from the previous five-year period. Thus, for the 1966-70 period, prices in intra-COMECON trade were established on the basis of average 1961-1965 prices. This procedure, which produced practically absolute stability of prices during five-year periods, was fully compatible with the national systems of planning. But at the same time, there was an extremely slow reaction to price changes in the world market, and thus to progressive tendencies in economic development. Sharp fluctuations in world market prices in the mid-1970s led to a new formula of pricing in intra-COMECON cooperation: the so-called sliding basis of prices. According to it, prices had to be reviewed and revised each year by averaging world-market prices of the five previous years.

It is quite clear that using any of the aforementioned methods of pricing inevitably leads to a deviation of COMECON's price structure from that of the world market. Some other factors added to this problem. It is a well-known fact that the possibility of "borrowing" at world prices is not the same for different commodity groups. Moreover, a great many problems arise when command economies try to develop industrial cooperation or to engage in joint ventures with one another. This is because, in most cases, it is not possible to determine genuine world market prices for components to be supplied in cooperation agreements, or prices for an industrial complex being erected in joint construction programs. Thus, it becomes necessary to create some artificial pricing algorithms. It should not come as a surprise that, under such circumstances, prices were not regarded as a barrier against inefficiency-producing economic decisions. Just the opposite: a price formula was sought that would support economic decisions previously coordinated on the basis of purely technocratic considerations.

In conditions under which the state assumes the role of both seller and buyer, it has the possibility to maintain the same overall effect of bilateral cooperation, provided deviations of contract prices form world prices for export and import goods are coordinated and mutually counterbalancing. But at the same time it is clear that such frequently used mutual concessions inevitably lead to a plurality of prices for the same commodity in the COMECON "market." The method of pricing based on borrowing world-market exchange parities inevitably created a parallel standard of values based on differences in "economic importance." This fact manifested itself in the division of goods into "hard" (that is, those that can be traded on the world market) and "soft" (that is, those that cannot be sold for hard currency). Accordingly, the understanding of exchange equivalents had to be modified: the aim was not only to assure a corresponding price structure within COMECON and on the world market, but also a roughly similar amount of "hard" and "soft" goods in the structure of mutual supplies.

We can draw the conclusion that, contrary to a widespread opinion, the division of commodities according to their economic importance was rather a result of the historically formed mechanism of cooperation than a manifestation of the existing gap in the quality of goods traded on world markets on the one hand, and on the COMECON "market" on the other. A qualitative uniformity of goods does not exist on the world market, either. But the supply-and-demand mechanism provides the formation of "equilibrium prices," which reflect differences in consumption characteristics of commodities.

Another potentially influential factor regarding the structure of exchange within COMECON is that of contractual prices. It would not be correct to say that command economies are totally indifferent to price fluctuations: all of them are quite sensitive to the terms of trade, because these determine how much national labor should be expended in order to acquire necessary products. But does this mean that the level of fluctuation between contractual and domestic prices is the main criteria for exporting or importing any goods?

The experience of economic cooperation within COMECON shows that contractual prices influence the directions of the "international socialist division of labor" only very little. The structure of trade was primarily determined on a bilateral basis, due to considerations resulting from the state of quantitative balances. This was not the result of a mere underestimation of the potential role of foreign trade relations in improving the efficiency of national economies, but it reflected that, within command economies, the quantitative side was always much more important than the value side. It is thus no surprise that deteriorating terms of trade were met with balancing efforts highly typical of command economies: neither their production nor the structure of foreign trade was adjusted, but an administrative reduction of "less important" imports and an increase in exports of all more or less "abundant" commodities took place, irrespective of costs. This is why, since the mid-1970s, when dramatic changes in the international economic cooperation occurred, economic and foreign-trade structures of the COMECON countries have remained practically the same.

## Bilateralism Versus Multilateralism

From 1969 onward, the bulk of mutual payments within COMECON were made in transferable rubles through the International Bank of Economic Cooperation, or IBEC. Initially, the idea was to make the transferable ruble an international socialist currency, to be used for the multilateral settlement of payments between the IBEC member states. In terms of banking techniques, this construct differed substantially from any multilateral clearing. A country could pay goods only if it had the necessary amount of transferable rubles on its current account. If it did not, it had to be credited first by IBEC. No limits for a passive balance of payments, characteristic of all forms of clearing, were established. Further, it had been envisaged to introduce deposit operations for national banks, an IBEC statutory and reserve fund in transferable rubles, and the distribution of IBEC profits in transferable rubles among the member states.

As far as multilateral payments were concerned, there were no obstacles from the point of view of banking techniques. Moreover, one had to admit that the system did function: upon receiving a payment order, the IBEC took the necessary amount from the current account of the importing country and transferred it to the account of the exporting country, no matter where the money came from. But this is only one, the formal, side of the story. In reality, the IBEC member countries were always eager to avoid bilateral imbalances in supplies and, as a result, the possibilities of multilateral settlements were rarely used. The prospect of accumulating transferable rubles on respective current accounts, i.e., a surplus of exports over imports, has never been viewed with great enthusiasm by the net exporter. Moreover, such situations were regarded as unfavorable to the owner of "money." All these "strange" attitudes are by no means accidental. They cannot be regarded as shortsightedness on the part of the IBEC members. The following reasons, which explain the dominance of a mutually balanced bilateralism within COMECON, are usually mentioned:

(1) One is the plurality of contractual prices, the reasons for which were analyzed above. This had the effect of making the "purchasing power" of transferable rubles in a country other than that in which they had been earned different from their "purchasing power" in a country where they had been earned.

(2) Another problem consisted in the necessity to balance not only exchangeable values but utility values as well, otherwise the surplus in a given country, accumulated as the result of exports of "hard" goods, might have been used for acquiring "soft" goods in another country. It is easy to understand that it proved practically impossible to realize such dual balancing on a multilateral basis.

(3) But the most important factor hindering multilateralism within COMECON had a systemic, as it were, character. As mentioned earlier, mutual supplies were determined not by market forces but by quantitative contingents coordinated beforehand. This is why, theoretically speaking, multilateral balancing could only be realized in the early stage of negotiating quantities. But we have already seen that this, too, failed in practice.

Thus we can draw the conclusion that the task of creating an efficient system of payment within COMECON turned out to be unrealizable because of its incompatibility with the main features of the mechanism that governed cooperation between command economies. Most elements of this multilateral system of payment did not function, or, more precisely, they did function, although in a superficial manner, i.e., without influencing real processes in economic cooperation. As a result, this system did not even meet the requirements of multilateral clearing: actually it should be regarded as a set of bilateral clearings within which the same accounting unit, the transferable ruble, was used.

"International socialist credits," as envisaged in the IBEC statute, were confronted with the same major problem of how to convert transferable rubles into commodities. Within the traditional mechanism of intra-COMECON cooperation, this could only be solved if necessary commodity supplies had been included in advance in bilateral trade agreements and protocols. It should be clear that the existence of international credit within COMECON was no evidence of a true capital market. This explains, in turn, why the mechanism of interest rates, as an integral part of such a market, was absent, and also why interest rates, used in credit relations, were of a totally artificial nature. Analysis of the mechanisms of payment, pricing and crediting within COMECON reveals that, in practice, the transferable ruble did not perform any money functions. It was simply an instrument of accounting for intergovernmental supplies. But owing to illusions about its being real money, the transferable ruble had, for a long time, a disorienting influence on setting practical targets. This became painfully clear in another particular case: the fixing of appropriate exchange rates.

## The Controversial Value of the Transferable Ruble

It was argued that the introduction of "economically justified" exchange rates of the transferable ruble to national currencies was one of the important prerequisites for its convertibility. But according to the classical definition of exchange rates, these were the prices of a currency expressed in another currency, and, therefore, a genuine currency market was needed in order to provide the necessary conditions for any "economically justified" exchange rate. In other words, convertibility and "real" exchange rates may not be treated as two different problems: they are two sides of the same coin. Thus, one has to conclude that, essentially, the so-called exchange rates of transferable rubles to both convertible capitalist and nonconvertible socialist currencies were, from a substantial point of view, no exchange rates at all. The same is true when it comes to calculating "real" exchange rates based on the purchasing power of respective currencies. In fact, this is similar to the common hope entertained by all socialist countries that they would find a basis for determining "scientifically justified" prices when calculating "socially necessary costs of labor." One cannot but regard such "purchasing power," applied to both national money units of command socialist economies and to the "currency" serving their mutual cooperation, as an artificial product. By definition, money that cannot be converted directly into commodities without state allocations and quantitative contingents has no purchasing power. This is why comparisons established in order to determine "rational" exchange rates make no economic sense.

The treatment of transferable rubles as genuine money sometimes led to curious situations. The efforts made to check the adequacy of the transferable ruble against the US dollar by comparing their respective purchasing power are a good example of this. In 1970, for the first time, experts from COMECON's member states examined the consistency of the exchange rate using a general methodology elaborated by the Standing Committee for Currency and Finance Problems. In 1971, the Comprehensive Program of Socialist Economic Integration submitted that the consistency of this exchange rate be reviewed periodically. As a result, such a review was carried out in 1978. It demonstrated that the official exchange rate significantly "overvalued" the transferable ruble relative to the US dollar. And the same conclusion was reached in yet another way -- by determining the transferable ruble/US dollar parity as a crossrate, on the basis of the foreign-exchange coefficients used in some COMECON countries to convert the transferable ruble and dollar earnings of enterprises into national currency. Thus, many experts came to the conclusion that a really consistent rate of the collective currency could only be obtained via these exchange rates of national currencies to the transferable ruble and the US dollar.

There were no arithmetic errors in all these calculations. It is true that the respective "purchasing power" of transferable rubles and US dollars did not coincide with their established exchange rate. Essentially, however, the problem was that such a coincidence was not possible, owing to the COMECON's pricing mechanism. Let us imagine that we establish today the "consistent" exchange rate of the transferable ruble to the dollar corresponding to the respective purchasing power of these currencies. Then, tomorrow, immediately after this exchange rate is introduced in the process of pricing according to COMECON's rules (that is, including all the factors that inevitably lead to deviations of contractual prices from those on the world market), the previous gap in the "purchasing power" between the two currencies will automatically be reproduced. And there is nothing strange in that. We should simply not forget that the transferable ruble itself did not take part in any price setting: it was only needed to express in another form prices borrowed from the world market and transformed according to a certain algorithm. If, for instance, the COMECON countries had used dollars as a means of accounting for mutual supplies in the same traditional way of pricing, then dollars would inevitably have suffered the same fate, creating two different purchasing powers for the same currency.

Summing up, we can say that, though a great many books and articles have been written about the "world socialist market," this notion has never had its counterpart in real life. Actually, within COMECON, products were not really traded; they were distributed in a very special manner. A proper pricing mechanism was absent, and there was thus no other way than adopting (with some corrections) exchange parities from the world market. The so-called collective currency -- the transferable ruble -- did not perform money functions, and, this is important, not because it was "bad" money, but because "good" money simply was not needed in such a mechanism. The skewed nature of national prices, interest rates and exchange rates (inherent in command economies), the absence of an organic relationship between them and of international market instruments led to a situation in which decisions on the division of labor were not so much based on efficiency criteria as on purely technocratic considerations and on the state of physical balances (or, more accurately, imbalances) in the economy. From both a theoretical and a practical point of view, it is now obvious that such features of the "world socialist economy" as the gap between the quantitative and the value side of exchange, the bilateral type of cooperation, the unsusceptibility to modern forms of transnational interaction did not reflect "difficulties of growth" but had a systemic character. It follows that until the lack of any prospect for the historically formed model of socialism was officially acknowledged, it was not possible to find a constructive way out of the miserable economic relations.

## A First Attempt to Restructure COMECON

It was only natural that the Soviet Union became the major initiator in the restructuring of intra-COMECON cooperation.[3] On the one hand, support for radical changes in this sphere was but the logical extension of Mikhail S. Gorbachev's efforts at fundamentally transforming his own domestic economy. On the other hand, it is absolutely clear that, since the USSR was the main trading partner of the other COMECON member states, changing the traditional mechanism of cooperation within this organization would have been inconceivable without the determination of the Soviet Union to renounce its own irrational economic system.

While formulating basic directions for improving the mechanism of mutual cooperation, the COMECON countries (except Rumania) came to the conclusion that the integration process among them needed to be reoriented toward creating a truly unified socialist market. In 1987, COMECON's 43rd session outlined necessary changes in all elements of the cooperation mechanism. A year later, at its 44th meeting, COMECON decided to consolidate this policy by creating a special "Temporary Working Group of the Executive Council," whose task was to finalize the "Integral Concept for Restructuring the Mechanism of Cooperation." These measures had some positive results. For example, it became clear that restructuring the mechanism of integration directly depended on the reform processes in the member states. Taking into account that these reforms were being realized in a rather uneven fashion (to say the least), the conclusion was drawn that new methods of cooperation should not necessarily encompass all the COMECON members. In addition, an agreement on the reduction of a number of goods delivered on the basis of quantitative contingents had to be reached, because, without any alterations here, it would have been impossible to introduce efficient market mechanisms. This, in turn, required improving the technique of applying world market prices for intra-COMECON trade, while, at the same time, introducing the possibility of free agreements between enterprises, the so-called direct ties. In the financial realm, both an improvement of the transferable ruble and the use of convertible currencies (as well as of the national currencies of the member states) was envisaged.

It is also necessary, however, to point to those difficulties that emerged in the process of implementation of the new policy and seriously affected the formation of a unified socialist market. Very soon after an agreement had been reached, it became clear that some of the member countries regarded their official approval as a kind of tactical trick, meant to accept "market terminology" but to fill it with rather old wine. This was true, though to varying degrees, for East Germany, Cuba, Czechoslovakia and Bulgaria. As far as Hungary and, to a lesser degree, Poland were concerned, one could discover an attempt not to bind their hands by real obligations because of fears that this could infringe upon their plans for a more active participation in the world economy. It was also obvious that virtually all the COMECON members displayed an unconcealed distrust of the seriousness of Soviet intentions, arguing that the Soviet Union was neither politically nor economically prepared to realize its own proposals. Soviet efforts to outline and fix in much detail both the unified market and the schedule of the suggested "marching path" greatly contributed to such an attitude.[4] Taking all this into account, one cannot be surprised that the first attempt to restructure the system of intra-COMECON cooperation in 1989 at the latest turned out to be a failure. The intention to overcome the crisis in economic cooperation on the basis of a unified market was gradually scaled down to a collective search for an elastic formula giving an image of unity but having no (or nearly no) practical importance.

## Reconsidering National Interests

The revolutions that swept East Germany, Czechoslovakia, Bulgaria, and Rumania in late 1989 created an entirely new situation. All the European members of COMECON became active and genuine supporters of market economies, which, as it might seem, could breathe new life into the strategy of market integration. Nothing of the sort happened, however. Quite the opposite: COMECON and the traditional system of cooperation between its members became a subject of unprecedented sharp criticism. In January 1990, for instance, on the eve of COMECON's 45th meeting, the Czecho-Slovak finance minister, Vaclav Klaus, openly declared his country's intention to propose a dissolution of COMECON and, should this proposal be rejected, to leave the organization unilaterally.[5]

Nevertheless, this 1990 session in Sofia was not to be the last one in the history of COMECON. Once more, its members agreed on a radical renewal of the organization, including substantial changes in its statute and the introduction of real market conditions. At the same time, however, talk about further integration within COMECON disappeared completely from the documents of this 45th session. Against the backdrop of widespread calls to "return to Europe," this was by all means an important signal. There can be no doubt that, in the sharp criticism leveled from within at COMECON, emotions reflecting the actual political situation in a number of countries played an important role. But one must also be aware that the profound changes taking place in these countries make it absolutely natural to reassess historically formed realities. The transition toward a market economy, though still at a rather early stage, creates the fundamental prerequisites for overcoming the division of the world economy into two sectors based on qualitatively different rules. It provides the countries of Central and Eastern Europe with new opportunities to choose their foreign economic strategy, thus making a re-evaluation of intra-COMECON integration inevitable.

Soon after the revolutionary wave of 1989 had ebbed, it became evident that most of COMECON's European members were neither interested in a separate regional market in the eastern part of the Continent nor in a continuation of the integration process. Instead, they opted for an active participation in the world economy, raising hopes of joining the European Community in the near future. It is no accident that, during the work of the Special Commission, set up at COMECON's 45th session in 1990, the delegations from Hungary, Poland and Czecho-Slovakia made strenuous efforts to prevent COMECON (or any other organization that might have replaced it) from being transformed into an efficient instrument of economic cooperation. Even in the official documents the Special Commission had to elaborate, the delegates strongly resisted any mention's being made of the preferential character of mutual economic ties.

Since then, the Soviet attitude toward COMECON has undergone a dramatic evolution, too. At that organization's 45th session, the Soviet delegation was still fighting for its preservation as the core of multilateral cooperation. It is symptomatic of the Soviet position at the beginning of 1990 that an interview with Mr. Ryzhkov (the former Soviet prime minister), on the occasion of COMECON's 45th meeting, was

published in Moscow News under the title "We have managed to preserve COMECON."[6] But even then, this position was far from being
shared by everybody in the country. Referring to the nature of Soviet
relations with other members of COMECON, Vasilii Seliunin, a well-
known analyst, wrote in the fall 1989 issue of *Novy Mir*:

> In essence, national economic interests are sacrificed for the
> sake of ideological postulates. In contrast to the way it was
> seen in Lenin's time, our motherland is not openly consider-
> ed a base for world revolution by today's authorities. But if
> we judge by deeds and not by words, today, the bowels of
> the earth (the country's wealth) are as never before being
> thrown open for the benefit of the socialist camp.[7]

Of course, this is a very emotional appraisal, but there is an element of
truth in it. It is a well-known fact that, until recently, the Soviet Union's economic relations with its COMECON partners were regarded
mainly from the point of view of their importance for consolidating political unity among the socialist countries. In purely economic terms,
significant losses for the Soviet Union are obvious. It is necessary,
however, to point out that these losses are relative rather than absolute:
they merely reflect the Soviet Union's "missed opportunities." Primarily, this has to do with the specifics of pricing in intra-COMECON
trade.

As mentioned earlier, the COMECON countries tried to use world
market prices. But whereas it was easy to find a world price for raw
materials such as oil, coal or for crops, it was much more difficult to
do the same in the case of complex industrial goods, which have widely
variant qualitative parameters and different utility values. Numerous
expert estimates and comparisons of prices for those goods, which were
traded on both socialist and capitalist markets, showed that intra-
COMECON prices for finished products were significantly higher than
those on the world market -- at least when taking the qualitative level
into account. The Soviet Union was a net exporter of fuels and raw
materials and a net importer of finished products. This is the real reason behind the losses incurred by the Soviet Union in trade with its European COMECON partners. According to the calculations of two
American economists, Michael Marrese and Jan Vanous, these losses
amounted to approximately US $196 billion (in 1984 prices) for the
1970-1984 period. On average, the accumulated per capita gains of socialist countries in the same period amounted to $1,760 (GDR: $3,493;
Bulgaria: $3,486; Czechoslovakia: $2,828; Hungary: $1,974; Poland:

$1,021; Rumania: $169).[8] Calculations made in different countries all showed that, if the 1989 Soviet trade with its COMECON partners had been conducted on the basis of world market prices, the balance of trade would have been favorable to the USSR and not to its partners, as it actually turned out to be the case.

It is therefore clear why it was beneficial for the Soviet Union to introduce world market conditions into COMECON. Thus, at the Sofia session, the Soviet delegation proposed the introduction of convertible currencies and world market prices in intra-COMECON trade as of January 1, 1991. At that meeting, however, it was not yet clear how this should be carried out. If, for instance, the established system of quantitative exchange between the COMECON member states had remained the exclusive channel of economic cooperation between them, then such a change could have had no effect. In such a situation, nothing but an even greater rigidity in the bilateral balancing of mutual supplies could have been expected -- a country, threatened by the prospect of a deficit in its balance of payment, would simply reduce its imports and do away with the possibilities of currency payments. The same is true for price-fixing, because, in such a case, there would be no free choice of trade partners, prerequisite for true market prices, and thus no prospect for COMECON and world market prices to approximate one another any further.

Another option was to combine the introduction of convertible currencies with the simultaneous renunciation of quantitative contingents. This actually happened and led to drastic changes in the mutual trade -- and to a significant slump in both quantities and prices for finished products offered by COMECON's European members. From the Soviet point of view, this was the most profitable solution, for it permitted its foreign trade to perform in conditions of absolute freedom of choice. It was primarily a radical reassessment of Soviet interests under fundamentally changed circumstances (not only was the union at stake, but public opinion also gained more prominence at a time when rhetorical salvos fired by some East European politicians at COMECON and at the USSR caused some irritation in Moscow) that led the Soviet leadership to reconsider its stance toward COMECON fundamentally. As a result, the Soviet side assumed a rather passive role, agreeing to convert COMECON into a research organization in which mutual experience in the field of economic cooperation would be shared. It also took the unilateral decision to drop the system of settlements in transferable rubles as of January 1, 1991. In fact, 1990 marked a decisive turning point in the Soviet attitude to economic matters. That this stunning turnabout was executed somewhat ruthlessly is reflected not only in such unilateral moves but also in breaches of contract regarding oil supplies to the former allies.

It would not be fair to perceive the reconsideration of their national interests by the COMECON countries as a one-sided act. Rather, we should regard it as a dynamic process. Thus, when the East European partners of the USSR turned toward the qualitatively new possibilities of integrating into the world economy, a series of obstacles became more and more obvious. Premier among these was the dependence of all those countries on the Soviet economy and Soviet supplies -- the legacy of the policy of socialist division of labor and economic integration pursued within COMECON for decades. While it was quite legitimate to criticize the economic inefficiency of such a policy, it was not possible to ignore that it had materialized under conditions of stable, if not rational, economic ties and of extremely extensive foreign trade among the COMECON partners (see table 1). The specific feature of the international division of labor within COMECON was that the Soviet Union was at the center of it, satisfying a significant demand of other COMECON members in terms of fuels, energy and raw materials (see table 2), while at the same time being a large and -- more important -- undemanding consumer of final products (see data in table 3).

Taking all this into account, it is quite natural that the more indifferent the Soviet position on problems of economic relations with other COMECON countries became, the more anxiety surfaced. It became increasingly clear that the process of transition to world market conditions was quite risky for them because the structure of their national economies was totally inconsistent with fundamental market requirements. Of course, the situation was not identical for all those countries. For example, Bulgaria, with an industry almost entirely geared to meeting Soviet needs, now finds itself in a most precarious position. But even a country like Czecho-Slovakia now regards the collapse of economic relations with the Soviet Union and its successor states as one of the most serious external obstacles on the way to reforming its economy. This was already stated openly in the plan of economic reform adopted in September 1990 by the supreme legislative body of that country.[9] The economic prospects of COMECON's European members were further dimmed by the crisis in the Middle East caused by the Iraqi aggression against Kuwait in the summer of 1990. According to official estimates at the time, Czecho-Slovakia stood to lose approximately US$1 billion as a result of that crisis.[10]

Yet, right after the introduction of the new system of convertible-currency payments at the beginning of 1991, an avalanche-like curtailment of mutual cooperation took place within COMECON. Though less seriously, it also affected the Soviet Union, shattering illusions that a "dollar rain" over the country would result from the switch to convertible currencies. True, the Soviet Union's terms of trade vis-à-vis its partners markedly improved, but, at the same time, the losses resulting from the abrupt break in traditional intra-COMECON economic ties turned out to be quite painful. The Soviet government proved to be totally unprepared as regards the consequences of its own proposal -- otherwise it would have created in due time a rational mechanism of currency distribution among importers. Absent such a mechanism, it was inevitable that those companies that used to import from COMECON countries did not have the necessary convertible currency to continue to do so, and that those that had it preferred to import from other countries.

Thus we can see that, at the end of 1990, beginning of 1991, a more or less sober attitude toward the future of mutual cooperation emerged. Though priority was still being given to the aim of integrating the COMECON countries into the world economy, these were not ready to accept an uncontrollable collapse of their long-time economic ties.

## What Is Ahead?

Taking all the above into account, it hardly comes as a surprise that COMECON's European member states were now seeking a way to make the transition to world conditions smoother, at the least keeping its possible negative economic and social consequences under control. This was even true for Hungary, which, initially, was a major advocate of introducing convertible currencies and current world market prices, hoping that the shock this was certain to inflict to its economy would accelerate the process of modernization rather than just deepening the country's economic crisis.

Specific proposals focused mainly on the introduction of bilateral clearing arrangements in convertible (or even national) currencies with the USSR This would have helped preserve a great many economic ties on the microeconomic level, limiting international competition and maintaining a somewhat isolated system of pricing. There were, however, various difficulties in implementing this proposal. They stemmed mainly from the lack of market relations within the Soviet Union itself and from the resultant complexity of creating at the national level there a rational mechanism involving individual companies in international economic cooperation. There were also plans to involve the West in the settlement of payment problems between East European countries and the USSR One was the idea introduced at Harvard University in 1990 by the Czecho-Slovak foreign minister, Jiri Dienstbier, aimed at attracting Western credits to the Soviet Union for financing imports from Czecho-Slovakia, Hungary and Poland. Similar loans from the recently founded European Bank for Reconstruction and Development, or EBRD, were under study.

All these projects are still being discussed from time to time -- with little enthusiasm, however. For a new factor outweighs all the others: the disintegration of the USSR, the pace of which has accelerated greatly in the wake of the events of August 1991. It would not be correct to say that the former socialist countries were wholly unprepared for such a course of events. Seeing that the balance of power in the Soviet Union had for quite some time began to tilt from the center to the republics, they did their best to establish economic ties with the republics. Unfortunately, however, in this transitional period, neither the center nor the republics have had much control over the situation. And with the Soviet Union having been replaced by the least ambitious alternative -- the Commonwealth of Independent States -- conditions for economic cooperation have not grown any better. Instead, the danger of an uncontrollable disintegration of the former Soviet market looms ever larger, and the prospects of forestalling it are quite dim indeed.

As for COMECON, its future appeared in a somewhat new light. At the very last moment, Hungary, Poland, and Czecho-Slovakia abandoned the idea of introducing bilateral clearing arrangements in convertible/national currencies, proposing instead to limit the agenda of the 46th COMECON meeting, originally scheduled for February 1991, to the dissolution of that body, as the creation of a new organization of international economic cooperation was to take place at a later stage. The separation in time of these two events was primarily aimed at preventing COMECON's non-European member states, especially Cuba, from joining the new organization. COMECON's 46th session, eventually held at the end of June 1991, spelled the doom of that organization, putting a formal end to more than 40 years of its activity. For easily understandable reasons, the prospects of a new regional economic organization in the eastern part of Europe have now become quite dubious.

# Notes

1. On the basis of current prices, the growth rate dropped from an average of 14 percent in 1971-80 to just 2.3 percent in 1981-90.

2. *Pravda*, November 4, 1986.

3. This can be seen, for instance, in the Soviet initiative to convene a "Special Working Meeting of the COMECON Heads of Party and State" in November 1986 in Moscow, where for the first time the idea of restructuring the mechanism of socialist economic integration was expressed.

4. To most of COMECON's European member states, this must have seemed another of the traditional Soviet attempts to continue the old game and impose all kinds of large-scale projects and programs with no prospect whatsoever of being realized.

5. See his interview with the Polish newspaper *Rzeczpospolita*, January 4, 1990.

6. *Moscow News*, No. 3, 1990.

7. Vasilii Seliunin, "Chernye dyry ekonomiki (Black Holes of the Economy)," *Novy Mir*, No. 10, 1989, p. 178.

8. M. Marrese, J. Vanous, "The Content and Controversy of Soviet Trade Relations with Eastern Europe 1970-1984," in: T. C. Brada, T. A. Wolf, (eds.), *Economic Adjustment and Reform in Eastern Europe and the Soviet Union*, (Durham: Duke University Press, 1988), pp. 202-3.

9. "Scênár economiké reformy (Scenario of Economic Reform)," *Hospodárské noviny*, September 4, 1990, p. IV.

10. *Ibid.*, p. IV.

## Table 1

Share of COMECON countries in foreign
trade of its European member-states (%)

|                 | 1980 | 1985 | 1988 |        |
|-----------------|------|------|------|--------|
| Bulgaria        | 72.8 | 75.6 | 79.2 |        |
| Czecho-Slovakia | 65.5 | 74.1 | 74.6 |        |
| GDR             | 62.7 | 63.6 | 66.4 |        |
| Hungary         | 49.6 | 52.1 | 45.1 |        |
| Poland          | 53.2 | 69.3 | 69.9 |        |
| Rumania         | 34.6 | 51.0 | 55   | (1987) |
| Soviet Union    | 48.6 | 55.0 | 59.7 |        |

Source: Calculated on the basis of national statistics.

## Table 2

Share of the USSR in imports of the
COMECON member-states of different commodities (%)

|                        | 1980 | 1985 | 1987 |
|------------------------|------|------|------|
| Machines and equipment | 33.3 | 32.5 | 30.1 |
| Coal                   | 67.3 | 65.7 | 67.6 |
| Oil                    | 75.0 | 76.2 | 78.7 |
| Oil products           | 85.0 | 77.3 | 85.5 |
| Natural gas            | 99.3 | 99.8 | 96.0 |
| Electric power         | 78.4 | 61.9 | 84.9 |
| Iron ore               | 71.3 | 71.5 | 66.4 |
| Rolled steel           | 68.5 | 65.7 | 65.7 |
| Copper                 | 60.7 | 51.3 | 89.7 |
| Zinc                   | 42.0 | 26.5 | 17.0 |
| Aluminum               | 70.5 | 74.0 | 70.6 |
| Cellulose              | 51.6 | 46.4 | 41.8 |
| Cotton-wool            | 49.8 | 62.5 | 63.2 |

Source: Calculated on the basis of national statistics.

Table 3

The structure of Soviet trade with COMECON countries (%)

|  | Export | | | Import | | |
|---|---|---|---|---|---|---|
|  | 1980 | 1985 | 1988 | 1980 | 1985 | 1988 |
| Machines and equipment | 23.5 | 17.0 | 19.7 | 45.8 | 48.9 | 48.4 |
| Fuels and mineral raw materials | 52.8 | 60.8 | 55.4 | 7.4 | 6.6 | 7.1 |
| Chemical products | 3.4 | 3.4 | 3.6 | 3.3 | 2.9 | 2.7 |
| Building materials | 0.5 | 0.3 | 0.3 | 0.8 | 0.8 | 0.9 |
| Raw materials of vegetable and animal origin | 5.6 | 5.0 | 5.0 | 1.6 | 1.1 | 1.1 |
| Live animals | 0.0 | 0.0 | 0.0 | 0.0 | 0.1 | 0.0 |
| Raw materials for the production of food-stuffs | 0.7 | 0.5 | 0.3 | 11.1 | 11.6 | 9.7 |
| Food-stuffs | 1.8 | 1.2 | 1.2 | 8.1 | 6.6 | 5.5 |
| Industrial consumer goods | 2.7 | 2.2 | 3.1 | 16.5 | 14.3 | 14.9 |

Source: Vnesnyaya Torgovlya SSSR (National Yearbook of Statistics), (Moscow: "Nauka," 1986), p. 25.

# 11

## The European Community: Nucleus of European Integration?

*Vladimir Zouev*

Soviet thinking was never truly geared into reflection on Western European integration. Most of what was written in the Soviet Union on this subject was aimed, at best, at simply providing a description of the phenomenon. At worst -- and this was particularly true of the media -- it aimed to disparage the process, predicting the imminent collapse of this grouping of countries which had ventured to unite their efforts and interests.

After the three days in August 1991 which set one-sixth of the world shaking, the question of finding a way into the process of European integration now stands high on the agendas of many of the former republics of the USSR. Their interest is not just theoretical but involves practical politics also. This change of attitude is not surprising: the EC displays a number of important characteristics that have transformed it into a major vehicle of pan-European cooperation. It has the greatest economic potential on the continent and forms the largest economic bloc. It is growing fast and has successfully exploited the advantages of free trade and transnational cooperation. It is an important instrument for regulating national economies and provides an institution through which efforts may be made to establish the rule of law on a common basis. It is an international body that displays transparency and a steady level of predictability in its policy-making. The overall line it follows is born of compromise, it is the "mean" of a number of individual policies, and thus avoids the potential extremes of individual countries. It has shown itself keen to defend the mutual interests of its member-states, and to ensure that those states prosper. It has discovered and captured the "golden mean" (a constantly changing phenomenon that has repeatedly to be recaptured) between market and regulation and between the economic and political elements in its system (compare the weakness of the CSCE process, in which real economic ties between the participants are lacking).

The EC has, overall, become a zone of peace and stability, and its efforts to foster democracy are well-attested. The increase in its power and economic potential has given it more scope to extend a helping hand to other countries and regions in need. Its agreements with the developing world (the Lomé accords) display many innovative features and have helped improve the atmosphere of the North-South dialogue. The community has also emerged as a coordinator of aid (G-24, PHARE) and as a leader in determining policy *vis-à-vis* the Eastern European countries. Finally, the EC structure has proved resistant to shock -- from both inside and out. The supranationality of certain of its institutions, the supremacy of its law, and a viable decision-making process are important features of the EC, and are what in large part determines its effectiveness and distinguishes it from other European organizations. All this makes the EC the most solid and stable of the existing structures -- unlike NATO, which has been forced fundamentally to reconsider its mission and nature in the wake of the radical changes that have taken place on the opposing side.

Given these attributes, and given the virtual disintegration of the USSR and the limited scope of, and loose cooperation amongst, other European organizations, it is clear that the EC will play a key role in determining the nature of the future political and economic architecture of Europe. It is indeed already playing a major role, but its impact will be even greater in the near future. It has gone beyond being simply a partner for other European states, and has become a major pole of attraction. The shift in priorities that has thus occurred for most of the countries on the continent provides one of the major starting-points for the development of Europe's political future. The European Community has become a reference-point for other countries (and not just European ones) in determining policy. It provides a model for problem-solving based on federal or federal-style approaches. The most recent evidence of this may be seen in the attempts to create an economic community embracing the former republics of the USSR, and in the foundation of the Commonwealth of Independent States, which comprises eleven of the USSR's successor states. Many of the elements of Western European integration will be extremely valuable in the construction of a pan-European order. Unfortunately, EC institutions are not yet perceived as completely immune to erosion, or as particularly conducive to pan-European cooperation -- but no doubt this will change.

In practical terms, the community has already contributed much to avoiding fragmentation in terms either of numerous sub-regional groupings or -- even worse -- of nineteenth-century-style national rivalries. On the other hand, there is little scope for any sub-regional federations other than the EC: associations of a different kind may be possible, but not federations. It seems that only the EC has the option of following this path. However, even some federal states in Europe have displayed instability resulting from nationalist unrest and economic problems; thus if any European state is ready to accept limitations on its sovereignty, I do not see any reason why it should not apply for membership in the community, as opposed to other regional groups that have not yet given proof of their viability.

In order to complete the picture, however, one has to add that many countries want to be in the community not just because it is a "pole of attraction," but also because they see it as a kind of "fortress" and are afraid that those left outside it will be at a disadvantage. Some states, jealous of their sovereignty and neutrality, would like just a cautious association with the EC. And other countries and political parties are prepared to give half-hearted support to further European integration as the lesser of two evils. For instance, the still fairly hypothetical risk of the reemergence of the "German threat" is viewed by some as justifying the sacrifice of sovereign rights, for the sake of a process of integration that keeps Germany firmly under control. In principle, however, although there is still a clear fear of a consolidated community, and although this provokes reaction, or rather counter-reaction, among certain politicians, this standpoint as a whole is gradually being superseded. The steady implementation of internal-market measures proves that a consolidated community will not necessarily have a negative impact on the countries outside its borders. Consequently, the emphasis has shifted from initially considering the consequences of 1992 in Europe as mostly negative in terms of the interests of non-members, to viewing the potential role of the EC in Europe at the close of the century as more positive. Talk is now much more balanced, with mention of "risks and opportunities," rather than concentrating purely on the threats inherent in the internal market.[1]

Any fear of the EC's becoming a "fortress" cannot, however, obscure the fact that the changes that have taken place have conferred a fundamental role on the community in terms of determining the political future of Europe. This role will, in all probability, be more important than that played by the CSCE, in which the EC is already becoming increasingly actively involved. In the past, the EC was not an instrument for regulating East-West conflict -- it played a rather passive role in this sphere; however, it is now about to become just such an instrument. Through active dialogue (already under way) and through a framework of agreements (currently being set up -- e.g. association arrangements), the EC has developed quite an active policy towards the East.

In the long term, the EC, incorporating or associating most of the countries of Europe, may even undermine the CSCE, the latter remaining mainly a forum for negotiation between North America, the EC, and certain other European countries, such as the successors to the Soviet Union. The first part of this task could be accomplished by NATO; for the second part, the community might prefer to deal directly, as a bloc, with its eastern neighbours. In this case, the incentive to maintain the CSCE would be slight. Such reasoning may seem odd at a time when the CSCE is flourishing, but in the light of recent developments inside and outside the European Community, and in view of the longer-term prospects, the EC appears more able to meet the challenges in Europe than is the CSCE.

## The EC: Entering a New Phase of Development

Progress has clearly been made towards the creation of a barrier-free economic space. Although there may be obstacles and delays involved in carrying out the programme leading to the establishment of the internal market, these will not really put the final outcome in any doubt. The point is not to what extent the measures envisaged will actually be accomplished; the point is rather that this progress in itself clearly signifies that a new type of structure is emerging within the EC. The new freedom of economic activity across the borders of the community's member states will lead to a new level of interdependence, and this in turn will necessitate new institutional and organizational changes in the EC's structures. The economic space that is being created requires appropriate institutions and regulatory mechanisms.[2] The process of integration thus becomes irreversible, and the single internal market is closely bound up with other EC policies. Because the relevant measures take the form of interlinked packages, the whole process rapidly intensifies and spreads. Some progress, at least, is inevitable.

Clearly, the establishment of the internal market will promote science and technology, and the increased economic activity which it will bring makes the development of a common ecological policy more urgent than ever. Clearly too, the removal of economic barriers will accentuate the vulnerability of weaker members of society in the community, and an eye should therefore be kept on social policy, in order to avoid the risk of increased social tensions and the aggravation of economic disparities which could come about.[3] In principle, however, the economic growth that will result from 1992 will provide additional resources for tackling social problems.

Supranational elements will, it seems, become more numerous in future EC policy. More areas will be subject to majority voting -- which has now come to be recognized as efficient and indispensable. One example of this trend was the argumentation in favour of majority voting as a means of making EC social policy work.[4] The spirit of the Maastricht agreements of December 1991 offers further clear proof of this tendency. At the same time, there is no prospect of the EC's moving towards federation without strict adherence to the principle of subsidiarity, and without preserving diversity as the community moves towards greater unity. Federal elements are multiplying within the EC -- although at the Maastricht summit the leaders of The Twelve dropped the term "federation" from the draft treaty on European Union, at the insistence of the British and in accordance with a proposal made by Denmark. Whether this idea will ultimately be accepted in full by the member states depends on those states' conviction that European unity can be a tool that preserves diversity and at the same time makes all those involved stronger and wealthier. Up to now, the community has pursued this path successfully, with only one major exception -- the "no vote" in the Danish referendum on Maastricht in June 1992. In most cases, community policy has assured support for the regions, and in some of those regions, people think of themselves more as Europeans than as members of their particular nation. However, it is now clear that future progress in European integration will not be possible without a further Europeanization of people's attitudes, and a change in behaviour on the part of the economic actors in the respective societies.[5]

The establishment of the internal market provides a base from which the community can continue the move towards economic and monetary union. Indeed, once the internal market is created, "the EC will have to develop along such lines so as to become a European Union."[6] It is likely that more steps will be taken in this direction, even if some of the countries involved hesitate along the way. The momentum of integration is so great, and the number of countries at its core are so numerous, that one cannot imagine the countdown to the creation of this new entity being stopped artificially at any point. Even in harder times, the EC has always managed to find a way through.

For an outsider from the eastern part of Europe, the transformation of the EC is that much more exciting, surprising, and crucial, given the rapid disintegration of alliances in the East, and of countries such as Yugoslavia and the Soviet Union. Even recourse to military action could not preserve the integrity of Yugoslavia. And in the Soviet Union, an attempt to use such force failed -- fortunately. But the current situation merely proves that there is no other kind of force to keep the republics together -- in radical contrast to the situation in the EC.

Yet even the EC's future is not entirely rosy. There is ample scope for conflict inside the community, and ther are several difficult problems to resolve. Convergence is one of them. One matter of growing concern to the EC is that the various economies of its member countries are not showing sufficient signs of convergence as the second stage of economic and monetary union, scheduled for January 1994, approaches. Henning Christophersen, EC Commissioner for Economic Affairs, is one of several people who have pointed to the need for clear and binding commitments on the part of member states to reduce inflation, budget deficits, and balance-of-payments discrepancies to acceptable levels within three to five years.[7] In order to be able to move on to the final stage of monetary union, some states will inevitably have to introduce major changes in their macro-economic policies.

This topic was one of the key issues at the Maastricht summit in December 1991. Uncertainty about the ability of all member countries to match the average macro-economic indicators of the top performing states prompted the elaboration of specific arrangements offering several options. If more than half the member states of the EC are in convergence, the final stage of monetary union can be declared earlier than 1999; after that year, the final stage may be implemented even if the number is less than half. This arrangement was arrived at because of widespread scepticism that all, or even the majority, of the countries involved would be sufficiently prepared by then. The importance of convergence is also reflected in the fact that progress in this area will be jointly monitored by the EC Commission and the European Monetary Institute, and that great efforts are being made -- in the shape of the Cohesion Fund, to be set up by the end of 1993 -- to bring forward those countries which are lagging behind. "Adjustment," as has been noted by one observer, "becomes inevitable."[8]

Compared with advances on monetary union, the results of the intergovernmental conference on political union are less spectacular. Nevertheless, in view of the delicate nature of this subject, the Maastricht agreement appears very promising in this regard: it broadens the scope in decision-making on foreign-policy issues and envisages a link with the West European Union. Given the sceptical attitude of experts towards political integration -- reflected in such statements as "The history of the EPC [European Political Co-operation] is no guarantee for the future"[9] -- even the less spectacular achievements of Maastricht seem a major step forward.

In fact, it is clear that economic and political integration are closely related. Sooner or later, arrangements for political union will have to match those for monetary union. The two are already bound by numerous ties, including legislative ones. The Single European Act, for example, provides for cohesion between the external policies of the EC (mainly economic) and the EPC.[10] A follow-up to this, in the shape of a common foreign and security policy (including common defence), has already been envisaged in the Maastricht decisions. The ultimate result is clear: the community is becoming stronger and more united; its capacity to speak with one voice is increasing; and its ability to incorporate other countries, even relatively large ones, is growing.

## The "Widening Versus Deepening" Controversy

The question of what impact a widening of the community would have on its ability to consolidate or deepen integration stands high on the EC's current agenda. It is not the first time that it has done so.[11] For the moment, clear priority is being given to deepening integration, by completing the programmes that have already been announced. A number of EC officials, as well as various representatives of member states of the community, had stated, before the Maastricht meeting, that the community was not ready to welcome new members. However, the Maastricht agreements greatly advanced the process of deepening, and thus cleared the way for further widening. The question then arises as to how far such widening could go, and to what extent new membership-agreements, due to be negotiated in 1993, might undermine the process of deepening.

The first enlargement that occurred, namely the accession of Britain, Denmark, and Ireland in 1973, did, it is true, slow down the pace of integration, and it resulted in a renegotiation of certain conditions of membership that was in conflict with the aim of deepening integration. However, as far as European political cooperation was concerned, the first enlargement did not seriously affect coherence.[12] On the other hand, Greece's entry into the EC in 1981 reduced coherence in the EPC and created additional problems in regard to economic integration, by increasing divergence and multiplying disparities. The entry

of Spain and Portugal in 1986, however, has proceeded smoothly: it
has not jeopardized existing levels of integration nor has it hampered
the intensification of the process of integration that has come in the
wake of the Single European Act. It has proved possible to tackle qualitatively new tasks in parallel with this third widening of the EC. Accommodation of these two new members has not prevented the EC
from announcing, and successfully introducing, its programme for the
establishment of the internal market.

In principle, therefore, there is no inherent contradiction between
the widening and the deepening of the community, as there may have
seemed to be after the first enlargement in 1973. This is especially true
in the case of the admission of the EFTA countries. These have structures that are in many respects similar to those of the EC, and on average they display a greater degree of economic development than the
EC. Perhaps one should rather say that they are closer in nature to the
original Six. Disparities between the EFTA countries and the Six are
smaller than between the new and old members of the community.
EFTA long ago launched programmes of legislative adjustment to EC
requirements, and on the occasion of negotiations with the EC about
the European Economic Space, it adopted further measures designed to
help it adjust to the EC internal market. In addition, EFTA countries in
some cases have more stringent regulations than the member states of
the EC. Economically, membership is therefore more problematic for
EFTA than for the EC. This is also true for the sensitive topic of the
migration of labour. Paradoxically, however, although EC membership
poses greater problems for EFTA, its member countries show greater
enthusiasm for accession than does the EC.

The changing nature of neutrality also helps clear the way for the
entry of the neutral countries into the community without the need for
special regulations.[13] In addition, the more members the EC has, the
more scope there will be to move towards the establishment of a
community *à deux vitesses*. However, it would be politically
embarrassing for the EC to admit some European countries and not
others. One particularly delicate example of this is the admission of
Turkey, as envisaged by the association agreement. Another disquieting
fact is that if one member leaves EFTA to join the EC, the others will
almost certainly follow. Following Austria's application for
membership, the attitudes of countries such as Sweden, Finland,
Norway, and even Switzerland have shifted in favour of application. In
practical terms this will mean that, having admitted one EFTA country,
the community will be hard put to it to find any justification for not
letting the others in. Opting for the community therefore does not

imply the entry of just one more member, but the entry of several more at a time.

Finally, to admit Western European applicants while leaving Eastern Europeans out would not be an easy option, despite the fact that the case of Eastern Europe is quite different. Yet the admission of economically weak candidates from the east need not necessarily hamper the deepening of integration: the community's experience with Portugal and Ireland, which are also weaker members, belies such a conclusion.

For a while it seemed as if liberalization in Eastern Europe might lead to intensified economic interaction between the countries of the East, on a new and voluntary basis. Traditional economic links between the countries in this region, compatible structures, and similar standards in terms of quality of products all pointed in this direction -- as did the experience of Nordic cooperation.[14] However, even in the case of the Nordic countries, only 23 per cent of foreign trade is carried out within the group, whereas 59 per cent is conducted with other Western European countries, notably the EC. A similar pattern could be produced in Central and Eastern Europe in the medium term, though at present this does not seem very likely.

Paradoxically, the future of the ex-COMECON countries depends largely on EC policy. Their political aspirations point in the direction of cooperation with the community, as a means of ensuring that their efforts at systemic change are successfully completed. It is the nature and form of ties between the EC and the Eastern European countries that will determine in large measure the future structure of "Greater Europe." The countries of Central and Eastern Europe display a willingness not just to enter into closer cooperation with the community, but ultimately to accede to it. For the moment, however, the community is not signalling any readiness to admit them in the near future -- although since autumn 1991 there have been some important changes in the positions of certain member-states on this question. On the occasion of his visit to Poland at the end of May 1992, for example, the British Prime Minister, John Major, declared his support for EC membership of the three Central European states by the year 2000.[15] Again, after Maastricht, the EC made it clear that it was prepared to speed up consideration of applications, starting in 1993, as opposed to the previously announced date of 1994. However, Central and Eastern Europe will not be the first in the queue. Nevertheless, by the beginning of the next century, the community will have to make up its mind about applications from Eastern Europe. Another important area of doubt concerns the willingness of the new democratic élites who have just come to power to cede a substantial part of that power to a supra-national authority and to give up any measure of their sovereignty.

Agreements of association might be an approach that suits both sides better, as well as accomplishing the task of creating closer ties between the countries of Europe. Such agreements would not jeopardize the consolidation of the community and would also allay fears in Central and Eastern Europe about the loss of a sovereignty that has only just been regained from the Soviet Union. This partly explains the rapidity with which the European Accords between the EC and Poland, Hungary, and Czecho-Slovakia were concluded in December 1991.

Another, more general, question concerns the number of members the EC would be able to digest. A limit on numbers may be justified, but is more important in the case of purely intergovernmental organizations, in which it is harder to achieve consensus. In the case of the EPC, it is relevant only in so far as the EPC is just an intergovernmental venture. The UN has twelve times the number of members and is still capable of resolving urgent international problems. Four times as many members participate in the CSCE process, and yet many countries consider the mechanism it provides as a valuable European asset. The position in regard to the EC, however, is very different, quite apart from the question of efficiency. In an organization with strong discipline, a powerful bureaucracy, and overriding communitarian law, the number of members has less of an impact. Moreover, the desire to comply with the rules of the community is steadily growing outside the community itself. As long as there is no question of granting anyone exemption from community law, worries about numbers are not justified.

The EC's position in not allowing the EFTA countries to participate in its decision-making processes without being full members was unequivocal: it was based on the simple argument that if one is to benefit from a process one has to share the responsibilities attaching to it. As the stronger party in negotiations on accession, the EC sets the terms. EFTA countries have no choice but to accept the stance of the EC and simply content themselves for the time being with the European Economic Space. For some this represents a variant of closer integration without full participation; for others it constitutes a step towards membership. However, this situation cannot last forever, or even for long. Pressure from European non-members will increase. It will become politically harder for the community to resist widening -- first in the direction of EFTA and then to the rest of Europe.

## The Soviet Legacy:
## A Stumbling-Block on the Path to Europe?

From the time of the creation of the EC up to the second half of the 1980s, the Soviet Union preferred to deal with each individual member of the community on a strictly bilateral basis. This corresponded with the Soviet notion of the preferred structure of East-West relations in Europe. Soviet reluctance to establish direct contacts with the EC persisted even after the official declaration of the desirability of having a "business relationship" between COMECON and the Common Market. Although this statement was made as early as 1972, by the then CPSU Secretary, Leonid Brezhnev, it took a long time to produce any results. By the late 1980s the situation had changed. Partnership with the EC was a must. The Soviet Union, and later Russia and the other major members of the Commonwealth of Independent States (CIS), began to consider relations with the EC an important feature of their policies on Europe, in addition to, and in parallel with, bilateral relations with individual countries, which they continued to favour. In the case of the USSR, this position was clearly reflected in its 1989 agreement with the EC; in the case of Russia, it was demonstrated during the visit of Jacques Delors to Moscow in May 1992; the Ukraine, for its part, made its policy clear on the occasion of the visit of the Ukrainian President, Leonid Kravchuk, to France in June 1992.

The question arises as to whether there will be any further changes in this area; whether relations with the community will be given a higher profile, and granted preference over bilateral links with individual member-states; whether these latter links, although still considered necessary, will now be regarded merely as an additional element, to be encouraged in parallel. In other words, will bilateral links this time be viewed as additional to the most-favoured relations with the community, instead of vice versa? Given both the prospects of the EC and the changes in the former Soviet Union, there is good reason to suppose that just such an approach is already gaining ground. However, mistrust of the EC is still prominent amongst many politicians and bureaucrats, even in the post-Soviet era. Much of this mistrust results from misapprehension or mere ignorance of EC policies, the extent of which is sometimes unbelievable. But this is only a natural consequence of a thirty-year absence of diplomatic relations with the community.

Recent EC action has had a decisive influence on attitudes to the community, particularly in Russia. Practical steps have been taken which are directly aimed at helping overcome the Soviet legacy in the economy and society. The EC has played an important role as coordinator of the G-24 aid to the Eastern European countries since the G-7 summit in Paris in 1989. It has arranged the direct allocation of funds to the USSR and its successors, including humanitarian aid and technical assistance.[16] A further clear illustration of the EC's stance in this area was its position on the creation of the European Bank for Reconstruction and Development, including the invitation to the Soviet Union to take part in this.[17] Unlike the other parties involved, the community wanted to grant the USSR equal status in the Bank right from the outset. These initiatives have done much to restore trust between the various parts of Europe. Indeed, recent polls show that roughly half the population in Central and Eastern Europe have a positive impression of the European Community.[18]

At present, the greatest risks to relations with the EC lie in the CIS, with its ethnic clashes, political instability, and economic deprivation. The federation that had appeared possible in August 1991 had definitely died by the end of the year. The Soviet republics became independent, progressively acquiring the attributes of sovereignty during 1992. Political and economic power is already concentrated in these new states, and for some of them, the only structure that could conceivably ensure the preservation of a minimum of unity is a pre-federal order along the lines of the European Community. From the time of the creation of the CIS, and particularly since summer 1992, the EC has even been suggested as a model for reconstruction within some of the independent states.[19]

However, the major actor in determining the nature and form of ties within the Commonwealth and with the EC will undoubtedly be Russia. It is therefore important to take a closer look at the Russian approach to relations with the community. The aim of the traditional, "narrow" approach that was cultivated in some of the former Soviet economic bodies, was to deal with the community only within the limits of its current competences in the economic sphere, particularly in the domain of trade. This approach has lost much of its former influence. Many people, particularly ministry officials, considered these limits offered quite a lot of scope -- more than enough for at least the next decade. They believed broader tasks should be carried out solely on a bilateral basis with individual countries, or within the framework of multilateral conferences where individual countries participated on an equal basis. However, since August 1991, the official administration has been seriously weakened, and a new generation of civil servants has entered institutional structures at all levels.

In contrast, supporters of an alternative, "broad" approach argue that, as far as the construction of a new Europe is concerned, the EC is an indispensable partner in all sorts of areas. Many individuals who have recently moved from the academic community into the new economic and political management-structures hold to this view. The Soviet share of world trade was very modest, but the economic potential of its successors is much greater. In order properly to exploit this potential, it is thought necessary to develop forms of economic cooperation other than trade: joint ventures, cooperation in industrial, scientific, and technological fields, etc. It also seems logical to move beyond economic cooperation, to search for solutions to ecological problems, to develop cultural contacts, and to look for institutionalized forms of political dialogue. This approach incorporates the vision of a future EC with extended competences, to match long-term prospects for relations with the EC.

Short-term scenarios for relations vary considerably, depending on the internal situation in the member states of the CIS, in particular Russia, and on the pace of reforms, the size and shape of the new states, and the attitude of the EC. However, some avenues of development are already visible. For example, the new independent states could -- either separately or jointly -- fully exploit existing opportunities for cooperation, as provided for in the agreement struck by the Soviet Union and the EC in December 1989. This has so far not been done, and it seems it will not be done until the relevant agreements have been concluded with the individual republics. For political reasons, these republics, including Russia, want something different from what they had during the Soviet period. In purely economic terms, however, the collapse of the Soviet economy greatly reduced the capacity of these states to cooperate with the outside world. In addition to straightforward economic cooperation, new relations will therefore necessarily have to include a large aid-component, to help the republics in their efforts to transform and reconstruct shattered economic links. Greater emphasis is already being placed on credit and other financial arrangements to support trade and establish economic links. On 4 March 1992, for instance, the EC and Russia singed an agreement providing for a credit of 500 million ECUs over three and a half years. The EC is preparing a further such arrangement worth 1250 million ECUs. In parallel with these arrangements, other kinds of aid and technical assistance are being granted on both ad hoc and regular bases. Two programmes of technical assistance worth 400 and 450 million ECUs respectively were agreed in the EC's budgets for 1991 and 1992. More than 155 tons of food aid were supplied over a six-month period in 1992. The very professional manner of its delivery could serve as a model for future actions of this kind by other international organizations.

A framework agreement that will be of great importance to Russia has been agreed in principle by the latter and the EC. It is important because the time is not yet ripe for sectoral arrangements, following the disintegration of the USSR (affecting fishing) and the breakdown of the economy (affecting coal and steel, textiles, science and technology). It is quite likely that progress will be more rapid in some areas than in others. One obvious possibility here is the formation of a pan-European energy community, or at least the establishment of links on the basis of jointly approved principles and conditions.

Another possibility is the initiation by the EC of specific, long-term measures to help individual republics. In this connection, one can conceive of a further extension -- the third -- of PHARE, to include the remnants of the Soviet Union. Some at least of the EC programmes, such as educational projects, could be extended geographically to cover some of the new states, as well as Central and Eastern Europe. A possible variant of this approach would be to adjust (rather than extend) PHARE to the specific circumstances in the former Soviet Union and announce the creation of a new one. The task of restructuring the Soviet economy and facilitating the transition to a market economy is an extremely ambitious one and will require much effort. Ways and means of cooperation should therefore be on a qualitatively higher level compared with the first scenario -- where activity is mainly restricted to trade -- or indeed with the traditional PHARE. Following the failed putsch in the USSR, and the resolute institution of economic reforms, such an approach is all the more urgent, and there is a much greater likelihood that resources will not be wasted. In addition -- and this is by no means the least significant factor -- Russia has proved that it is prepared to accept assistance under strict international control. However, the task to be tackled in Russia is so huge that it will be difficult to accomplish without the involvement of other Western countries. Yet although some efforts at coordinating Western assistance and mobilizing resources on a broad scale were made during this year's conferences in Washington, Lisbon, and Tokyo, it is still the community which has provided nearly 80 per cent of all assistance.

A new agreement on cooperation between Russia and the EC, involving more openness in the economic field and greater emphasis on cultural and political ties, was proposed during Jacques Delors's visit to Moscow in May 1992. It was the EC representatives who emphasized the importance of a comprehensive approach (covering political, economic, and cultural cooperation) and the readiness of the EC to help the Russian economy adapt to world economic standards. Exploratory talks have begun, with the aim of concluding such an agreement by the end of 1992. Politically the community feels compelled to propose something new for Russia (as the initiator of change in Europe); but it seems reluctant to conclude the same kind of agreement with the successors to the Soviet Union as it concluded with Central and Eastern Europe -- in the form of the European Accords. Nevertheless, positing the most ambitious scenario, it is still possible to imagine the conclusion, in the long term, of association-type agreements with at least some of the former republics of the USSR. This might take place in the following order: first the Baltic states, then the Ukraine, Belarus, and Russia, and finally Kazakhstan. Frans Andriessen, Vice President of the EC Commission, suggested, on 2 March 1992 in Brussels, that cooperation agreements might be concluded in the following sequence: Russia, Belarus, the Ukraine, Kazakhstan. In this connection, it is worth mentioning that the EC and the republics of Lithuania, Latvia, and Estonia initialled agreements on trade and cooperation as early as February 1992. Indeed, these were the first such treaties with successor states of the USSR.

In the past there were a number of explicit obstacles to closer ties between the EC and the Soviet Union: the size of the country -- a deterrent to potential partners; a lack of predictability; a lack of stable economic, legal, and political conditions inside the USSR; and, finally, the Union's sizeable Asian component. These objections no longer hold good: disintegration of the Union has reduced the dimensions involved; the independent states are smaller and, at least from this point of view, more amenable to closer ties with the community -- in any case, as far as some of the republics are concerned, size no longer necessarily reflects power; in addition, the European republics are looking to establish links individually; and, finally, the stronger the community grows, the easier it will become for it to cope with bigger partners and to influence the process of transition.

The earlier stance adopted by the EC, namely allocating aid to central authorities in the Soviet Union, in order to help preserve stability and prevent the immediate, violent disintegration of the country, was quite understandable. Once independent states had been created, however, the EC had the legally founded option of selecting the more European amongst these, and of having deeper relations with them than with the others. Hence the EC's options in regard to the CIS are similar to its differentiated approach to Eastern Europe prior to the disintegration of the USSR.

However, it is Russia that will probably become the EC's major partner, provided democratic and market reforms continue to be implemented. This does not necessarily mean that relations with Russia will in fact be the closest of all those with the CIS states; but they will undoubtedly have the most weight. An indication of this was given by the President of the EC Commission during his visit to Moscow, when he said that the intent of the proposed agreement with Russia was "to make the partnership between the EC on the one hand, and Russia on the other, more comprehensive, thus creating two supporting pillars on our great continent, one being the community, the other being Russia."[20]

The future shape of relations will depend not just on developments in the former Soviet Union, but also, and to a large extent, on the European Community. Recent developments have shown that the EC has markedly stepped up its efforts in this area, and is displaying much greater interest in getting involved in the erstwhile Soviet Union. Does this mean that Russia, or any other member-state of the CIS, will one day be admitted to the community? It seems clear that this issue will not appear on the agenda before the end of this century. Nevertheless, during his visit to France in June 1992, the Ukrainian President, Leonid Kravchuk, urged French support for such a measure. Similarly, the Russian ambassador to the EC, Ivan Silaev, recently stated that "It is imperative for Russia to create the necessary conditions for joining the EC."[21]

As far as the community itself is concerned, it has other priorities than the admission of the (European) remnants of the USSR. Besides, most of the republics are clearly not yet ready for entry to an EC-type organization (and will not be for a long time). One obvious reason for this is the supranational nature of the EC, and the supremacy of EC law, which together form a hurdle which it is almost impossible to envisage surmounting. Another factor is superpower attitudes, particularly in the case of Russia. For comparison, we may recall how difficult it was for the disintegrating British empire to adapt to new realities. At the time when the European Communities were being set up, Britain could not accept that a supranational authority should take decisions on its internal affairs. In the case of Russia, adaptation may be even more painful. There is an obvious reluctance on the part of those politicians who have only recently come to power to submit any element of national policy to the scrutiny of an international authority with broad competences.

Changes in the perception of the EC have done much to modify the policies on Europe pursued by the new élites in the former USSR. But this is only part of the story. Present circumstances are such that the ex-Soviet republics have little choice in regard to the future. Some important international rivals of the community have the option of counterbalancing European unification by gathering together the countries in their own vicinities: the US has launched an initiative to dismantle barriers and create a free-trade area in North and Central America; similar options are open to Japan in the Asian-Pacific region. At the same time, all efforts to reconstruct COMECON have proved ineffective. And attempts to create a Soviet federation, confederation, or economic union have been met with strong opposition. Certain republics in Central Asia and on the southern flank of the former USSR are the only ones who appear to be pressing ahead with regional cooperation of a kind that is not yet visible in central and western parts.

If the former European republics of the Soviet Union decide to maintain their distance in regard to the EC, they will face the risk of becoming ever more separated from the rest of Europe, which is now becoming their most natural ally. Given the increasing pull exerted by the European Community on the rest of Europe, all these republics have to do in a sense (and luckily for them) is simply to join the other European states in the pan-European process of unification.

## Notes

1. J. van Brabant, *1992, the Revolutions in Eastern Europe, and Relations Among East, South, and North. The Implications of the Single Market Act for Non-Member Countries* (New York: United Nations, 1991), pp. 1-40.

2. Cf. J.-V. Louis, "L'Acte unique européen," in: *L'instauration du Marché Intérieur le 1 Janvier 1993* (Bruxelles: Editions du Jeune Barreau, 1989), p. 40.

3. See, for instance, *Europe: le défi social* (Bruxelles: Editions CIACO, 1989), pp. 21-33.

4. "Tribune pour l'Europe," *Informations du Parlement Européen*, No. 8, Septembre 1990, p. 3.

5. As was emphasized by P.Cecchini, M. Catinat, A. Jacquemin, *1992 Le Defi. Un rapport issu du projet de recherche sur le cout de la non-Europe* (Paris: Flammarion, 1988), p. 222.

6. J. Pinder, "The Single Market: a step towards European Union," in: Juliet Lodge (ed.), *The European Community and the Challenge of the Future* (London: Pinter, 1989), p. 105.

7. *International Herald Tribune*, June 1-2, 1991, pp. 1, 10.

8. F. Serre et al. (eds.) *Les politiques étrangères de la France et de la Grande Bretagne depuis 1945. L'inévitable ajustement* (Paris: Fondations des Sciences Politiques, 1990), pp. 13-21.

9. A. Pijpers et al. (eds.) *European Political Cooperation in the 1980s. A common foreign policy for Western Europe?* (Dordrecht: Kluwer Academic Publishers, 1988), p. 271.

10. See *Single European Act*, Article 30, (Luxemburg: Office for official publications of the EC, 1986).

11. See H. Wallace, *Widening and deepening: the European Community and the new European agenda* (London: RIIA Discussion paper No. 23, 1989), pp. 13-9.

12. *New Europe*, Vol. 13, No. 1, 1987, p. 18.

13. P. Schori, *Sweden and new developments in Europe* (Los Angeles: World Affairs Council, 1991), pp. 2-6.

14. *Monitoring European integration. The impact of Eastern Europe* (London: CEPR Discussion Paper, 1990), p. 4.

15. *Izvestia*, May 27, 1992.

16. *Izvestia*, June 20, 1991.

17. *La Communauté et la Banque Européenne pour la Reconstruction et le Développment* (Bruxelles: Commission des Communautés Européennes, May 7, 1990).

18. *Evropa, Magazine of the EC for Russia* (Moscow: Delegation of the Commission of the EC to Moscow, May, June, 1992), p. 6.

19. This happened, for instance, in the case of Moldova where the leaders of *Pridnestrovye* (Transdnestr) definitely rejected any federation at the end of June 1992, see *Izvestia*, June 23, 1992, and *Nezavisimaya Gazeta*, June 24, 1992.

20. Press conference of J. Delors, May 30, 1992, Moscow, *Russian Foreign Office Press Release*, p. 3.

21. *Evropa (op.cit.* in note 18), p. 13.

# 12

## The Difficult Return of the Prodigal Son: Central and Eastern Europe on the Threshold of the 21st Century

*Pavel Kandel*

When contemplating the destiny of Central and Eastern Europe one frequently refers to the following lines by the Russian poet Osip Mandelstam: "Europe of the Cesars! For the first time in a hundred years since Metternich directed his pen to Bonaparte, your mysterious map is changing before my very eyes." These lines come to mind not accidentally: both, the Second World War and the post-war settlement changed the contours and colours of the European map fundamentally, and the antitotalitarian revolutions of 1989 have raised expectations as well as fears of another equally fundamental change. Since Europe has responded to international cataclysms and social upheavals twice in this century by changing its borders and entering into violent conflicts, it would be quite logical to expect a similar though hardly desirable change again.

Be it the historical fate of the peoples of Central and Eastern Europe or be it a matter of geo-politics or of the logic of socio-economic and socio-political development, ever since it has served as an arena for rivalry of the great European powers fighting for the trophy; the specific role of the region in European economic and political life appears indisputable. It never managed to become a subject rather than an object of world politics, and remained the least stable zone between the dynamically developing West and the dreamy and stagnant East. Moreover, this region, though lagging behind Western Europe's social, economic and political developments, surpassed Russia and later the Soviet Union in these fields, which led to additional international tensions in Central and Eastern Europe's relations with both the West and the East. But even on those rare occasions which saw the young states of Central and Eastern Europe acting on their own for short intervals, most of them could not resist the temptation of challenging their neighbours, thus failing to establish a reasonable balance between their much cherished historical aspirations and their real political weight.

Although history does not repeat itself -- except as a caricature -- the current changes in Central and Eastern Europe which call for historical analogies do not promise immediate peace despite the pro-European orientation in both domestic and international policy. The USSR-centered system of international relations that existed in the region for more than 40 years is giving way to a Europe-centered one. No less dynamic and important are the changes in Eastern Europe's internal development where the totalitarian social order is being replaced by a pluralistic system. However, the existing society and the one Eastern Europe is trying to establish are nearly antipodes in their major economic, social, ideological and political parameters. And this is compounded by the current state of international legal amorphousness, dangerously frought with the potential of external interference. Therefore, these countries must yet overcome a dangerous period of instability which can be described as the battle between future challenges and the inertia of the past.

Whatever the obstacles ahead, they will scarcely undermine the irreversible changes. There is abundant evidence for this. These changes are the logical result of previous developments common to the whole of Eastern Europe: an array of bitter social antagonisms unresolvable within the totalitarian system and in conditions of socio-economic and political crisis, which has hit every country in the region, and the dangerous escalation of social and political tensions which at the end of the 1980s revived the spectre of 1956 only in larger dimensions. However, contrary to 1956, change in Eastern Europe was met with an unexpectedly calm reaction on the part of the USSR: the Soviet Union denounced military resistance as an answer to the sweeping wave of revolutionary changes either after thorough consideration of its weakening power and the difficulty of the task, or because it was typically unable to realize the historical dimension of the events taking place.

## Towards the Post-Totalitarian Society:
## Problems of Transformation

The most salient symptom of the irreversible choice made by Eastern Europe is the strategic defeat of the communist movement -- the
socio-political subject of the previous social order which now seems to
be disappearing from the political arena for good. "Real socialism" created by the communist movement as a historical substitute and rival of
capitalism has failed to carry out its task and has wound up in disgrace,
having ruined the very movement that brought it to life. Having recognized the complete failure of the social system built under the communist party's autocratic rule, a fact almost universally recognized, the
communist parties have revealed their total historical uselessness. Once
they were compelled to turn to the ideas of a market economy, a civil
society, a constitutional state and of political pluralism, which they had
previously strongly denounced, the communist parties lost their own
ideological and political identity and were no longer trustworthy. A series of amazingly similar tactical errors committed in different countries, provoked by a significant inability of these state "super-agencies"
in the monopolistic system to transform themselves into real political
parties, has clinched the matter.

Neither the still sizable communist party membership nor the relatively strong electoral results for the Party of Democratic Socialism
(PDS) in (east) Germany, the Communist Party in Czecho-Slovakia,
and for the communist heirs in Rumania, Serbia, Montenegro and Albania will be long-lived; for numerous indicators show that neither the
communist parties nor their predominantly "socialist" successors will
have the slightest chances for success in the near future. The seemingly
contradictory results of the 1991 general elections in Poland and Bulgaria, whereby the Polish Alliance of the Democratic Left (DLA) and
the Bulgarian Socialist Party (BSP) won enough seats to become the
second strongest group in their respective parliaments do not stand
against this assessment of Eastern Europe's political evolution. The
BSP, supported by one third of the electorate, is no longer the ruling
party. And 12% of the votes for the DLA account for no more than
50% of the former Communist Party's membership. With the new political elites in both countries so determined and even aggressive in
their attempts to oust the "ex-elites" from political and social life, the
former communists have had to fight hard. This might be one reason
for the less obvious "ebb" of communism in these cases. However, the
defeat suffered by most of the ex-communist parties in conditions of financial, organizational and material advantage over their rivals only

indicates that, once deprived of all these assets, they will turn politically insolvent.

In addition, the blows suffered by reformist-communist and other leftist but decisively anti-communist organizations such as "Das Neue Forum" in the former GDR are indicative of a deep public distrust in anything somehow reminiscent of the communist idea or not radical enough in rejecting "real socialism." The same holds true for the isolation of communist parties and their heirs in the political arena: even when centrist or leftist parties are pushed into alliances by the logic of political and parliamentary competition, they are not yet ready to furnish agreements with communists or those who are still viewed as such.

Even more significant were the defeats of the social democrats, despite their expectations of much greater success on the basis of their self-presentation as the party most capable of bridging the gap between the past and the future and as a guarantor of a gradual and smooth transition. The reason for this failure is not so much the weak historical roots of social democracy in Eastern Europe. Far more important is that evolutionary reformism, the traditional aspiration of social democrats, which relies on institutions such as the state and public ownership, is becoming more and more questionable even in Western Europe and amongst social democrats themselves. In Central and Eastern Europe, where people long for rapid and fundamental reforms, these aspirations find even less sympathy. They simply do not correspond to the fundamentally different topics on today's political agenda such as radical denationalization and rapid transition to a market economy. And, furthermore, the long-standing ideological and political monopoly of "leftist" ideas and forces has transformed the former opposition into a "rightist" movement.[1]

The current situation in which "rightist" values such as the market and private ownership are fused with the genealogically "leftist" ideas of *liberté, egalité, fraternité* provides ample evidence of the depletion of the leftist political tradition during the period of its allegedly unshared dominance. In the political tradition of the West, this ideological synthesis was represented by classical liberalism. However, in Central and Eastern Europe, liberalism with few exceptions has never taken root and its impact has been minimal. This reflects the low level of socio-economic development in the region, where the tardy introduction of capitalism is causing sharp political and ideological divisions within societies previously unaccustomed to such social change.

All that suggests a drastic weakening of the leftist political spectrum as such: another swing of the historical pendulum. Particularly in post-socialist societies, the defeat of the leftist movement is largely determined by the "rightist" tasks which need to be tackled with regard to economic disarray. Only when a market economy and political pluralism are firmly established can one envisage a reshaping of the currently right-biased political spectrum along the typically Western European lines characterized by regular though moderate fluctuations to the right or the left. And then the time might be ripe for a new leftist movement emerging in accordance with the needs of a pluralistic society and not in reaction to historical inertia, as was the case, for instance, in pre-October Russia. Meanwhile, there is hardly anything to prevent the societies in the East from enormous social, economic and political overloads unavoidable in the unique transitional period from totalitarianism to pluralism. As experience shows this period may entail a further economic decline, social unrest, bitter political clashes and international tensions.

Well-known are the economic problems due to the inherited macroeconomic disequilibra as well as the transition to a market economy. The latter necessitates deregulation on a large scale, denationalisation and nothing less than far-reaching structural changes in production and employment in order to facilitate integration into the world market. But, more than two years after the first "revolutionary" measures were introduced, the results are still unsatisfactory. Even in unified Germany, a single prosperous state, the economy in the eastern part is still in turmoil. All the other countries of the region will have to go through a long and painful transition period with most companies, and in particular the typical huge conglomerates, finding themselves sandwiched between a not-quite-clear market future and a no-longer-working centrally planned economy of the past.

The social transformation embedded in this process will also encounter serious obstacles. A society with an almost undifferentiated social structure, in a way just divided between "them" -- the *nomenklatura* -- and "us" -- the overwhelming majority of the population -- will have to develop into a system of self-organized, widely differentiated interests. The old system, in which the leading parts were played by those in power and their administrators, must be replaced by a system in which those assuming individual responsibility for production and distribution (be it the businessman or the blue-collar worker) are the key figures. In this process of rapid transition, a single generation will witness major changes in life-style, in the correlation between social status and range of public authority, and in established social roles, links, and patterns of interaction. However, beside the redundant *nomenklatura* and the rising market economy elite, there is a large group of people who have been forced out of their social niche without yet occupying a new one. Thus, a politically dangerous situation, in which a sizable number of people are becoming temporarily marginalized, can easily arise. These people are receptive to all sorts of populist and extremist sentiments. In this way -- leftist radicalism having exhausted itself --, an increasingly strong rightist extremism can play on the vulgar egalitarian sentiments of the lower walks of life who used to man the communist reserve and lure these people with empty hopes.

This phenomenon is well-known in history, for instance, during the last years of the Weimar Republic in Germany. But there is also more recent evidence. The effective manipulation of national sentiments by communist leaders (particularly in Slovakia, Rumania, Bulgaria, Serbia and Montenegro) shows that the communists' traditional social base is not at all immune against the virus of nationalism, contrary to their internationalist ideological postulates. The actions of Rumanian miners who in June 1990 secured the survival of the *neo-nomenklatura* regime of President Iliescu by staging a pogrom on the opposition forces and in September 1991 toppled the government and almost deprived the ruling party of power, are on the other hand indicative of the different shapes which extremist populism can take. Public polls and the results of the 1991 parliamentary elections in Bulgaria and particularly in Poland are ample proof of the rise of radical populism on both ends of the political spectrum. Arguably, a potential for radical tendencies was also manifested by the 50% abstentions in these Polish elections -- the possible recruits for a future non-parliamentary opposition.

Quite a similar picture can be observed in the sphere of party-democracy. Although the large number of political formations set up immediately after the revolutions in most of the East European countries might signify tough competition and a rich variety of political interests, true ideological and political differentiation and, moreover, an adequate political channeling of social interests have only just begun. Many of the emerging parties have been trying to borrow names and programmes of existing Western parties or of parties that operated in the inter-war period. In many cases, however, it was and to a large degree still is difficult to identify more than small -- if any -- distinctions amongst the post-revolutionary political parties in programme and practice.

Reference to an idealized past is but a poor imitation of continuity. Today, the main task is to move peacefully from totalitarianism to a post-totalitarian system. And for this, no recipe is readily available in Western party arsenals, nor do the predecessors' experiences help much. Attempts to apply merely borrowed political and ideological concepts to a reality that is fundamentally different must therefore have alienating effects on many people. They can hardly feel represented by political platforms which do not reflect the specific post-socialist conditions in terms of social interests, behavioural patterns or value systems. This very fact can easily prepare the ground for simple answers to a fairly complex and demanding task, ending up in protest actions in the streets directed by extremist and nationalist forces.

It is not accidental that Bolshevik-like anticommunists are appearing in Eastern Europe, conservatives ready to raise everything to the ground, christian democrats slipping into clericalism, and liberals whose attitude to the state is a replica to that of anarchists. The "Tyminski effect" in Poland, where a Canadian-Peruvian businessman of Polish origin with an extravagant political habit suggested the simplest solutions and got 25% of the overall vote to finish second in the presidential elections, was the first manifestation of this inherent danger. Although this remained an isolated case so far, the example is significant in that under prevailing circumstances, charisma turns out to be more important than a political reputation. Similarly, it has shown the extent to which rational and efficient policy is impotent against miracle-working illusions, eclectical populist programmes and nationalistic sentiments. And this is understandable, for the essence of social relations in "real socialism" -- be it feudo-industrial or, more precisely, clientèle-like in character -- was nothing but pre-capitalist, pre-industrial and "pre-European." Hence the lack of articulated political programmes in present day Eastern Europe. Like hardening lava, the process of social, ideological and political crystallization will take time and cover the entire transitional period before a stable political structure within a true civil society will take shape.

This process has started and the "negative consensus" (i.e. the battle against "real socialism") is gradually being replaced by the need for the elites of the 1989 revolutions to determine constructive political aims and means on their own. In most cases, parties with the most convincing record of fighting socialism in whatever shape are still dominated by right-wing neo-liberal and neo-conservative forces: here, the question arises as to whether this shift to the right will be confined to parliamentary competition or turn into a witch-hunt. As mentioned above, the rise of right-wing political forces in the initial stages of transformation in Eastern Europe was hardly surprising. But, will this lead to a Western-type democracy and are the new political figures in power really capable of laying the groundwork for stable and lasting democratic institutions? Under present circumstances, this is undoubtedly a demanding task as we can already observe a number of severe splits within the new elites precisely along these lines. Here, I do not have in mind so much the inevitable break-up of the broad and fairly amorphous revolutionary movements such as Solidarity in Poland or the Czech "Civic Forum" and the Slovak "Citizens Against Violence." More alarming is a growing confrontation between pro-European versus nationalist and traditionalist movements calling for "originality" and "national values," between secular versus clerical circles, and between liberal democrats as well as conservatives versus advocates of authoritarian rule.

It would be premature to make any definite judgements about the outcome of these controvercies, but there are sound reasons to argue that in Eastern Europe, with its weak democratic tradition, the new democratic institutions will be able to withstand the tough economic, political and social pressures they encounter. Though many of these countries used to have a parliamentary democracy in the inter-war period, these had an unmistakably autocratic touch. And still today, political stability and decision-making rests to a much lesser extent on viable and transparent democratic institutions than on the reputation -- and determination -- of venerable political figures such as Lech Walesa, Vaclav Havel, Zhelu Zhelev or Josef Antall. One can neither rely on indispensable political virtues such as common sense or the readiness for compromise nor is it appropriate to invest much hope into the experience and intelligence of the new generation of politicians. An age of new idols and new values seems to be emerging.

### Nationalism: The Most Dangerous Escape Route

Traditionally, weak democratic institutions have had their counterpart in strong national sentiments in Eastern Europe, a region where ethnic tensions and the problems connected with nation-building have been on the political agenda since the 19th century. For a number of reasons, this sentiment resurfaced after more than forty -- and in the case of the erstwhile Soviet Union even seventy -- years of a forced-upon freeze. Apart from many still unresolved nationality problems, two major causes are behind the recent reemergence of nationalist sentiments and of nationalism in the region. On the one hand, there is the unexpectedly rapid and relatively easy political change of 1989, which has served as a favourable psychological basis for fomenting nationalist sentiments. The subsequent elation has made people feel that no goals are unattainable and that any obstacle can be overcome. Such emotions can easily be transformed into nationalistic euphoria which quite often makes state borders look as brittle as the Berlin Wall. On the other hand, economic crisis and growing social tensions are underscoring a trend in which people are switching their attention from these domestic problems to issues of a compensatory nature. Relief from the whole range of pressing problems is then expected solely from clear-cut answers to the many national questions.

Obviously, states with a multiethnic composition are most severely affected and threatened by the rise of nationalism all over Eastern Europe. Given forty years of limited or even suppressed sovereignty, for quite a while there was also a particularly prominent object for hostile national feelings: the Soviet Union. These feelings have, however, largely receded due to the collapse of the CPSU and the break-up of the union. But other feelings may easily take their place, resentments with abundant historical roots such as Russophobia and Ukrainophobia. The sovereign Ukraine in particular, which has good chances of becoming a dominant power in the region, may soon become an object of cupidity in terms of border disputes as well as a large variety of minority conflicts.

Considering the covert nationalistic and territorial claims most Central and Eastern European countries hedge against each other, the rise of nationalism in any one of them is principally fraught with the danger of violent conflicts. There is not only the war over control of Serb enclaves in Croatia as well as in Bosnia and Herzegovina, but other republics and autonomist regions inside former Yugoslavia (Kosovo, Macedonia, Vojvodina) are about to become new trouble spots. The position of the Turks in Bulgaria and that of the Hungarians in Slovakia, Transylvania, Vojvodina and the Ukraine may highten tensions both inside and outside these countries. A similar reaction cannot be ruled out in countries blown up from inside as a result of growing social discontent. Albania, Rumania and Bulgaria are likely to be the first in this respect. Although history will decide upon the order, we can be sure that many of the countries enumerated above will enter the list.

But, undoubtedly, the most dramatic events are now taking place in what used to be Yugoslavia, which has become a "European Lebanon." If its neighbours start claiming their share to the Yugoslavian legacy, then a series of national and territorial crusades in the whole region seems inevitable. So Yugoslavia serves as a kind of litmus test for the region's -- and Europe's -- readiness to enter the new post-cold-war era. The Yugoslav situation also serves to illustrate the violent potential inherent in nationalism and its limited dependence on the overall economic situation. It is generally assumed that in a situation of economic crisis the gap between different ethnic groups widens. The Yugoslav example, however, has shown that this is only one aspect. Though the country was confronted with serious economic problems before the civil war broke out, Yugoslavia had achieved remarkable results in its readjustment efforts, curbing inflation and reducing imbalances in trade and payment. Prospects of a Dinar-convertibility looked real, foreign credits were guaranteed and closer relations with the EC were within reach. But in the end, economic logic was discarded and nationalism got the upper hand.

No wonder nationalism has become the most powerful force in the post-totalitarian societies. The collapse of totalitarianism has left behind a social wasteland, and the elementary forms of socialisation appearing in that wasteland are both primeval and natural: i.e. nationalism. At the same time, the structural kinship of totalitarian and nationalist consciousness (monism, mythologism, the priority of the community as opposed to the human personality) make it very easy to replace the class-based myth by the nationalist myth. Viewed from this angle, the "Balkanization" of Central and Eastern Europe is by no means an only theoretical perspective. The same is true for the region's internal development, where in a worst-case-scenario one might be confronted with the uncomfortable alternative of either a Latin American-type of "wild" capitalism or an African-type of intermittent development with its specific amalgamation of private enterprise and bureaucratic state monopoly. Social and political consequences of both alternatives are easy to predict.

## Central and Eastern Europe Between East and West

The situation in Eastern Europe -- threatened by a deep economic crisis, social unrest and lacking political stability -- will be further endangered by the security vacuum that emerged with the collapse of integrative Eastern institutions such as COMECON and the Warsaw Treaty Organisation. Moreover, non-compliance with treaties of bilateral cooperation and badly eroded economic relations reveal a change that runs far deeper. The aftermath of the 1989 revolutions has brought a fairly different set-up of military, economic, political and ideological power factors to the fore in the region, at the same time putting an end to the only political and economic power center that previously existed.

With the transformation of the European bipolar system of international relations into a unipolar one, Central and Eastern Europe has become an area in which two main tendencies confront each other: the call for "Europeanization" on the one hand -- integration into a single

European community within the shortest possible period of time -- and, on the other hand, the risk of "Balkanization" which inevitably will come out of widespread attempts to concentrate political efforts on cleaning up the ethnic and territorial mess within and among most of the countries concerned. Economic and long-term state interests encourage the first tendency while the opposite has become prominent due to domestic developments, the legacy of the past and the destructive consequences of regional instability (the notable examples are Yugoslavia and the former Soviet Union), not effectively contained by the somewhat slow and sluggish efforts on the part of Western Europe.

The two tendencies in question are unevenly present on the region's map. The "Europeanisation" is firmly established in Czecho-Slovakia, Hungary and Poland. So one can reasonably expect that it will remain dominant in the foreign policy of these countries, provided the Czecho-Slovak Federative Republic remains a single state. As against it, a "Balkanization" is more probable in the South-Eastern European countries and maybe the former Soviet Union, where the orientation towards Europe does not appear strong enough.

Which tendency in the end prevails depends to a considerable degree upon the resolution of the crisis in and around Yugoslavia. The fear of "balkanizing" the whole area may be drastically reduced, provided a viable post-war settlement in Yugoslavia is found by the world community with active European participation and in compliance with CSCE principles. Such a solution must be based on the right of self-determination, i.e. the official recognition of the Yugoslav republics in international law. Similarly, minority rights have to be ensured and it might also entail a negotiated change of borders under international supervision. In case Serbia succeeds in carving out sizable parts from Croatia and Bosnia and Herzegovina by means of force, however, an extremely dangerous and provocative precedent will have been made. Such a turn of events would encourage further violations of the status quo or of CSCE principles by force because the offender can easily get away with it, while purely rhetorical condemnations by the international community need not be taken into account. In such circumstances Yugoslavia's neighbours, who still feel strongly about the injustice of the Versailles Treaties and the subsequent Yalta agreements imposed upon them, would certainly raise concerns about the security of their compatriots in neighbouring countries. This might give them a golden opportunity for justifying a military build-up and for exercising pressure on these countries in order to satisfy seemingly legitimate territorial claims.

But whatever scenario will follow Yugoslavia's break-up, tensions in the Balkans will continue to grow. This would in all probability have a negative impact on the disarmament process and on much-needed confidence-building measures in the region. Without a significantly higher degree of attention and coordinated interference on the part of the leading powers it will be hard to overcome the instability in the Balkans. In any case, if rivalry gets the upper hand, the situation in the area will further deteriorate and the danger of violent confrontation spreading into Europe will increase likewise.

Whereas in the Yugoslav case a black hole appeared on the political map in the south-east of Europe, developments in the former Soviet Union have blurred the eastern demarcation of Europe. As a result, a greater Central and Eastern Europe has emerged with various new countries as its constituent parts. However, the ill-structured and conflict-laden political space may easily give rise to additional trouble spots, even though the character of possible conflicts has fundamentally changed. In the months preceding the August coup in Moscow, the Central and Eastern European countries timorously watched the rising counter-reform in Soviet domestic and foreign policy, fearful of setbacks by the use of force. Once the coup failed and true revolutionary changes started, the bugaboo-bear of a Soviet threat took on a new meaning: it was no longer the power of the second superpower but its weakness and its dismemberment that became the cause for great concern. The volatile situation in the region renders any prognosis about future developments fairly hypothetical, as the union that turned into a commonwealth also turned from a recent stronghold of stability in Europe into a country exporting instability.

Against this background, Hungary, Czecho-Slovakia and Poland in particular began to seek NATO and WEU membership or at least security guarantees. The emphasis Lech Walesa, Zhelu Zhelev and many others constantly lay on the necessity of retaining a US military presence in Europe in order to ensure European security, should be considered in the same context. The peaceful break-up of the USSR and the emergence of fifteen new sovereign states, however, does in itself not necessarily affect the European process, except in the quantitative sense that more actors have appeared on the international political floor, many of them of a rather complicated nature.

Yet, the emergence of such a large number of new states with, in many cases, contested borders and governed by reborn politicians with strong national sentiments but no experience whatsoever in conducting foreign policy, may also have an opposite effect. Here, Eastern Europe is particularly vulnerable and may become a battle-field for the Ukraine and Belarus versus Poland, Poland versus Lithuania, Lithuania versus Belarus, the Ukraine versus Rumania and/or Moldova as well as Hungary. A kind of "multiple Balkanization" can by no means be ruled out. The same is true with respect to Russia. The risk of hostilities between Russia and the other republics (particularly the neighbouring ones) runs high and is intensified by multiple problems facing the numerous ethnic Russians in the republics outside Russia.[2] The arbitrary character of the former inter-republican borders and the previously badly hurt feelings of national self-respect adds to the explosive potential of relations with Russia. Hence the famous notion that in case of a failure of the efforts at peaceful realignment, the war in Yugoslavia will look like a shabby amateur rehearsal as compared to a large-scale performance of *Khovantchina* (*à la Bolshoi*) in the former Soviet empire.

Obviously, there is an urgent need for external powers to secure stability and progress in the eastern part of the European continent. The withdrawl of the Soviet Union from the international scene calls for an adequate political replacement. It is true that a search for new approaches in the Eastern multilateral network had begun prior to the definite Soviet withdrawal. When the Soviet Union dropped its militarist policy of control over the region it became aware of the necessity to develop new methods of a more balanced cooperation. This was particularly true for the economic field, but at that advanced stage, the dual economic and constitutional crisis compelled the country to concentrate exclusively on its specific internal problems. Besides, transition to trade on the basis of world market prices and hard currency, unilaterally introduced as of January 1991 after lengthy talks within COMECON, has caused a sharp decline in Soviet foreign trade. In 1989, trade between the USSR and Eastern Europe amounted to 68 billion rubles, in 1990 it dropped to nearly 52 billion rubles and in 1991 trade was only half of the preceding year.[3]

The post-Soviet reconstruction of the national economy -- aimed at integration into the international division of labour -- will further accelerate the process of overcoming the economically irrational and excessive ties once established between the USSR and its Eastern European allies (Soviet foreign trade with COMECON countries used to make up almost 40% , while the EC share did not exceed 14%).[4] However, from a purely economic point of view, the lacking competitiveness on the world market, the desire to prevent immediate bankruptcies of large parts of inefficient industries and to hold back soaring unemployment should have encouraged Eastern Europe as well as the successor states of the Soviet Union to maintain as much cooperation as possible. Yet, though the advantages of trading in mutually unpretentious markets at least in the transitional period seem obvious, this did not prevent the established links from virtually collapsing. Political irrationality and the inherent dynamics of disintegration have swept away economic rationality across the board.

Instead, elsewhere in the East of the continent, many and sometimes rather desperate hopes are being invested into the European Community, i.e. desires for rapid integration into the European economic structures. One of the first notable steps on this path was the associate membership status granted to Hungary, Poland and Czecho-Slovakia by the EC in November 1991. But, in principle, the EC -- preoccupied with the demanding task of deepening its integration -- is still reluctant to play a role in accordance with Eastern expectations and to shoulder an additional burden, in particular as the short-term interests of Western firms are but a poor stimulus for an expansion eastwards. In fact, the EC is supposed to play the role formerly performed by the Soviet Union at a time when political and ideological considerations largely determined the scope of excessive economic ties. There is no other power, neither the United States or Japan nor any single European state capable of setting goals and providing sufficient resources in the process of economic reconstruction and political realignment. In a long-term perspective, Europe is doomed to integration. This is the only way, not just for the EC but for those Europeans beyond its present confines, of making sure that Europe will retain its say in world politics and occupy a stable position in the tough economic competition with the other two centers of world economic power. On the contrary, disintegration in whatever part of the continent, often likely to be accompanied by violent conflicts, would open the door to interference in European affairs by external powers; Europe's weakness would then have greatly contributed to the rise of other powers. This was unmistakably proven by history only some fifty years ago. Thus, politically as well as economically, the future of Eastern Europe should in a very substantial sense also be a concern for Western Europe, which would be ill-advised in enjoying its "splendid isolation" much longer.

In the interim period, however, the East is bound to find a balance on its own. This is why the sometimes desperate efforts at detecting a common denominator among the successors of the USSR -- in the shape of the Commonwealth of Independent States -- are as valuable as is communication and coordination on a regular basis among Poland, Hungary and Czecho-Slovakia even in the absence of formal treaty obligations. Similarly, bilateral undertakings can be observed in the case of Bulgaria and Rumania and their respective neighbours. Constant fears of being isolated and of taking a wrong turn, intrinsically characteristic of Bulgaria's and Rumania's foreign policy, have much contributed to their current flexibility.

However, in the longer run, with ineffective CSCE institutions, neither a system of bilateral agreements nor regional political and economic cooperation (along the lines of the Vishegrad accord or the "pentagonale" that on the verge of Yugoslavia's break-up was nearly replaced by a "hexagonale") alone will manage to stabilize the situation in the region. The developments in Central and Eastern Europe at the end of the 1930s may serve as a reminder of the bitter experience when the well-elaborated system of collective security and numerous coalitions were smashed by fierce national ambitions. The current situation, with an upset balance of forces and dangerous internal instability, is in many respects not that different. In such a situation, the instruments of bilateral or multilateral political cooperation alone do not work. There is a pressing need to create efficient mechanisms of European security imbued with powers of enforcement in a crisis situation.

For quite a while, NATO's unilateral eastward expansion was ruled out by NATO itself in order to avoid alienating the Soviet Union. Now, with Russia and many other successors applying for NATO membership, the situation is different. Nevertheless, there are valid reasons against an eastward NATO extension. For instance, by exercising influence from outside, NATO now is in a position of keeping that zone of instability in check. Should NATO choose to enter into this zone, it runs the risk of turning into an intra-NATO battlefield of endless conflicts of the Greek-Turkish type in Cyprus, not exactly adding to the alliance's efficiency.

As long as the Soviet Union appeared to be a viable entity two possible solutions could be envisaged in order to meet the pressing security concerns with respect to post-socialist Eastern Europe. A first solution would have consisted of an agreement on Soviet-NATO guarantees to maintain security either in the shape of a comprehensive regional treaty or of separate tripartite treaties between the Soviet Union, NATO and respective countries. That solution, however, is no longer feasible as Russia -- under the new situation -- can hardly take the place of the USSR. The alternative solution stipulates a restructuring and upgrading of the CSCE in order to establish an efficient body of a UN Security Council-type and to create European peace-keeping and peace-enforcement forces. Here, too, prospects look fairly dim.

Since the end of the East-West conflict, irrespective of whether it was ready to play it or not, Europe's role has grown considerably. The West has emerged victorious from the cold war but the taste of victory is mixed if not bitter. The Soviet Union's history in the aftermath of the Great Patriotic War shows that victories can easily be gambled away. The current situation in Eastern Europe provides sufficient opportunities for committing similar mistakes. But, there is also the unprecedented opportunity of unifying the continent. It largely depends on the wisdom and the readiness of the West whether Europe will be able to make use of that.

## Notes

1. Both terms "left" and "right" are used here in the traditional European sense not in the distorted meaning adopted in the Soviet Union, where advocates of a market economy and of parliamentary democracy were labelled the "left" and their opponents advocating communist dogmas referred to as the "right."

2. The share of Russians living in the Ukraine, Kazakhstan and Moldova as well as in Latvia and Estonia is quite sizable.

3. S. Semendayev, "Krug zamknulsya. SSSR-Vostochnaya Evropa: snova kliring (The Wheel Comes Full Circle. New Honesty in Soviet-East European Relations)," *Nezavisimaya Gazeta*, April 20, 1991, p. 4.

4. R. Grinberg, K. Legai, "Stupeny dezintegratsii. Problemy torgovli SSSR s Vostochnoi Evropoi (Steps of Disintegration. Trade Problems Between the USSR and Eastern Europe)," *Nezavisimaya Gazeta*, May 5, 1991, p. 4.

# 13

---

## Towards a European Economic Space?
## The Political Changes in the East
## as a Challenge to the West

*Hans-Joachim Spanger*

The days when Europe came in two permutations, each ranged against the other, are coming to an end. The opening-up of the Hungarian border, the fall of the Berlin Wall, the withdrawal of Soviet troops from Central and Eastern Europe, the dissolution of the Warsaw Pact and COMECON, and, finally, the confederal reorganization of the Union of Soviet Socialist Republics, hard fought for in the civil war and defended in the "Great Patriotic War," mark the close of the era of bipolar, bloc-based division of the old continent. What remains is the legacy -- itself divisive -- of over forty years of schism: a deep gulf between a prospering, politically and militarily integrated western part of Europe, and an economically devastated, disintegrating eastern part.

The time-honoured ideological antagonism, has, it is true, already been replaced -- in the form of the CSCE Paris charter -- by a profession of belief, on the part of all European states, in liberal democracy and a market economy based on private property. Whether a new European order can be established on this basis, however, depends crucially on the removal of the continuing socio-economic asymmetries. This is a matter that affects both sides: the eastern part of Europe, which faces the task of radically reorganizing its whole political, social, and economic system; and the western part, whose willingness to open up and provide material support is a precondition of the success of the process of transformation that has been set in motion.

The burdens and risks in this process are extremely unequally divided. Whereas the eastern part of Europe faces a task that is qualitatively unprecedented, is uncertain in its outcome, and will involve considerable social costs, the western side is moving on familiar ground to the extent that it is able recall the origins of its own success -- namely the European Recovery Programme or Marshall Plan. At the time of the plan, however, integration and the transfer of resources took place under the banner of a clearly identifiable external threat. Consequently, it was political-cum-strategic considerations that helped economic rationality to prevail. In the present situation, however, any potential threat is fragmented into a number of much less concrete risks. Not only does the task of countering these risks seem a much less urgent one; because of their variety, no single response is really possible -- a fact which, in terms of classic cost-benefit analysis, hardly stimulates willingness to make strategic sacrifices. Yet the Moscow *coup d'état*, the civil war in Yugoslavia, and the Albanian boat-people all offer proof of how quickly and effectively the omnipresent risks can cast their shadow into western Europe. What has also emerged, however, is that neither Europe as a whole nor western Europe alone has at its disposal an effective range of instruments for political, or indeed military, intervention -- a fact which confers an even higher priority on preventive measures.

This is where the European Community comes in. Not only is it the "object of desire" of every conceivable disputant, which means that the prospect of the reemergence of rival power-alliances on the pattern of those that existed in the nineteenth and early twentieth century is largely blocked; it also has at its disposal the most effective range of economic incentives and sanctions. The outcome of the "contest between the forces of integration and fragmentation," of the tussle between the "new Europe" of the Paris charter and the old competing nation-states that has taken the place of bloc-confrontation since the end of the Cold War, will depend largely on the Community.[1]

Of course, there is little chance of any short-term reduction in economically induced pressure to migrate. And the ethno-nationalist conflicts in the erstwhile Soviet Union and in eastern Europe are the product not so much of sober calculations of economic interest but of the fact that for decades these conflicts were forcibly put on ice, in the cause of a transnational idea. None the less, the profound economic crisis being experienced by these countries, and the concomitant loss of prosperity, security, and political stability, make the management of these conflicts more difficult and aggravate them, in many cases to the point of irreconcilability. All the more so since, following the collapse of Marxism-Leninism and the adverse effects of the transformation to capitalism, few options remain beyond taking refuge in nationalist atavism. In the changed circumstances of today, the economic stabilization of eastern Europe thus also acquires political/strategic significance -- not as a means of countering communism but as a way of containing nationalism. Yet the fragile political framework is not the only factor jeopardizing the transformation of the system that is now under way. The reorganization and reconstruction of the economy are inconceivable without extensive financial and technical help from the West.

## Economic Reconstruction, or
## the Unscrambling of the Egg

It is in the economy that the real revolution is taking place in central and eastern Europe, and in the Soviet Union. It was primarily in this area that real socialism lost the much-trumpeted "international class struggle." Its absolute inability to achieve ever increasing output for ever decreasing input, and its relative inability to satisfy the consumer needs of the population -- an inability that gradually became absolute during the 1980s -- finally robbed it of any prospect of success. It should therefore come as no surprise that it is within the economy that the most radical and painful changes are taking place. Whereas not much more than an initial push was sufficient to bring about the removal of the authoritarian systems of government, the desired "unshackling of productive forces" (Karl Marx) requires not only that the economy be turned from its head on to its feet, in a very basic sense, but also that it be taught to walk. This applies literally to every aspect of economic life, from the organization of national economies and business concerns, through economic structure, to the individual attitudes and behaviour of economic actors.

During the early phase of the revolutions in eastern Europe, the vision of a "third way," between Marxist-Leninist socialism and liberal capitalism, enjoyed considerable popularity. There appeared to be a historically unique opportunity, in the changes that were about to be made to the economic systems, of combining the socialist achievements of state welfare, distribution, and control with capitalist efficiency and innovation, to the benefit of all. However, talk of such a course soon ceased, even amongst the residual communist parties in their new, social-democratic guises. In view of the Polish and Hungarian experience of the 1980s, it is not difficult to see that such a strategy would soon have foundered on the realities.

State intervention in order to contain productive forces -- a containment that is certainly necessary -- presupposes, by definition, the existence of properly functioning markets and thus also of the ability of those same productive forces to assert themselves economically. There could not -- and still cannot -- be any question of such a situation within the socialist economic systems. As a result, had a third path been adopted under conditions of fundamental change in the system, it would not have been the positive elements of socialism and capitalism that would have made their effects felt, but purely the negative ones, namely dirigist idleness, with increasing attempts at regulation on the one side, and individual lack of responsibility on the other.

A glance at the way in which socialist economic systems function is sufficient to show why radical changes are needed in which, for the time being, the role of the state is restricted to initiation and social back-up. In theory, the socialist economy is the most rational form of production and distribution: supply and demand are coordinated not by the anarchical market but by a central authority, on the basis of feedback from consumers and producers; in addition, this can be done directly, without having to go by way of the money-cycle. The outcome for the economic actors is laid down in binding form in the relevant plan. In practice, however, this form of economic organization has proved a complete failure. It has foundered on the processing of information and on the economic actors themselves. The latter's behaviour, responding to the imperatives of the system, increasingly assumed a character which, though hardly rational from the economic standpoint, was entirely comprehensible in terms of the maximization of benefits to the individuals themselves. It was a pattern of behaviour that was often diametrically opposed to what is required in capitalist economies.

Thus business concerns in centrally planned economies strove to ensure that the plans to which they were bound were "soft," i.e. they strove to maximize input and minimize the output required. This guaranteed that plans were fulfilled (the decisive criterion of success) and also guaranteed bonuses in terms of income (material incentives where plans were exceeded). In capitalism, the situation is precisely the reverse. There, the criterion of success is profit, as a function of maximum (sold) output and minimum input. Given that in socialist economies the marketing of the goods produced was also centrally planned, supply and demand played no regulatory role as far as the exchange of goods was concerned. Consumers had no way of influencing quantity, quality, price, or supply via the income and assets at their disposal. They were forced into a passive role.

In this kind of system, money too could only play a passive part. It was needed solely as an accounting unit, as an expression of how goods related to each other for the purposes of exchange. Consequently, the prices -- also planned -- bore no relation to supply and demand or to scarcities; they merely reflected a sometimes bizarre mixture of the supposed utility value of a good, the costs involved in its production (based on what was in any case a distorted price-structure), and a range of political guidelines. The same is true of the credit-system extensively used by the state and the various concerns: it involved no risks and no great costs, since money, having very limited significance, had (practically) no price. This again is unique, since in capitalism money not only functions as the decisive means of exchange on commodity markets; there is also a money market, on which money itself is treated as a scarce commodity.

The purpose of this brief glance at the way in which socialist economies function is to make clear that, unlike the structural adjustment in developing countries, one thing above all is required here: a radical change in the attitude and behaviour of economic actors, one that demands much more than a simple adjustment to new circumstances. Given that change in attitude is a very time-consuming undertaking, an important dilemma arises here. Basic institutional change can be carried out in a limited period of time, provided there is social consensus and sufficient determination on the part of political actors. Such change is indeed required in order not merely to stimulate but to enforce market-oriented behaviour on the part of economic actors. But this alone will not produce properly functioning markets, because this in its turn presupposes that the necessary modifications in behaviour of the economic actors have already taken place. This is the fundamental dilemma before which all the reforming economies of eastern Europe currently find themselves. Another, no less serious, problem consists in the paradoxical fact that economic activity must be "denationalized" (i.e. taken out of state control), but at the same time the state is compelled to create stable and reliable framework conditions, in the shape of new legal regulations and a properly functioning administration.

These are the dilemmas which explain the unique character of the transition from a centrally planned economy to a market economy, and the uncertainties and risks that go with it. No model for this exists in economic history, nor is established economic theory able to point to an ideal solution that can guarantee success. However, the goal of transformation is not in dispute, and a range of basic premises has emerged which the economic reformers in eastern Europe have followed, albeit each in their own way.[2] These include, specifically:

(1) A *price reform,* involving the abolition of planned prices on all commodity and factor markets and their replacement by market prices plus -- less rather than more -- state price-control. The aim is to do away with the distorted price-structure typical of the socialist economies and to restore the price-mechanism to its status as the decisive instrument for coordinating economic activities.

(2) A *reform of business enterprises,* involving both the break-up of the highly monopolized business-structure and the "commercialization" of enterprises, their transformation into joint-stock companies. The intention is to enable business concerns to adapt their behaviour to the market and gear their decisions solely to criteria relating to business management, without frequent bureaucratic intervention from the state share-owners.

(3) A *legal guarantee of property rights,* laying down the conditions, forms, and regulations governing private economic activity. This is also the precondition for another essential measure,

(4) the *privatization of state property.* This may be carried out by one of a number of very varied means (sale, auction, distribution, restitution) and embraces every conceivable area (land, housing, small businesses, large-scale industrial enterprises). This category would also cover the distribution of quasi-state property such as that of cooperatives in trade, the crafts, and agriculture. The aim here is to replace the organized lack of responsibility of all with the individual responsibility of the entrepreneur, the efficiency of the latter being governed by the opportunities and risks of the market.

(5) A *reform of the banking system,* in which, in contrast to the former situation, a two-tier system of banking is created, separating the issue of money by the national bank from the operations of the commercial banks on the money and capital markets. This also uncouples the macro-economic responsibility for the stability of the currency from the micro-economic responsibility for the efficient use of deposits.

(6) A *reform of external trade,* whereby the state-planned, bilaterally agreed exchange of goods and services is replaced by mechanisms of state control and regulation of individual activities, through customs duties, quotas, norms, and exchange-rates. The principal question that arises in this connection is whether and to what extent an improvement of one's own econ-

omy -- in the broadest sense -- can be imported through a liberalization of external trade.

(7) A *reform of the legal system*, which must not only include the
creation of an independent third power enabling individual
rights to be asserted in the face of the once-powerful state, but
must also establish the principle of contractual freedom as the
core of a market economy.

(8) *Social reform*, in which social security is no longer ensured
through the absolute guarantee of a job, but through compensatory welfare provided by the state or by a social security system. This is necessary because on the one hand business concerns must be freed of the duty to provide employment and a
properly functioning labour market must be created, but on the
other hand something has be done to counter the unemployment
that will result from these measures.

(9) A *reform of taxes and contributions*, required firstly in order to
set state income on a new and stable footing, and secondly as a
means of creating a range of tools for indirect fiscal control of
the economy that is consonant with the requirements of the
market.

(10) Finally -- and in most cases this is the chief factor -- there is a
need for *macro-economic stabilization* measures, in order to
tackle the inherited imbalances, which take the form of a monetary overhang and budget deficits.

That all the reforms listed above will have to be undertaken sooner
or later is not disputed, either by the new political elites in eastern Europe or by their western advisers. On the other hand, there is much less
agreement about the order and pace of the individual steps. A comprehensive, simultaneous liberalization of all markets, based on a reform
of business concerns and privatization and backed up by a restrictive
monetary and fiscal policy, is viewed as "shock therapy." The alternatives are more gradualist schemes that favour step-by-step deregulation,
for example in external trade or in the determination of prices. The
danger with the radical approach is that it may result in the overbur-
dening of economies that are already in a fragile state, plunging them
into deep recession and threatening the social consensus. In the case of
a gradual approach, on the other hand, there is a danger that the individual steps will result not in a "spill-over" effect but in blockades,
which, though smoothing out the recession associated with transformation, would also cause it to last a good deal longer. Both approaches
could seriously threaten the success of the reforms. In principle, the adequacy of whatever strategy is adopted depends essentially on the con-

crete conditions prevailing in the respective countries and national economies. In Russia and Hungary, for instance, these are fundamentally different.

The required steps to reform do, indeed, harbour a whole range of risks, and thus also the danger that the whole process of reform will end in an impasse. This is particularly true of the kinds of variables to which very little attention is given in the purely economic deliberations, namely political stability and the social consensus. However, it is also true of a range of conflicting economic goals.[3] Thus a general *lifting of controls on prices* is undoubtedly an essential component of any kind of reform, ensuring that supply and demand are linked together in such a way that the economy receives the correct signals. Given the high degree of concentration, however, this will inevitably lead to monopolistic pricing, bringing galloping inflation and new distortions.

One solution to this might be a rapid *reform of business enterprises*. But here again there are limits. Thus, for example, break-up should not be confused with demonopolization, since even where the huge conglomerates in trade and industry are broken up, this scarcely affects the supply side: at the national level and, what is equally significant given the poor infrastructure, at the regional and local levels, there is often only one supplier left. This hardly stimulates competition, and incentives to change patterns of behaviour moulded by decades of extensive growth consequently remain insignificant. In conditions such as these, having to identify viable concerns is a difficult job. It presupposes the existence of properly functioning markets, and also necessitates tackling a whole range of inherited problems in relation to the operation of business concerns. Chief amongst these are the current liquidity-problems resulting both from the excessive financing of credits in the past and from the present disruption of economic cycles. If, for example, all those firms in Czecho-Slovakia which are currently insolvent were forced to declare themselves bankrupt, this would spell ruin for almost half the national economy.[4] One can hardly conceive of doing this, however true it is that the closure of unproductive companies is an essential component of any kind of market economy. As long as business concerns have some prospect of eventually being bailed out by the government, the urgently required change in attitude and behaviour on the part of management and staff will not materialize.

The problems in regard to *privatization* are much the same. Leaving aside the fact that in a market economy private monopolies are scarcely any less damaging than state ones, one of the main obstacles to rapid privatization has proved to be the valuation of the concerns that are on offer. In addition, there are widespread problems associated with restitution (in the sense of a credible restoration of property rights), as well as a dearth of capital, combined with political resistance to the alleged sale of national wealth to foreigners, and controversial debates as to who should really own public concerns (the state, society, the employees) and whether it would not be better to restore businesses to profitability before any move to privatize them is made. However indispensable privatization is considered by the reformers in eastern Europe, up to now it has contributed very little to the emergence of properly functioning markets.[5]

In view of the difficulties involved in establishing a market economy solely with national resources, one possibility is to import competition and market prices through a *liberalization of external trade*. However, this strategy too harbours considerable risks -- and not just in regard to the balance of external trade. These risks manifest themselves primarily in the problem of fixing exchange rates and currency values in a way that is socially defensible. In order to offset the poor competitivity of the national economy as against the generally superior foreign competitors, a -- marked -- undervaluation of the country's own currency is required. But such a step also results in considerable losses in income, which are only defensible if exports are providing stimuli to growth.

Finally, there is the problem of the *removal of macro-economic imbalances*, which is not only closely tied up with the need for structural reform but which itself also leads to another conflict of objectives. In order not to aggravate the burdens of transition, one might think it imperative that a correction of these imbalances by means of a restrictive monetary and fiscal policy should precede structural reform. This is how the Soviet prime ministers Ryshkov and Pavlov have argued, though it has not stopped them from doing precisely the opposite. On the other hand, these kinds of measures promise lasting success only if one also removes the mechanism that has put the relevant national economies out of kilter. This applies equally to the financing of the public debt through the printing of money and to the broad spectrum of government compensation for individual company losses. Only "hard budget constraints," on the heels of macro-economic stabilization and institutional change, can put corrective pressure on the economic actors.[6] But this considerably narrows the scope for much-needed social security as well as for any active industrial policy on the part of the state, a policy that can hardly be dispensed with, given the specific problems of transition. These problems range from the indebtedness already mentioned, through short- and medium-range problems of adjustment experienced by business concerns, to the requirements imposed by regional economic policy. Since there are not really any other sources of finance available, and since privatization has as yet not brought in anything like the expected profits, the only option here is the national budget.

To sum up, one may note that provided there is the necessary political consensus and determination, minimum preconditions for a market economy can be established relatively rapidly. This alone, however, does not create properly functioning markets. And whilst the burdens of the transition are felt immediately, in the shape of increasing imbalances, the benefits take a long time to show themselves. As previous experience has shown, bridging this gap can be critically important for the success of the process of reform.

## Trapped in a Vicious Circle?

In both theory and practice, the economic reforms being undertaken in eastern Europe continue to display considerable variation, even though more than two years have passed since the collapse of the communist regimes. These differences are due chiefly to delays in adjustment and democratization in those countries where the old elites managed to retain important positions of power for quite a time. In contrast, in those places where communist parties and their successors were relegated to the periphery in free elections, there was, for the most part, a tendency to press ahead with radical programmes of economic transformation, in the shape of the much-quoted "shock therapy."

*Poland* was the first country to set out on this path, beginning on 1 January 1990. It was closely followed by the *GDR*, which, on 1 July 1990, formed a currency, economic, and social union with the Federal Republic. A similar path was chosen by *Czecho-Slovakia*, which on 1 January 1991 implemented its "scenario for economic reform." The federal parliament of *Yugoslavia* had agreed on a similar package of reforms in December 1989, but this was scuppered during 1990 by the increasing rivalries and by the introduction of a range of unilateral measures by the individual republics. *Hungary* had already introduced important reforms under the last communist government led by Miklos Nemeth, and these merely had to be continued and extended by his conservative-liberal successor, Jozsef Antall. At the end of 1990, as a result of the slow pace of privatization, growing imbalances, and strong public protest, a vehement debate took place about the need for some kind of shock therapy (this debate led to the resignation of Finance

Minister Rab). Despite this, the Antall government has so far held fast to its vision of a "soft landing" into a market economy.

In contrast to these countries, *Bulgaria, Rumania,* and the erstwhile *Soviet Union* had for a greater part of the new era done no more than introduce individual measures. Thus the Bulgarian government adopted a radical programme of reform, but only isolated components of this (removal of price controls, land reform, the introduction of laws regulating competition and foreign investments) were approved by parliament during 1991. It was only when the anti-communist opposition secured victory at the general elections of late 1991 that more far-reaching advances were possible here. A number of similar steps were taken in Rumania, but here, in contrast to Bulgaria, the government still lacks both a coherent strategy of reform and the willingness to contain new macro-economic imbalances. Instead, after the assumption of power by the National Salvation Committee, the government turned away from Ceausescu's austerity programme and pursued an expansionary monetary and fiscal policy which was clearly aimed at buying short-term, short-sighted political legitimation. This contributed greatly to the current macro-economic imbalances, and the government has only recently started to address these.

The situation in the Soviet Union and its fifteen successor states, eleven of which are associated in a loose -- and in all probability short-lived -- Commonwealth of Independent States (CIS), is even more problematic and unclear. Following the failed coup of August 1991 by the representatives of centralized communist power, decisive competencies were transferred from Moscow to the politically and economically highly heterogeneous republics. This meant that the laws on reform that were passed before this -- e.g. those on private commercial activity -- as well as the "main directions" programme of stabilization and reform put forward by the Ryshkov government as an answer to the Shatalin plan, and approved by the Supreme Soviet in October 1990, became invalid.[7] Moreover, after the coup, inter-governmental economic policy was reduced to a kind of crisis management which merely tried to ensure the minimum degree of cooperation and joint responsibility that seemed to be required to prevent the complete collapse of the economy. The dissolution of the Soviet Union in December 1991 was therefore of decisive importance in this regard, since it cut short the death throes of the central institutions and gave the now sovereign republics sole responsibility for their affairs, thus making it possible for Russia in particular unilaterally to implement its radical programme of reform, derived from the Polish model. However, the development of the CIS has also demonstrated that, contrary to all economic rationality, the unitary economic space, with a single currency and centralized -- or at least co-ordinated -- control of monetary and fiscal policy, is about to disappear.

Notwithstanding the differences in the way reform is proceeding, there are some important similarities in the macro-economic situation in this region. All the countries involved are currently experiencing a deep recession, with plummeting production and an equally marked drop in the value of money. And they are all undergoing a series of shocks in relation to foreign trade, caused by the decline (in 1990) and virtual collapse (since the introduction, on 1 January 1991, of convertible currencies as the basis for settlement in mutual trade) of COMECON trade, and as a result of the Gulf war. These similarities, attributable to the fact that all the countries concerned started out from the same conditions, should not blind us to the fact that there are considerable differences in the nature, depth, and causes of the economic crisis in eastern Europe. Whereas in the case of the most advanced countries (the former GDR, Poland, Czecho-Slovakia, Hungary), that crisis is clearly the result of the transition to a market economy (transitional recession), in the other countries, it is -- still -- the product of inconsistent strategies of reform and the vacuum left by the collapse of central planning.

In making any comparison, one should therefore bear in mind that the aggregate macro-economic data give only a very limited indication of the positive (or disastrous) changes that are going on at the micro-economic level. Thus, as the Polish and Hungarian governments in particular are repeatedly pointing out, it has not as yet been possible for private economic activity to be properly reflected in the official statistics. In addition, the reforms have done away with the specific costs of former insufficiencies. And finally, the production of obsolete goods has been halted, which has also helped to clean up the formerly politically distorted economic statistics.[8] These facts to some extent temper the loss in prosperity signalled in the statistics, although one should note that the way those losses are distributed is now much more unequal than in the past, and this is leading to increasing disparities in income. It should also be noted that almost all advocates of "shock therapy" have underestimated the real shocks to which the national economies in eastern Europe are subject when this kind of treatment is applied.

The worst affected was undoubtedly the *GDR*. Despite all the voices raised against such a course, from the president of the Bundesbank to the combined forces of economic expertise, the introduction of capitalism and the removal of all protective barriers to the outside (including the exchange-rate-buffer) were implemented overnight.[9] The consequences were devastating. Literally overnight, the majority of GDR enterprises lost their markets, which were taken over by their superior western -- and especially West German -- competitors. In the one year since the inauguration of the currency union, industrial output in the former GDR has practically halved, with the consequence that today, 20 per cent of the German population, inhabiting 30 per cent of German territory, are responsible for only 8.3 per cent of German GNP.[10] It was only the implementation of extensive, publicly financed aids, in the shape of numerous business-credits, export guarantees, and a general moratorium on debt-repayment, that averted immediate mass bankruptcies. Nevertheless, within a few months, the number of jobless rose drastically, and had already reached 1 343 000, or 17 per cent, by January 1992. In addition, there are 519 700 "short-time workers," most of whom are actually without work, but because of special regulations remain employed by their place of work. In all, the unemployment rate is therefore about 30 per cent -- a figure unparalleled in eastern Europe.[11]

On the other hand, the GDR's integration into the West German economic sphere enabled another negative effect of the transformation of the system to be kept under control: inflation. In the course of 1990, the cost of living in eastern Germany rose by only 1.4 per cent, though with the removal of other GDR-specific subsidies, this had rapidly risen to 26.7 per cent by the end of 1991. However, this was more than compensated for by the marked increase in income, which far exceeded the growth in productivity.

The only reason why the GDR was able to cope politically, socially, and economically with this kind of crash-landing into the market economy was that, in the shape of the Federal Republic, it had available to it a mighty economic power which, however reluctantly, was prepared, and continues for the foreseeable future to be prepared, to finance the damage. In 1991 alone, the net transfer of public money from west to east is running at 140 billion DM, a figure approximately equal to two-thirds of the gross domestic product produced in the "five new *Länder*." Of this, 67 billion DM are to be classified in the broadest sense as subsidies, covering fields ranging from housing, through local transport and energy provision, to the servicing of debts and economic incentives.[12] The other countries undergoing reform can hardly allow themselves this kind of luxurious approach to economic reconstruction. Their resources are just enough to ensure a minimum of social security, and already begin to be overstrained when it comes to managing domestic or foreign debts, or implementing urgent measures in the sphere of industrial policy.

*Poland*, for example, which comes second to the former GDR in terms of the radicalness of its approach and of the latter's consequences, has so far failed to achieve any of the targets of its reforms, and it seems to be hopelessly caught in a vicious circle of galloping inflation and declining production. Both these developments were expected when the programme of reform began in January 1990, particularly since a highly restrictive fiscal, monetary, and incomes policy had been introduced, with a view to macro-economic stabilization. But in 1991 also, the decline continued almost unchecked and this has thrown into doubt even the limited successes that had been achieved in 1990 with regard to stabilization, namely containment of the budget deficit and the reduction of the hyperinflation of 1989. In 1990 gross domestic product decreased by 13 per cent, and industrial production by 23.3 per cent. In 1991, contrary to expectations, which predicted a rise of about 4 per cent, there was a further decline in production of 15 per cent, and a drop of almost 10 per cent in gross domestic product.[13] As far as inflation was concerned, here too developments did not stop at the one-off 76 per cent "corrective inflation" that was aimed at when price-controls were removed at the start of 1990.[14] Instead, prices continued to rise at a monthly rate of 5 per cent, and this rise has hardly slowed during 1991, with an annual rate of 60.4 per cent.

As a result, the important nominal anchor of monetary policy has begun to totter: the exchange-rate of the Polish currency against the US dollar, fixed in January 1991 at a very low level roughly corresponding to its black-market value on that date. The marked undervaluation of the zloty, coupled with declining domestic demand, resulted, in 1990, in considerable export-successes in the OECD area. However, these were not repeated in 1991, not least because inflation had eroded the currency-related benefits. In spring 1991, the government was therefore forced to put through a further devaluation of the zloty, of 15 per cent, followed, in spring 1992, by a further devaluation of 12 per cent. This, together with the imposition of import duties on agricultural and consumer goods, was the first clear corrective which the government, under pressure of growing criticism, was forced to make to Finance Minister Balcerowicz's reform-plan. In other words, the Polish example shows what a tough task it was to secure (relative) macro-economic stabilization, but also how extremely fragile that stability remains. At the same time, it shows up the limits of the political consensus, which largely collapsed under the social burdens. During the parliamentary elections, all the parties with the exception of the Liberal Democrat Congress, led by the then prime minister, Bielecki, and the Democratic Union, led by his predecessor Mazowiecki, directed their campaigns chiefly against Balcerowicz and his economic policy. The alternative they proposed was: to fight the recession rather than inflation, and to stimulate demand and protect domestic production in agriculture and industry instead of imposing strict monetary and fiscal discipline.

That scope for action is extremely limited for *any* government under the present conditions became obvious after the elections, which had ended in a clear victory for the critics. Despite all the rhetoric, the new cabinet, under prime minister Olszewski, was able to make only marginal adjustments: the agricultural lobby was granted credit subsidies and minimum prices; businesses were relieved of the (in any case senseless) duty to pay taxes on their working capital; and financial rehabilitation programmes were introduced for some state enterprises. Other cornerstones of economic reform which had previously been sharply criticized -- for example the tax on wage gains or *popiwek* -- remained untouched. Last but not least, the pressure of the maximum limit fixed by the IMF for the budget deficit, 5 per cent of GDP, meant that all further thoughts of an expansionary monetary and fiscal policy were dismissed.

The situation in *Czecho-Slovakia* is less dramatic. Yet here too the political consensus is under grave threat. Because the costs of reform are much more strongly felt in Slovakia than in the western parts of the country, demands for a modification of Prague's liberal economic policy, and in particular for a more expansionary monetary and budget policy, are growing in Bratislava. Since the recession brought about by transformation is expected to worsen and continue into the election year 1992, this could easily put a question mark not only over the federal government's programme of reform, but over the continued existence of the federation itself.

It is true that a decline in economic activity had already set in in 1990, in other words before the introduction of the reforms associated with the "scenario;" but this had remained within relatively narrow limits. Thus produced national income fell by 3.1 per cent only. At the same time, in the wake of the first of a series of removals of subsidies, the cost of living rose by 10 per cent (this removal of subsidies was, however, offset by compensations in income). The unemployment rate also remained low, at 1 per cent. In contrast, in 1991 there was a marked acceleration in the decline. By the end of the year, industrial production had fallen by 23.1 per cent, and the unemployment rate risen to 6.3 per cent (11.1 per cent in Slovakia). Following the removal of price controls, inflation too has accelerated, with the result that at the end of 1991 consumer prices were 53.6 per cent higher than the previous year's levels. In contrast to the situation in Poland, however, the upward movement has slowed down markedly since mid-1991, and only a 10-15 per cent inflation rate is expected in 1992 (unlike in Poland, where forecasts envisage rates of up to 70 per cent). With the restrictive measures implemented by the government, this has led to a fall of more than 20 per cent in real income.[15]

The 1991 decline in the *Hungarian* economy is not of the same magnitude, but began as early as 1988. Here too, there is no prospect of any remarkable upturn, though there are hopes that the bottom of the depression may be reached by mid-1992.[16] In 1990, gross domestic product fell by 5.5 per cent, and industrial production by 4.5 per cent. Inflation reached 28.9 per cent, whilst unemployment remained at only 1.7 per cent. This trend was more or less continued in 1991. Thus gross domestic product has again fallen by more than 6 per cent, unemployment was at 8.3 per cent at the end of the year, and depreciation reached about 36 per cent.

In contrast to the situation in the countries just mentioned, the macro-economic position in *Bulgaria, Rumania,* and the former *Soviet Union* is very similar to that which prevailed in Poland before the introduction of the reforms in 1989. As a result of partial liberalization and -- particularly in Rumania and the Soviet Union -- an expansionary monetary and fiscal policy up to the end of 1991, all three countries currently find themselves in a downward spiral characterized by galloping inflation, growing problems of supply, and declining production. The specific data in this connection are as follows:[17]

|  | 1990 (%) | 1991 (%) |
|---|---|---|
| *Bulgaria* |  |  |
| Gross domestic product | -12.2 | -19.5 |
| Industrial output | -14.1 | -27.3 |
| Inflation | 19.3 | 550 |
| Unemployment | 1.8 | 11 |
| *Rumania* |  |  |
| Gross domestic product | -15 | -15 |
| Industrial output | -19.8 | -22 |
| Inflation | 5.6 | 278 |
| Unemployment | 1.8 | 3.7 |

*Soviet Union*

| | | |
|---|---|---|
| Net material product | -4 | -15 |
| Industrial output | -1.2 | -9 |
| Inflation | 5.3 | 365 |
| Unemployment | no reliable data | |

All three countries have yet to tackle the problems of adjustment involved in the change-over to a market economy, and the positions from which they have to start have been made markedly worse by the accumulation of imbalances. The militant action taken by the Rumanian miners at the end of September 1991 indicate how difficult it will be to cope politically with the social costs engendered by macro-economic stabilization.

The fact that it has so far not been possible to slow down the decline in the reforming economies of eastern Europe is not due solely to the problems of transition, which were expected though underestimated. It is also due in large part to the changes in the flow of goods within the erstwhile COMECON, and particularly with the Soviet Union. In 1990, it was already clear that falling production-rates would have negative multiplier-effects, but in 1991, following the introduction of the new accounting methods, further collapses -- some of them dramatic -- occurred. There was, however, a difference in the extent to which these affected eastern Europe and the Soviet Union. Thus terms of trade became substantially less favourable for the eastern European economies, given that they were now obliged to pay for their imports of energy and raw materials from the USSR in convertible currency and at world-market prices. On the other hand, because Soviet importers had very little foreign currency at their disposal, the eastern Europeans forfeited their largest, least demanding and therefore most profitable export-market. According to data from the Polish government, two-thirds of the fall in production in 1991 is attributable to this situation.[18]

The end of COMECON may serve as an illustration of the consequences which the break-up of the Soviet economic space -- a much more tightly knit entity -- entails for the individual republics. Numerous efforts were made by the members of the CIS to halt the collapse. Thus at the Minsk summit in mid-February 1992, a framework agreement was concluded which was intended to regulate economic relations during the current year, though it had little effect in practice. In view of the growing unilateralism in the republics, expressed, amongst other things, in their resolve to introduce their own currencies, the members of the CIS will, for the foreseeable future, have little choice but to continue on the path which the erstwhile members of COMECON had already set out on in 1991, namely to countermand the rules of the market and conclude bilateral barter-trade agreements on the classical model. This guaranteed the necessary supplies of raw materials and stabilized exports at a low level, but it is hardly likely to stimulate competitiveness on the world market.

This points to another reason for the continuing economic problems: even where the institutional preconditions for a market economy have already been established, a long time is needed to fulfil these. This is demonstrated by the slow progress in the setting-up of private businesses or in foreign commitments. But all this is indispensable if one wishes to establish competition, innovation in production, and cost efficiency -- in short if one wishes to establish properly functioning markets. By way of illustration: whereas in the former GDR about 40 per cent of the state-run concerns offered for sale had been disposed of by mid-1991, the figure for this "large-scale privatization" in Hungary was only about 10 per cent, and in Poland as low as 4 per cent. In the other countries, meanwhile, large-scale privatization has scarcely begun, and there has been little advance even in the break-up and transformation of state companies.[19]

Yet these are not the only factors that have so far impeded the establishment of markets and the adoption of market-oriented behaviour. There is also the socialist legacy of a distorted economic structure, with its concentration on (heavy) industrial production, its internal and external insolvency, caused by the eccentricities of a centrally planned system of allocation of liquid assets, and its inappropriately qualified personnel and distortions in the employment sector, reflected in now obsolete jobs and in the overmanning of most business concerns and of the state apparatus. Experience to date has shown that this situation can hardly be tackled solely with the instruments of the market, or that this would be possible only at the price of wide-ranging social disparities and political destabilization. What is needed, therefore, is an admittedly tricky balancing-act between state-led initiative, regulation, and spending on the one side, and the development of market forces on the other. In addition, in order to smooth the way for the reforms, there should be strategic support from outside.

## Western Assistance:
## A Prerequisite of Strategic Importance

That the market-oriented reform-programmes being implemented by the erstwhile socialist countries depend on extensive support from the western industrial nations is no longer a matter of dispute. But it took a long time for this realization to gain acceptance in all the capitals of the West; and even today there are still considerable differences of opinion as to the degree of need, the potential recipients, and the extent of resources that should be transferred. Willingness to rearrange the burdens of the Cold War in a way that benefits those who brought it to an end is by no means uniformly strong.

As far as the amount of capital required for the economic reconstruction of eastern Europe and the Soviet Union is concerned, there are currently only vague estimates as to what this should be. They range up to a figure of 2 000 billion US dollars, as proposed by the European Bank for Reconstruction and Development (EBRD). However, these kinds of global data are not based on any solid calculations. It is therefore much more sensible to gear oneself to previous and current programmes of economic aid, particularly since this allows one to assess conditions of success and the extent of required aid in a more reliable way. In this connection, even before the introduction of the programmes of reform, there was a suggestion, from political quarters, that there could be a Marshall Plan for eastern Europe -- a suggestion that immediately provoked a storm of controversy. The sceptics thought such a Marshall Plan was merely "a hackneyed synonym for throwing large amounts of money at large problems."[20] Advocates of the plan, on the other hand, pointed to the important psychological effects both then and now: "The Marshall Plan worked by employing small amounts of economic assistance to produce large psychological effects." Thanks to its correct "timing, its targeting and its publicity," it helped "to shift the expectations of its recipients from the belief that things could only get worse to the conviction that they would eventually get better."[21]

Marshall aid between 1948 and 1951 amounted to 12.4 billion US dollars and benefited sixteen western European countries. This figure corresponded to just over 1 per cent of US GNP for the four-year period, or 2 per cent of GNP on average on the recipient side. Applied to the erstwhile socialist countries per capita at current price-levels, this would mean an annual sum of 4.8 billion US dollars for eastern Europe, and 16.7 billion US dollars including the former Soviet Union. This is still only equal to 0.1 per cent of the combined GNP of the USA, Japan, and the EC.[22] The president of the EC Commission,

Jacques Delors, chose a different reference-point as an illustration: if the six eastern European countries were to receive the same amount as that given to the underdeveloped EC regions under the terms of the structural funds, this would require an annual sum of 14 billion ECUs (17 billion US dollars) over the next 5 to 10 years, on top of which there would be 5 billion ECUs for the European Investment Bank (EIB). This is equivalent to about 0.45 per cent of the Community's GDP, and is thus noticeably higher than the updated Marshall Plan figures.[23]

In practice, up to 1992, the OECD states (G-24) had agreed financial assistance totalling about 30 billion ECUs. This sum is intended to finance the PHARE programme being coordinated by the EC Commission. The EC is financing more than two-thirds of it, and it is due to run until the end of 1992.[24] The total sum also includes 8 billion ECUs to be deposited with the EBRD by 1995. In addition, the IMF and the World Bank have agreed sums of 4.1 and 5.3 billion US dollars respectively for eastern Europe. There is also extensive bilateral support, and growing multilateral support, for the remnants of the Soviet Union which are not covered by the PHARE programme. This includes most notably the 24-billion-dollar package agreed in April 1992 by the group of leading industrial nations (G-7), although this is destined chiefly for Russia. This sum includes: 11 billion dollars previously promised within the framework of bilateral humanitarian aid; 2.5 billion dollars in deferral of debt payments; 4.5 billion dollars available from the Bretton Woods institutions; and finally 6 billion dollars for a stabilization fund for the ruble.[25] Here too, commitment on the donors' side is conspicuously unequally divided. Since 1989, the Federal Republic of Germany alone has promised -- and for the most part already paid out -- about 57 billion DM to the Soviet Union. This includes export credits and guarantees as well as the financial price of German unification, in the form of payments intended to facilitate the withdrawal of Soviet troops or to provide "safeguards of trust" with regard to the economic relations of the former GDR. Taken together, it has, over the last two years, provided 56 per cent of all western aid given to the Soviet Union.[26]

In all, therefore, the maximum financial pledges made to date lie between the Marshall Plan equivalent and the Delors analogy. But the size of the pledges alone are relatively uninformative. Thus, the provision of 7 billion DM for the construction of housing for dependants of the Soviet troops being withdrawn from Germany will hardly stimulate the transformation and reconstruction of the economy in Russia, the Ukraine, and Belorussia. The same applies to the transfer of resources from western to eastern Germany, 75 per cent of which is going on consumption and is thus mainly stimulating the west German economy. Although the provision of a minimum degree of social security and political stability must be one of the basic preconditions of the current process of transformation in eastern Europe, western support should primarily benefit those areas which are likely to produce the greatest multiplier effects as far as self-reliant economic growth, as envisaged in the schemes of reform, is concerned. This means above all that it must facilitate investment and provide technical assistance. In addition, in striking contrast to the Marshall Plan, the proportion of grants -- about 30 per cent (from PHARE) -- is relatively low, which means that short-term relief is being bought at the price of a new long-term burdening of the balance of payments. Moreover, the donors have a marked strong interest in stimulating their own exports by granting credits.

The Marshall Plan was successful because it facilitated high rates of growth and investment in a receptive environment without having to finance these through inappropriate losses in income. Hence, if western help is to have the same effect in the erstwhile socialist countries, coherent, binding programmes of reform are needed. Only on this basis will it be possible, to any reasonably reliable extent, to identify and quantify the need for external support and to calculate its effects. In so doing, however, one must not overlook the specific problems associated with the transition to what, for the majority of eastern Europeans, is completely unknown territory; nor should one lose sight of the risks which social deprivation and political destabilization constitute for the success of reform.

In both its volume and its targeting, western support has up to now only done partial justice to the requirements cited above. There are basically five distinct areas to consider: humanitarian aid, technical and financial assistance, cooperation on trade, and, finally, moral support.

The least demanding and least controversial of these is undoubtedly *humanitarian help*. Its aim is to ensure the supply of food and medicines, which in a number of countries is under grave threat. To date, recipients of this kind of aid have included Poland, Bulgaria, Rumania, and the former Soviet Union, and these countries, together with the remnants of Yugoslavia, will continue to be given this help in the future.[27] In 1991 the European Community pledged 40 million ECUs to Bulgaria, 60 million to Rumania, and another 20 million for a programme of aid to children. The volume of humanitarian help to the Soviet Union agreed in autumn 1991, after lengthy debate, by the seven leading industrial nations (G-7) is far greater than this. Even before that date, the EC had made available 250 million ECUs free of charge, as well as credit guarantees of 500 million ECUs for food imports. Following an original request of 15 billion US dollars from Moscow, this amount was topped up to 2.4 billion US dollars, a similar figure being pledged by the United States and Canada, and by Japan.[28] In contrast to the bilateral German "Aid to Russia," which, in winter 1990/1991, attained a volume of 340 million US dollars, only a limited proportion of the assistance now agreed can be classed as humanitarian aid. Most of it is made up of export credits, which in the medium term will swell the country's debt-burden and which has been publicly guaranteed solely because the USSR, and its successors, precisely for this reason, are no longer regarded as creditworthy on international money-markets. These credits also serve clear national interests such as the traditional desires of American farmers in regard to exports.

Of central importance to the success of the economic reforms in the former socialist countries is *technical assistance*. It will help to improve infrastructure, telecommunications, transport, administration, education, and business management -- all the framework conditions that are indispensable to a properly functioning market-economy. Given that market economies will have to be newly learned and built up literally from the ground, wide-ranging western aid-schemes will be most useful here, in contrast to the Marshall Plan.

The main providers of multilateral technical assistance are the EBRD and the World Bank. The activities of the EBRD, which began operating in April 1991, have so far remained modest: in its first twelve months it provided aid for a total of twenty projects, with a combined volume of 621 million ECUs.[29] In fiscal year 1991-2, the World Bank increased the volume of its pledges of credit to eastern Europe by 60 per cent, to 2.9 billion US dollars, a figure almost equal to the reduced amount of 3.39 billion US dollars pledged for the African continent.[30] In addition, there are the 215 million ECUs made available to Hungary and Poland through the EIB (for infrastructure, privatization, and the modernization of small and medium-sized businesses), as part of an 820 million ECU technical-assistance package for eastern Europe agreed by the EC in 1991. Although the Houston Four Study, in which -- at the behest of the 1990 G-7 summit -- the IMF, the World Bank, the OECD, and the EBRD jointly analysed the Soviet economy, proposed the provision of technical assistance to the USSR, no substantial sums have as yet been made available for this. Sums worth mentioning here are the 400 million ECUs agreed by the European Council at its session in Rome in December 1990, and a further 500 million ECUs pledged for 1992. Further assistance is envisaged for the successors to the Soviet Union after the conclusion of the IMF admission procedure.

Whereas the transfer of know-how and resources for technical projects is an integral component of the reform process, *financial assistance* plays an important back-up role. The main activity here is the bolstering of national currencies and the resolution of short-term balance-of-payments problems, from which practically all the former socialist countries suffer to a more or less marked degree. An attempt has been made to use this route to help stabilize the macro-economic situation: since 1990, priority has been given to eastern European countries undergoing reform in the granting of a number of bilateral and multilateral credits, governed by IMF provisions. These were intended also to cushion the effects of the drastic rise in import-prices for energy. These grants include the three-year extended arrangements made by the IMF to Poland and Hungary and one-year stand-by credits to Czecho-Slovakia, Bulgaria, and Rumania totalling more than 6.1 billion SDRs. In addition, in 1990 the EC granted Hungary a further credit of one billion US dollars. It also declared its willingness to finance half the medium-term loans of one billion US dollars envisaged in 1991 for Czecho-Slovakia and Rumania, and the credit of 800 million US dollars for Bulgaria. So far, the Soviet Union and its successors have been refused similar assistance, on the grounds that before this can be granted, a coherent programme of reform must be agreed with the IMF, the servicing of current debts must be clarified, and a plausible monetary and fiscal policy must be introduced.

Another serious problem -- inherited for the most part from socialist times -- remains largely unsolved. This is the problem of external indebtedness in convertible currencies. According to data provided by the Economic Commission for Europe (ECE), this totalled 147.7 billion US dollars (gross debt) in mid-1991:[31]

| | |
|---|---|
| Bulgaria | 11.0 |
| Czecho-Slovakia | 8.8 |
| Hungary | 19.7 |
| Poland | 46.0 |
| Rumania | 2.1 |
| Soviet Union | 60.0 |

Only Poland managed, in negotiations with the Paris Club, to have its publicly guaranteed debts halved in spring 1991, securing a reduction of about 17 billion US dollars. A similar request to the banks of the London Club has, in contrast, so far remained unsuccessful thus blocking the whole endeavour. Bulgaria and -- after lengthy argument -- the Soviet Union have had to be content with rescheduling. However, in the case of Russia and the Commonwealth of Independent States in particular, the discussion about adequate repayment and servicing of debts -- mostly accumulated in the recent past -- is by no means over yet. Although a generalized remission of debts is not very likely, and, given its unequal effects on both donors and recipients, does not seem a very sensible course, there should at least be some consideration as to whether further relief-measures would not be possible in the case of Bulgaria, Hungary, and Poland. They are being forced to pay for mistakes for which they are not responsible: the money was received -- and squandered -- by the old regimes, with the sole effect of restricting the financial scope of their successors.

An expansion of *external trade* could facilitate debt-servicing. But here too, with the exception of Hungary, the picture is not a very encouraging one. Whilst trade with former COMECON partners has virtually halved, the European Community shows little inclination to open up its firmly barricaded doors in certain critical areas. On the basis of the bilateral accords concluded between 1988 and 1990, and within the framework of the PHARE programme, the EC took Hungary and Poland (from January 1990) as well as Czecho-Slovakia and Bulgaria (from January 1991) into the General System of Preferences. But this was just a first step, the effect of which was merely to grant these countries a status inferior to that of the Mediterranean countries. That the EC's willingness to grant concessions reaches its limits at the point where sensitive areas of its national economies are affected was also demonstrated in the negotiations on association completed with Hungary, Poland, and Czecho-Slovakia in December 1991. The negotiations were blocked for months not least because the EC steadfastly refused to open up its market in sensitive and thus highly protected sectors such as coal, steel, textiles, and agriculture. Only Britain and Denmark argued from the outset for a broad opening-up, whilst France sought right up to the end to impose limits, in particular on the export of agricultural products. The compromise arrived at provides for a gradual removal of EC import duties and quotas on coal and steel, textiles, and most agricultural products over the next four to six years.[32]

In view of the production structure which they have inherited, and of their poor competitivity in the sphere of industrial goods, the export of the goods mentioned above, accounting for almost 40 per cent of total exports, is of crucial importance to the countries concerned -- at least during the transitional period. But there is another reason why the opening-up of the EC markets is vital to economic reconstruction in eastern Europe: only when that opening-up is guaranteed will there be sufficient incentives for foreign investors, in addition to comparative wage-cost benefits, to build up production there. The example of the southern European members of the EC shows that where there is inadequate internal capital formation, foreign commitment provides important stimuli for economic recovery. This is all the more true for eastern Europe, because of its much weaker capital base and because of its proximity to the receptive markets of central and western Europe.

Western receptivity, however, should have more facets and it is here that the final aspect of assistance, namely *moral support*, comes in. This does not sound overly ambitious: as we all know, morale can hardly be translated into economic terms. And in any case, this is not the prime object. What is meant, rather, is an unequivocal undertaking on the part of western Europe to think of the reforming countries of the east as a part of Europe as a whole. And this requires an equally unequivocal willingness, if need be, to smooth these countries' path to (what has up to now been western) European integration.

The "European treaties" or agreements on association with Hungary, Poland, and Czecho-Slovakia would have provided an excellent opportunity of establishing the conditions and a possible timetable for the inclusion of these countries in the European Community -- not just as a general statement in the preamble, but in concrete terms. Simply on technical grounds, this is hardly likely to take place, as, among others, the former Polish prime minister Bielecki would like it to, within the present decade.[33] It should, however, be possible for negotiations on membership to begin once the single European market has begun operating and in the wake of negotiations with the EFTA members who have applied to join.

One cannot, however, overlook the fact that there are considerable reservations in regard to such a rapid expansion of the EC, and that there are a number of objective difficulties associated with it. These concern available resources and their distribution, the risk that, as the Danish referendum has shown, the ambitious task of integration may be sacrificed for the sake of expansion, and, last but not least, the question of the established balance of power, which has, as it is, already been put under great strain by German unification and the opening-up to the east. In addition there is the fact that if the economic and monetary integration that is currently being prepared is pursued, it will hardly be possible any longer to maintain the traditional style of community consensus, whereby the slowest member determines the pace. If, therefore, on top of the variations in levels of integration that appear on the horizon, there are political differences -- with France as the mouthpiece of the integrationists, for example, and Germany as the advocate of expansion -- centrifugal tendencies could easily break out, and the EC could degenerate into nothing more than a free-trade area. This would jeopardize its role as an anchor of economic and political stability and cooperation on the continent, and eastern Europe would be no better off than if it remained "outside the gates."

Even though almost all the arguments that were put forward in relation to the southward expansion of the EC, ranging from the fostering of systems based on the market economy to the strengthening of democratic stability, can validly be applied to eastern Europe today, it does not seem possible that we should follow the same route. A suitable alternative would seem to be some kind of graduated integration with clearly defined political and economic conditions for both potential and existing members. This would make it possible for the EC to open up, without at the same time calling into question its targets in relation to integration and without exposing existing structures to unjustifiable strains. However: even in such a case, the European Community would have to undergo a radical reform in order to be able to live up to its own name.

## Conclusions

The ability of the new political elites in eastern Europe and the successors to the Soviet Union to implement radical reforms in the economy and in society is not the only thing that is currently on trial. So too is the capacity of western Europe not merely to observe the process of transformation benevolently from outside, but to mobilize the material and conceptual resources that are indispensable to its success. The experiences of the first two years have shown that this is a task of unanticipated proportions. This is true of economic policy, which is agreed on the objectives but has underestimated the distance to be travelled and the imponderability of the terrain; as a result, shock-therapists and gradualists alike have been left standing before the ruins of their illusions, and little more remains of their conflicting ideas on transformation than the classical dispute between monetarists and Keynesians. It is also true of the state of the national economies themselves, which currently find themselves in the midst of a recession comparable only to the world economic crisis of the 1920s. The consequences of that crisis are well known. In eastern Europe too, there are signs that political disorientation and social deprivation are entering into a disastrous alliance.

Properly functioning market economies represent more than the mere sum of the institutions, norms, and procedures involved. They are an achievement of civilization which demands inevitably long processes of adaptation and learning. Therefore, in the conditions now prevailing in eastern Europe, the aim must be to bridge the critical gap between the idea and the reality, and to open up some kind of perspective. Things being what they are, only western Europe is in a position to do this. Western commitment in quantitative terms show that the size of the challenge has been recognized; the qualitative shortcomings that still persist, however, indicate that the same recognition has not yet been given to the pan-European nature of that challenge. But readiness to make financial sacrifices cannot compensate for a lack of willingness to open up and integrate. Nor does insistence on neo-liberal-inspired schemes for reform do justice to a situation in which the new political authorities have to perform a difficult balancing-act between state and market, between old bureaucracy and new administration, between the pull towards the periphery and the urge to integration in the world market -- in short between the demands of the new capitalist economy and the legacy of its socialist predecessor. It was European capitalism's capacity for innovation that brought it victory in the Cold War; whether this will also be true for peace-time will depend on its capacity for absorption.

## Notes

1. John Lewis Gaddis, "Toward the Post-Cold War World," *Foreign Affairs*, Vol. 70 (Spring 1991), p. 103.

2. See, for instance, Economic Commission for Europe, *Economic Survey of Europe in 1990-1991* (New York: United Nations Publications, 1991), pp. 122-36; Paul Marer, Salvatore Zecchini, *The Transition to a Market Economy*, 2 vols. (Paris: OECD, 1991); Jozef M. van Brabant, *Remaking Eastern Europe -- On the Political Economy of Transition* (Dordrecht: Kluwer, 1990); Alan H. Gelb, Cheryl W. Gray, *The Transformation of Economies in Central and Eastern Europe. Issues, Progress, and Prospects* (Washington, D.C.: The World Bank, 1991).

3. See Jeffrey Sachs, David Lipton, "Poland's Economic Reform," *Foreign Affairs*, Vol. 69 (Summer 1990), pp. 52-4.

4. See Kamil Janacek, "Widespread Insolvency of State-owned Firms," in: Radio Free Europe Research Institute, *Report on Eastern Europe*, Vol. 2, No. 31, 1991, pp. 1-4.

5. See, for instance, Marvin Jackson, "The Progress of Privatization," in: Radio Free Europe Research Institute, *Report on Eastern Europe*, Vol. 2, No. 31, 1991, pp. 40-5.

6. See Bert Hofman, Michael J. Koop, "Makroökonomische Aspekte der Reformen in Osteuropa," *Die Weltwirtschaft*, No. 1, 1990, pp. 166-71.

7. For both concepts, see Marie Lavigne, *Financing the Transition in the USSR: The Shatalin Plan and the Soviet Economy* (New York: Institute for East-West Security Studies, 1991).

8. Bank für Internationalen Zahlungsausgleich, *61. Jahresbericht* (Basel, June 10, 1991), p. 56.

9. See, for instance, Lutz Hoffmann, "Wider die ökonomische Vernunft," *Frankfurter Allgemeine Zeitung*, February 10, 1990, p. 15.

10. *Handelsblatt*, October 4, 5, 1991, p. 7.

11. See *Handelsblatt*, February 6, 1992, p. 1. This per cent figure also includes the many people currently engaged in retraining and job creation schemes under the auspices of the German Labour Exchange.

12. Alfred Boss, "Subventionen in den neuen Bundesländern," *Die Weltwirtschaft*, No. 1, 1991, pp. 67-75.

13. *Neue Zürcher Zeitung*, January 26, 27, 1992, p. 14.

14. According to Sachs, Lipton (*op. cit.* in note 3), p. 56.

15. See Jiri Kosta, "CSFR -- Die Transformation des Wirtschaftssystems: Konzepte, Probleme, Aussichten," *Vierteljahresberichte der Friedrich-Ebert-Stiftung*, No. 125 (September 1991), pp. 249-50; *Handelsblatt*, January 16, 1992, p. 7.

16. According to expectations of the vice-president of the Hungarian National Bank; see *Handelsblatt*, September 17, 1991, p. 9.

17. See, for instance, ECE (*op. cit.* in note 2), pp. 39-65; ECE, *Economic Bulletin for Europe*, Vol. 43, 1991, pp. 24-39; *OECD Economic Outlook*, No. 49 (July 1991), pp. 39-40; "Privatization: A Special Report," *RFE/RL Research Report*, Vol. 1, No. 17 (April 24, 1992).

18. Louisa Vinton, "Walesa, "Special Powers," and the Balcerowicz Plan," in: Radio Free Europe Research Institute, *Report on Eastern Europe*, Vol. 2, No. 29, 1991, p. 19.

19. See Jackson (*op. cit.* in note 5), p. 43.

20. Cf. Economic Commission for Europe, *Economic Survey of Europe in 1989-1990*, (New York: United Nations Publications, 1990), p. 9.

21. Gaddis (*op. cit.* in note 1), p. 115.

22. According to ECE (*op. cit.* in note 20), pp. 11-3.

23. *Ibid.*, p. 13.

24. PHARE (Pologne, Hongrie, Assistance à la Restructuration Economique) was originally agreed at the economic summit in Paris in 1989 as a programme of aid by the OECD states to the two countries mentioned and was

subsequently extended to include Czecho-Slovakia, Bulgaria, Yugoslavia, and Rumania.

25. See *The Japan Times*, April 3, 1992, pp. 1, 4.

26. See *Handelsblatt*, October 10, 1991, p. 11. In the case of the USA, however, the figure was only 2.1 per cent, whilst Britain provided only 0.12 per cent.

27. For subsequent data, see European Parliament, *Report of the Committee on External Economic Relations on a General Outline for Association Agreements with the Countries of Central and Eastern Europe*, compiled by Christa Randzio-Plath (DOC EN/RR/105815), p. 19f; ECE (*op. cit.* in note 2), pp. 113-4.

28. See *Handelsblatt*, October 8, 1991, p. 1, and October 9, 1991, p. 10.

29. See *Handelsblatt*, April 1, 1992, p. 2.

30. See *Handelsblatt*, September 23, 1991, p. 1, and September 30, 1991, p. 10.

31. See ECE, *Bulletin* (*op.cit.* in note 17), p. 105.

32. See *Handelsblatt*, September 19, 1991, p. 8, and December 17, 1991, pp. 2, 10.

33. See his interview with *Die Zeit*, October 11, 1991, p. 34.

# About the Book and Editors

In this timely book, distinguished scholars from the Peace Research Institute Frankfurt and institutes of the Russian Academy of Sciences in Moscow take up the challenge passionately articulated in the Foreword by Eduard Shevardnadze. Considering the unprecedented opportunities for unifying a region split into antagonistic blocs for more than forty years, they explore the rapidly shifting context of cooperation in Europe.

The preconditions for establishing a new order—integrating both halves of Europe—are much more favorable than they have ever been, especially in the realm of arms reductions. However, the disintegration of the bipolar order has unleashed multifarious regional conflicts that now shape the security agenda in Europe.

The contributors argue that without comprehensive Western support, the still-shaky transformation cannot succeed. And they believe this support is all the more urgent in that the future of the whole continent will be decided in eastern Europe.

**Vladimir Baranovsky** is head of the European Studies Department at the Institute of World Economy and International Relations (IMEMO) of the Russian Academy of Sciences, Moscow. **Hans-Joachim Spanger** is senior fellow at the Peace Research Institute Frankfurt.